Arthurian and Other Studies

PRESENTED TO SHUNICHI NOGUCHI

Shunichi Noguchi

Arthurian
and
Other Studies

PRESENTED TO

SHUNICHI NOGUCHI

EDITED BY

TAKASHI SUZUKI AND TSUYOSHI MUKAI

D. S. BREWER

© Contributors 1993

All Rights Reserved. Except as permitted under current legislation
no part of this work may be photocopied, stored in a retrieval system,
published, performed in public, adapted, broadcast,
transmitted, recorded or reproduced in any form or by any means,
without the prior permission of the copyright owner

First published 1993 by D. S. Brewer, Cambridge

D. S. Brewer is an imprint of Boydell & Brewer Ltd
PO Box 9, Woodbridge, Suffolk IP12 3DF, UK
and of Boydell & Brewer Inc.
PO Box 41026, Rochester, NY 14604, USA

ISBN 0 85991 380 5

British Library Cataloguing-in-Publication Data
Suzuki, Takashi
 Arthurian and Other Studies Presented to
 Shunichi Noguchi
 I. Title II. Mukai, Tsuyoshi
 820.9
 ISBN 0–85991–380–5

Library of Congress Cataloging-in-Publication Data
Arthurian and other studies : presented to Shunichi Noguchi / edited
 by Takashi Suzuki and Tsuyoshi Mukai.
     p.   cm.
 Includes bibliographical references.
 ISBN 0–85991–380–5 (hardback : acid-free paper)
 1. English literature – Middle English, 1100–1500 – History and
 criticism. 2. Malory, Thomas, Sir, 15th cent. Morte d'Arthur.
 3. Arthurian romances – History and criticism. 4. English
 literature – History and criticism. I. Noguchi, Shun 'ichi, 1933– .
 II. Suzuki, Takashi, 1949– . III. Mukai, Tsuyoshi, 1952– .
 PR251.A78 1993
 820.9'001 – dc20   92–40726

This publication is printed on acid-free paper

Printed in Great Britain by
St Edmundsbury Press Ltd, Bury St Edmunds, Suffolk

Contents

Abbreviations	vii
Editors' Preface	ix
Sonnet to Shunichi Noguchi on his sixtieth birthday † GEORGE MOOR	xi
Our Friend Shunichi Noguchi JOHN LAWLOR	xiii
Publications of Shunichi Noguchi	xv
Tabula Gratulatoria	xix
Power as a Measure of Humanism in *Beowulf* and *Sir Gawain and the Green Knight* RAYMOND P. TRIPP, JR.	1
Jesus, A Trickster in the York Passion Plays MIKIKO ISHII	15
'Greyn' of Martyrdom in Chaucer's *Prioress's Tale* ISAMU SAITO	31
A Note on 'Nature' in *Hamlet* SHINSUKE ANDO	39
'Allegory of Happiness' in *The Merchant of Venice* SOJI IWASAKI	45
Hamlet and 'Modesty' SHIRO SHIBA	57
Cathleens in Yeats and Joyce: Love's Bitter Mystery TAKASHI SUZUKI	65
The Narrator's Function in *The Great Gatsby* EIICHI HAYAKAWA	69
The Significance of Latin Teaching in British Education ANTONY DICKINSON	77

† deceased

Hauberk and Helm in Malory's *Le Morte Darthur*   87
DEREK BREWER

Hunting, Hawking, and Textual Criticism in Malory's *Morte Darthur*   95
P. J. C. FIELD

Malory's "Noble Tale of Sir Launcelot du Lake", the Vulgate *Lancelot*,   107
and the Post-Vulgate *Roman du Graal*
EDWARD DONALD KENNEDY

Chaucer and Malory: Signs of the Times   131
GREGORY K. JEMBER

Editor/Compositor at Work: the Case of Caxton's Malory   143
TOSHIYUKI TAKAMIYA

Modernity of the Middle English Stanzaic Romance *Le Morte Arthur*   153
JÁN ŠIMKO

The Structure and Tone of the Stanzaic *Morte Arthur*   169
TADAHIRO IKEGAMI

De Worde's Displacement of Malory's Secularization   179
TSUYOSHI MUKAI

Some Scribal Differences in Malory   189
TOMOMI KATO

On the Relationship Between the Winchester Malory and Caxton's   201
Malory
YUJI NAKAO

Texts of 'Be Cynestole' in Wulfstan's *Institutes of Polity*   211
TADAO KUBOUCHI

Chaucer's Use of Words of Old Norse Origin   219
JUN SUDO

'Myn deere herte' in Chaucer's *Troilus and Criseyde*   231
FUMIKO OKA

Negation in the Wycliffite Sermons   241
SHUICHI AITA

Spelling Variations in Cambridge, St John's College MS. B 12 (34)   247
YUZURU OKUMURA

Caxton's Revisions: the *Game of Chess*, the *Mirror of the World*, and   257
Reynard the Fox
KIYOKAZU MIZOBATA

Discourse Properties of Initial and Final *When*-Clauses in English   263
Written Narratives
KAZUO FUKUDA

Abbreviations

E.E.T.S.	Early English Text Society
E.E.T.S., o.s.	Early English Text Society, Original Series
E.E.T.S., e.s.	Early English Text Society, Extra Series
E.E.M.F.	Early English Manuscripts in Facsimile
J.E.G.P.	*Journal of English and Germanic Philology*
M.E.D.	*Middle English Dictionary*
O.E.D.	*The Oxford English Dictionary*
P.M.L.A.	*Publications of the Modern Language Associations of America*
R.E.S.	*Review of English Studies*
S.A.T.F.	Société des Anciens Textes Français

Editors' Preface

This wide-ranging collection of essays is dedicated to Shunichi Noguchi by his friends, colleagues, and pupils on the occasion of his sixtieth birthday. The collection is focused on his major professional field, Malorian studies, hence the title, *Arthurian and Other Studies*. We express our sincere thanks to all the contributors who have assisted in this project, among whom are many eminent medievalists both at home and abroad. The line-up of the contributors is in itself a clear indication of Noguchi's highly regarded scholarship and scholarly integrity, qualities which have deeply impressed many people who know him.

Shunichi Noguchi, born on the 24th of March, 1933, the son of Yoshitaka Nakamura, primary school headmaster, and Yuriko Nakamura (Noguchi), was educated at Hiroshima University, where he was taught by Michio Masui and Jiro Ogawa. After teaching for nine years at Fukui University as lecturer and associate professor of English, he moved to Osaka University of Education in 1971. Since then, while devoting himself to research in medieval English studies, he has been teaching undergraduates and graduate students for more than twenty years at Tennoji, the busy centre in the south of Osaka City. He has made an important contribution to Malory textual criticism (developed principally by Eugène Vinaver, editor of the Winchester Manuscript of Malory), and has published many significant essays and articles on Malory and on medieval English literature and language, among them: 'Malory and the Consolation of Style' (1971); 'Caxton's Malory' (1977); 'Englishness in Malory' (1981); 'Caxton's Malory Again' (1984); and a new edition of *Le Morte Arthur* (1990). These works have had a remarkable influence on recent directions in medieval English studies. Outside Osaka University of Education, he has given lectures at Kagoshima and at other Universities as visiting lecturer. He worked for the Editorial Committee and the Organising Committee of the English Literary Society of Japan and was a leading member of the Editorial Committee of Medieval English Studies (Japan). He has been associated with the International Arthurian Society since 1976 and he read a paper about Malorian chivalry at the International Congress on Medieval Studies at Kalamazoo, Michigan, in 1988. As a teacher, Noguchi has enlightened many students by his keen and subtle reading of texts, a reading which is an expression of his gentle, well-balanced and solid personality. His instructive supervision and his authentic lectures on Malory and on other medieval writers have encouraged not a few promising medievalists, who have, more or less, been inspired by his exorbitant(!)

suggestion that, in approaching texts, medievalists should try to be both 'orthodox *and* original'. Noguchi's strength as a teacher is further emphasised by the fact that he does not limit his teaching to medieval studies: he has a wide intellectual interest in English literature in general and offers helpful advice on any subject or any writer or poet that his pupils want to study. The variety of their scholarly publications, most of which are written in English, is another evidence of his distinction.

The sixtieth birthday is called 'Kanreki' in Japanese, which means the completion of a sixty-year cycle in the Japanese calendar. It is, therefore, the time for celebration both of his past achievement and of the commencement of a new era in his life. We wish Shunichi Noguchi a fruitful and healthy future in presenting him with this volume.

We are happy to express our deepest gratitude to Derek Brewer (he was Noguchi's supervisor when he was a British Council scholar at Birmingham University), for his warmhearted understanding of English studies in Japan and for the acceptance of publication from Boydell and Brewer. We also acknowledge our indebtedness to John Lawlor, Richard and Marie Axton, all of whom constantly encouraged us and willingly gave us their cordial assistance. It is indeed a pity that George Moor did not live to see the publication of this book, adorned with his beautiful and moving sonnet. George Moor was, Noguchi often tells us, the person who made him certain of the significance of writing articles in English by continuously giving him considerate and invaluable advice on his English style. *Requiescat in pace*. Thanks to their support and that of many other people, our project is now completed, we believe, most successfully.

March 1993   Takashi Suzuki
Tennoji, Osaka, Japan   Tsuyoshi Mukai

Sonnet to Shunichi Noguchi
on his sixtieth birthday

Long buried here in Lancashire was found
  The body of a knight in perfect state,
    As if his death had been of recent date
And still the rider's limbs all strong and sound,
Fresh from the joust borne with a fatal wound.
  So in your studies you brought light and air
    And made the past alive. With insight rare
You from your Isles old lore of ours unbound.

The Golden Climateric now like a bell
  Bids you to contemplation, Vesper hours
    Of Milton's learnèd ease among the flowers.
In the rich Autumn, harvesting complete,
The toiling bees have filled the cells with sweet.
  Long may your studies and yourself be well.

George Moor

Our Friend Shunichi Noguchi

JOHN LAWLOR

It is a special pleasure to recall that my first link with Shunichi Noguchi was a Library – or rather, a Librarian, one whose memory flourishes wherever scholars fortunate enough to have met him are to be found. Jack Blakiston had in his loving care The Fellows' Library at Winchester and kept an exact record of those who came to see the prize of the collection, the Manuscript of 'some 480 leaves, paper not vellum . . . about King Arthur and his Knights, but lacking a beginning or an end'.[1] Thus far Walter Oakeshott, discoverer of what came to be known as 'The Winchester Malory'.

The long duration of Vinaver's work (he had been preparing an edition of Caxton's printing, undertaken in 1931 and necessarily interrupted by Oakeshott's discovery in 1934) meant that all scholarly enquiry had, in effect, to be suspended. I well recall my own Tutor, C. S. Lewis, heading me off from Malorian studies, my first hopeful proposal on returning from War service in November 1945. It was of course Lewis who wrote the full-length review of Vinaver in *The Times Literary Supplement*.[2] It is perhaps not without interest that, having already bought his own set of Vinaver, Lewis passed the review copies to his friend and close ally of those days, J. R. R. Tolkien, who became my postgraduate Supervisor, though not alas! for Malory. Later comparisons of *The Lord of the Rings* with Malory were, Tolkien ruefully said, 'too much for my vanity',[3] though they may not seem to others wholly beside the point.

The reader will see that when my turn came to journey to Winchester, it was with indelible associations of old friends and revered mentors in English studies. Turning leaves of the MS. under Blakiston's watchful eye, I heard his whole-hearted commendation of a Japanese scholar whose scholarly energy and assiduity were matched only by his natural gifts of consideration and courtesy. Here, it seemed, was the prospect of a new friend to join an honoured line. Let it suffice to say that when Jack Blakiston's absorbing pages on 17th century French memoirs and letters came to be posthumously published,[4] the frontispiece showed him

---

1 *Essays on Malory*, ed. J. A. W. Bennett (Oxford, 1963), p. 3.
2 Reprinted in C. S. Lewis, *Studies in Medieval and Renaissance Literature*, ed. Walter Hooper (Cambridge, 1966), pp. 103–10.
3 *The Letters of J. R. R. Tolkien*, ed. Humphrey Carpenter (London, 1981), p. 181.
4 *Reminiscing in the 17th Century*, published by The College, Winchester, 1985.

proudly holding the Winchester MS. – the photograph (unaccredited) being by Shunichi Noguchi.

It was not long after my first encounter with Blakiston that Noguchi and I met. Characteristically, learning of my interest in the Winchester MS. he sent me a sheaf of exact notations on the differences between the Winchester MS. text and the printed transcript. Since then, our meetings have been many and various – in Japan and in England, in class-rooms and under hospitable roofs – I in his house near Nara and he in the house of my boyhood in Plymouth. We have even, and indeed memorably, been under sail together when, learning of my interest in all things maritime, he asked his great friend the gifted architect Mende to skipper us in Japanese home waters for a day. Memorably, a fish was caught and, later at Mende's house, ceremoniously eaten! It was a particular joy for Kimie Imura and me to have their company at our wedding-celebration in Tokyo. The reader will readily see that Noguchi's is the true gift of friendship – the circle is ever-widening.

The contributors to this book are sufficient testimony to the range and quality of Noguchi's interests. *Amicitia semper prodest* runs the old tag. In friendship there is always an unceasing and ever-expanding range. It lies not merely in the acquisition of new members of the circle, precious and vital as that is, but also, and principally, in the renewal of those who have gone before. I recall not only those in the British tradition (as, Lewis, Tolkien, Blakiston) but also such firm and lasting friends as Toshikazu and Toshiko Oyama – vividly present in the insights and affirmations of a creative scholarship that, before all else, is obedient to the principle that English studies, wherever pursued, must be contributions to a worldwide forum, not merely 'ei-bun-gaku-ken-kyu' [written in Chino-Japanese characters].

That is, and most happily continues to be, the watchword for all Shunichi Noguchi has achieved. Long may it continue, to our lasting profit and delight!

Publications of Shunichi Noguchi

Article (and Edition)

1961

'Malory's English – An Aspect of its Syntax', *Hiroshima Studies in English Language and Literature*, Vol. 7, No. 2 (Hiroshima: The English Literary Association of Hiroshima University, 1961), 130–7.

'The Language of *Sir Gawain and the Green Knight*', *Hiroshima Studies in English Language and Literature*, Vol. 8, No. 1 (Hiroshima: The English Literary Association of Hiroshima University, 1961), 76–91.

1962

'Notes on the Language of the *Paston Letters* in Relation with London English', in Michio Masui's "A Joint Study of the Language of *the Paston Letters*", *Hiroshima University Studies (Literature Department)*, No. 20 (Hiroshima, 1962), 291–300.

'Kindai-hyōjun-eigo-no Kigen-ni Kansuru Ichi-chōsa' (in Japanese) ['A Research Concerning the Origin of Modern Standard English'], *Bulletin of the Faculty of the Liberal Arts, Fukui University, Part I, the Humanities*, No. 11 (Fukui, 1962), 1–16.

1963

'Richard Rolle-no "fire of love" – Shūkyōteki-na Keiken-o Arawasu Hiyu-hyōgen' (in Japanese) ['Richard Rolle's "fire of love" – Figurative Expression of Religious Experience'], in Michio Masui's "Hyōgen-to-shite-no Eigo-gaku" ["English Philology as a Study of English Expression"], *Eigo-Kyoiku [Journal of English Teaching]*, Vol. 12, No. 9 (Tokyo: Taishukan, 1964), 20–1.

'Malory-no Sakuhin-no Winchester MS-to Caxton's Edition-to-no Gengoteki-sai-ni-tsuite-no Nōto' (in Japanese) ['Notes on Linguistic Differences Between the Winchester MS. and Caxton's Edition of Malory's Works'], *Bulletin of the Faculty of the Liberal Arts, Fukui University, Part I, the Humanities*, No. 12 (Fukui, 1963), 1–7.

1964

'Separability in Malory's Syntax – the Group-genitive', *Bulletin of the Faculty of the Liberal Arts, Fukui University, Part I, the Humanities*, No. 13 (Fukui, 1964), 1–4.

1967

'The Paradox of the Character of Malory's Language', *Hiroshima Studies in English Language and Literature*, Vol. 13, No. 2 (Hiroshima, 1967), 115–34.

'Corrigenda' (in Collaboration with A. O. Sandved and Ján Šimko), *The Works of Sir Thomas Malory*, 2nd Edition, ed. Eugène Vinaver (Oxford: Clarendon Press, 1967), pp. 1753–6.

1971

'Malory and the Consolation of Style', *Studies in English Literature, English Number 1971* (Tokyo: The English Literary Society of Japan, 1971), 35–53.

1977

'Caxton's Malory', *Poetica*, No. 8 (Tokyo: Shubun International, 1977), 72–84.

1979

'Caxton-ga Malory-no Buntai-kara Manandakoto' (in Japanese) ['What did Caxton Learn from Malory's Style?'], *Chusei-Eibungaku Danwakai Kaiho* [*Bulletin of the Colloquium for Medieval Studies*], No. 17 (Tokyo: Colloquium for M.E.S., 1979), 6–7.

1980

'Eugène Vinaver: in Memoriam', *Eigo Seinen* [*The Rising Generation*], Vol. 125, No. 11 (Tokyo: Kenkyusha, 1980), 510–1.

1981

'Englishness in Malory', *Aspects of Malory*, ed. Toshiyuki Takamiya and Derek Brewer (Cambridge: D.S. Brewer, 1981), pp. 17–26.

'Writing in Malory', *Poetica*, No. 12 (Tokyo: Shubun International, 1981), 82–93.

1982

'Robin Huddo-to Āsā-ou' (in Japanese) ['Robin Hood and King Arthur'], *Igirisu-no Seikatsu-to Bunka Jiten* [*A Dictionary of British Life and Culture*], ed. Shinsuke Ando and others (Tokyo: Kenkyusha, 1982), pp. 916–25.

1983

'On a Certain Poem in Yeats's *Last Poems*', *Masui Michio Sensei Taikan Kinen "Eigo-Eibungaku Kenkyu"* [*Studies in English Language and Literature Presented to Professor Michio Masui on the Occasion of his Retirement*], ed. Hiroshige Yoshida (Tokyo: Kenkyusha, 1983), pp. 411–9.

1984

'Caxton's Malory Again', *Poetica*, No. 20 (Tokyo: Shubun International, 1984), 33–8.

1985

'Malory-to Shārotto-no Otome Erein' (in Japanese) ['Malory et puella de Escalot'], *Gengo-Bunka* [*Lingua et Humanitas, Universitas Meiji-Gakuin*], Vol. 3 (Tokyo: Meiji-Gakuin Studium Linguae Humanitatisque, 1985), 66–70.

'Āsā-ou Densetsu', 'Chūsei' (in Japanese) ['Arthurian Legend', 'Middle Ages'], *Hikari-no Imejarī* [*Imagery of Light*], ed. Bunsei Uesugi (Tokyo: Kirihara-shoten, 1985), pp. 228–51 and 369–78.

'To "make it good" upon Malory Scholars', *Mediaeval English Studies Newsletter*, No. 13 (Tokyo: Centre for Mediaeval English Studies, 1985), 3–4.

1986

'W. B. Yeats: his "Memory" and Memories', *Eishi Hyōron* [*Essays on Poetry*], No. 3 (Hiroshima: Chugoku-Shikoku Igirisu Romanha Gakkai [Chugoku-shikoku Circle for Studying English Romantic Poetry], 1986), 3–7.

1987

'Dom', *Key-Word Studies in Beowulf 2* (Tokyo: Centre for Mediaeval English Studies, 1987), 1–4.

'Chaucer's Use of *Coward* and *Cowardice*', *Key-Word Studies in Chaucer 2* (Tokyo: Centre for Mediaeval English Studies, 1987), 75–7.

1988

'Beowulf and *Sothfæstra Dom*', *Terasawa Yoshio Kyoju Kanreki Kinen Ronbunshu* [*Philologia Anglica: Essays Presented to Professor Yoshio Terasawa on the Occasion of his Sixtieth Birthday*], ed. Kinshiro Oshitari and others (Tokyo: Kenkyusha, 1988), pp. 251–8.

1989

'Malorian Knights: Their Humility and Patience', *In Geardagum X* (Denver: Society for New Language Study, 1989), 19–27.

1990

Le Morte Arthur, ed. Shunichi Noguchi (Tokyo: Centre for Mediaeval English Studies, 1990).

1992

'*Fair* in Chaucer and *Unfæger*', *Key-Word Studies in Beowulf and Chaucer 4* (Tokyo: Centre for Mediaeval English Studies, 1992), 35–40.

'Chaucer's Concept of Nature', *Chaucer to Shakespeare: Essays in Honour of Shinsuke Ando*, ed. Toshiyuki Takamiya and Richard Beadle (Cambridge: D. S. Brewer, 1992), pp. 25–31.

Review

1967

Aya Shimizu, *Asā-ou Densetsu* (in Japanese) [*A Study of Arthurian Legend*] (Tokyo, 1966), *Eibungaku Kenkyu* [*Studies in English Literature*], Vol. 44, No. 1 (Tokyo: The English Literary Society of Japan, 1967), 100–1 (in Japanese).

1968

Eugène Vinaver, ed. *The Works of Sir Thomas Malory*, 2nd Edition (Oxford: Clarendon Press, 1967), *Hiroshima Studies in English Language and Literature*, Vol. 15, No. 1 (Hiroshima, 1968), 41–6.

1978

Mark Lambert, *Malory: Style and Vision in Le Morte Darthur* (New Haven: Yale University Press, 1975), *Studies in English Literature, English Number 1978* (Tokyo, 1978), 120–4.

1984

Beverly Taylor and Elizabeth Brewer, *The Return of King Arthur* (Cambridge: D.S.Brewer, 1983), *Eigo Seinen* [*The Rising Generation*], Vol. 129, No. 12 (Tokyo: Kenkyusha, 1984), 608–9 (in Japanese).

Tabula Gratulatoria

Contributors

Shuichi Aita
Shinsuke Ando
Derek Brewer
Antony Dickinson
P.J.C. Field
Kazuo Fukuda
Eiichi Hayakawa
Tadahiro Ikegami
Mikiko Ishii
Soji Iwasaki
Gregory K. Jember
Tomomi Kato
Edward Donald Kennedy
Tadao Kubouchi

John Lawlor
Kiyokazu Mizobata
George Moor
Tsuyoshi Mukai
Yuji Nakao
Fumiko Oka
Yuzuru Okumura
Isamu Saito
Shiro Shiba
Ján Šimko
Jun Sudo
Takashi Suzuki
Toshiyuki Takamiya
Raymond P. Tripp, Jr.

Subscribers

Masahiko Agari
Junko Asakawa
Richard and Marie Axton
Chosei Azuma
Thomas and Margaret Beaumont
Kazutoshi Becchaku
Norman Francis Blake
James P. Carley
The Centre for Medieval English
  Studies, College of Arts and
  Sciences, University of Tokyo
Reginald T. Davies
A. Eileen Dickinson
Yumi Dohi
Ikuko Fujimoto
Reiji Fujimoto
Hiroshi Fujiwara
Yuri Fuwa
Keiko Hamaguchi
Tamotsu Harada
R. M. Hare
Masami Hatano
Hiroko Hayakawa
Tadashi Hiraga

Keiko Ikegami
Sumie Iwao
Akiyuki Jimura
Keiichiro Kamino
Masahiko Kanno
Tsunenori Karibe
Takao Kato
Teruoki Kawakubo
Kenichi Kitahata
Nobuhiko Kobayashi
Tsunehiro Kobayashi
Takashi Kunikata
Keiko Kuriyagawa
Nicholas Lee
Hideichi Matsubara
Takami Matsuda
Noriko Matsui
Hiroyuki Matsumoto
Etsuko Mega
Hideo Mende
Kiyoshi Miyagawa
Yoshie Mizobata
Katsumi Morita
Nobuhiko Motoyama

TABULA GRATULATORIA

Junko Mukai
Mitsuie Nagamachi
Satoshi Nagao
Genichi Nakamura
Takeo Nakamura
Toru Nakamura
Kunio Nakashima
Keiko Nakasuga
Keiichi Narita
Kinji Natsumeda
Junko Nitao
Ryoji Noguchi
Tetsuichi Nyunoya
Shigeyuki Oenoki
Yoshiaki Ohata
Saburo Oka
Miyuki Okumura
Shigeru Ono
Toshiaki Oya
Hisaaki Sasagawa
Shuji Sato
Toshihiko Sato
Isao Seo
Mikiko Seyller
Kazuyo Shiba
Reiji Shibata
Hisashi Shigeo
Naoko Shirai
Kuniko Shoji
George J. Sutton
Reiko Suzuki
Yutaka Tabuchi

Masaji Tajiri
Ken-ichi Takami
Tohru Takeuchi
Katsuya Taki
Masahiko Takizawa
Yuzo Tamaki
Harumi Tanabe
Mitsuhiro Tani
Takashi Terauchi
Haruo Tetsumura
Hisao Tsuru
Elisabeth Vinaver
Yoko Wada
Tsuyoshi Wadazumi
Harumi Yagi
Hiroshi Yamada
Manabu Yamada
Hiromitsu Yamagata
Hiroyuki Yamasaki
Hiroshi Yamashita
Tomosaburo Yamauchi
Takeshi Yanase
Jun Yasuda
Kiyoshi Yokoi
Takashi Yoneda
Junko Yoshida
Koji Yoshimura
Nobuyuki Yuasa
Toshiro Yui
Hyo-Yun Yun
Zhu Huan
Peter Singer

Power as a Measure of Humanism
in *Beowulf* and *Sir Gawain and the Green Knight*

RAYMOND P. TRIPP, JR.

I

Since Professor Noguchi's interests span more than one period of English literature, I am emboldened to return to the subject of continuity, in particular, to the beginnings of *native* English humanism as this appears in the preoccupation with power which marks many early English works.[1]

In C. S. Lewis's judgement Anglo-Saxon is the 'taproot' for all later English studies. He was convinced that:

The taproot, Anglo-Saxon, can never be abandoned. The man who does not know it remains all his life a child among real English students. There we find the speech-rhythms that we use every day made the basis of metre; there we find the origins of that romanticism for which the ignorant invent such odd explanations. This is our own stuff and its life is in every branch of the tree to the remotest twigs. That we cannot abandon.[2]

A look at the way power is handled in Old and Middle English poetry will show that the same may be said of English humanism. This also springs from native stock, whose 'taproot' reaches through scholarly engrafting of numerous 'odd explanations' deeply into Anglo-Saxon.

II

That characteristically western style of man-centredness called humanism, to be sure, has taken and continues to take myriad forms; but

---

[1] See my 'On the Continuity of English Poetry Between *Beowulf* and Chaucer', *Poetica*, 6 (1976), 1–21; 'The Arming Topos and the Comparative Modernity of Chaucer, The *Gawain* Poet, and Malory', *The Bulletin of Hirosaki College*, 3 (1981), 179–87. 'The Dialectic of Debate and the Continuity of English Poetry', *Massachusetts Studies in English*, 7:1 (1979) [for 1978], 41–51; and 'Beowulf and Chaucer's Walter: Memory and the Continuity of Compulsion', *In Geardagum*, 9 (1990), 59–74.

[2] Roger Lancelyn Green and Walter Hooper, *C. S. Lewis, A Biography* (New York, London: Harcourt Brace Jovanovich, 1974), p. 151. From a letter? Source not given.

these all have an existential centre, and one way or another devolve into a question of power. It is necessary, therefore, to understand the growth and structure of the preoccupation with power.

As men come again to believe they are the measure of all things, the shape of life appears to change, and the world to look like a much different place. Consequently the origin and progress of humanism itself can be measured by the new concerns this re-orientation occasions. Of these a growing preoccupation with power of all kinds, actual and symbolic, is one of the most revealing. The gnomic pronouncement, for example, *Cyning biþ anwealdes georn* (*Maxims I*, 58b) does more than assert a perennial fact of life. The self-consciousness in this Anglo-Saxon conviction that 'A king is eager for *all* the power' heralds a new epoch.

Mere tribal power ceases to satisfy; it is natural, bounded, and assumes rather than subsumes the individual and society. Intoxicated by the 'sweet poison of the false infinite',[3] men want to conquer space and time, and ultimately death itself. This pursuit of power over nature, however, results in the power of fewer and fewer men over more and more other men:

> . . . what we call Man's power over Nature turns out to be a power exercised by some men over other men with Nature as its instrument.[4]

Unchecked this trends continues until private and social life are absorbed into the collective personality of the 'leader'. Somehow conquering nature turns into abolishing man. A shrinking circle of self, self-will, and survival traps whole populations in a quest for unlimited power, 'begotten by the hatred of death upon the fear of true immortality'.[5]

There is more to the world than power. Power is but one aspect of reality – the good, the true, and the beautiful are others. But from the outset the personality preoccupied with survival fixes upon power with an intensity which excludes other things, both secular and divine. At first God-language dominates the idiom of the preoccupation with power, so that 'as a useful concept for the development of ideas in moral theology, . . . the *potentia Dei absoluta* enjoyed its fullest bloom in the first half of the fourteenth century.'[6] But insofar as a 'sense of selfhood necessarily

---

3 C. S. Lewis, *Perelandra* (New York: Collier Books, 1962 [1944]), p. 82.
4 C. S. Lewis, *The Abolition of Man* (New York: Macmillan, 1965), p. 69.
5 *Perelandra*, p. 82.
6 Laurence Eldredge, 'The Concept of God's Power in the Later Fourteenth Century', pp. 211–26, in David L. Jeffrey, ed., *By Things Seen, Reference and Recognition in Medieval Thought* (Ottawa: University of Ottawa Press, 1979), p. 211. Later in the century, he argues, the distinction between *potentia absoluta* and *potentia ordinata* became confused and disregarded. This loss of interest, however, in the theological distinction suggests, not that God's absolute power disappeared, but rather that it was materialised into the laws of biology and physics. In any case, the humanist concern with power in the context of radical survival precedes and survives its narrow theological expression.

involves an awareness of one's tacitly adversarial relationship to environment and external values',[7] outside of theology a concern with power appears well before and continues long after the fourteenth century.

Psychologically speaking, the self-conscious personality projects its own preoccupation with power upon God. The more willfully assertive the personality becomes, the more arbitrary it deems God to be, and the more it sees death as God's arbitrary agent. In this way, step by step the humanist personality abandons transcendental thinking and falls back into the vegetative archaism of the classical world. Achilles's complaint to Odysseus describes the condition to which the humanist unwittingly returns:

> Let me hear no smooth talk of death
> from you Odysseus, light of councils,
> Better, I say, to break sod as a farm hand
> for some poor country man, on iron rations,
> than lord it over all the exhausted dead.   (XI, 64–8)[8]

For all his posturing and rhetoric, the humanist becomes a clever animal, for whom staying alive means everything, and the only important power is the power not to die.

III

The beginnings of what might be called the power preoccupation syndrome of the humanist personality can be seen in both Old and Middle English works, such as *Beowulf* and *Sir Gawain and the Green Knight*. Each work – often directly through spokesmen figures – presents a paradigm of man's predicament in terms of death and power, and in ways which justify applying Lewis's view of romanticism to humanism. In these works power expands into a network of narrative parallels, so that point for point one can observe the growth and structure of the preoccupation with power. As one would expect, the problem is first presented in terms which are more theological than psychological or political; and the Old English poet shows himself to be predictably less man-centred than his Middle English counterpart. The earlier poet still commands enough faith to wonder rather than to rebel against life. His

---

[7] Robert L. Reed, Jr., *Middle English Debate Poetry, and the Aesthetics of Irresolution* (Columbia, Missouri, London: University of Missouri Press, 1990), p. 251. See my *Beyond Canterbury: Chaucer, Humanism, and Literature* (Cross-Ways, Church-Stretton, England: Onny Press, 1977), for a discussion and history of this idea of the self's 'adversarial' relationship with the world.

[8] I am citing Robert Fitzgerald, trans., *The Odyssey, Homer* (New York: Doubleday, 1963), p. 201.

good characters accept their powerlessness before death, while the bad ones resist. The more intensely man-centred Middle English poet psychologises the problem of power, but leaves the question of survival unresolved.

In *Beowulf* the poet's spokesman, Hrothgar, reacts with wonder at God's power and His distribution of the good things of life:

> 'Wundor is to secganne,
> hu mihtig God   manna cynne
> þurh sidne sefan   snyttru bryttað,
> eard ond eorlscipe;   he ah ealra geweald.'   (1724b–7)[9]
>
> ('A wonder it is to say
> How mighty God to every kind of man
> Through His boundless mind dispenses wits, land,
> And rank. He owns the power over everything.')

But as positive as wonder may be, dialectically it implies a split between natural and supernatural and thus the seeds of future doubt. But in *Beowulf* men like Heremod, who rage rather than wonder at God's distribution of *snyttru . . . eard ond eorlscipe* (1726b–7a) 'wits . . . land, and rank', not to mention longevity, are blamed and damned *hellbendum fæst* (3072b), 'fast in hell-bonds'. The fleeing man-dragon (2221–6a) desperately complains, *Heahþrymm bruce nu* (2247a), 'The great power I now enjoy', but to no avail.[10]

God indeed 'owns the power over everything', including that power which is the strength of heroes. God's monopoly permeates the poem.[11] Beowulf is not one of those *egna kraftens män*, 'self-might men', we meet in the Icelandic *fornaldarsǫgur*.[12] This last man to have power has it, in fact, because he has it from God. Grendel's Mother, for one, complains that Beowulf defeated her son because:

> '. . . he gemunde   mægenes strenge,
> gimfæste gife,   ðe him God sealde,

[9]   Citations before line 2208b are from Fr. Klaeber, ed., *Beowulf and the Fight at Finnsburg*, 3rd ed., with 1st and 2nd suppls. (Boston: D.C.Heath, 1950). Translations are adapted from my *Beowulf, An Edition and Literary Translation, In Progress* (Denver: The Society for New Language Study, 1991).

[10]   Here I depart from the Klaeber consensus and follow my *More About the Fight with the Dragon, Beowulf 2208b–3182, Commentary, Edition, and Translation* (Lanham, New York, London: University Press of America, 1983). In my judgement the conventional fleeing thief is in fact an evil king who became a dragon; in my considered judgement the manuscript at 2247a appears to read as presented.

[11]   To a degree, as a matter of fact, which should have prevented editors from emending *mægenes* (2628b), to *mæges*, etc.

[12]   Folke Ström, *Den egna kraftens män: en studie i forntida irreligiositet*, Göteborgs högskolas årsbok, 54:2 (Göteborg: Elanders boktryckeri AB, 1948). Cited from Stephen A. Mitchell, *Heroic Sagas and Ballads* (Ithaca, New York: Cornell University Press, 1991), p. 114.

ond him to Anwaldan are gelyfde,
frofre ond fultum; ðy he þone feond ofercwom,
gehnægde helle gast.'   (1270–4a)[13]

('. . . he took his mighty legacy in hand,
The huge gem of strength God had given him,
And trusted the mercy, aid, and comfort
Of the Lord, by which he overcame his foe –
He felled his house-guest from hell.')

The poet's revisionary theme is that the heroes of old, whose strength is proverbial and not to be disputed, all in fact had their power from God. Those *mægenagendra* (2837a), 'holders of power', who abused the gift of power, *dryhtmaðma dæl deaðe forgolden* (2843), 'bought their tiny share of gold with death',[14] and concluded this *lænan lifes* (2845a), 'loan of life', as we have seen, *hellbundum fæst* (3072b), 'fast in hell-bonds'.

The classic case of rebellion and abuse of God's gift of power is Heremod, who became a terrible burden to his people:

'ðeah þe hine mihtig God mægenes wynnum
eafeþum stepte, ofer ealle men
forð gefremede.'   (1716–8)

('Though mighty God had with the joys of strength
Served him mightily, fostering him far
Beyond all other men.')

Heremod serves as a foil to Beowulf, who uses his gift of power well. Hrothgar tells him, *hit geþyldum healdest, mægen mid modes snyttrum* (1705b–6a), 'You hold it all with patience, might with the force of your mind.'

God *is* all-powerful, and there are few other things that the poet is more fond of repeating in his gnomic way than this inexorable fact of human life. Even in the olden days:

Metod eallum weold
gumena cynnes, swa he nu git deð.   (1057b–8)

(God the Measurer ruled then
All the race of men, as He still does now.)

God also holds sway over the elements and the seasons, and is presented almost as identical with them. The way Beowulf's sword melts in the heat of Grendel's blood strikes a proto-empirical note:

---

[13] See also lines 942b–6a, 1700–3a, 1841–2, 2247 ff., and 9422b–46a, *et passim*. Grendel's Mother, like Beowulf himself (2806–8), speaks in the third person about her own situation.

[14] Literally, 'From Beowulf was this tiny share of gold bought with death'.

Þa þæt sweord ongan
æfter heaþoswate   hildegicelum,
wigbil wanian;   þæt wæs wundra sum,
þæt hit eal gemealt   ise gelicost,
ðonne forstes bend   Fæder onlæteð,
onwindeð wælrapas,   se geweald hafað
sæla ond mæla;   þæt is soð Metod.   (1605–11)

(Then his sword below,
After its battle-slavering bite, began
To wane like ice sickly. It was a wonder
That it all melted most like icy bodies
When frosty time the Father unbinds in death,
Bodily unwinds water-ropes, He who folds
Time's tangled edges – the true Measurer.)

God, the physical world, and surviving in the world, all become freshly congruent – with power.

More telling, perhaps, is the obverse of God's hegemony. Sometimes God refuses to use His power. He may decide, as in the case of the raging Grendel, not to rescue people from evil. Hrothgar reminds us of this disturbing possibility when he tells Beowulf about Grendel's ravages. These remarks of the old king upon divine power look forward to the exchange between Sir Gawain and the Green Knight.

When Hrothgar begins, he is ashamed. For reasons of age or doubt, he interrupts himself and reflects upon how easily God could kill Grendel:

'Sorh is me to secganne   on sefan minum
gumena ængum,   hwæt me Grendel hafað
hynðo on Heorote   mid his heteþancum,
færniða gefremed;   is min fletwerod,
wigheap gewanod;   hie wyrd forsweop
on Grendles gryre.   God eaþe mæg
þone dolsceaðan   dæda getwæfan!'   (473–9)

('A heartbreaking thing it is for me to say,
To any man, what Grendel has done to me,
Low insults to Heorot and thoughts of hate,
Swift stinking sorties – my floor-troop, gone,
My war-band weakened. Fate has swept them
Into Grendel's horror – God with death could
Easily part this cruel madman from his deeds.')

To this comment on what God could do Hrothgar juxtaposes a tale of slaughter. No matter how the Danes tried to dislodge Grendel, every morning Heorot would be a bloody mess (480–8). And Grendel would have continued to devour Danes had not God finally intervened (1055b–7a).[15]

The implications of Hrothgar's reflection persist and have the effect of reminding the audience that God could indeed easily have dispatched Grendel long – twelve years (147a) – before he did. Ultimately God does help the Danes, just as he had helped them before (12–8). Hrothgar rejoices that this help has arrived in the form of the young Geat (381b–4a).[16] But the unsettling fact of human slaughter and God's inactivity remains.

This hint of ambivalence reappears in Hrothgar's apparent forgetfulness. Even though he recognises Beowulf as God's agent, he later blames the hero for starting a feud which cost his beloved Æschere's life (1333b–7a); but Beowulf cannot, of course, be blamed without implicating God. Hrothgar, however, never openly complains; evil characters do that. The poem as a whole exhibits a faith still strong enough to wonder at death:

> Wundor hwar þonne
> eorl ellenrof ende gefere
> lifgesceafta, þonne leng ne mæg
> mon mid his magum meduseld buan.   (3062b–5)

> (A wonder it is, then,
> Where an arm-famed earl should meet his end,
> Cut from life – after the man no longer
> Dwells as a man among his mead-hall kin.)

The poet's relentless praise of God's power, nonetheless, does run the Miltonic risk of making 'satan' into a hero. The man-dragon makes his own seductively 'satanic' speech in hell:

> 'Hwæt, hyt ærror,
> ðe gode begeaton, guðdeað fornam,
> feorhbealo frecne, fyrma gehwylcne
> leoda wanra.'   (2248b–51a)[17]

> ('All this, long ago
> What good they got from God, Warring-Death took,
> Suicidal-Slaughter, each mortal delight
> Of men.')

Later this demonic grutching receives a gnomic answer. God 'hands out' (3055b) the good things of life, like longevity, wealth, and victory, *þam ðe*

---

[15] For reasons of metrical and prosodic theories *ðæs mannes mod* (1057a) has erroneously been taken to describe Beowulf's cooperating with God; but the phrase applies to Grendel and should be translated 'that man's arrogance'. See 730b, *et passim*.

[16] As he does again in lines 1397–8.

[17] From my edition; macrons omitted. Revised translation.

he wolde . . . swa him gemet ðuhte (3055b–7b), 'to those whom He wishes . . . as it seems fit to Him'.[18] Such words would likely fall upon deaf ears among Danes being devoured by a Grendel or among Geats at the mercy of a fiery dragon. The Danes' desperate apostasy reminds us that the peculiar logic of the pagan priest Cefi, in Bede's famous conversion story, cuts both ways. Cefi was willing to try Christianity because his paganism was not working. The Danes, to the poet's disapproval (178b–88), obviously made the reverse argument and reverted to paganism in order to rid themselves of Grendel (171b–8a).[19]

But Beowulf is the poet's man, and the poet, in his own way, seems to be God's man and to respect the chain of command. God is *sigora soðcyning* (3055a), the 'true King of Victories', and the poet shows us a grateful Beowulf, and a grateful Hrothgar before him (1778b–81). Before the hero dies, we hear him say, *Ic ðara frætwa Frean ealles ðanc, Wuldorcyninge wordum secge* (2794–5), 'I say words of thanks to God, the King of Wonders . . .' Not everyone, however, is as grateful. 'Self-might men' like Grendel and the man-dragon, who had the power not to die until God took it away from them through Beowulf – and a new theology – rage at God's monopoly of power.

The world according to Hrothgar is a catalogue (1761b–8) of natural and handmade horrors. Like the symbolic Grendel Mere, *nis þæt heoru stow* (1372b), 'it is not a pleasant place'. The long or rather the short of it is that men die; in one form or another *deað oferswyðeð* (1768b), 'death overpowers', them. The *Beowulf* poet, like the *Gawain* poet, presents us with an inventory of men's attempts, one way or another, to escape Death, by fleeing (into a barrow), fighting back (against demons), and by applying their wits (to paganism). But man's *snyttrum* (942a), 'natural powers', are actually *unsnyttrum* (1734a), 'useless follies'. Human cunning leads to disaster, and success is only *þurh Drihtnes miht* (940a), 'through the Lord's might'.

Clearly, in *Beowulf* the age of good heroes is with one partial exception over. A preoccupation with power and the yawning gap between God and man informs the poem. The poet has enough faith to bridge this gap, but the 'taproot' of humanism probes even the healthy *hæleþa hleahtor* (611a), 'laughter of men', in Heorot. The situation in *Sir Gawain* and Arthur's court is more advanced. Arthur's wonder is ominous and challenges rather than rejoices in belief (467–70), and the laughter in his court (2512–3) is sophisticated and shrill. If the age of heroes is over, so it

---

[18] Cf. line 678b.

[19] *Historia Ecclesiastica Gentis Anglorum*, Book II, Chapters viii–xi. The desperate and problematic recidivism of the Danes (171b ff.) seems to be so explained.

seems is the age of martyrs. Action in general has been even further internalised.[20]

In spite of the brutally realistic hunting scenes and the two beheading games,[21] action as such has become unimportant to the degree that it has been transformed into a symbolic language of existential battles. The sense of man as man has become stronger, the faith to bridge the gap this creates between God and man has weakened, and the gap has grown wider. Lacking the faith to wonder at death, the poet balks at human powerlessness, struggles to resolve it, and fails.

In terms of the humanist preoccupation with power, the importance of the three hunting scenes lies in the fact that they obviate self-deception. Taken together they underscore the fact of death and the futility of trying to escape it, while at the same time they show the corrupting effects of the effort to do so. As in *Beowulf*, the serial fate of the animals catalogues the repertoire of existential alternatives: flight, force, and cunning fore-thought.[22] The deer's running away, the boar's fighting, and the fox's cunning all fail. Boudoir parallels and complementary distinctions of cowardice, arrogance, and dishonesty serve only to reinforce the ba-nality of the human predicament. In the end we all die whether we run away, fight back, or cheat.

Through a paradigmatic opposition of reversible and irreversible be-headings, Gawain's story presents death as the climactic fact of life. The irrevocable loss of one's head dramatises God's immunity and man's vulnerability to death. In particular, the poet's engrossing sense of man as man leads to an unmediated sense of biological death. Such raw mortality has the additional effect of making matters even more humiliating by reducing the supernatural side of the equation to a creature of folklore.

Man's opponent is no longer anything as grand and elevating as God Himself or a hero who is clearly God's agent. The killer works for a witch, and he has become a 'Green Knight', whose colour suggests the mindless vegetable power of nature, in that he can have his head cut off and survive, as it were, by growing another one. To be killed by God may be an unwelcome honour, but at least it is not an insult; whereas to be dispatched by a man-vegetable literally adds insult to injury by dehumanising death into a process. Such an opponent, who is not divine but merely a natural undying something, points to a more deeply

---

[20] For the partial internalisation of action in *Beowulf*, see my 'The Arming Topos and the Comparative Modernity of Chaucer, the *Gawain* Poet, and Malory', note 1 above.

[21] The hunts: III, 1126–77, 1319–71 (deer); 1412–67, 1561–618 (boar); 1688–732, 1894–923 (fox). The beheadings: I, 279–459 (at court); IV, 2212–330 (at the chapel).

[22] When the *Beowulf* poet says *Forþan bið andgit æghwær selest* (1059) ('Therefore is looking ahead always best'), he means Christianity, not the *snyttrum* (942a) ('cleverness') of man's natural powers, which always fails and cannot solve the problem of death. See Loren C. Gruber, 'Forethought: The New Weapon in *Beowulf*', *In Geardagum*, 12 (1991), 1–14.

9

ARTHURIAN AND OTHER STUDIES

materialised consciousness. This horror is further heightened by the paradox that this man-vegetable talks – and *you* answer *it*. The dignity of the third person epic perspective is supplanted by the hellish intimacy of conversing with a second person who is not fully a person.[23]

The pivotal scene in *Sir Gawain*, of course, is the second beheading game at the Green Chapel. In outline, the Green Knight threatens with his ax, and Gawain flinches. The Green Knight then chides him for cowardice; and Gawain replies with the obvious answer that he cannot replace his head, but nonetheless he bides his blow. The Green Knight then nicks Gawain, who leaps up to defend himself, only to be told to calm down. The Green Knight then goes on to explain why he did not decapitate the hero, in effect saying: 'You failed only a little and really should not feel too badly about it.' Gawain, however, will have none of this and refuses to forgive himself. Man's powerlessness before death remains central here, but needless to say the way it is handled differs profoundly from the way the cowardly retainers in *Beowulf* are treated.

In plain language, the Green Knight explains to Gawain, who has been dishonest and concealed the green girdle to save his neck, that it is all right to cheat to save one's life.

'Bot here yow lakked a lyttel, sir, and lewté yow wonted
Bot þat watz for no wylyde werke, ne wowyng nauþer,
Bot for ȝe lufed your lyf – þe lasse I yow blame.'   (2366–8)[24]

This compromise is utterly unlike either Germanic heroism or Christian martyrdom, both of which involve death before dishonour. Clearly, the doctrine of perfection, martial or moral, has been abandoned. Here is no 'Be ye perfect like the Father' – or die trying – nor anything like Wiglaf's heroic, if somewhat tardy, 'Death is forever better for every man than a witless life of shame' (2890b–1). The Beowulfian equivalent would be to have Wiglaf withhold the *grim andswaru* (2860b), 'grim answer', the cowardly retainers deserved and got, and then to have him go on to explain to them that it was all right to flee into the woods to save their lives (2596–9a). The nearest thing to this would be the earlier attempt to convince Beowulf not to fight the man-dragon (2345–7a, 3079–83). But at least one voice in *Sir Gawain* asserts outright that it is not such a bad thing to be 'only human'.[25]

---

[23] In *Beowulf* the creature at which the hero shouts his challenge (2250–8a) was once a person.

[24] Here and elsewhere, *The Poems of the Pearl Manuscript*, ed. Malcom Andrew and Ronald Waldron (Berkeley, California: University of California Press, 1978).

[25] For different reasons the people at court think it is a sad thing to waste the life of such a man as Gawain (558–61) just to keep a silly oath. For a similar attitude against voluntarily dying for the cause – or anything else for that matter – in Chaucer's *Knight's Tale*, see 'Beowulf and Chaucer's Walter: Memory and the Continuity of Compulsion', note 1 above.

The naked contrast between power over and powerlessness before death, however, is best seen in Gawain's answer to the Green Knight's accusation of cowardice. When Gawain flinches, the Green Knight chides him:

> 'Nawþer fyked I ne flaȝe, freke, quen þou myntest, . . .
> And þou, er any harme hent, arȝez in hert'.   (2274–7)

But Gawain's distinction between reversible and irreversible beheadings tells the human side of the story:

> Quoþ Gawayn, 'I schunt onez,
> And so wyl I no more;
> Bot þaȝ my hede falle on þe stonez
> I con not hit restore.'   (2280–3)

Men die. A Green Knight can easily replace his head; a man cannot. The parallel to *Beowulf* is immediately apparent. God, 'Who owns the power over everything', as Hrothgar reminds us, can easily dispatch a Grendel; young warriors, let alone an old king, cannot. Even a hero with God on his side eventually meets his match.

Compared to the *Beowulf* poet, the *Gawain* poet obviously flirts with a problematic, if not openly softer moral line: 'death before dishonour' is softened to, well, 'a *little* dishonor before death'. This perplexing compromise is further complicated by Gawain's reaction to it. Unlike his judge he will not rationalise his failure, but takes a hard line of his own of a markedly different – and modern – kind.[26] If Gawain fails of perfect knightly behaviour, he succeeds in the existential anxiety of self-condemnation. These conflicting interpretations of Gawain's behaviour make the poet's position hard to pin down. The message may be survival at any cost, justice tempered with mercy, or a new existential consciousness.[27] We must fault Gawain or displace the Green Knight as the only spokesman of the poem, because Gawain does fail of the 'wisdom' delivered at the Green Chapel. If we approve of his heroic self-condemnation and psychological martyrdom, we must justify disagreeing with the humanistic acceptance of human frailty. After all Gawain may be prideful.

But the Green Knight and Gawain are not the only voices in the poem. The choice of reactions to Gawain's behaviour extends to his fellows at court. They laugh. These people, who never approved of Gawain's

---

[26] The situation is exactly like that between God and Jonah in the poem *Patience*. God forgives the Ninevites as the Green Knight forgives Gawain; while Jonah would condemn them as Gawain blames himself. See lines 481–523.

[27] *Pace* Robert E. Bjork, 'Sundor Æt Rune: The Voluntary Exile of The Wanderer', *Neophilologus*, 73 (1991), 119–29, existential isolation is not Christianity. After the Green Chapel Gawain is also *snottor on mode sundor æt rune* (*The Wanderer*, 111).

departure (558–61), appear to agree with the Green Knight in not taking the girdle too seriously (2514–8). But their dismissal of Gawain's failure springs from a suspect combination of shallowness and sophistication. They had earlier laughed, along with a nervous Gawain and a sobered Arthur, when the Green Knight galloped out of the hall with head in hand (557–66). Their laughing now at Gawain's return trivialises the green girdle into the latest courtly fashion. Yet we must weigh their courtly laughter against the Green Knight's compromise theology and Gawain's existential stubbornness.

In this way the *Gawain* poet like his Old English predecessor also presents us with an inventory of solutions to the problem of death. The Green Knight's common sense, Gawain's altruism, and the court's sophistication – all questionably partial – parallel the advice not to fight the dragon, Beowulf's determination to do so, and Wiglaf's switch to politics.[28] Taken together, the 'It is *un*important', the 'It *is* important', and the 'Who cares?' Gawain hears respectively from the Green Knight, himself, and the court closely parallel the message of the hunt scenes. But it is clear that these competing reactions can no more explain death than flight, force, or cunning forethought can escape it. If such options admit of degree, the *Gawain* poet has carried them considerably beyond *Beowulf*. He has exceeded the parent preoccupation with power and arrived at a pluralism which despairs of a solution. Elevating rebellion thus into an epistemology points to a deeper humanism, far more modern than merely maintaining a 'tacitly adversarial relationship to environment and external values'.[29]

---

[28] Wiglaf's speech (3076–86) amounts to an early version of Antony's 'Friends, Romans, countrymen . . .'

[29] If the *Beowulf* poet's characters are either far worse or far better than anyone could hope to be, and Chaucer's no better than they ought to be and frequently a little worse, and seldom self-condemnatory, the *Gawain* poet's character is one better than most but still not good enough. Chaucer's people, like Gawain, do in fact 'extreme' things: they kill daughters, torture wives, butcher people on a whim, and for their own advantage happily deceive and otherwise abuse their fellow human beings. But they do so for unique reasons – they are survivors. They act out of a peculiarly intellectual or at least emotional consciousness which sacrifices themselves and others to wrong-headed and perverse abstractions, economic, legal, or religious. Chaucer presents his own interpretative choices. His narratives implicitly attack certainty of any kind, elevating the irrational compulsion of needs and drives, called 'experience', over and against books and 'authority'; and his readers must decide whether this opposition is moral or epistemological. And we must question: is Chaucer's stance a deeply humble and charitable response to the limitations of man's natural powers, or simply a confused yet sinister materialism which is at once too timid or too expedient to throw the dead baby out with the holy water? It is significant, as *Sir Thopas* shows us, that Chaucer could not sustain a romance even as a narrative framework. In this regard, the *Gawain* poet is the more old-fashioned. Knights, castles, and bitchy witches have not become so laughable that they no longer can be made to serve storial purposes. Compared to *Beowulf*, however, he does reduce certain more heroic sequences to one-liners. The poet is too busy, for example, to elaborate on the miscellaneous monsters Gawain encounters en route to Bertilak's castle:

12

IV

In *Beowulf* and *Sir Gawain* we can see, therefore, not only a central preoccupation with power, but also a complementary sense of man's powerlessness. This self-centred preoccupation with survival generates corollary narrative strategies which point to a humanistic frame of mind. Varying in context and degree, the humanism of each poet represents a new development in 'the psychological history of the West'.[30] As men turn to themselves, they forget as much as they learn and begin to wonder at what they once knew. Faith then begins to fail, and a growing resistance to death changes wonder into complaint, as the self seeks refuge in willful ignorance. To be sure, this road to the likes of Nietzsche and Sartre has been paved with the help of foreign labour from the Near East. Just the same, closer to home, a look at *Beowulf* and *Sir Gawain and the Green Knight* shows that power can be a measure of English humanism, which like English romanticism springs from native stock whose 'taproot' reaches into Anglo-Saxon.

> So mony meruayl bi mount þer þe mon fyndez,
> Hit were to tore for to telle of þe tenþe dole.
> Sumwhyle wyth wormez he werrez and with wolues als,
> Sumwhyle wyth wodwos þat woned in the knarrez,
> Boþe wyth bullez and berez, and borez oþerquyle,
> And etaynez þat hym anelede of þe heȝe felle. (718–23)

The poet internalises a considerable portion of archaic freight in his desire to get to the psychological meat of his story. Yet his dwelling on such courtly and martial mechanisms as Gawain's elaborate armour shows greater than Chaucerian tolerance for 'enacted ideas' as these take shape in meaningful objects and actions.

[30] C. S. Lewis, *The Discarded Image* (Cambridge: University of Cambridge Press, 1964), p. 42. Lewis like his friend Owen Barfield was keenly aware of the importance in literary studies of heeding qualitative changes in consciousness.

Jesus, a Trickster in the York Passion Plays*

MIKIKO ISHII

The Passion sequence in the York Cycle, ranging from the Entry into Jerusalem to the Death of Christ, and consisting of twelve plays, has been the focus of critical attention. As early as 1907, C. M. Gayley distinguished and attributed seven (plays XXVI, XXVIII–XXXIII) out of these twelve plays to a single author, whom he identified as the York Realist.[1] Gayley was also aware of the influence of the same dramatist in all the York Passion plays, except *The Last Supper* (XXVII). In 1951 J. B. Reese, after a thorough examination of the versification of the York Passion, noted that eight plays are written in skilfully elaborated alliterative verse, arranged in stanzaic patterns,[2] and recognised more than one author as responsible for these plays. He included *The Death of Christ* (XXXVI) among the works by the York Realist. Hardin Craig, however, asserted that at least the plays written in alliterative verse are the work of a single author.[3] More recently J. W. Robinson presented more precise evidence to elucidate the characteristics of the dramatist's concern for realism and for dramatic language. He insists that the eight plays 'stand apart as a group and may be referred to as the work of the York Realist'.[4] Most scholars are now inclined to accept this idea, although some believe that his criticism and interpretations need some qualification.[5]

A close examination, however, shows that the plays should not be discussed solely in limited terms, such as the realistic presentation of human behaviour or the use of dramatic language; all the twelve plays

---

* This is a revised version of my paper presented at the Conference on Feasts and Festivals (organised by the Folklore Society and the Traditional Cosmology Society), at Glasgow University, 25th–28th March, 1987.

1 G. M. Gayley, *Plays of our Forefathers* (New York, 1907), p. 158.

2 J. B. Reese, 'Alliterative Verse in the York Cycle', *Studies in Philology*, 48 (1951), 639–68.

3 Hardin Craig, *English Religious Drama of the Middle Ages* (Oxford, 1955), p. 228

4 J. W. Robinson, 'The Art of York Realist', *Modern Philology*, 60 (1962–1963), 241–51, rpt. in *Medieval English Drama: Essays Critical and Contextual*, ed. Jerome Taylor and A. H. Nelson (Chicago & London, 1972), pp. 230–44.

5 E.g., Clifford Davidson, 'The Realism of the York Realist and the York Passion', *Speculum*, 50 (1975), 270–83, rpt. in *Medieval English Drama*, ed. Peter Happé (London, 1984), pp. 101–17: 'More urgently, we need a more precise understanding of the York Realist's *realism*, especially since this term as used in literary criticism has come under increasing attack. Furthermore, any such understanding of the realism of this dramatist must then be balanced with an evaluation of the traditional and iconographic elements in his plays' (p. 102).

constitute a complete unity in terms of festivals, although festive elements are more conspicuous in the plays attributed to the York Realist: they are presented with a greater sense of vividness and with more dramatic effect. No other medieval dramatist was so concerned with festivity as the York Realist. This fact implies that the York Realist might have also contributed to some extent to the presumably older portions such as *The Entry into Jerusalem* (XXV), *The Last Supper* (XXVII), and *The Crucifixion* (XXXV); or it may imply that when he was requested to improve the eight plays, he might have set out to create a world more elaborately charged with festivity than had hitherto been presented in York. It is, therefore, my contention that Robinson's assertion that the eight plays 'stand apart as a group' should be reconsidered. The comparison of the festive elements in the York Passion with the same elements in the other Cycles will suggest that they are unique to the English cycle-drama. This is not surprising, since the Feast of Corpus Christi provided the occasion for this particular dramatic genre.

The first play of the Passion sequence, *The Entry into Jerusalem*, is not considered as the work of the York Realist, but performs a very important function not only in initiating the events leading up to the Passion, but also in setting up an internally consistent and recognisable world of festival. It brings in a strong sense of festivity, which becomes the essential quality of the whole series of the York Passion. The most important terms of mirth and game and 'hail' speeches are first introduced, and the character of Jesus as a trickster is created in this play.

Now let us examine *The Entry into Jerusalem* in detail. As Jesus and His disciples come near Jerusalem, Jesus sends two disciples, Peter and Philip, to go into the town and fetch an ass and her foal. Jesus says to them that He needs the ass for the festival: '. . . I ȝou charge loke it be wrought/ Þat schal ȝe fynde/ An asse þis feste als ȝe had soght./ Ȝe hir vnbynde/ With hir foole, and to me hem bring' (XXV, ll. 18–22).[6] Jesus's reference to the 'feste' should be noted, for there is no such reference in the Scriptures (Matthew 21:2; Mark 11:2–3). The time is set at the festival. This is important, because it helps to create the dramatic world of festival and defines the nature of all the actions in the Passion sequence that follows. Peter and Philip exult with joy; they believe that the time has come for their master to win the victory and that they could celebrate it in the capital at the time of the Passover. The scene introduces a new character, the Porter, who forms a link between the disciples and the citizens. He asks the disciples for whom they need the ass; the ass is 'common', that is, for the use of the poorest in the city. Peter answers that they need it for Jesus, king of the Jews (ll. 80–1). The Porter gives them the ass and declares the news to the citizens, who rejoice at it. Jesus is spoken of as a king, 'sovereign', 'lord', and 'knight', upon which, of

---

6   York Plays are cited below from *The York Plays*, ed. Richard Beadle (London, 1982).

course, important theological meanings in the Christian story are imposed. Particularly the term 'king' becomes important at this stage. It is used nineteen times in this play. By frequent repetition, the imagery of Jesus as the King, the Saviour of mankind, is strongly emphasised. Later, ironically, those who hate Jesus are shown creating the character of Jesus in a fool-king elected by the folk for the festival. We shall also see Jesus, the heavenly king, presented in sharp contrast to Herod, a worldly king, and scorned as an idiot, only to grasp that the true roles are the reverse of those presented in the play.

Hearing the joyful noise of the people, a citizen suggests that they should go to see Him who has brought them joy:

> Go hym agayne vs blisse hath brought,
> With *myrthe* and *game*. (XXV ll. 251–2)
>> (emphases mine, in this and the subsequent quotations)

A new set of words such as 'myrth' and 'game' are introduced for the first time. They help to heighten the joyful atmosphere of the festival. In the scenes that follow, however, the same terms are used again and again to signal a series of the demonic actions by which Jesus is scorned and killed.

In the joyful atmosphere of the festival, typical episodes from Jesus's ministry, how Jesus healed the injured, are recounted. The healing of the blind man and the lame man, and the tale of Zacheus in the sycamore tree (Luke 19:2–9) present the imagery of Christ as a great healer. This is significant, because later, Jesus is erroneously interpreted as a magician or trickster by His opponents for His prophetic, healing powers. The term 'mirth' is again taken up by the blind man. He asks the poor man about the mirth that he has heard (ll. 302–6). The poor man explains that a prophet, full of grace, is coming (ll. 307–8). When they have Jesus with them, Zacheus worships the great healer, saying, 'Lord, may you eternally be worshipped by men and women' (ll. 459–60). The physical weakness of the sick men is often interpreted as representing fallen mankind's flawed spiritual state. Thus, the first scene serves to create a joyful, festive world where the bliss of the heavenly king is exhibited to everyone.

The mirth and joy of the citizens culminates in their passionate 'hail' speeches, which are as long as 55 lines. A citizen calls Jesus the *mark of mirth*, that is, the object of joy, in worshipping him:

> Hayll florisshand floure þat neuere shall fade,
> Hayll vyolett vernand with swete odoure,
> Hayll *marke of myrthe* oure medecyne made,
> Hayll blossome bright, hayll oure socoure,
>   Hayll kyng comely.
> Hayll menskfull man, we þe honnoure
>   With herte frely.   (XXV, ll. 496–502)

It should be reminded that the 'hail' speeches echo the 'Hail' lyrics previously spoken in *The Nativity* (XIV) by Joseph and Mary, and by the Three Kings in the play of *Herod and the Magi* (XVI) in worship of the Child Jesus. Later, in his betrayal at the Garden, Judas shamefully greets his master with an 'all hayll', (XXVIII, l. 248), and asks to kiss him. When Jesus is brought before Pilate for the second trial, the torturers worship Him in 'hail' marked by gruesome mock-reverence.

The joy of the citizens reaches the highest point when they triumphantly sing songs in celebrating the entry of their king. The Stage Direction does specify which songs should be sung, but it is likely that the songs were drawn from the liturgy of Palm Sunday. The stage is filled with songs, laughter and talks of mirth. The minute the people celebrate the victorious entry of their king, a strange and disturbing mood is created; the audience will be reminded of the scene where Jesus predicted that He would soon be betrayed and tortured with hatred and derision in the town.

Jesus has also predicted Peter's denials of Him, saying to him that his mirth will be soon taken away: 'Thy *game, þi gle,* al fro þe refte' (XXV, l. 477). Before His arrest, He refers again to the denials (XXVIII, ll. 147–52), which are to be dramatised in play XXIX, while Jesus is being brought before Caiphas.

Thus, *The Entry into Jerusalem* brings in the essential dramatic actions of the Passion sequence, together with 'hail' speeches and the key words such as 'king', 'game', and 'mirth'. As we shall see, these speeches and key words depend for their effect on the plays that will immediately follow, when the first scene is made to cohere dramatically through the cleverly manipulated actions and ironies.

In the next play, *The Conspiracy*, the portrait of Jesus as a trickster is first created by Pilate, who takes Jesus's entry for a joke, when he is informed of His entry into the town, and of the folk's enthusiastic welcome of Him as their king. Pilate says:

> And if so be, þat *borde* to bayll will hym bryng
> And make hym boldely to banne þe bones þat hym bare.
> (XXVI, ll. 117–8)

'þat borde' means 'that trick'; it is clear that Pilate decides in advance that Jesus is a trickster, an absurd imposter, one of the potentially disorderly men who often turn up at a time of festivals.

Pilate is historically described as an ambivalent character. It has been pointed out by critics that the characterisation of the York Pilate is inconsistent and that contradictory traditions are fused in him.[7] It is true that

---

[7] E.g., Arnold Williams values the Townely Pilate for economy of effect and for consistency of character (*The Characterization of Pilate in the Towneley Plays* (East Lansing, 1950), p. 16).

the Pilate in the first trial is sharply contrasted with the Pilate in the second trial: the former is an essentially fair judge, who shows great sympathy for Jesus when he knows that the Jews are irrationally plotting agaisnt Jesus; the latter is characterised as a Herod-like evil tyrant who swears by Lucifer and threatens Jesus with death. A close examination of his attitudes toward Jesus, however, shows that Pilate is treated with consistent dramatic manipulations. In the early part of the first trial he is portrayed as a politician who is keenly conscious of the vulnerability of his political position. The moment he feels his position is threatened, he abandons the role of the fair judge and begins cooperating with the Jews. Pilate becomes angry only when told that Jesus teaches the people to withhold the tribute to the Emperor and cails himself king of the Jews.

Caiphas[8] insists that Pilate should place charges of treason, witchcraft, and other evil doings against Jesus. He does not fail to make use of the occasion for presenting Him as a threat to social stability when Procula, Pilate's Wife, sends her son to ask her husband to save Jesus; Satan has appeared in her dream and persuaded her to do the right thing for Jesus: if Pilate dooms Jesus, he will be sorely punished. Caiphas assures Pilate that Jesus has worked the jest with his witchcraft (to disturb the society). 'Ya sir . . . þis is but a *skaunce* ['jest'],/ He with *wicchecrafte* þis wile has he wrought' (XXX, ll. 292–3).

When Jesus is brought before Pilate, Caiphas does not hesitate to call Jesus a fool that has caused many disturbances, charming the people with His witchcraft: 'The deffe and þe dome he delyuered fro doole/ By *wicchecrafte*, I warande – his wittis schall waste –/ For þe *farles* in fere þat he farith with loo how þei folowe yone *fole*,/ Oure folke so þus he frayes in fere' (XXX, ll. 442–5).

When Pilate delivers an official order to capture Jesus, he identifies Jesus as a fool and reminds his men that they should not injure the body of the fool, since they have to release him if he turns out to be harmless: 'For if þe sotte ['fool'] be sakles, vs sittis hym to saue' (XXVI, l. 288). The torturers spontaneously understand Jesus to be a trickster, a festive fool, and are ready to enjoy the wholesale action.

Formal charges are made against Jesus in various names, but it is

---

Kolve is, however, opposed to this and says that to present a character as 'bad, all bad' is an uninteresting dramatic fiction, since all men are a mixture of good and bad (Kolve, *op. cit.*, pp. 233– 4). Robert Brawer interprets the York Pilate as a realist, and remarks that the two seemingly competing conceptions of Pilate's character are consistent (Brawer, 'The Characterization of Pilate in the York Cycle', *Studies in Philology*, 69 (1972)). Lawrence M. Clopper insists that medieval playwrights did not think it necessary to maintain the character consistently throughout the sequence (Clopper, 'Tyrants and Villains: Characterization in the Passion Sequence of the English Cycle Plays', *College English*, 41 (1984), 3–20).

[8] In the Towneley Cycle it is Caiphas who is irrationally insistent on killing Jesus without going through even buffeting. Annas and Caiphas are usually distinguishable and their portraits are nearly the same from Cycle to Cycle.

surprising that all of them involve the sense of trickster: 'japer'=deceiver (XXXII, l. 44), 'faytor'=deceiver (XXVI, l. 47; XXXII, l. 47), 'warlowe'= traitor (XXIX, l. 185; XXX, ll. 140, 259; XXXII, ll. 66, 105; XXXIII, l. 190; XXXV, l. 63; XXXVI, l. 278), 'traitor' (XXIX l. 232; XXXII ll. 42, 64, 254), 'harlott' (XXIX, l. 283; XXX, l. 380; XXXII, l. 81), 'fool' (XXIX, ll. 197, 358, 376; XXX, ll. 444, 489; XXXI, ll. 91, 342, 345; XXXIII, l. 387; XXXIV, l. 28), 'sotte' (XXVI, l. 288; XXIX, l. 260).

The miracles of Jesus are described in terms of tricks: 'wicche-crafte'=witchcraft (XXIX, l. 58: XXX, ll. 293, 443), 'cautellis'=magical tricks (XXXV, ll. 206, 278), 'socery' (XXIX, l. 97; XXXIII, l. 288), 'fendes-craft'=devil's craft (XXX, l. 298), 'farles'=marvels (XXX, l. 444; XXXI, ll. 118, 188; XXXII, l. 80), 'trante'=tricks (XXIX, l. 232; XXXII, l. 254; XXXVI, l. 73), 'trayne'=deceit, trick (XXVI, l. 267), 'bourdyng'=trick (XXXI, ll. 146, 173, 174), 'gaudis'=tricks (XXXVII, l. 160), 'mervaylis'=marvels (XXXI, ll. 191, 200, 363; XXXII, ll. 46, 91), 'selcouth'=marvel (XXXI, ll. 140, 216), 'foly' (XXXI, ll. 352, 360), 'wile' (XXX, l. 159, 293).

Judas in the *Cornish Cycle* describes Jesus in the same image when he offers to the Jews to betray his master:

> It is good for you to be cautious:
> The fellow is very sharp, without a doubt,
> And he knows many tricks.[9]

We understand that the conception of Jesus as a trickster is not the invention of the York dramatist, but in the York Passion it is presented with dramatic intensity by being frequently asserted. In the *Conspiracy*, it is made more impressive by a new scene introduced into the Passion story. Curiously enough, the conspiracy takes place at Pilate's mansion. A scene is devoted to the process by which Judas has gained admission to the place. The Porter decides that he does not like Judas's appearance, and refuses to consult with his masters about letting him in. Judas twice says that he has come to offer the lords a 'mirth', which will surely keep them out of trouble: '. . . I mene of no malice but *mirthe* meve I moste' (XXVI, l. 173); '. . . but and þe truthe shulde be tryed,/ Of *myrthe* are þer materes I mell,/ For thurgh my dedis youre dugeperes fro dere may be drawen' (XXVI, ll. 181–3).

The Porter gives in, and Judas is brought before the Jews. They gladly accept Judas's betrayal. Their expectation of a good amusement is well expressed in the First Doctor's greeting to Judas:

> My blissing sone haue þou forthy –
> Loo, here is a *sporte* for to spye.   (XXVI, ll. 221–2)

---

[9] *Cornish Drama: The Ancient Cornish Drama*, ed. and trans. Edwin Norris, 2 vols. (Oxford, 1859), I, 301 (ll. 999–1001).

The dramatic events leading up to the Crucifixion are set in motion when Judas, Pilate, and the chief priests conspired to have Jesus arrested. Nothing is more tragic than this, because in the scenes that follow, Jesus is arrested, brought to trial, scourged and finally killed by the action of mirth and game first plotted by Judas, whom Jesus loves. In the Betrayal, Judas's mirth is shown as an ironic shadowing of the mirth presented in *The Entry into Jerusalem*. Moreover, in the next play, *The Last Supper*, the dramatist seeks to reveal the divine purpose of the Redemption.

In *The Last Supper*, a new scope of mirth is added to the story. Jesus makes his ominous prophecy that one of the disciples will betray Him when confronted with a critical situation. John cries in sorrow, 'Allas, oure *playe* is paste'(l. 100). Jesus comforts them, and predicts that he will rise again; when he rises, he will restore the mirth: '. . . whanne I ryse agayne/ Þan schall youre *myrthe be mende*'(ll. 150–1). He points to the truth of the Christian story, a truth which is also applicable to the actual experience of the audience who look upon the spectacle. No one would fail to understand the profound meaning of the mirth that Jesus is referring to. He speaks of the mirth designed to give men new life. It is placed in parallel to the mirth offered by Judas. Jesus's reference to the mirth has considerable ironic potential. He knows that the mirth and game of His enemies will result in catastrophy and tragedy for Him, but it is apparent on a divine level, because He has chosen the way of restoring the mirth through His sufferings. Judas's ignorance of what he is really doing is superbly illuminated. The York dramatist obviously has in mind the parallelism between the mirth spectacularly displayed by Jesus's opponents and the mirth to be restored by Him. The paradox of mirth is presented here with great emotional intensity to reveal the divine purpose of the Redemption as well as Jesus's dignity and love. They are communicated in such a way as to gain emotional response from the audience. From this time on, Jesus's physical sufferings in fact become the focal point for all the action, because His body is the supreme gift of God redeeming man's sin.

The series of sufferings that Jesus encountered is well documented in iconography. The most surprising element is perhaps the tormentor's indulgence in their task. The *Hours of Catherine of Cleves* and *Les Belles Heures de Jean Duc de Berry*, both of which are contemporary with the work by the York Realist, for example, illuminate Jesus being mocked and scourged in play and game. In the Mocking of Christ in the *Hours of Catherine of Cleves*, one man is blowing a horn, while the others are hitting Christ Jesus whose face is covered with a veil. Another tormentor in the margin beats a metal basin with a stick.[10] In the Way to Calvary and Christ nailed to the Cross in the *Les Belles Heures de Jean Duc de Berry*,

[10] *The Hours of Catherine of Cleves*, introduction and commentaries by John Plummer (New York, 1966), plate 19.

the soldiers in brightly coloured costumes are sounding a horn or raising a banner transforming the sad events into festive pageants.[11]

The Passion plays in England, which have close ties with the cultures that produced book illuminations such as these, depict Jesus's sufferings in the same way, although the York dramatist in his drama substitutes Roman soldiers for the Jewish tormentors throughout the whole sequence until the Mocking in play XXXI. V. A. Kolve has pointed out how their actions may be analysed in terms of game: 'They are shown killing Christ in outbursts of great energy, violence, laughter, and delight; they are shown turning the tasks assigned by their masters into a sequence of formal games, into a changing metamorphosis of play, and adding to them further games of their own devising.'[12] Although Kolve has not noted it, in the English cycle-drama it is Annas and Caiphas who give game motivation to the sequence and allow the torturers the opportunity for indulging in irrational behaviour. Like Herod, they are portrayed as having a frenetic appetite for diversion. From the very beginning (when they are offered mirth by Judas), they are determined to draw as much amusement as they could from the present case. Caiphas's personal intention of sending the soldiers to the Garden of Gethsemane is clearly shown in his dialogue addressed to Annas: '. . . I haue sente for þat segge halfe for hethyng ['amusement'](XXIX, l. 33). The soldiers assigned this task by the priests take the arrest for a sport, as it is shown in one soldier's swearing that Jesus shall curse this sport: 'By þe bonys þat þis bare, þis bourde schall he banne'(XXVIII, l. 297). When they come back, they shout the news of the arrival of Jesus, 'My lorde, my lorde, my lorde, here is layke and ȝou list'(XXIX, l. 190).

Caiphas asks them if they have found the fool: 'Why, and is þe foole fonne?'(XXIX, l. 197). Then, Caiphas and Annas amusingly proclaim the opening of their great fool show of the festival:

Caiphas	Pese now sir Anna, be stille and late hym stande,
	And late vs grope yf þis *gome* be grathly begune.
Anna	Sir, þis *game* is begune of þe best,
	Nowe hadde he no force for to flee þame.
	(XXIX, ll. 203–6)

Jesus is brought in, his hands tied. Caiphas spontaneously declares that he does not want to play with an 'animal' that is bound, for it is not fun: 'Itt is no burde to bete bestis þat are bune'(XXIX, l. 243). And he orders the soldiers to untie Jesus. Annas does not conceal his appetite for diversion either: 'We will haue *joie*/ To spille all thy *sporte* for thy

---

[11] *Les Belles Heures de Jean Duc de Berry*, ed. Millard Meiss and Elizabeth H. Beatson (London, 1974), fols. 138ᵛ and 141ᵛ.

[12] *The Play Called Corpus Christi* (Stanford, 1966), p. 180. See also C. Davidson, 'Civic Concern and Iconography in the York Passion', *Annuale Mediaevale*, 15 (1974), 142.

spellis'(XXIX, ll. 274–5), and insists that Jesus should be beaten straight-way. Caiphas, who has more discriminating taste in good amusement, urges the torturers to slow down the pace of the game since it is more amusing: 'Nay, sir, none haste, we schall haue game or we goo./ Boy, be not agaste if we seme gaye'(XXIX, ll. 288–9). In the trial before the priests Jesus is a sort of medieval fool that was made the butt of cruel popular entertainment.

Jesus is accused of everything from witchcraft to treason. In contrast to Jesus before Herod, He gives answers to all the accusations and refutes them, but these answers are too profound for the priests to comprehend. The soldiers believe that He is playing a joke with their masters, and they threaten Him with death. One of the soldiers says: 'What, fye on the, beggar, who made þe so bolde/ To bourde with our busshoppe? Thy bane schalle I bee'(XXIX, ll. 326–7). The interesting thing is that Jesus tempts them to the actual beating with explicit comments upon their actions by using the game words Himself. He reminds them that, if what He says is true, they shall pay dear for their game of beating that is too improperly conceived:

> Sir, if my wordis be wrange or werse þan þou wolde,
> A wronge wittenesse I wotte nowe ar 3e;
> And if my sawes be soth þei mon be sore solde,
> Wherfore þou *bourdes* to *borde* for to bete me. (XXIX, ll. 328–31)

His comments place the whole mood and manner of their actions in the true perspective of a Christian story. However, the torturers, who are concerned with the game, are never directly aware of Jesus, and believe that He has now started playing with them. And for this, they beat Him again.

To the torturers' eyes, Jesus is nothing but a braggart, a man not unlike themselves, one who pretends to be something greater. From this under-standing they create a new game of buffeting over Jesus's prophetic powers. Thus the cruellest game of Hot Cockles is engendered. It is an ancient game ultimately drawing upon the Bible (Luke 22:63–5), but is transformed into medieval terms. It has many names, but all seem to be the same. In the York Cycle, it is called 'popse'(XXIX, l. 355), 'whele and pylle' in the *Ludus Coventriae*,[13] 'new play of yoyll'[14] in the Towneley Cycle, and 'bobbid game' in a medieval sermon, as pointed out by G. R. Owst.[15] It corresponds to the modern Blind Man's Buff. The torturers blindfold Jesus and strike Him by turn, urging Him each time to guess who has struck Him. Jesus is made 'It' in their new game. In order to hit

---

[13] *Ludus Coventriae or The Plaie Called Corpus Christi*, ed. K. S. Block (London, 1922), p. 277, l. 170.

[14] *The Towneley Plays*, ed. George England and Alfred Pollard (London, 1897), p. 239, l. 344.

[15] G. R. Owst, *Literature and Pulpit in Medieval England*, 2nd ed. (Oxford, 1961), p. 510.

Him properly, they try to make Jesus sit on a stool. The term 'fool' is again applied to Jesus by the first soldier who has found a suitable stool for the task. He says, 'Lo, here is one full fitte for a foole'(XXIX, l. 358). Once the game of 'popse' starts, Jesus does not show any response. He refuses to play their game. Accordingly, the more they play, the more they are frustrated. Finally they believe Jesus is napping, though in fact he is losing consciousness due to the heavy beating. The first soldier makes a noise in order to keep Jesus from falling asleep: 'Nay, nowe to nappe is no nede, Wassaille! Wassaylle! I warande hym wakande'(XXIX, ll. 368–9). And they begin beating him again. Kolve asserts that the York torturers, being tired of their game of Hot Cockles, varied it with another, and identifies 'Wassaile' as another medieval game reminiscent of a drinking ceremony.[16] In the context, however, the cries seem to be nothing but rude sounds, but these surely help to establish a grotesque atmosphere of festivity. In spite of the torturers' desperate effort, the game of 'popse' does not seem to have been successful, because Jesus refuses to play it. They label Jesus as a witless trickster to be shown in a ceremony for a fool:

IV Miles	It semys by his wirkyng his wittes were awaye.
I Miles	Now late hym stande as he stode in a foles state,
	For he likis no3t þis layke my liffe dare I laye.
	(XXIX, ll. 375–7)

Any game has certain rules and requires a certain formal sequence of actions. Once involved, all the participants are required to follow the rules and sequences for the duration of the game. In the game of 'popse', however, Jesus spoils the game by refusing to accept this principle and by remaining silent, because they do not deserve the joyful mirth; the game of the Passion and Resurrection must go as He wants. Finally the torturers are obliged to give up the game, and have to take the spoil-sport back to the High Priests, grudgingly reporting that they have carried out their order but have not enjoyed the task at all:

III Miles	My lorde, we haue *bourded* with þis boy
	And holden hym full hote emelle vs.
Cayphas	Thanne herde ye some *japes of joye*?
IV Miles	The devell haue þe worde, lorde, he wolde telle vs.
	(XXIX, ll. 380–3)

Jesus has successfully destroyed the soldiers' game world, with his calm, silent, and patient endurance, revealing himself to be the ultimate leader of the game.

Jesus is sent to Pilate again to be finally judged. Caiphas again substitutes a game for the task: 'Sir Anna, þis *sporte* haue ye spedely aspied'

---

[16] Kolve, *ibid.*, p. 186.

(XXX, l. 205). The soldiers take Jesus to Pilate's mansion with noise, violence, jests and laughter. They are reprimanded by Pilate's servant, Beadle, and told to cease the noisy revel: 'O, what *javellis* are ye þat *jappis* with gollyng?/ . . . / I saye, gedlynges, gose bakke with youre *gawdes*' (XXX, ll. 235–7). The scene is set at night. Pilate is in bed asleep. He has strictly ordered that he should not be disturbed, but he wants fun quite as much as the others. When he is awakened, he is anxious to know whether the noisy revel has brought him some pleasure. He orders Beadle to inquire about it: 'Spedely spir þam yf any *sporte* can þei spell' (XXX, l. 246). The demonic nature of the mirth of Jesus's opponents is again suggested within the structure of play and game when Pilate's most faithful servant defies his master, and is compelled to describe the day when Jesus was welcomed and worshipped as the source of the mirth by the citizens: ' "Osanna" þei sange, "þe sone of Dauid",/ Riche men with þare robes þei ranne to his fete,/ And poure folke fecched floures of þe frith/ And made *myrthe* and *melody* þis man for to mete'(XXX, ll. 343–6). Jesus has brought mirth to the folk, but refuses to give any fun to Pilate. The conception of Jesus as a poor entertainer becomes prominent when Pilate's son accuses Jesus of failing to show respect to his father; 'O Jesu vngentill, þi *joie* is in *japes*'(XXX, l. 389). Ironically, the audience may realise that the inappropriate behaviour is really applied to the torturers, whose speeches reveal their complete lack of awareness of what they are doing.

It is in the trial before Herod, however, that the festive elements in the York Play become cohesive motifs. Herod, as in the Scripture (Luke 23), is particularly anxious to meet Jesus, because of the latter's reputation for witchcraft. Herod is presented as a king who has an anarchic appetite for fun. When the soldiers turn up at his palace with Jesus, Herod warns them that their errand should portend good sport and that he must be amused with it, otherwise they shall heavily pay for it: 'Sirs, but youre message may *myrthis* amende,/ Stalkis furthe be yone stretis or stande stone still'(XXXI, ll. 61–2). The soldiers assure Herod that they have come to offer him a good sport: 'Yis certis ser, of *myrthis* we mene'(XXXI, l. 63). One of the dukes announces Jesus's arrival: 'My lorde, þei bryng you yondir a boy boune in a bande/ Þat bodus outhir *bourdyng* or bales to brewe' (XXXI, ll. 79–80). It is reminiscent of the speech that Pilate uttered (XXVI l. 117) when he was told of Jesus's entry into the town. In the presentation of Jesus, a soldier promises Herod that they will punish the fool, if He turns out to be a poor entertainer: 'My lorde, we fare *foolys* to flay / Þat to you wolde forfette'(XXXI, ll. 91–2). Herod shows great pleasure at the presentation of such a good game:

> And in faith I am fayne he is fonne,
> His farles to frayne and to fele;
> Nowe þes *games* was grathely begonne.   (XXXI, ll. 117–9)

Addressing Jesus in French, which is broken, Herod begins the game, but is soon frustrated, because Jesus does not show any response. A soldier advises Herod that it is useless to play the game with Him: 'Nay my lorde, he can of no *bourdyng*, þis boy'(XXXI, l. 147). But this stimulates Herod's propensity for fun:

> O, my harte hoppis for joie
>   To se nowe þis prophette appere.
> We schall haue goode *game* with þis boy –
>   Takis hede, for in haste ȝe schall here.
> I leve we schall laugh and haue likyng
>   To se nowe þis lidderon her he leggis oure lawis.
>
> (XXXI, ll. 163–8)

The rowdy king is set against the dignified, silent Lord Jesus. Eventually Herod begins to be disturbed by the sullen look of the entertainer. In an attempt to encourage Herod, one of the dukes informs him that Jesus has been amusing many people with His tall tales: 'Mi lorde . . . of his *bordyng* grete bostyng men blawes'(XXXI, l. 174). Herod, willing to listen to them himself, devises a new game for fun. Believing that Jesus does not know how to behave at court because of His low birth, Herod asks Jesus about His birth: 'Saie firste at þe begynnyng withall, where was þou borne'(XXX, I l.186). The scene reminds us of the Wakefield *Buffeting*, where the torturers compare Jesus to the seasonal Christimas Fool and decide to teach him a harsher game:

> II Tortor Go we now to our noyte ['business'] with this fond foyll.
> I Tortor We shall teche hym, I wote, a new play of Yoyll ['Yule'],
>   And hold hym full hote.   (ll. 343–5)[17]

Sandra Billington's interpretation of this scene helps us to comprehend the deep meaning of the York buffeting. She remarks, 'The Yule game being enacted (the passion and death of Christ) is the fulfilment of the prophecy of his Yule-time birth. On a social level, Christ's birth is the reason for the rejoicing which permitted the pagan Fool games to which the torturers refer.'[18] The new game invented by the York Herod is comparable to the Wakefield Yule game. Herod asks Jesus about his birth and forces Him to play the role of the Christmas fool. Jesus remains silent. His silence implies that Herod, the evil pagan king, is not allowed to enjoy the Yule-time joy. Although it is beyond Herod's comprehension, the medieval audience might have fully understood the underlying meaning. Before the remaining sequence moves into the climax, the

---

[17] *The Six Pageants in the Towneley Cycle*, ed. The Society for Medieval English Drama (Tokyo, 1987), p. 182.

[18] Sandra Billington, *The Social History of the Fool* (Brighton, 1984), p.18.

Cruicifixion, Jesus's Yule-time birth should be referred to again to make sense of the Nativity-Passion-Resurrection story.

However, it is not Jesus but the torturers who actually tell Herod tall tales of Jesus's miracles. In so doing, they assign themselves the role of the Christmas fool, although they are not aware of this. The scene has considerable ironic implications, since it points out a theological truth that those who deny salvation are real fools.

Herod is amused to be told how Jesus boasted that he would ordain each man's reward at the Last Judgement, how He fed five thousand people with five loaves of bread, how He brought the dead Lazarus to life and so on. Herod exclaims in wonder, 'We, such *lesyngis* lastis to lange'(XXXI, l. 223). What has amused him most, however, is the story that Jesus calls himself king of the Jews. Herod immediately identifies Jesus as a seasonal fool-king elected by the folk, and wishes to know where Jesus comes from (XXXI, l. 231). When one of his men tells him that Jesus claims himself to be the king just to make matters easy for himself, Herod hits on another new game. He decides to elect Jesus king of his court, and invites him to sit on the throne with him: 'Comes nerre, kyng, into courte. Saie, can ȝe not knele? / We schalle haue *gaudis* full goode and *games* or we goo'(XXXI, l. 236–7).

However, Herod does not gain any response from Jesus.[19] Finally, Herod loses his patience. The moment Herod shouts at Jesus, the courtiers explain to him that his shouting and goading frighten Jesus into silence. Herod is extremely pleased with this idea and calls it 'a *bourde* of þe beste'(XXXI, l. 254). He gets more excited and finally puts his sceptre, the symbol of authority, into Jesus's hand. Ironically enough, the sceptre is placed in the hand of the true King, who is the source of mirth for new life. Of course, Herod lacks any glimpse of illumination of what he himself is really doing.

Herod's attempts to cajole Jesus into performing miracles and playing the role of court jester has finally failed. He becomes outraged at Jesus's silence. One of the soldiers lies to him that Jesus has done many marvels while being brought there from Pilate, and this makes Jesus's refusal seem more grudging. It invites the most insulting game, the dressing of Jesus in the white robes of a fool for punishment.

As for the white robes of a fool, Richard Beadle and Pamela King remark, 'Herod and his sons discuss the possibilty that Christ is frightened into silence by the court's finery, erroneously considering this to be the mark of the divine. The audience will recognise the sumptuous tawdriness the court presented before their eyes as one of the common

---

[19] As for the significance of Jesus's silence, see Rosemary Woolf, *English Mystery Plays* (London, 1972), p. 257. She has noted that it draws upon the tradition of Pseudo-Bonaventura's *Meditationes*, but Jesus's silence before the accusers is referred to in the Scriptures (Matthew 27:11–4; Mark 14:61, 15:5).

marks of misplaced pride. Hence in Christ's white fool's gown, though contemporary nonsense as such, they are presented with a visual contrast of simplicity and purity which in turn enhances his silent grandeur.'[20] It should be noted that in the later part of the play, Herod and his men treat Jesus as an idiot who has failed to amuse them, as is shown in the repeated advice of Herod's son to his father that it is no use dealing with the madman (ll. 294, 302). Earlier, Jesus was welcomed to the court as a gifted entertainer but now He is degraded to the status of an object for derision, entirely useless to the court. So, there is no need for them, it seems, to prepare for Jesus the motley gown of the professional fool. Viewed in this way, the act of dressing Jesus in white, and not in motley, is by no means 'contemporary nonsense'. In an illuminated miniature from the *Psalter in Latin and French of Jean de Berry*, a fool, who is very much like a beggar, biting at cheese, is actually shown in white robes with a fool's staff in his left hand.[21] The picture implies that an innocent fool is ruling the universe symbolised by the round shape of the cheese.

Jesus's refusal to accept the role of a successful trickster is presented as a strong contrast to His willing acceptance of His role as the seasonal king of the Passover at the time of His entry into Jerusalem. Jesus has never provided His opponents with joy, since they do not deserve it. In the trials and buffeting, game blends into game in an endlessly changing series, only to clarify Jesus's identity. The games of the festival are also sought to reveal the demonic affiliations of Jesus's enemies, as is most conspicuously shown in Herod's devilish cry: 'What, deuyll, whedir dote we or dreme?'(XXXI, l. 270) uttered when he realises that he has been defeated. This can be called one of the greatest achievements of the York dramatist, when it is remembered that, in many contemporary vernacular accounts of the Redemption, only the buffeting, the dicing for Jesus's gown and the dressing of Jesus in a fool's white gown are actually called game or play.

The executioners, who are assigned the task of taking Jesus to Calvary, immediately substitue Jesus for the fool-king in their games and display a game of mock-reverence, as it is clearly shown in First Soldier's speech: 'We haue bene besie all þis morne/ To clothe hym and to croune with thorne,/ As falles for a *fole-kyng*'(XXXIV, ll. 26–8). They constantly develop games and jokes on the road to Calvary and turn even the cruellest task of the Crucifixion into a series of games of competition. The more deeply they are absorbed in their games, the more utterly they forget with whom they are dealing. Never do they properly see Him or hear

---

[20] *York Mystery Plays: A Selection in Modern Spelling*, ed. Richard Beadle and Pamela King (Oxford, 1984), p. 175.

[21] Bibl. nat., fr. 13091, fol. 106, dated 1384–1411, reproduced in *Medieval Seasons in Europe*, by Shunsuke Kijima (Tokyo, 1983), p. 44. A drunken Jewish fool in *The Psalter of Bonne de Luxembourg* dated mid 14c, The Cloisters Museum, The Metropolitan Museum of Art, New York, fol. 83ᵛ, is also wearing a white robe.

Him. As they noisily quarrel over what to do with Him, they lose sight of the Saviour's identity; at the same time, His identity becomes clearer in the mind of the audience, who surely accept the Passion as joyful in meaning, for they know that, through the Passion, Jesus will confuse those who believe themselves as being wise and confute those who believe themselves as being mighty. It might be appropriate to conclude the present paper by quoting from the bull by Pope Urban IV, who instituted the Corpus Christi Feast in 1264: 'This is a glorious act of remembrance, which fills the minds of the faithful with joy at their salvation and brings them tears mingled with a flood of reverent joy. For surely we exult as we recall our deliverance and scarce contain our tears as we commemorate the passion of Our Lord through which we were freed . . . because on this occasion we both rejoice amid pious weeping and weep amid reverent rejoicing, joyful in our lamentation and woeful in our jubilation.'[22]

---

[22] Reproduced and translated by Kolve, *op. cit.*, p. 45.

'Greyn' of Martyrdom in Chaucer's
*Prioress's Tale**

ISAMU SAITO

"This welle of mercy, Cristes mooder sweete,
I loved alwey, as after my konnynge;
And whan that I my lyf sholde forlete,
To me she cam, and bad me for to synge
This anthem verraily in my deyynge,
As ye han herd, and whan that I hadde songe,
Me thoughte she leyde *a greyn* upon my tonge."
(VII, 656–62; emphasis mine)[1]

A 'litel clergeon' (VII, 503), seven-year-old boy, whose throat has been cut by the Jews, continues to sing an antiphon 'Alma redemptoris mater' in virtue of a 'greyn' laid on his tongue by the Blessed Virgin Mary. When the 'greyn' is removed from his mouth his soul ascends to heaven 'softely' (VII, 672). F. N. Robinson, whose text of Chaucer has long been a popular one among critics, explained the 'greyn' as a 'pearl', because the pearl was a recognised symbol of the Virgin.[2] James Winny's text comments on the 'greyn' as a 'small pearl: an appropriate emblem of purity',[3] following probably Robinson's explanation. In L. D. Benson's new edition, however, a great variety of interpretations of the 'greyn', inclusive of Robinson's, is summarised so as to make us realise that the symbolism of the 'greyn' is still a problem awaiting solution.[4]

---

[*] This is a revised version of the paper I read at the 8th Congress of the Japan Society of Medieval English Studies held at Aoyamagakuin University in Tokyo on 5 December, 1992.

[1] References to and citations of Chaucer's text are made from L. D. Benson, ed., *The Riverside Chaucer*, 3rd ed., based on *The Works of Geoffrey Chaucer*, ed. F. N. Robinson (Boston: Houghton Mifflin, 1987).

[2] F. N. Robinson, ed., *The Works of Geoffrey Chaucer*, 2nd ed. (London: Oxford University Press, 1975), p. 736.

[3] James Winny, ed., *The Prioress' Prologue and Tale* (Cambridge: Cambridge University Press, 1975), p. 58.

[4] L. D. Benson, *op. cit.*, p. 916.

I

Since the 'greyn' is placed on the tongue of the boy so that he may continue singing *Alma*, it is certain that the 'greyn' is the sign of the Virgin's favour towards the person who unconditionally devotes himself to her, and that the tale seems to be designed as an anecdote of the miracles of the Virgin. However, if the tale were told wholly to illustrate the Virgin's boundless mercy, it would seem desirable that the boy should be restored to life by the mercy of the Virgin. In some other analogues the boy is miraculously dug up from the earth alive and unharmed. The thirty-three analogous versions of the miracle are classified and arranged by Carleton Brown as A, B, and C.[5] In Group A, apparently the earliest form of the legend, the boy's anthem leads to the discovery of his body, and he is restored to life by the miraculous efficacy of the Virgin, and his resurrection excites the conversion of the Jews. In Group B the contrivance is almost the same except that the episode of the boy's mother drops out of the story. Only in Group C, of which *The Prioress's Tale* is one, the boy's life is not restored physically and he yields up his soul leaving tear-stained people behind. Groups A and B retain the genuine type of Marian miracles – a happy ending from the medieval Christian point of view, but Group C adopts the legend of child-martyrs, in which the boy is the victim of the Jews' ritual murder.[6] Chaucer, most likely, chose the source of the tale from among Group C and worked over his *Prioress's Tale*. *The Prioress's Tale*, therefore, is not merely a story of a Marian miracle, but also a story of martyrdom. The key to solve the meaning of the 'greyn' seems to lie in this point.

In Group C, there are four versions in which miraculous objects are found in the mouth of the boys. In C 5 (Vernon version (Bodeleian MS. 3938)) it is 'A lilie flour, so briht and cler' (*S & A*, p. 473), in C 6, Chaucer's version, 'a greyn', in C 9 (Alphonsus a Spina, Fortalicium fidei (Basil, *c.* 1475)), 'a precious stone' (*lapidem . . . preciosum*) (*S & A*, p. 478), and in C 10 (Trinity College, Cambridge, MS. 0.9.38, fol. 37), 'a white pebble' (*lapillum album set saxo simillimum*)(*S & A*, p. 482). Whatever symbolism they may bear, it is necessary to examine whether or not these objects, inclusive of Chaucer's 'greyn', suggest the logic of martyrdom.

To begin with, let us go into the meaning of martyrdom from a medieval Christian point of view. A martyr is a person who has given and exposed his life in testimony to the truth of Christian faith. Clement I, in his *Epistle*, referring to the endurance of St. Peter and St. Paul in their suffering, says that a martyr is the person who 'because of unrighteous jealousy suffered . . . and having thus given his testimony went to the

---

[5] *Sources and Analogues of Chaucer's Canterbury Tales*, ed. W. F. Bryan and G. Dempster (London: Routledge & Kegan Paul, 1941), pp. 447–50; hereafter cited as *S & A*.

[6] *S & A*, pp. 647–9.

glorious place . . .'[7] Ignatius of Antioch insisted that the martyr was one who perfectly imitated Christ in his suffering and death.[8] For Origen, martyrdom was a testimony of the victory already achieved over the evil power and an assertion of the resurrection.[9] Tertullian considered martyrdom the second baptism since it removed all sin and assured the martyr of his eternal crown.[10] For Origen, likewise, martyrdom was the baptism of blood, because, 'just as the Savior brought cleansing to the world,' martyrdom does 'cleanse many'.[11] Martyrdom, paradoxically speaking, is to obtain 'a life in death', or 'the everlasting spiritual life in physical death'.

Three conditions are required for a martyr: (1) that physical life has been laid down and real death undergone; (2) that death has been inflicted in hatred of Christian life and truth; (3) that death has been voluntarily accepted in defence of these.[12] The boy's death in *The Prioress's Tale* meets the first and the second conditions. As for the third one, however, there is some question. His death is not a voluntary one, but passive and accidental. Is the boy's death, then, not martyrdom? Perhaps it may not be. But the Prioress (and Chaucer behind her) had probably no concern for such a rigorism of theology. People's affectionate sentimentality in the fourteenth and fifteenth centuries could accept, without reserve, the slain boy as a martyr, and Chaucer was well aware of people's elasticity of mind. But the final condition is not necessarily beyond question. Cajetan, a theologian in the fifteenth century, allows that a man might be martyred in his sleep, and holds that unbaptised babies can be saved in the faith of their parents.[13] (We have to remember here that the boy's mother, a widow, always taught her little boy to 'worship . . . Cristes moder deer' (VII, 510–1).) For this reason the Church did not hesitate to enroll the Holy Innocents among the martyrs. Nor did the Prioress feel reluctant to compare the boy to the Holy Innocents who follow the white Lamb in Revelation.

What, then, is the symbolism of 'a lily', 'a precious stone', and 'a white pebble' in each of the other three analogues of *The Prioress's Tale*? Has it something to do with the formation of the legend of martyrdom adopted to the traditional legend of Marian miracles? 'Lily', as the symbol of purity, has traditionally been considered an attribute of Christ, Mary and

---

7 *The Apostolic Fathers*, Vol. I, ed., and trans. Kirsopp Lake, The Loeb Classical Library (London: Heineman, 1912), p. 17.

8 F. X. Murphy, 'Martyr', *The New Catholic Encyclopedia*, Vol. IX (Washington, D. C.: The Catholic University of America Press, 1967).

9 *Ibid.*

10 *Ibid.*

11 Origen, *An Exhortation to Martyrdom, Prayer, First Principles: Prologue to the Commentary on the Song of Songs, Homily XXVII on Mumber*, trans. Rowan A. Greer (New York: Paulist Press, 1979), pp. 61–2.

12 T. Gilby, 'Theology of Martyrdom', *The New Catholic Encyclopedia*, Vol. IX.

13 *Ibid.*

other Virgin-Mothers,[14] and would naturally be accepted as the sign of the Virgin's grace. The image of the lily serves to associate the boy's purity with Mary's and is appropriate for the legend in which a Marian miracle is the central topic. 'Lily' is moreover the symbol of immortality, eternal love and resurrection, for it grows again from the seed remaining in the ground[15] and is a suitable image for the legend of martyrdom. But it is arbitrary to assume that Chaucer's 'greyn' is directly concerned with the image of a lily, because one is of a cereal plant and the other, of a flowering one. If we took 'a precious stone' or 'a white pebble' as 'pearl' which, for its parthenogenesis, shares the same attribute with the Virgin,[16] it would not be so farfetched to conclude that the 'greyn' is the symbol of a 'pearl', as F. N. Robinson did. The 'greyn'-equals-'pearl' theory therefore would be possible, so far as *The Prioress's Tale* is considered as the adaptation of the legend of the miracle of the Virgin with no element of martyrdom.

In the Middle English *Pearl*[17] we can find the image of 'pearl' associated with the Holy Innocents, the infant martyrs. A 'faunt' (161), or 'precious perle' (4, 48, 82, 192, etc.), who passed away at the age of two is found in bliss among the 144,000 infant followers of 'Þe Lombe þe sakerfyse' (1064) in Jerusalem. But in the *Pearl*, the 'faunt' is privileged to be one of the followers of the white Lamb not because she is murdered as a martyr but because she died pure and unstained (Vmblemyst . . . wythouten blot (782)). The example of the *Pearl* does not necessarily support the grain-equals-pearl-equals-martyrdom theory.

'Greyn' is grain, and 'pearl' is pearl. Each has its own entity as an object. Even if 'greyn' symbolises any abstract ideas, and 'pearl', the same one, it is only because either shares the same attribute. But it does not follow that 'greyn' is equivalent to 'a precious stone' or 'a pearl'. 'Greyn' is not a gem or a stone but a 'single seed of plant . . . which is small, hard, and roundish in form' (*O.E.D.*). In Latin, 'granum' is 'the seed of a cereal plant' (*Oxford Latin Dictionary*, ed. P. G. W. Glare, 1982). The question is what the cereal plant or its 'semen' does symbolise in accordance with its vegetable property. Sherman Hawkins, in his 'Chaucer's Prioress and the Sacrifice of Praise',[18] contrasts the commonness of a grain to a pearl comparing two Biblical parables in Matthew, 13:31 and 13:45. One is that 'The kingdom of heaven is like to a grain (*grano*) of mastard seed,'[19] and the other is that 'the kingdom of heaven is

---

[14] 'Lily', Ad de Vries, *Dictionary of Symbols and Imagery* (Amsterdam: North-Holland, 1974); James Hall, *Dictionary of Subjects and Symbols in Art* (London: John Murray, 1974).

[15] Ad de Vries, *ibid.*

[16] 'Pearl', Ad de Vries, *ibid.*

[17] *Pearl*, ed. E. V. Gordon (Oxford: Clarendon Press, 1952).

[18] *J.E.G.P.*, 63:4 (1964), 614–7.

[19] All quotations from the English Bible are from the *Authorized Version* unless otherwise stated.

like unto a merchant, seeking goodly pearls (*bonas margaritas*)'. Thus he explains that the 'greyn' signifies *verbum Dei* as the 'goodly pearls' do. The kingdom of heaven, however, in Matthew, 13, is variously compared to other things. Sometime it is 'leaven' (*fermento*) (33), and sometime, 'a net' (*sagenæ*)(47). As far as the attribute of the object is concerned, the 'greyn' must be also synonymous to both 'leaven' and 'a net'. A dozen other objects would have served just as well. Most likely Hawkins pointed out only the commonness of 'greyn' to 'pearl' taking the solidity of both objects into consideration.

Paul E. Beichner hesitates to interpret the 'greyn' as a pearl, because 'if the [magical] "greyn" were a precious stone or a pearl, anyone with an ecclesiastical mentality would have preserved it properly as a relic,'[20] as was done in the two analogues (C 9 (*S & A*, p. 477); C 10 (*S & A*, p. 483)). But in *The Prioress's Tale*, when the 'greyn' is removed from the boy's mouth, nothing more is said about it. And Chaucer nowhere used the word 'greyn' for a gem, a precious stone, or a pearl. For Beichner the 'greyn' is a grain of paradise, the throat soother. The image therefore is that of a loving mother who uses medicine to relieve the pain and distress of the injured throat of her child.[21] To express the maternal affection of the Virgin in relation to the boy's mother's, and the narrator Prioress's, the image is possibly fitting so far as the tale is told only as the panegyric of Marian mercy.

II

The Prioress, the narrator, judges the murdered boy as the martyr (VII, 579, 610, 680). She likens the boy to 144,000 virgins who follow the Lamb, having been purchased from among the men on earth as a consecrated offering to God and the Lamb (Rev., 14:3f.), saying 'Now maystow syngen, folwynge evere in oon the white Lamb celestial' (VII, 580–1), and compares him, in closing her tale, to a famous child-martyr, Hugh of Lincoln, 'slayn also / With cursed Jewes' (VII, 684–5).[22] If *The Prioress's Tale* were to be considered as a legend of martyrdom which is adopted to Marian miracle, the 'greyn' should be interpreted in that line. This boy is assumed to be one of the innocents who were redeemed as the first fruits (*primitiæ*) to God and the Lamb. In heaven 'he is now' (VII, 683). It is the surrender to a higher order, or the triumphant victory over the evil power. The 'greyn' is not so much a mere sign of the Virgin as the symbolism of the victory through martyrdom.

---

[20] Paul E. Beichner, 'The Grain of Paradise', *Speculum*, 36 (1961), 303.

[21] *Ibid.*

[22] For the details of Hugh of Lincoln confer my article 'Is *Prioress's Tale* Adapted to its Teller?', *Doshisha Studies in English*, 52 and 53 (1991), 8–29.

In the time of Chaucer, Osbern Bokenham (1392–1477), a Suffolk man, an Augustinian friar, in his account of St. Agatha in *Legendys of Hooly Wummen*,[23] talks of her martyrdom with the metaphor of 'greyn'. Tormented by Quintianus, the consul, she rather rejoices in her pain:

> For þis I wyl þou knowe certeyn,
> That, lych as þe nobyl *greyn* whete,
> Tyl yt be weel trosshyn & bete
> And from þe chaf be partyd so clene
> That no fylth þer-in be sene,
> It ne shal be put in-to þe garnere
> Of þe lord; & so in lych manere
> May not my soule, depuryd fro*m* vyce
> Entryn yn of gloryous paradyce
> By palme of *martyrdam* to þe place
> But þou my body do al to-race
> Wyth þi tormentours ful dylygently.   (8570–81; emphases mine)

As the 'greyn' is beaten off from the chaff and put into the granary of the Lord, so Agatha's soul is received into the realm of heaven with the consul's torments (beating). Bokenham's description of St. Agatha's fortitude is a free adaptation from the same scene in Jacobi a Voragine's *Legenda Aurea*. ('Greyn' in Bokenham is the translation from 'triticum' (threshed grain of wheat) in *Legenda*, and 'By palme of martyrdam', from 'cum palma martirii').[24]

This sort of metaphor in relation to sufferings and martyrdom is seen in Augustine's writings. In his *In Joannis Evangelium Tractatus*, Augustine, referring to the cry of a sufferer, says that it is not the voice of one man because the faithful are 'many grains (*grana*) groaning amid the chaff (*paleas*), scattered through the whole world'.[25] Martyrs who have been groaning in the chaff are to be delivered and scattered as the seeds of new life. The same sort of metaphor appears in the second vespers of the Feast of the Holy Innocents (28 Dec.) in *Sarum Breviary*.[26] Its responsory runs as follows: 'Jacet *granum* oppressum palea, / justus caesus pravorum framea. / Caelum domo commutans lutea' (The grain lies crushed from the chaff, the just man is felled by the sword of the sinner, changing

---

[23] *Legendys of Hooly Wummen*, ed. Mary S. Serjeanston, E.E.T.S., o.s., 26 (London: Oxford University Press, 1938).

[24] Jacobi a Voragine, *Legenda Aurea*, resensuit de Th. Grasse (Dresden, 1890, repr. 1969, Osnabrück: Otto Zeller), p. 171.

[25] *In Joannis Evangelium Tractatus*, CXXIV, *Patrologiae cursus completus*, ed. J. P. Migne, Series Latina, 35, 1438; St. Augustine, *Tractates on the Gospel of John, 1–10*, trans., John Rettig, The Fathers of the Church, 78 (Washington, D. C.: The Catholic University of America Press, 1988), p. 154.

[26] Nicholas Maltman, 'The Divine Granary or the End of the Prioress's "Greyn" ', *Chaucer Review* 17:2 (1982).

his house of clay for heaven) (emphasis mine).[27] The day following the Feast of the Holy Innocents is the Feast of Thomas of Canterbury (29 Dec.) and the second vespers of Holy Innocents is sung when the procession reaches the altar of Thomas of Canterbury, and the prosa *Clangat pastor* is sung. In the prosa there are such lines as 'Martir vitae donatus laurea / Velut *granum purgatum palea.* / In divina transfertur horrea' (The martyr, given the laurel wealth of life, is, like the grain purged from the chaff, transported into divine granaries) (emphases mine). Here again we come across the metaphor of the 'greyn' being beaten out of chaff and transported to the realm of new life in heaven.[28]

III

The Prioress, referring to Herod who ordered the murder of all the children in Bethlehem, compares the sorrow of the boy's mother to that of Rachel who weeps for her lost children (Mat., 2:18). Rachel's weeping is originally in Jeremiah, 31:15, and adapted to the murdered innocents in Matthew, 2. On the loss of Rachel's sons, Ambrose comments with the metaphor of plowing and explains that what is sown is not the seed of grain, but the seed of martyrs (*martyrum seges*) and that Rachel's weeping for her children is 'to offer for Christ her babes washed with her tears' (. . . *ut lacrymis ablutos suis, pro Christo offeret infantulos*). The loss of her children is rather a sort of triumph.[29] This is the exegesis which probably takes into consideration the Holy Innocent slain by Herod. The Prioress also, as stated previously, likens the murdered boy to the Holy Innocent, paraphrasing Revelation, 14:16, sings in apostrophe that the martyr would ever sing 'a song al newe' (VII, 584), amidst the virgins that follow the celestial Lamb. The boy, now that he is in heaven, will triumphantly continue to sing a new song just as, while he was on earth, he sang *Alma*:

Alma Redemptoris Mater, quæ pervia cæli / Porta manes, et stella maris succurre cadenti . . .[30]

---

[27] *Ibid.*, 164–5; English translations are Sister Maltman's.

[28] I cannot endorse J. C. Werk's opinion that the 'greyn' is 'the most worthless grain of seed of sand as compared to eternal existence with God'. The 'greyn', he asserts, was taken away from the child's tongue as a worthless earthly existence. Werk therefore insists that even the boy's song is only 'the brief burst of song' compared to 'the eternal symphony of praise which sounds to God, who is everlasting'. ('On the Source of the *Prioress's Tale*', *Mediæval Studies*, XVII (1955), 219). The 'greyn', however, in my opinion, is a thing which incites the boy to sing *Alma* leading him to 'the eternal symphony'.

[29] Migne, *Patrologia Latina*, 16 1139; Saint Ambrose, *Letters*, *1–91*, trans. Mary M. Beyenka, The Fathers of the Church: A New Translation, 26 (Washington, D. C.: The Catholic University of America Press, 1954), p. 269.

[30] *Officium Parvum Beatae Mariae Virginis*, editto amillor secunda (Tokyo: Komyosha, 1965), p. 98.

'Bountiful Mother of the Redeemer, you (who) are the passage to heaven. You remain the gate and star of the sea. Hasten to give help to the fallen one.' Thus the boy sang. The Virgin will help us even if we fall, because she is 'the passage to heaven' (*pervia cæli*). The Virgin's action of putting a 'greyn' on the boy's tongue is that of sowing the seed of martyrdom. Once the 'greyn' is removed, the boy would, as the good seed (*bonum . . . semen*), or one of the children of the Kingdom (*filii regni*) (Matt., 13:38), join the 144,000 infants in heaven through 'the passage' and sing a new song (*canticum novum*) (Rev., 14:3). The boy's *Alma* on earth is 'the passage' to *canticum novum* in heaven.[31] If martyrdom is, as Origen explained, the testimony of victory, 'a new song' is the song of victory. In medieval exegesis *canticum* signifies a joy over eternal things and the sign for faith, charity, and grace.[32]

In Maccabees, 7,[33] there is the story of seven martyred brothers who endured terrible torments and finally were slain by the heathen king, believing in 'an eternal renewal of life (*æternæ vitæ*), (II Macc., 7:9) in the hope that they shall be raised up again by Him (*spem exspectare a Deo, iterum ab ipso resuscitandos*) (II Macc., 7:14). Their mother, looking on her seven sons perishing within one day endured the sight with a good courage for the hopes that she had set on the Lord (II Macc., 7:14). Origen, referring to this mother's endurance, says that it is the power of love for God, for 'The Lord is my strength and song' (Ps., 118:14).[34] Bernard suggests that songs are sung for victory won (*pro obtentu victoriae*).[35] The seven-year-old boy's song is the *canticum* of martyrdom which opens the way to a new song of victory and the 'greyn' is laid on his tongue as 'the passage' to heaven where a new song is sung. The Virgin, the passage to heaven, put it on his tongue. The 'greyn' qualifies the boy to be the martyr, raising his status from mere victim to inspirer of Christian action. Hereupon *The Prioress's Tale* is rightly explained as the combination of the legend of Marian miracles and that of martyrdom.

---

[31] Audrey Davidson also took note of the phrase 'pervia cæli' in *Alma* and interpreted it as 'the open door to heaven' (464), emphasising the motherliness of the Virgin, whose role was 'intermediary between the ordinary person and the Lord of heaven' (464). But Davidson did not make special mention of the phrase in terms of martyrdom. She was primarily concerned about the origin of the anthem's text and tune and its appropriateness. ('*Alma redemptoris mater*: The Little Clergeon's Song', *Studies in Medieval Culture*, IV (1974), 3).

[32] David Chamberlain, 'Musical Signs and Symbols in Chaucer: Convention and Originality', *Signs and Symbols in Chaucer's Poetry*, ed. J. P. Herman and J. J. Burke, Jr. (Alabama: The University of Alabama Press, 1981), pp. 58–9.

[33] *The Apocrypha*, translated out of the Greek and Latin Tongues, The World Classics, 294 (London: Oxford University Press, 1926).

[34] Origen, *op. cit.*, p. 59.

[35] *S. Bernardi Opera*, Vol. I, *Sermones super Cantica Canticorum*, ed. J. Leclercq, C. H. Talbot and H. M. Rochais (Romae Editiones Cistercienses, 1957), p. 6; Bernard of Clairvaux, *On the Song of Songs*, I, trans. Killan Walsh (Kalamazoo: Cistercian Publications, 1981), p. 4.

A Note on 'Nature' in *Hamlet*

SHINSUKE ANDO

The protean word 'Nature' in Shakespeare's plays is obviously a hard nut to crack. A Japanese translator cannot but encounter great difficulty in interpreting it with the single Japanese word 'shizen', whose meaning in fact only vaguely corresponds to that of 'Nature'. Similar difficulties arise with such words as 'love', 'order', 'peace', 'law', 'custom', 'fortune', 'reason', 'time', 'form', 'fashion', all of which are essentially inherent in the medieval and Renaissance conception of the term 'Nature'. Needless to say, the difficulty is not only for translators nurtured in a different history of ideas and semantics. The term itself, in Shakespeare, implies extremely complex and varied conceptions, and it is crucial to know the proper connotation of the term in order to understand the ethical ideals behind Shakespeare's dramatic representation.

John F. Danby's *Shakespeare's Doctrine of Nature: A Study of "King Lear"* (London, 1949) is one of the most splendid analyses of the complicated idea of Nature in Shakespeare.[1] By accentuating the characteristic contrast between medieval and modern doctrines of Nature, he clarifies the structure of *King Lear* as essentially based on the dramatic conflict between these two opposing conceptions of what the word signifies. His interpretation of *King Lear* as a drama of ideas is pre-eminent. However, it is on the single word Nature that Shakespeare relies throughout the whole play, – of course, irrespectively of Danby's semantic differentiation of the concepts of the word. Naturally, when we read the text, the subtle ambiguities of the word allow us to choose our associations. Moreover, it should be asked if Danby's clear-cut classification of the meaning of 'Nature' into two distinct categories, 'medieval' and 'modern', is entirely satisfactory. Did the word Nature acquire a new meaning, or did its meaning expand into a more complex and even contradictory one? This is not an easy question to answer. The problem is that Danby's impressive argument may lead us to an excessively schematic categorisation of the idea of Nature, to fail to grasp the total message of the word, which had been enriched throughout human history.

---

[1] Cf. E. C. Knowlton, 'Nature and Shakespeare', *P.M.L.A.*, LI (1936), 719 ff.; E. M. W. Tillyard, *The Elizabethan World Picture* (London, 1943); and Theodore Spencer, *Shakespeare and the Nature of Man* (London, 1949).

'In the beginning was the Word, & the Word was with God, and the Word was God'. This statement at the beginning of the Gospel according to St. John is certain to remind us that linguistics as well as theology is a discipline fraught with danger. Is it not that the 'Word' is as dangerous a subject to talk about as is 'God'? As one is perplexed when asked the question 'What is God?', one is cast into doubt as to the meaning of any single word. The doubt grows all the more as one strives to clarify the meaning. This is what we usually experience with poetic language, but we cannot expect any definitive solution of semantics. Junzaburo Nishi-waki, a representative modernist poet of Japan, once declared that 'Poetics is as dangerous a subject as theology. All the theories of poetics are dogmata.'[2] One may here be allowed to replace the word 'poetics' with 'linguistics'. Just like the history of theology, the history of both poetics and linguistics is nothing but a tradition of casuistic dogmata. Thus, Danby's interpretation of medieval and Elizabethan Nature is often quoted almost as dogma, although what should be emphasised is his least dogmatic critical insight into the ambiguous subtlety of meaning. With this in mind, I here intend to draw a tentative sketch of 'Nature' in *Hamlet*.

One of the most important key-words in *King Lear* is the word Nature; and, as mentioned above, the dramatic structure of the play is based on the conflicting conceptions of this word. The character of this play as 'a drama of ideas' obviously reinforces the idea that morality played an important role in fostering Shakespeare's dramatic genius and sensibility. It is not impossible to describe *King Lear* as a 'drama of allegories' of the two kinds of Nature. In comparison with this play, Nature cannot be said to be such an important key-word in *Hamlet*. However, Nature in this play, as in *King Lear*, also shows its semantic change or expansion characteristic of the period of transition from the Middle to the Modern ages.

First, I should like to quote Hamlet's words, addressed to the itinerant players, which can be accepted as an exposition of Shakespeare's own idea of drama.[3]

> *Hamlet* [*to the First Player*]. Speak the speech I pray you as I pronounced it to you, trippingly on the tongue, but if you mouth it as many of your players do, I had as lief the town-crier spoke my lines. Nor do not saw the air too much with your hand thus, but use all gently, for in the very torrent, tempest, and as I may say whirlwind of your passion, you must acquire and beget a *temperance that may give it smoothness* . . .
> *Hamlet*. Be not too tame neither, but let your own *discretion* be your tutor, suit the action to the word, the word to the action, with this special observance, that you *o'erstep not the modesty of nature*: for *any*

---

2 Junzaburo Nishiwaki, *Surrealistic Poetry* [Chogenjitsushugi Shiron] (Tokyo, 1930), p. 1.
3 All quotations from *Hamlet* are taken from *Hamlet*, ed. J. D. Wilson (Cambridge, 1971).

A NOTE ON 'NATURE' IN *HAMLET*

thing so o'erdone is from the purpose of playing, whose end both at the first, and now, was and is, *to hold as 'twere the mirror up to nature* to show virtue her own feature, scorn her own image, and the very age and body of the *time* his form and pressure . . .

(III. ii. 1–24; emphases mine in this and in the subsequent quotations)

Hamlet warns the players against exaggerated or insufficient dramatic presentation, and asserts that Nature should be the fundamental ideal of the art of playing. One may say that playing is a mimetic art, and no expression by means of 'Mimesis' can be 'Nature' itself. As regards the relationship between Art and Nature, however, Shakespeare had a clear view, which is shown in the following words of Polixenes towards Perdita (*The Winter's Tale*, IV. iv. 89–92)[4]:

> . . . nature is made better by no mean,
> But nature makes that mean: *so, over that art*
> *Which you say adds to nature, is an art*
> *That nature makes*. . . You see, sweet maid, we marry
> A gentler scion to the wildest stock,
> And make conceive a bark of baser kind
> By bud of nobler race. This is an art
> Which does mend nature. . . change it rather, but
> *The art itself, is nature.*

Hamlet's words should be taken as emphasising that 'Nature' makes 'an art' in drama. If Art itself is Nature, the art of playing must be governed by the ideal of Nature, which demands that the players 'speak the speech trippingly on the tongue' and play temperately and with 'smoothness'. Both 'discretion' and 'modesty' were ideas which inherently pertained to the orthodox Nature of the Middle Ages. The act of overstepping the 'modesty of nature' in disregard of the rules of 'discretion' would have been described as being against Nature. The Renaissance ideal of the golden mean is obviously heir to the medieval conception of Nature.

Hamlet declares that the purpose of playing, including the art of playwright, has always been 'to hold as 'twere the mirror up to *nature*'. The idea of nature in this context is also medieval. It signifies the sublunary world of human beings, the earthly world of time as opposed to eternity.[5] John Dover Wilson comments that Hamlet implies that this mirror should 'not reflect nature but show human nature the ideal'.[6] The purpose of all Renaissance arts was certainly to represent the essential

---

4 *The Winter's Tale*, ed. A. Quiller-Couch and J. D. Wilson (Cambridge, 1931).
5 Cf. 'Thou know'st 'tis common, all that lives must die, / Passing through *nature* to *eternity*.' (*Hamlet*, I. ii. 71–2)
6 Wilson, *ibid.*, p. 196.

qualities of humanity. My feeling is that the subsequent words – 'to show virtue her own feature, scorn her own image, and the very age and body of the time his form and pressure' – were something like Shakespeare's own commentary in order to make more concrete the abstract connotations of Nature.

The 'time', here, also pertains to the meaning field of the orthodox Nature. Thus, Hamlet's words:

> The time is out of joint, O curséd spite,
> That ever I was born to set it right!   (I. v. 188–9)

can be interpreted as a solemn lament of the tragic hero. The disjointed 'time' indicates the destruction of Nature as a manifestation of Order, Reason, Law, Justice, and Harmony. Hamlet's predicament comes from his fear that everything has been cast into complete chaos. My conviction is that Hamlet's ethical principles are firmly based on the normative code inherent in the ideal of medieval Nature. Ophelia sees in Hamlet the ideal of humanity and also an embodiment of the ideal of medieval Nature. Her sorrow is profound when she sees Hamlet completely changed:

> *Ophelia.* O, What a noble mind is here o'erthrown!
>   The courtier's, soldier's, scholar's eye, tongue, sword,
>   Th'expectancy and rose of the fair state,
>   The glass of fashion, and the mould of form,
>   Th'observed of all observers, quite quite down.
>   And I of ladies most deject and wretched,
>   That sucked the honey of his music vows,
>   Now see *that noble and most sovereign reason*
>   *Like sweet bells jangled, out of tune and harsh,*
>   That unmatched form and feature of blown youth,
>   Blasted with ecstasy! O, woe is me!
>   T'have seen what I have seen, see what I see!   (III. i. 153–64)

The loss of Reason also indicates the destruction of Nature. I should like to quote here an interesting example which shows the close relationship between Nature and Reason. Although admiring Hamlet's filial piety towards his father, Claudius implores him to cast aside his 'unprevailing woe', and says:

>   But to persever
> In obstinate condolement is a course
> Of impious stubbornness, 'tis unmanly grief,
> It shows a will most incorrect to heaven, ...
>   ...   'tis a fault to heaven,
> A fault against the dead, *a fault to nature,*
> *To reason most absurd,* ...   (I. ii. 92–103)

Claudius's words 'To reason most absurd' are again Shakespeare's own commentary, clarifying the meaning of 'a fault to nature'. According to the orthodox concept of medieval Nature, Reason is Nature itself.

Claudius himself pretends to lament the death of King Hamlet, but says:

> Yet so far hath *discretion* fought with *nature*,
> That we with wisest sorrow think on him
> Together with remembrance of ourselves: (I. ii. 5–7)

It is noteworthy that Claudius uses the word 'discretion' here in the sense of an opposite to 'nature'. The sense of the word 'nature' here is clearly contradictory to that in which Claudius used it to admonish Hamlet's 'obstinate condolement'. It also differs from the concept of Nature, inseparable from 'discretion' and 'modesty', with which Hamlet instructed the players in the purpose of playing. One may say, according to Danby, that medieval and modern concepts of Nature are confused in Claudius. But we should be careful not to overstep the modesty of nature in this kind of examination of the word. What is important is to try to grasp the complex meaning of Shakespearean Nature in its entirety. Any semantic analysis of the word is merely a preliminary to the appreciation of 'human nature the ideal' shown in Shakespeare's mirror held up to nature.

It is well known that Stendhal, in *Le Rouge et le Noir*, used as an epigraph an aphorism he attributes to Saint-Réal, that 'Un roman: c'est un miroir qu'on promène le long d'un chemin'.[7] He propounds the same idea in another chapter:

> Eh, monsieur, un roman est un miroir qui se promène sur une grande route. Tantôt il reflète à vos yeux l'azur des cieux, tantôt la fange des bourbiers de la route. Et l'homme qui porte le miroir dans sa hotte sera par vous accusé d'être immoral! Son miroir montre la fange, et vous accusez le miroir! Accusez bien plutôt le grand chemin où est le bourbier, et plus encore l'inspecteur des routes qui laisse l'eau croupir et le bourbier se former.[8]

Stendhal may have conceived this idea of the novel, singularly characteristic of his own works, on the basis of Saint-Réal's definition of

---

7 P. G. Castex, ed., *Le Rouge et le Noir* (Classiques Garnier, 1973), I, xiii, p. 72. 'A novel: a mirror which one takes out on one's walk along the high road.' [*The Red and the Black*, trans. H. B. Samuel] (London, 1922), p. 79.

8 'Yes, monsieur, a novel is a mirror which goes out on a highway. Sometimes it reflects the azure of the heavens, sometimes the mire of the pools of mud on the way, and the man who carries this mirror in his knapsack is forsooth to be accused by you of being immoral! His mirror shows the mire, and you accuse the mirror! Rather accuse the main road where the mud is, or rather the inspector of roads who allows the water to accumulate and the mud to form.' *The Red and the Black*, trans. H. B. Samuel, p. 366.

ARTHURIAN AND OTHER STUDIES

history; although the commentators seem to have failed to locate the precise words in Saint-Réal's works.[9] My hypothesis is that it was also through Hamlet's words on the purpose of playing that this eminent novelist acquired the idea. Stendhal was a great admirer of Shakespeare. In particular, his great interest in *Hamlet* led him to create his own version of it in the form of political tragedy (1805). Although the mirror of Stendhal must of course have been quite different from that of Shakespeare,[10] one is almost tempted to describe Stendhal's statement as a remarkable variation on the theme presented by Hamlet. Certainly Stendhal was a great novelist, one who could most intuitively recognise the true meaning of Nature in *Hamlet*.

[9] Castex, *ibid.*, p. 540.
[10] Cf. Hidekatsu Nojima, 'Hamlet's Mirror' [Hamlet no Kagami], *Essays on Hamlet* [Hamlet-Dokuhon], ed. Takashi Sasayama (Tokyo, 1988), pp. 4–26.

'Allegory of Happiness' in
The Merchant of Venice

SOJI IWASAKI

I

The Merchant of Venice is a moral play. Morality here is a problem of choice between good and evil, the higher moral value and the lesser. Economic value and its problematic aspects are also of great significance.

In the casket-choosing scenes, three caskets are set before the choosers: the golden casket bears the motto, 'Who chooses me, shall gain what many men desire'; the silver one, 'Who chooseth me shall get as much as he deserves'; and the lead one, 'Who chooseth me, must give and hazard all he has.' The Prince of Morocco chooses the casket of gold and finds a skull with a scroll in its empty eye:

> All that glisters is not gold;
> Often have you heard that told.
> Many a man his life hath sold
> But my outside to behold.
> Gilded tombs do worms infold.
> Had you been as wise as bold,
> Young in limbs, in judgement old,
> Your answer had not been inscrolled.
> Fare you well, your suit is cold.   (II. vii. 65–73)

These words and the skull, together with the motto 'Who chooseth me, shall gain what many men desire', practically comprise an emblem, which very closely resembles Geffrey Whitney's emblem 'Ex maximo minimum',[1] whose application goes:

> Where liuely once, Gods image was expreste,
> Wherein, sometime was sacred reason plac'de,
> The head, I meane, that is so ritchly bleste,
> With sighte, with smell, with hearinge, and with taste.
>> Lo, nowe a skull, both rotten, bare, and drye,
> > A relike meete in charnell house to lye.[1]

---

[1] Geffrey Whitney, *A Choice of Emblemes* (Leyden, 1586), p. 229.

Shakespeare in his casket scenes is an emblematist, and his emblem on a skull teaches us the vanity of 'gold' or 'what many men desire'.

The Prince of Arragon chooses the silver casket. Knowing better than to be deceived by the golden appearance, he yet is proud enough to choose 'as much as he deserves.' He finds the head of a fool with an application: '. . . Some there be that shadows kiss; / Such have but a shadow's bliss' (II. ix. 65–6). Arragon's proud belief in his empty self reminds us of King Lear, who believes in his absolute self and drives away Cordelia's reticent 'truth' ultimately to discover his own folly; Lear, who once thought he was 'everything', is utterly disillusioned and comes to know he is 'nothing'. The fool accompanying Lear in the tempest scene is a reflection of the foolish king himself, and in the same way the fool's head coming out of the silver casket in *The Merchant* is a visual correlative of the folly of Arragon the chooser. A fool addressing to his image on his bauble – this is a motif we find in Holbein's well-known illustrations to Erasmus's *Praise of Folly*.[2]

While Morocco's choice of the golden casket predicts the ruin of Shylock as personified Avarice or Cupidity, Arragon's choice of the silver casket foreshadows the downfall of the Jew as Rigorous Justice, who holds a knife and scales in his hands in the law-court scene. To demand 'what he deserves' is foolish. A proverb in Tilly's *Dictionary* goes, 'No man ought to be judge in his own cause',[3] and this is what Portia means when she says, 'To offend and judge are distinct offices, / And of opposed natures' (II. ix. 61–2). Shylock in the court scene commits this offence of 'judging in his own cause', the result of which is predicted in Arragon's choice of the silver casket.

After Morocco and Arragon, Bassanio comes to choose among the caskets. Portia has music played and a song is sung, implying a warning against 'fancy' that 'is engend'red in the eye, / With gazing fed, and . . . dies / In the cradle where it lies' (III. ii. 67–9). Perhaps taking the song's warning, Bassanio rejects the golden casket. He rightly feels that a beauty's golden hair often belongs to a buried skeleton. He also rejects the silver casket because silver is 'pale and common drudge / 'Tween man and man' (III. ii. 103–4), and by thus scorning the association of love with money, Bassanio avoids the fortune Arragon found. Bassanio therefore decides on the lead casket whose plainness is more pleasing than eloquence – 'truth' was found in the 'plain plowman' in Langland, or in plain Kent and true Cordelia in *King Lear* – and he dare 'give and hazard

---

[2] See William Willeford, *The Fool and His Scepter* (Northwestern University Press, 1969; rpt. 1980), plate 9. Also see F. Saxl, 'Holbein's Illustrations to the *Praise of Folly* by Erasmus', *Burlington Magazine*, 83 (November, 1943), 276.

[3] M. P. Tilley, *A Dictionary of the Proverbs in England in the Sixteenth and Seventeenth Centuries* (Ann Arbor, 1950), M341.

'ALLEGORY OF HAPPINESS' IN *THE MERCHANT OF VENICE*

all he has'. Bassanio in fact foresees the truth hidden in the plain casket and, opening it, he finds the image of 'true love', Portia's portrait:

> You that choose not by the view
> Chance as fair, and choose as *true*.
> Since this *fortune* falls to you,
> Be content and *seek no new*.
> If you be *well pleased* with this
> And hold your fortune for your bliss,
> Turn you where your lady is,
> And claim her with a loving kiss.   (III. ii. 131–8; emphases mine,
> in this and the subsequent quotations)

The moral lesson given here is that only he who gives and hazards all will win good fortune and true love, and, if we read the words more attentively, it may also be that chastity and pleasure are implied in 'seek no new' and 'well pleased', reminding us of the Three Graces – Love, Chastity and Pleasure – in Botticelli's *Primavera*.

So far the general lesson of the three caskets seems to be that a true lover should reject both the glistening gold all men desire and the pale silver that grants what one deserves and choose the plain lead casket so that he can find true love. But is this all we are expected to grasp? Should one merely turn away from gold and silver and choose lead? Is it that one must cease to be a merchant and be a lover? Must we leave Venice and turn to Belmont?

A clue to these questions is given in Bassanio's words when he has chosen the right casket, making himself qualified to demand Portia:

> A gentle scroll! Fair lady, by your leave,
> I come by note to give, and to receive.
> . . .
> So, thrice fair lady, stand I even so,
> As doubtful whether what I see be true,
> Until confirmed, signed, ratified by you.   (III. ii. 139–48)

Bassanio wants his successful suit to be 'confirmed, signed, ratified' by Portia's kiss; he tells of his love in commercial terms. Certainly it was conventional to speak of love in commercial terms[4] and, for example, call a lover's kiss the seal confirming the lover's words, but in *The Merchant* love and commerce seem more closely related. We find Portia expressing her love to Bassanio in commercial terms:

> . . . for you
> I would be trebled twenty times myself,

---

[4]   Cf. Spenser, 'Epithalamion', ll. 31–3, and 315–20. For examples in Shakespeare, see J. R. Brown, 'Introduction' to his Arden edition of *The Merchant* (1955, 1961), pp. l–lii.

A thousand times more fair, ten thousand times
More rich, that only to stand high in your account
I might in virtues, beauties, livings, friends,
Exceed account. But the full sum of me
Is sum of something: which to term in gross
Is an unlessoned girl, unschooled, unpractised. . . (III. ii. 152–9)

Portia wishes to be sixty, thousand, and ten thousand times more fair
and rich than she is now, but this is no sign of cupidity in her, for she
wants in order to 'give all'. Her idea of number is not the same as Lear's
when he measures his elder daughters' love by the number of knights
they grant him. The balances in Lear's mind with which to measure love
in proportion to the number of knights granted do not exist in Portia.
Her number tends to grow huge only to increase the gifts for her love.
Thus Portia 'gives all she has' – house, servants and herself – together
with her ring and calls Bassanio her 'lord', 'governor', and 'king' (III. ii.
165). When Bassanio has chosen lead, he is one who 'gives and hazards
all', and so is Portia. Their act of giving is not that of 'give and take' but
that of 'give and hazard', no return expected just as with a pelican giving
blood to her young.[5]

However, another person is there whose love is of the same nature:
Antonio. His love of Bassanio recalls the Biblical passage, 'Greater love
hath no man than this, that a man lay down his life for his friends' (John,
15:13). How is he related to the theme of the play? Does he belong with
Shylock and Venice? Is his 'commercial' value to be reconciled with the
love of Belmont people?

II

In the Elizabethan theatre, when an actor stood on the stage with a
pair of scales and a knife in his hands, he inevitably reminded the
audience of the Goddess of Justice. In the court scene of *The Merchant of
Venice*, Shylock an emblem of Avarice, equipped with scales and a knife,
might well have been a parody of the Goddess.[6] The iconic figure of
Justice depicted in tapestries and painted cloths was so familiar that
Dekker in *The Magnificent Entertainment Given to King James* (1604) writes:
'Hauing tolde you that her name was *Iustice*, I hope you will not put mee
to describe what properties she held in her hands, sithence euery painted
cloath can informe you.'[7]

The Elizabethan idea of justice was in a sense very near to that of

---

5   See Whitney, p. 87; *King James' Bible: or The Authorized Version* (1611), title page.
6   Cf. Samuel Chew, *Virtues Reconciled* (Toronto, 1947), p. 48.
7   Thomas Dekker, *The Magnificent Entertainment Given to King James* (1604); *Dramatic Works*,
    ed. F. Bowers (Cambridge, 1955), II, p. 295.

'ALLEGORY OF HAPPINESS' IN *THE MERCHANT OF VENICE*

revenge, and sometimes Justice and Nemesis were not clearly distinguished.[8] In Lydgate's *Falle of Princes* (1431–38, reissued 1554) and William Baldwin's *A Mirror for Magistrates* (1554, 1559), the wheel of Fortune was Nemesis-Justice's instrument to punish the proud men of high degree, and in Jean Baudoin's *Iconologie* (Paris, 1644) this idea of 'Revenge Justice' or 'Rigorous Justice' was allegorically represented by a figure of Death equipped with a pair of scales and a sword.[9] Shylock armed with a knife and scales in the law-court scene is in fact a dramatic version of the icon of Rigorous Justice, his knife approximating to the sickle of Death rather than the sword of Justice. Shylock's justice, however, is defeated before a higher justice. This higher justice is that equitable justice represented by Britomart in Spenser's *The Faerie Queene*, Book Five, the pliant female justice in contrast to the rigorous male justice represented by Artigal.[10] As Britomart is an allegorical image of Queen Elizabeth I, so the Queen's portraits were often allegories of Astraea, and as Astraea, Elizabeth had the sword of Justice in her hand. The same iconic image appeared in August 1554 when the marriage of Mary Tudor and Philip of Spain was celebrated: one of the London pageants represented the royal couple, accompanied on one side by allegorical figures of Justicia with a sword and Equitas with a pair of scales, and on the other side by Veritas with a book and Misericordia with a heart of gold.[11]

Justice, Equity, Truth and Pity are traditionally called the Four Daughters of God, the idea originating from Psalm 85: 'Pity and Truth met, and Justice and Peace kissed each other.' (Thus Equity in the above-mentioned pageant might have been replaced by Peace.) The gist of the idea of the Four Daughters is that as jury in God's court Justice and Truth should be reconciled with Pity and Peace (or Mercy), thus tempering God's wrath. The image of justice moderated by pity or mercy, is what Portia represents in *The Merchant of Venice*. The book in her hand is symbolic of law and truth. Thus the opposing causes of justice and mercy in the law-court scene may better be understood as the opposition of Rigorous Justice and Equitable Justice, or revengeful justice *vs.* justice moderated by mercy.

The argument can be confirmed in the text of the play. Shylock in the court scene rejects the 'mercy' which the Duke and Portia-Balthazar ask of him, and he demands for his 'bond', 'law', and 'justice'. But since his

---

[8] Cf. Chew, *Virtues*, p. 98.

[9] 'IVSTICE-RIGOVREVSE' in Jean Baudoin, *Iconologie*, II, 56 (Paris, 1644); reproduced in Jane Aptekar, *Icons of Justice* (New York, 1969), p. 56.

[10] Cf. Aptekar, p. 55. Also cf. Hermann Sinsheimer, 'Now the fable comes to illustrate the progress from the rigidity of law, *rigor juris*, or from the strict letter of the law, *jus strictissimum*, to fairness and humanity in the interpretation of deeds and bonds, to *equitas*.' *Shylock* (1947; New York, 1963), p. 80.

[11] John Nichols, *The Chronicle of Queen Jane* (London, 1850), pp. 150–1.

knife is essentially Death's sickle, his 'justice' is nothing but 'malice', which is mentioned by Bassanio:

> Yes, here I tender it [the money] for him in the court,
> Yea, twice the sum; if that will not suffice,
> I will be bound to pay it ten times o'er
> On forfeit of my hands, my head, my heart.
> If this will not suffice, it must appear
> That *malice* bears down truth. And I beseech you
> Wrest once the law to your authority;
> To do a great right, do a little wrong,
> And curb this cruel devil of his will.   (IV. i. 205–13)

Iconographically, Truth's enemies are Envy and Fraud,[12] and the 'malice' in Bassanio's speech here is an equivalent to Envy in Renaissance iconography. (Gratiano indeed mentions 'envy' in IV. i. 126.) And, though Envy is persecuting Truth, the judge or any other authority cannot straightaway rescue the victim if the persecution is authorised by law.

Since Shylock obstinately insists on having his 'bond', Portia as the judge asks him to 'season' or 'mitigate' justice:

> *Portia.* . . . earthly power doth then show likest God's
> When mercy *seasons* justice. Therefore, Jew,
> Though justice be thy plea, consider this:
> That in the course of justice, none of us
> Should see salvation. We do pray for mercy,
> And that same prayer doth teach us all to render
> The deeds of mercy. I have spoke thus much
> To *mitigate* the justice of thy plea,
> Which if thou follow, this strict court of Venice
> Must needs give sentence 'gainst the merchant there.
> *Shylock.* My deeds upon my head! I crave the law,
> The penalty and forfeit of my bond.   (IV. i. 192–203)

Shylock insists on rigorous justice with the result that he is defeated by the 'law' he obstinately upholds. (Portia's argument is of course legally controversial but we are concerned with the iconographical interpretation here.) And a higher justice, not rigorous justice but justice seasoned by mercy, falls upon Shylock; his life is spared and he has his fine remitted, though he deserves death and confiscation for seeking the life of a Venetian citizen. Living for 'what all men desire' and living for 'what one deserves' have both been invalidated, and the values of gold and silver are loaded on Shylock the scape-goat and driven away.

---

[12] In Whitney, the persecutors of Truth are Envy, Slander and Strife. In 'The Calumny of Appelles' Calumny is of course the persecutor. See Whitney, p. 4; Vincenzo Cartari, *The Fountain of Ancient Fiction*, trans. Richard Linche (London, 1599), sig. Bbij^v–Bbiv.

'ALLEGORY OF HAPPINESS' IN *THE MERCHANT OF VENICE*

Shylock's greed is called by Gratiano 'wolfish, bloody, starved, and ravenous'(IV.i. 138), this vice being traditionally associated with a wolf.[13] When Antonio compares Shylock to a wolf, saying that the animal 'Hath made the ewe bleat for the lamb'(IV.i. 74), we are reminded of the Biblical parable of 'the good shepherd'[14] where the wolf attacking the lamb stands for Satan attacking man. In this play, as in the parable, the good shepherd is expected to come, and it is Portia who eventually comes. This is why Portia refers to 'salvation' in her speech above, and thus she approximates to the Saviour when she has seasoned justice by mercy, saying, 'earthly power doth then show likest God's / When mercy seasons justice.'

III

To Belmont come those who 'give and hazard all they have', Bassanio choosing the casket of lead and finding Portia's portrait, and Antonio hazarding all for Bassanio and finding new life. What is newly found by them is not 'fancy' but constant and true love tempered by trials. Portia's spacious estate at Belmont is, as it were, a Garden of Love free from the threat of knife-wielding Death. The moon is up in the sky, and Lorenzo and Jessica are singing a duet:

> *Lorenzo.*   The moon shines bright. In such a night as this,
>   When the sweet wind did gently kiss the trees,
>   And they did make no noise, in such a night
>   Troilus methinks mounted the Troyan walls
>   And sighed his soul toward the Grecian tents,
>   Where Cressid lay that night.
> *Jessica.*   In such a night
>   Did Thisbe fearfully o'ertrip the dew,
>   And saw the lion's shadow ere himself,
>   And ran dismayed away.
> *Lorenzo.*   In such a night
>   Stood Dido with a willow in her hand.   (V. i. 1–10)

By the anaphoric repetition of 'In such a night . . .' Shakespeare establishes a mood, and at the same time, the great lovers' names possibly recall the tragic endings of romantic love: Cressida's betrayal, Thisbe's unhappy death, Medea's jealousy and revenge. Passionate love often came to a sad ending – this will make the lovers in the play feel them-

---

[13] In Bronzino's tapestry 'L'Innocentia', for example, a wolf is a symbol of avarice. Cf. Erwin Panofsky, *Studies in Iconology* (Oxford, 1939), p. 84.
[14] See George Ferguson, *Signs and Symbols in Christian Art* (1954; New York, 1961), p. 21. Cf. Spenser, *The Shepheardes Calender*, 'August', ll. 31–4. This icon, of course, originally comes from John, 10:7–16.

51

selves the more fortunate and blessed. The loving couples – Portia and
Bassanio, Nerissa and Gratiano, and Jessica and Lorenzo – will have to
learn the realities of life before they can enjoy the full pleasure of their
married life (as the young King of Navarre and his courtiers had to learn
in *Love's Labour's Lost*). What the dramatist is doing here in the final act of
The Merchant is to build an understanding of love in the audience's mind:
the full pleasure of love must spring from full knowledge of human
reality. A nightingale sounds sweet, Portia says, when she sings on a
dark night:

> How many things by season seasoned are
> To their right praise and true perfection.   (V. i. 107–8)

Love, like justice, must be seasoned – seasoned by love's possible sor-
rows.

Before these two sententious lines of Portia's, Lorenzo and Jessica's
duet recalls the thematic opposition of the two justices, rigorous and fair,
together with the motifs of love and money:

> *Lorenzo.*   In such a night
>   Did Jessica steal from the wealthy Jew
>   And with an unthrift love did run from Venice
>   As far as Belmont.
> *Jessica.*   In such a night
>   Did young Lorenzo swear he loved her well,
>   Stealing her soul with many vows of faith,
>   And ne'er a true one.
> *Lorenzo.*   In such a night
>   Did pretty Jessica (like a little shrew)
>   Slander her love, and he forgave it her.   (V. i. 14–22)

The two seemingly irreconcilable aspects of justice are not to be found in
Belmont, for here the problem has already been solved. Jessica's and
Lorenzo's stealth, her slander and 'unthrift' love (love is again looked
upon as if it were a matter of commerce), and Bassanio's and Gratiano's
broken promises in parting with their marriage rings – all these offences
have been forgiven through mercy, or corrected by mitigated justice. The
Four Daughters of God are all reconciled, the heavenly music and the
harmony of minds echoing each other in one 'lunar synthesis'. The
heavenly spheres turning in their proper order are symbolic of the perfection of love, endowing the lovers' rings with blessings. The word
'ring' recurs, summing up the themes of love and music.[15]
   Throughout the action of the play, economic value and moral value

---

[15] The very last word of the play is 'ring'. Gratiano implies obscenity in this word, and the
sexual implication contributes to the theme of the play.

'ALLEGORY OF HAPPINESS' IN *THE MERCHANT OF VENICE*

have been examined side by side, matters of love being described in monetary terms. Justice and mercy are reconciled in the court scene and confirmed in the moonlit-garden scene, and the meaning of the word 'bond' shifts from the 'bond' of money-lending to the 'bond' of love symbolised by a ring, both meanings eventually merging. Even the values of gold and silver are not straightforwardly rejected here. Portia's court in Belmont is a garden of music and love, but it is also a place of great wealth, unlike, say, the forest of Arden. Wealth is evil when it serves the cupidity of gold or the give-and-take commerce of silver, but when people like Antonio, Bassanio and Portia 'give and hazard', it has a positive value. While mercy rains like manna from heaven (IV. i. 181), wealth overflows out of the horn of plenty. When Lancelot refers to the messenger's bugle horn as a 'horn full of good news' (V. i. 46–7), the horn suggests the cornucopia. Portia is not only an icon of Equitable Justice but she is associated with the cornucopia and approximates to the image of Queen Elizabeth attended by Plenty and Justice.[16]

On the other hand, Portia may be more aptly compared with the image of Happiness in Bronzino's emblematic picture 'Allegory of Happiness' (Fig. 1),[17] where Happiness seated in the centre is also Venus attended on her right by Cupid aiming at his mother's breast. On her left stands Justice with her usual attributes, a sword and scales, and in front Fortune kneels with a forelock and her wheel, which she no longer turns. On Happiness's right, next to Cupid, is Prudence with two faces, young and old, reminding us of such passages in *The Merchant* as: first, Dr. Bellario's letter mentioning Portia-Balthazar's wisdom and prudence, 'I never knew so young a body with so old a head' (IV. i. 159–60); secondly, Shylock's ironical remark, 'O wise and upright judge, / How much more elder art thou than thy looks!' (IV. i. 246–7); and lastly the phrase in the scroll from the lead casket, 'Young in limbs, in judgement old' (II. vii. 71). In front of the bifrontal or 'Janus-like' Prudence, Father Time kneels, showing his hour-glass to Happiness (the sand seems to have stopped running, like Fortune's wheel, preventing any change from this state of happiness). The mask of a fool and the mask of Death lying beside the fallen figure of Unhappiness correspond, it seems, to the emblematic images that come out of the golden and silver caskets in Shakespeare's play. All in all, Bronzino's picture is an allegory of Happiness, how she is obtained, or how she is served and supported by Love, Justice, Fortune, Time and Prudence.

Another thing we should note in Bronzino is that Happiness has a caduceus in her right hand as well as a cornucopia in her left. The caduceus is of course an attribute of Mercury the god of commerce, and

---

[16] Cf. Samuel C. Chew, *The Pilgrimage of Life* (New Haven, 1962), p. 293.
[17] This picture is usually called 'Allegory of Fortune'.

Fig. 1 Agnolo Bronzino, 'Allegory of Happiness' (c. 1560).
Uffizi Museum, Florence

also of theft, eloquence, good fortune, prudence and music, and his snake-twined staff is a symbol of peace. Thus Happiness is endowed with peace[18] as well as plenty, and commerce and wealth join the harmony of Happiness. It is in this atmosphere of harmony and peace that Antonio in *The Merchant* is informed of the good news that three of his richly-laden ships have suddenly come to harbour.

[18] In Dekker's *The Magnificent Entertainment*, Plenty with a cornucopia and Peace with a caduceus appear on the stage of the pageant.

'ALLEGORY OF HAPPINESS' IN *THE MERCHANT OF VENICE*

The Merchant of Venice is Shakespeare's 'Allegory of Happiness'. Portia is 'a lady richly left, / And she is fair, and . . . / Of wondrous virtues' (I. i. 160–2). She is a Shakespearean allegory of Happiness, an image of the blessed human being of modern capitalistic society tinged with Medieval pastoral idealism. A money bag is an attribute of the Medieval icon of Avarice, yet, when held in Portia's hand, it becomes a cornucopia, a Renaissance symbol of plenty.

Hamlet and 'Modesty' *

SHIRO SHIBA

Learning was becoming fashionable in Renaissance courts. As L. Ryan says, courtiers and princes were becoming aware of a knowledge that could make them nobler in character and more cultured in manners.[1] Erasmus wrote a comment illustrative of this tendency in 1516: 'To be a [moral] philosopher and to be a Christian is synonymous in fact. The only difference is in the nomenclature'.[2] Sir Thomas Elyot's *The Book Named the Governor* (1531) was probably the most popular among those books on the education for the nobility in Renaissance England; its popularity was such that it might have exerted considerable influence on Sir Philip Sidney.

This paper is aimed at focusing on the concept of 'modesty', one of the most fundamental virtues required of the Renaissance nobility. As Elyot suggests in his *The Governor*, the word 'modesty', with its adjective form 'modest', was a relatively new one in the 16th to early 17th centuries. But the word had come to have a great significance by Shakespeare's time; and actually it is, according to Marvin Spevack's *Concordance* (1973), used more than 50 times in his works. The employment of 'modesty' at well-chosen moments in *Hamlet* (1601) very strongly evinces Shakespeare's own way in bending eagerly to the neo-classicism as well as in positively diverging from this literary concept. There is most probably no other play in which Shakespeare betrays his keener awareness of the neo-classical or academic tradition, and in which the academic principle and the popular or anti-academic tradition are in more striking contrast than in *Hamlet*. The two main movements, popular and academic, in the play, whose directions are quite opposite, are sharply accentuated by the word 'modesty'. The word is therefore, I believe, worth an independent discussion.

In *The Governor*, which is typical of what we call courtesy books, such

---

* This is a revised version of a paper I read at the 29th General Meeting of the Shakespeare Society of Japan, held in Hirosaki on 20 October, 1990.
[1] Roger Ascham, *The Schoolmaster* (1570), ed. L. V. Ryan (Charlottesville: Virginia University Press, 1967), p. xxiv.
[2] *The Education of a Christian Prince* (1516; pr. 1540), tr. L. K. Born (1936; rpt. New York: Octagon, 1965), p. 150.

as Castiglione's popular *The Book of Courtier* (1528; tr. 1561),[3] Elyot not only discussed courtesy but also, being, as he was, versed in the classical literature, made an attempt to defend poetry, which he believed was 'the first philosophy', from the Horatian viewpoint (some fifty years earlier than Sidney's similar defence in *An Apology for Poetry*, 1579–1580). In Book 1, he writes that 'the virtue called Modesty', as defined by Cicero, is 'the knowledge of opportunity of things to be done or spoken, in appointing and setting them in time or place to them convenient and proper'. He continues,

> ... *Modesty*; which word not being known in the English tongue, nor of all them which understood Latin, except they had read good authors, they improperly named this virtue discretion.[4]
>
> (emphasis mine, in this and the subsequent quotations)

O.E.D. (2nd ed.), quoting the above passage as the first instance of the actual use of the word, gives a definition to 'modesty': 'Moderation; freedom from excess or exaggeration; self-control; clemency, mildness of rule' (s.v. 'modesty', †1). 'Modesty', closely associated with the idea of moderation, freedom from excess, is of much importance in terms of principles of human behaviour in the Renaissance.

Elyot, associated with Sir Thomas More's 'school' of humanists, was also Chief Clerk of the King's Council; his observation on 'modesty', therefore, deserves our special attention. He had every reason to lay stress on the notion of 'modesty' as forming the basis of the Renaissance social order. The above definition of 'modesty' (by Cicero) has much in common with the concept of decorum, the seventeenth-century French and Italian academic tenet which represented the triumph of social order, reason and self-control. When 'all decorum' goes 'quite athwart', as the Duke says in *Measure for Measure* (1604), 'liberty plucks justice by the nose;/ The baby beats the nurse' (I. iii. 29–31).[5] The thought of decorum in terms of literature, which, as M. T. Herrick suggests,[6] has a long tradition since Aristotle, Cicero, and Horace, is one of the

---

[3] Sir Philip Sidney is said to have carried this book in his pocket when he went abroad; and Ascham, in spite of his dislike of all things Italian, heartily recommends it in his *Schoolmaster*. See J. E. Mason, *Gentlefolk in the Making: Studies in the History of English Courtesy Literature and Related Topics from 1531 to 1774* (1935; rpt. New York: Octagon, 1971), p. 34.

[4] *The Book Named the Governor* (1531), ed. S. E. Lehmberg (London: Dent, 1962), p. 87. Elyot offered in his Latin-English dictionary (pr. 1538) 'modestie, temperaunce' as the definition in English for the Latin word 'Modestia'.

[5] All quotations (with line references) from Shakespeare, are, unless otherwise specified, from the edition of G. B. Evans and others, *The Riverside Shakespeare* (Boston: Houghton, 1974).

[6] *The Fusion of Horatian and Aristotelian Literary Criticism, 1531–1555* (Urbana: Illinois University Press, 1946), pp. 48–57.

HAMLET AND 'MODESTY'

indispensable elements in the Renaissance theory of mimesis for verisimilitude.

The first few lines in the Prologue to *The First Part of Tamburlaine the
Great* (1587)[7] reveal Marlowe's leaning as a playwright to the neo-
classical theory of drama, or they are as it were his own manifesto of
neo-classicism; Hamlet's advice to the players might also be taken as
Shakespearean manifestation of the same kind of inclination. But both
Marlowe and Shakespeare, on the other hand, disclose in their works
quite a different inclination, a strong denial of classical precepts. The
case of Shakespeare involves much more complex and difficult problems.

Gabriel Harvey observes that there is something in *Hamlet* 'to please
the wiser sort'; in the same way we can find there some elaborated
devices which satisfactorily appeal to 'the judicious' (III. ii. 26). Our first
example is a passage from 'an excellent play'(II. ii. 452–518) Hamlet
heard the player rehearse before. Actually such Marlovian bombast,
mighty purple epic pomp, moving utterance of emotion, and long-
echoing lament of Hecuba (though through the tale told by Aeneas to
Dido)[8], all these in that 'excellent' play may remind lots of *Hamlet*'s
readers and audience of the title figures' lamentations in *Cornelia* (1594)
and *The Virtuous Octavia* (1598), in the same way as do those dramatic set
speeches of lamentation found in *Richard III* (1592). Although the language of the Hecuba scene in *Hamlet* is rather of epic vigour, and the
language of the Cornelia's and Octavia's grieving scenes are of lyric
vehemence, what is found in all these alike is, most probably, what
Hamlet regards as 'an honest method, as wholesome as sweet, and by
very much more handsome than fine' (II. ii. 444–5). To put it another
way, what Shakespeare has here in mind is perhaps very close to the idea
of the Countess of Pembroke circle. Kyd's version of Garnier's *Cornelia*
(dedicated to the Countess's aunt) and Samuel Brandon's *Virtuous Octavia* are written on the basis of the neo-classical principle: stately
speeches, moral or philosophical schemes (rather than dramatic conflicts
between individuals), and propriety of style or decorum are highly regarded. The passage in the 'excellent play' contains 'a passionate speech'
(II. ii. 432), which Hamlet calls for; and 'stately speeches', which Sidney
had in mind when he, in his *Apology*, wrote in defence of poetry, and
against indecent 'mongrel tragicomedy'.

The play in question, 'excellent play', Hamlet remembers, was 'caviary

---

[7] 'From iygging vaines of riming mother wits,/ And such conceits as clownage keeps in
pay,/ Weele lead you to the stately tent of War', *The Works of C. Marlowe*, ed. C. F. T.
Brooke (1910; rpt. London: Oxford University Press, 1969), ll. 1–3.

[8] Jenkins notes that there is no justification for identifying this with Marlowe and Nashe's
Tragedy of Dido (1586), which also gives 'Aeneas's tale to Dido', but from which Shakespeare's version is not taken. See *Hamlet*, ed. H. Jenkins (London: Methuen, 1982), p. 477.

59

ARTHURIAN AND OTHER STUDIES

to the general', and did 'not' please 'the million', and therefore 'was never acted', or 'not above once'; but it was 'well digested in the scenes, set down with as much *modesty* as cunning', and there was 'no matter in the phrase that might indict the author of *affection*' (II. ii. 436–43). First of all, *'affection'* (=affectation)[9] was the fault in diction, which, together with obscurity, was most strenuously condemned during the Renaissance. A much more significant word in the passage is, of course, *'modesty'*, which, as we saw earlier, means 'moderation or freedom from excess'. The 'excellent play' was, in Hamlet's view, written down with propriety of style, restraint, and without any affectation (though not popular in the debased lower taste of the masses). The virtue of modesty, which forms one of the principles with which order, harmony, and balance are kept in the Renaissance society, also denotes propriety in dramatic style and speech.

In this connection, Guarini's remarks are very noteworthy. The author of *Il Pastor Fido* (*The Faithful Shepherd*, 1589) argues that the mingling of tragic and comic pleasure does not allow hearers to fall into excessive tragic melancholy or comic relaxation; as a result we don't sin against 'the *modesty* and decorum of a well-bred man'.[10] Here what we must bear in mind is that the concept of the word 'modesty' was very similar to that of 'discretion', 'mean', 'measure', 'mediety', 'mediocrity', 'moderation', 'prudence', and 'temperance' (the latter two, with 'fortitude' and 'justice', were among the cardinal virtues); and that the meaning of all these words and their derivatives was of great import in the Renaissance. All these virtues helped to develop the Renaissance sense of propriety, decorum.

The word 'modesty' (moderation) is meaningfully used in a crucial context in Act III, Scene ii, too, where Hamlet gives directions to the players. His central criterion, unmistakably aristocratic, is 'that you o'erstep not the *modesty* of nature' (19), which is another way of expressing the theory of mimesis: 'to hold, as 'twere the mirror up to nature'(21–2). Jenkins states that the 'widespread Renaissance theory of drama as an image of actual life derives from Donatus on comedy, where it is attributed to Cicero'.[11] Hamlet's claim that the player must on no account 'o'erstep . . . the modesty of nature' involves necessity to cultivate

---

9 affection] *Qq2–4*; affectation] *F1. F1: A Facsimile of "The First Folio"* (1623), prepared by C. Hinman (New York: Norton, 1968). *Q: A Facsimile Series of Shakespeare Quartos*, issued under the supervision of T. Otsuka (Tokyo: Nan'un-do, 1975).

10 *Compendium of Tragicomic Poetry*, tr. and ed. A. Gilbert, *Literary Criticism: Plato to Dryden* (New York: American, 1940), p. 512.

11 Jenkins, *Hamlet*, p. 288. See 'Comaedie . . . Imitatio vitae, Speculum consuetudinis, Imago vertatis' (attributed to Cicero), *Everyman out of Humour*, III. vi. 206–7, *Ben Jonson*, ed. C. H. Herford and P. & E. Simpson (1927; rpt. London: Oxford UP, 1966), vol. III. Cf. Lope de Vega, *The New Art of Making Comedies* (1609); and Lise-Lone Marker, 'Nature and Decorum in the Theory of Elizabethan Acting', *The Elizabethan Theatre*, 2 (1970), pp. 89–90.

HAMLET AND 'MODESTY'

'temperance' (7) and exercise all his 'discretion' (17) in avoiding those extremes of excess and deficiency which make 'the unskilful laugh' (25–6) and which 'cannot but make the judicious grieve' (26). 'Temperance' and 'discretion', Maurice Charney suggests, are synonyms for this ideal of 'modesty'.[12] Furness defines 'modesty of nature' as 'that symmetrical harmony by which the acts of everyday life are made to fit the situation, that "temperance and smoothness" '.[13] McAlindon indicates that the essence of all this advice on acting is deeply connected with the familiar doctrine that decorum is the chief consideration in action and delivery: 'Suit the action to the word, the word to the action' (17–8).[14] The rule of decorum, as Thomas Heywood shows in his *An Apology for Actors* (1612), aids the actor in fitting his phrases to his action, and his action to his phrase, and his pronunciation to them both. In addition, we must remember that Hamlet's (or Shakespeare's) art of acting was in part based, it seems, on the simple stagecraft of early Elizabethan travelling players, and perhaps even of medieval amateur players.

Decorum or propriety of style, which signals harmony and proportion on the one hand, and social adjustment on the other, coalesces with the mighty concept of world order and also with the notion that nature's order rests on degree. As Elyot's account of order shows, decorum or something decorous was thought to be natural order as perceived by the senses, or the aesthetic imagination, in the Renaissance. Age also has to be considered: amorous and sporty old gentlemen who put out the banner of youth (one thinks of Sir John Falstaff) are held to be particularly graceless.[15] In this way, since modesty, in the Renaissance context, means 'moderation' and 'self-control'; modesty and decorum are found to be the Renaissance twin brothers.

To his remarks on dramatic style and playing in terms of 'modesty', Hamlet adds another important use of 'modesty'.[16] When countering Gertrude's 'What have I done?' (III. iv. 39), he blames her for having blurred 'the grace and blush of *modesty*' (41), that is, for having disgraced

[12] *Style in "Hamlet"* (Princeton, NJ: Princeton University Press, 1969), p. 263.

[13] A New Variorum Edition: *Hamlet*, ed. H. Furness (1877; rpt. New York: Dover, 1963), vol. I, p. 179.

[14] T. McAlindon, *Shakespeare and Decorum* (London: Macmillan, 1973), p. 47, and p. 8. The interrelation of decorum, the art of Elizabethan acting, and oratory or rhetoric is not our concern here. Cf. Cicero, *De Oratore*; and Quintilian, *Institutio Oratoria*. It is noteworthy that the idea of decorum in speaking and behaviour found in *The Civile Conversation* (1581; vol. 1, Book II; by S. Guazzo, Mantuan Ambassador to Charles IX of France, and then to Pius V) is very similar to Hamlet's opinion on the decorum of playing.

[15] See McAlindon, *ibid.*; G. Cinthio, 'On the Composition of Romances' (1549); and B. Castiglione, *The Book of the Courtier*, esp. Book II (1528; tr. 1561).

[16] In *Hamlet*, there are five occurrences of the word 'modesty' in all (there is only one occurrence (II. ii. 440) in *Q1*); and it is worth noting that all of these are spoken by the prince. Other occurrences of the word, which are not mentioned here, are 'modesties' (=the quality of being modest or having a moderate opinion of oneself; II. ii. 280), and 'modesty' (=moderation; V. i. 208). Its adjective form 'modest' is not used in *Hamlet*.

the 'womanly propriety of behaviour' (*O.E.D.*, s.v. 'modesty', 3). Thomas Salter discusses the education of women in his *The Mirror of Modesty* (1579), which, it is said, is virtually a translation of Giovanni Michele Bruto's *La Institutione* (1555). He observes:

> Therefore concerning the Matrone to whom any yong Maiden is to be comitted (I saie) she ought what so ever she be, to be Grave, Prudent, *Modest*, and of good counsell, to thende that suche Maidens as she hath in tutyng, maie learne her honeste and womanlie demeanoure . . .[17]

Gertrude is remarried to her deceased husband's brother 'With such dexterity', 'within a month' after the husband's death; never shame-faced; and far from the ideal of 'modesty', at least from Hamlet's point of view.

Hamlet's notion about literary style and acting is directly or indirectly influenced by the theory of verisimilitude which was prevalent among those Renaissance literary theorists (such as Scaliger and Castelvetro) who followed Cicero, Horace, and Quintilian; Hamlet's view on 'modesty' owes something to other cultural principles, those found in such books as *The Governor*, *The Schoolmaster*, *The Mirror of Modesty*, and *The Complete Gentleman*. In our text, these literary theories and academic principles in many cases sharply contrast with popular elements.

We must say that Hamlet's aristocratic academic view on drama or human behaviour (which probably reflects Shakespeare's own aware-ness of the neo-classicism or aristocratism) reveals serious and complex problems of life and reality. In other words, there are, in the whole tragedy of Hamlet, familiar sorts of contrast (which have been already pointed out by many critics) between reality and appearance, between the right and the wrong, between words and actions, reason and emo-tion, between god and beast, mind and body, agent and patient. Above all, we find the aristocratic, academic dramatic theory in puzzling con-trast with the popular dramatic tradition, especially in the action of the protagonist. Hamlet himself emphatically advocates the ideal of 'mod-esty', while he actually does things which are quite contrary to this virtue. What I should like to emphasise here is that each of those kinds of contrast is one in which two opposed forces will hold their own direc-tions; and that most of these forces are kept and maintained as they are presented before the audience, and not reconciled or settled, until the end of the play.

Now we shall see some actual examples of the most marked contrast or conflict, which is represented mostly in the action and words of the

---

[17] *A Critical Edition of "The Mirrhor of Modestie"*, ed. J. B. Holm (London: Garland, 1987), p. 69. Salter was a schoolmaster of Upminster, Essex. In Renaissance England, books on 'chastity' for women were popular. See, for example, R. Greene's pamphlet, *The Myrrovr of Modestie* (or *Myrrovr of Chastitie*, 1584).

prince. Besides regarding the propriety of dramatic style, words and action, and womanly demeanour, Hamlet seems to concede decorum of type character (II. ii. 320–4). He himself is Prince of Denmark, 'the glass of fashion', 'the mould of form'; and yet in fact he pretends to be mad in several scenes. In the 'Mouse-trap' scene, he goes far beyond the 'modesty' of 'chorus' (III. ii. 245), and ardently explains the next anticipated action on the stage before the players have performed it. Above all, he calls himself, though jokingly, 'jig-maker' (III. ii. 125).[18]

As elucidated by Francis Fergusson, who regards the text as a play of improvisation, and by Anne Barton, who views it as a tragedy dominated by the idea of the play,[19] *Hamlet* is full of theatrical designs: the hero can be said to be playwright, stage director, 'jig-maker' of the play within the play, and chief actor surrounded by the character-audience he sways (cf. V. ii. 334–8). We might even say that Hamlet is in a way playing the part of clown or fool, displaying his extempore wit through the tragedy: he exhibits puzzling jocular behaviour when he addresses the ghost under the ground (I. v; also cf. his similar behaviour with Horatio just after the play-scene). In the person of Hamlet can be found a complex mingling of the king (or the king to be) and the fool: he is his own fool with grim, sarcastic or outspoken jest; ironical commentator on himself, on other persons and the action of the whole play. This behaviour of Hamlet grossly deviates from the very ideal of the Renaissance courtier, and too far away from the ideal of 'modesty'.

Hamlet himself confirms the drastic change in the clown's role within Elizabethan drama (III. ii. 38–42): traditional clowning, with extempore wit and improvisation, has become out of place in the more self-contained artistic unity of the Renaissance play.[20] His reprimand for over clowning is simply a reflection of the aristocratic impatience with knock-about, loud laughter and extempore speeches. It is intriguingly ironic that the improvisational, extempore Hamlet criticises the traditional clowning of extempore wit. 'Mongrel tragicomedy' (which mingles kings and clowns) was none other than the target which those neo-classical writers, George Whetstone, Sidney, and Joseph Hall, attacked; and 'loud laughing' was denied by Sidney and John Lyly. All these writers were probably strongly influenced by the then academic theory in the continent.

---

[18] A. Patterson points out Hamlet's alienated fragmentary adoption of a popular voice as the symptom of troubled intellectualism from the viewpoint of the relation of culture to society in her *Shakespeare and the Popular Voice* (Oxford: Blackwell, 1989).

[19] *The Idea of a Theater: A Study of Ten Plays: The Art of Drama in Changing Perspective* (1949); and *Shakespeare and the Idea of the Play* (1962). Among recent studies of this issue are D. Young, *The Action to the Word: Structure and Style in Shakespearean Tragedy* (1990); and J. Hubert, *Metatheater: the Example of Shakespeare* (1991).

[20] Cf. R. Weimann, *Shakespeare and the Popular Tradition in the Theater: Studies in the Social Dimension of Dramatic Form and Function*, ed. R. Schwartz (London: Johns Hopkins University Press, 1978), p. 191.

In fact, besides the well-known sorts of contrast we have seen, there are in the prince himself several pairs of vector working which drive him into opposite thoughts or actions. Hamlet is torn, both mentally and in terms of behaviour, between being an active man (like Hercules) and a passive passionate man, between being Prince Hamlet and director-player Hamlet, between being a hater and an approver of passion, between being a warm-hearted and a cruelly callous man, between being a 'minister' and a 'scourge', between being a reluctant intellectual and a fierce passionate avenger, between being an honest prince and a deceiving strategist. It is true that this sort of Hamletian complex mental state or action is actually inseparably associated with the background facts: the corruption in the state of Denmark; Claudius's killing of the rightful king; the unseemly haste with which Hamlet's mother joined with the usurper; Hamlet's 'distracted globe' which these abnormal events have caused eventually; and more specifically, his melancholic mental state identifiable with that described by Timothy Bright in his *A Treatise of Melancholy* (1586).

As regards Hamlet's mutually conflicting reactions to the ideal of 'modesty' (which are not found in the sources of the Hamlet story), it could be said that these diametrically opposed reactions are experimental devices elaborated by Shakespeare who tries to show how difficult it is to make a compromise between the two cultural traditions, academic and popular; or adversely how effective it is to employ them synchronisedly in one and the same tragedy while representing the hero's complex character at once by manipulating the two traditional principles deftly and by holding a subtle, delicate balance between every sort of extremes in the play. At least, we might say that Shakespeare violated the neo-classical principle to the extent that he did not 'o'er-step the modesty of nature'; that he transcended the neo-classical concept of tragedy in creating *Hamlet*, a work achieving the most successful and unprecedented kind of fusion of the two traditions.

In closing this paper, I should like to express my heartfelt thanks to Professor Andrew J. Gurr of the University of Reading for his kind reading of the draft and his valuable suggestions.

Cathleens in Yeats and Joyce: Love's Bitter Mystery

TAKASHI SUZUKI

When Yeats asked his most critical question in "The Man and the Echo",

> Did that play of mine send out
> Certain men the English shot?

that particular play in his mind was, of course, *Cathleen ni Houlihan*, especially its first performance at the Abbey Theatre in 1902, with Maud Gonne as the old shabby woman who made, in the end of the play, a 'magnificent' transfiguration into a most beautiful young girl with 'the walk of a queen': the rejuvenation was only possible at the sacrifice of total devotion of Irishmen to her, to their mother country, to their nationhood. The effect was obvious and instant. The performance visualised in the audience's mind an elated image of the revived nation. Though a poor old woman as a symbolic figure of Ireland was not at all original, the play's individual power of visualisation of resurrection of 'the nation once again' might have served some people, in their political propaganda, to produce or reproduce, or even to abuse this image of nationhood as a most beneficial one to their cause. Whether the play actually spurred 'Certain men' to take violent actions or not is still an open question. The answer will vary from one extreme such as Auden's confirmation that 'Poetry makes nothing happen' to the other: Stephen Gwynn's reflection when he asked to himself on his way home from the theatre 'if such plays should be produced unless one was prepared for people to go out to shoot and be shot.'[1] Can poetry and drama precipitate violence? As it is an open question, it would be desirable for amateur Yeatsean to add several things at the risk of being quite wrong.

It was, perhaps, inevitable for Yeats and is most admirable to ordinary people like us that Yeats so sincerely and self-accusingly scrutinised his responsibility as a poet when he was nearing his death. The play, which seems enthusiastically to celebrate the violent beauty of nationalism, at the same time displays the cruelty of that beauty, and the danger of such

---

[1] See Conor Cruise O'Brien, *States of Ireland* (London: Hutchinson, 1972), p. 70; or Peter Costello, *The Heart Grown Brutal: The Irish Revolution in Literature, from Parnell to the Death of Yeats, 1891–1939* (Dublin: Gill & Macmillan, 1977), pp. 2–3.

jingoism. Cathleen ni Houlihan demands 'all', and this demand directly leads to total denial of personal identity and integrity and finally to denial of one's own existence: the demand to die 'for love of' her, for love of one's nation. She erodes people's humane feelings by the epidemic power of the disguised beauty of violence. She also engenders a die-hard solidarity between people who are united by a specific anger, an anger fuelled by the revelation that they have lost the *true* beauty which was once of their own. The enticement is overwhelming and bewitching because what drives them is love, not hate; and the effect of this enticement incessantly works on people's imagination, alluring them to limitless violence without a tinge of remorse. *Cathleen ni Houlihan* fully betrays the root of this cruelty, this inhumanity and brutality. Even though this betrayal was not the conscious motivation in Yeats's creative imagination, it might have been part of Yeats's unconscious potentiality as a poet. We are not sure whether it was more Yeats's *Cathleen ni Houlihan* than O'Grady's *History of Ireland: Heroic Period* that fostered, for instance, Padraic Pearse's revolutionary vision.[2] To one of his contemporary audience, Cathleen ni Houlihan was a terrible image of 'ghoul', 'hyena' and 'corpsechewer' and he was haunted by her domineering threat. That one was James Joyce, who later tried to overcome her oppression by representing his version of Cathleen ni Houlihan in a disgracefully caricatured form and also in a child-devouring Terrible Mother image specifically embodied in his own mother's ghost. To Joyce, *The Countess Cathleen*, the play which was fiercely repudiated a few years ago, seemed to be, in terms of the audience's reception and the play's political impacts, no less nationalistic than *Cathleen ni Houlihan*.[3]

A Portrait of the Artist as a Young Man dramatises the riotous scene where *The Countess Cathleen* was first performed at the Antient Concert Room in 1899: 'The cat calls and hisses and micking cries ran in rude gusts round the hall from his scattered fellow students.' The background of this dramatisation was that students of University College felt that their national and religious pride was bitterly offended by the immoral and unfair representation of Irish peasants. When they composed a letter of protest and asked students to sign it, Joyce 'contemptuously' refused

---

[2] See, for instance, William Irwin Thompson, *The Imagination of an Insurrection: Dublin Easter 1916: A Study of an Ideological Movement* (New York, 1967), p. 25.

[3] Among many studies on the Terrible Mother theme in Joyce are: Ben L. Collins, 'Joyce's Use of Yeats and of Irish History: A Reading of "A Mother" ', *Eire-Ireland*, Vol. 5, No. 1 (1970), 45–66; Hugh Kenner, 'The Look of a Queen', *Woman in Irish Legend, Life and Literature*, ed. S. F. Gallagher, (Gerrards Cross, Bucks, 1983), pp. 115–24; Patrick J. Keane, *The Terrible Beauty: Yeats, Joyce, Ireland, and the Myth of the Devouring Female* (Columbia, 1988). These studies almost solely deal with *Cathleen ni Houlihan*. Thomas Flanagan's 'Yeats, Joyce, and the Matter of Ireland', *Critical Inquiry*, Vol. 2, No. 1 (Autumn, 1975), 43–67, finely analyses Joyce's absorption of *The Countess Cathleen* in *Ulysses* (unfortunately, he misrepresents the poem as 'Aleel's lovely lyric from *The Countess Cathleen*').

it.[4] In this context of Joyce's, 'that play' in "The Man and the Echo" could as well be *The Countess Cathleen*, which itself encouraged people, even intelligent elites, to nurture or forge a nationalistic spirit and solidarity by that peculiar power of bitterly wounded pride. With respect to how Joyce regarded the intimacy between these two plays, it is suggestive that, in writing to Stanislaus about the similar riot over Synge's *The Playboy in the Western World* which was performed at the Abbey Theatre in 1907, Joyce made a very symbolic mistake: 'Yeats . . . appeals as the author of "Countess Cathleen" ',[5] when, in fact, Yeats appealed to the audience as the author of *Cathleen ni Houlihan*.

Joyce seems to have recovered the balance in some way. He deliberately humiliates the image of Cathleen ni Houlihan and praises the poetic beauty of *The Countess Cathleen* and the depths of its theme. One such humiliation is harshly done in the opening of *Ulysses*, where an old milkwoman, assumed to be Ireland, is represented as 'Silk of the kine' and a 'poor old woman' in Stephen's imagination. In *Ulysses*, as is expected, no mystical transfiguration happens. Most ironically, the milkwoman, though she eagerly wanted to take all she could demand as her proper right, could not get it fully from Mulligan, who cajolingly sang back to her: '*Ask nothing more of me sweet, | All I can give you I give.*' When the 'Cathleen' in *Ulysses* receives a coin which Stephen, saying 'We'll owe twopence', has put in her 'uneager' hand, she poignantly mocks the 'Cathleen' in *Cathleen ni Houlihan* who defiantly declared, 'It's not silver I want.' As there is no imminent rising in *Ulysses*, she calmly responded, 'Time enough, sir'. Mulligan's succeeding chant increases the scene's irony: '*Heart of my heart, were it more, | More would be laid at your feet.*' Irony becomes stingingly acute because this incomplete sacrifice to the milkwoman-queen is initiated by an Englishman, Hains: 'Pay up and look pleasant'. His naive innocence, marked by his smiling face, changes all mythical and romantic elements implied in Yeats's play to a farcical nonsense. Every sacrifice either to a poor old woman or to a beautiful young girl 'with the walk of a queen' is meaningless and ludicrous when the sacrifice itself is meant to make Irishmen look pleasant to an Englishman.

Such is only one example of Joyce's demythologising reaction against Yeats's Cathleen ni Houlihan, but his attitude to Countess Cathleen is a

---

4   There are contradicting views and explanations about whether Joyce was, as described in Gorman's biography and as Joyce himself proudly said, the only person who 'contemptuously' refused to sign the protest. Perhaps C. P. Curran's explanation that Joyce was not the only person who did is nearest to the truth (see *Under the Receding Wave* (Dublin, 1970), pp. 100–2), but, as Father Noon's comment suggests, Joyce was the only person who 'made not signing it a public gesture' (see Ellmann, *James Joyce*, rev. ed. (Oxford Univ. Press, 1982), pp. 67 ff.), and, as a result, people believed that Joyce was the only person who refused it, and were against him (see O'Brien, p. 61, and Ellmann, p. 90).

5   *Letters of James Joyce II*, ed. Richard Ellmann (London: Faber & Faber, 1966), p. 211.

ARTHURIAN AND OTHER STUDIES

favourable one. A few minutes before the milkwoman's arrival, Stephen watches the sea from the top of the Martello tower. A verse from *The Countess Cathleen* of 1895 edition merges with his visual perception and brings forth the most lyrical and poetic prose in *Ulysses*. I have deliberately specified the edition, for here is implied Joyce's criticism towards Yeats's attitude at that time. The verse is 'Who Will Go Drive with Fergus Now'. Yeats composed it as Oona's consolatory song for Countess Cathleen when he first published the play in *The Countess Kathleen and Various Legends and Lyrics* in 1892, and he preserved it in its 'expanded' and 'strengthened'[6] version contained in *Poems* in 1895 which was eventually performed at the Antient Concert Room. He removed it from the text during the final, drastic revision which was made after the riot in order to make the play 'suitable for performance at the Abbey Theatre'.[7] A new text appeared in 1912. Joyce greatly admired the original *Countess Cathleen* and evaluated 'Who Will Go Drive with Fergus Now' so highly that he set music of his own to it.[8] Yeats's 1912 revision, where he removed Joyce's favourite verse, may have seemed to Joyce to be a sacrifice of artistic integrity to an unreasonable demand of the audience. Joyce made his admiration of the original play public and permanent by reviving the verse lost in the 1912 edition in his own work.

Stephen sang 'Who Will Go Drive with Fergus Now' for his dying mother, when he was insistently being asked to pray, that is, to obey. Here is Joyce's determined response to Yeats's self-enquiry which this article began with. It culminates in Stephen's vivid memory. May Dedalus 'in her wretched bed', who haunts Stephen's mind even in this early morning as 'Ghoul', was moved by the verse and cried, 'for those words, Stephen: love's bitter mystery'. Cathleen ni Houlihan cried because of Countess Cathleen's 'love's bitter mystery'. A small victory of the self-sacrificing love over the demanding love. Even if Stephen Dedalus knew that 'the word known to all men' is love, Stephen has not understood yet what the bitter mystery of love is. Love may be a bitter mystery to Yeats and Joyce in different ways, but they both accepted the bitterness courageously, sincerely and patiently without losing their trust in love itself.

---

6 Yeats says in his preface to his *Poems* (London, 1895) that 'He [Yeats] has . . . expanded and, he hopes, strengthened *The Countess Cathleen*.'

7 Note to *The Countess Cathleen* (London, 1912), p. 122.

8 C. P. Curran, *James Joyce Remembered* (London, 1968), p. 41.

68

The Narrator's Function in *The Great Gatsby*

EIICHI HAYAKAWA

Jay Gatsby, the title figure of this novel, is a ridiculously contradicting character when seen objectively. Despite his social activities presenting him as an experienced adult, his personal behaviour, especially when he is involved with Daisy, reveals his immaturity. He represents, as the narrator aptly comments in the opening chapters, 'everything for which [he has] an unaffected scorn';[1] wanting to regain Daisy, his 'first "nice" girl'(177), and making an enormous amount of money after the Great War through a dubious business, Gatsby purchases a 'factual imitation of some Hôtel de Ville in Normandy'(6) just across the bay from Daisy's mansion and waits for her to wander into one of his parties. His 'career as Trimalchio'(135) and his passive approach to Daisy reveal more than his immaturity; they reveal his absurdity as well. 'Great' seems an unbecoming epithet to Gatsby unless it is taken ironically.

Gatsby and his personal behaviour, however, assume some greatness in the interpretation of the narrator, Nick Carraway. Nick, after scornfully rejecting Gatsby's appearances, introduces him to the reader by saying, 'there was something gorgeous about him, some heightened sensitivity to the promises of life'(2), adding decisively that 'Gatsby turned out all right at the end'(3). The other characters' ideas of Gatsby, their reactions to him and their judgements upon him, however, are quite different: they are negative reactions and judgements, which are clearly shown by Nick's recognition that, after Gatsby's death, he finds himself 'on Gatsby's side, and alone'(197), and by the fact that his funeral is attended by no mourners except his father, the owl-eyed man, and Nick, the narrator.

In spite of these negative evaluations by the other characters, why does Nick, after all, judge Gatsby to be 'all right' and 'worth the whole damn bunch put together'(185)? What qualities in Gatsby lead Nick to such a sympathetic understanding? What qualities in Nick contribute to his affirmative reaction to Gatsby? To answer these questions, we must first know how much we can trust Nick, for the first-person narrator is liable to mislead the reader as to his story; he may be honest, but he may

---

[1] F. Scott Fitzgerald, *The Great Gatsby* (New York: Charles Scribner's Sons, 1925), p. 2. All references are to this edition.

not be able to penetrate the truth.[2] Only when we realize his limitations can we identify what he superimposed on facts, what he wanted the reader to believe.

This novel, which, as is expected, assumes the reader's trust on the validity of the narration, begins with Nick the narrator's self-introduction. He tells in the opening paragraphs that he is 'inclined to reserve all judgments, a habit that has opened up many curious natures'(1) to him. This is a very convenient device for a narrator who happens to be a witness. He is supposed not only to see happenings but also to hear various secret stories about people. He often seems to be a reliable narrator when he reports objectively what he sees and hears, but, when he adds that 'the intimate revelations of young men . . . are usually plagiaristic and marred by obvious suppressions'(1–2), the reader realises he has an inclination to make inaccurate generalisation, which casts doubts upon his reliability as an objective witness-narrator.

Nick the narrator presents us with an analytic and rather cynical depiction of his nature and his family tradition, making us expect in this way that he will try honestly to tell us what he actually witnesses. We find, however, that we cannot always trust his comments and interpretations because of his inclination to generalise in misleading ways and his inability to reserve judgement 'after a certain point'(2). That is, we can believe the genuineness of the facts and episodes, but, at the same time, we must presume that they may be those selected through the filter of the narrator's morals and ideas, and that his comments and interpretations may sometimes be biassed.

After betraying his limitations as the narrator, Nick informs the reader of his identity, his family's social status, his education and his war experience: Nick is a middle-class young American; he participated in 'that delayed Teutonic migration known as the Great War', and enjoyed 'the counter-raid so thoroughly that [he] came back restless'(3); he, thus, shares a common experience, common interest, with the other young Americans; he decides 'to go East and learn the bond business', simply because everybody he knows is 'in the bond business'(3).

Nick, a character in the novel, seems to be a more ordinary young American, hardly acting on his own initiative: he follows his father's advice and does things as other young men do; he does not seem to have his own ambitions at all. His ambition in the spring of 1922 is,

---

[2] Since R. W. Stallman pointed out Nick's hypocrisy in 'Gatsby and the Hole in Time', *Modern Fiction Studies*, I (Nov., 1955), 2–16, Nick's character and the reliability of the narrator seem to have become indispensable subjects for the serious critics dealing with interpretation of the work. Some of the articles in which the narrator's reliability is doubted are as follows: Gary J. Scrimgeour, 'Against *The Great Gatsby*', *Criticism*, VIII (Winter, 1966), 75–86; Ron Neuhaus, '*Gatsby* and the Failure of the Omniscient "I" ', *The Denver Quarterly*, XII (Spring, 1977), 303–12; David O'Rourke, 'Nick Carraway As Narrator in *The Great Gatsby*', *The International Fiction Review*, IX (Winter, 1982), 57–60.

like that of other young men, to succeed in the East and to become a millionaire. We first meet him in 1922, an inexperienced, naive young man: a man who, showing the way to a newcomer, feels as if he were 'a guide, a pathfinder, an original settler'(4); who feels 'a dozen volumes on banking and credit and investment securities' on his shelf promising to 'unfold the shining secrets that only Midas and Morgan and Mæcenas knew'(5); who can on occasion make an accurate and rather cynical observation.

Nick the narrator sometimes tries to modify the reader's impression concerning Nick as a character in the novel, as when he comments that the three parties he attended 'were merely casual events in a crowded summer'(68), and that these parties absorbed him 'infinitely less than [his] personal affairs'(68). In order to convince the reader, the narrator, after detailed, vivid depiction of the parties, briefly adds Nick's ordinary life during the time, a life any aspiring young man might lead in a big city; he worked hard, had 'a short affair with a girl'(68) working in the same company, and sometimes felt 'a haunting loneliness'(69) at the enchanted metropolitan twilight. In spite of his apparent effort to modify the reader's impression, we cannot take his words at their face value: in describing the parties vividly in detail, for example, he belies his own comment on the casualness of the events.

That is to say, Nick the narrator sometimes obscures the significance of events: the parties, for example, have given Nick chances to meet people from various social classes, and to be enchanted and repelled by their life. Nick the character visits the Tom Buchanans in fashionable East Egg and sees the life of the established rich; he peeps into Myrtle's New York apartment and finds the life and hope of the lower-middle classes; he attends the party at Gatsby's mansion and notices almost all kinds of people gather together. Although Nick's narration does not sufficiently make it clear, his attention is now focused on the people's lives, especially on their abortive attempts to realise their dreams.

Tom and Daisy, for instance, though enjoying themselves with their enormous amount of money, seem to have been leading purposeless lives: 'They had spent a year in France for no particular reason, and then drifted here and there unrestfully wherever people played polo and were rich together'(7); and Daisy, whose impersonal eyes showed 'the absence of all desire'(15), made 'only a polite pleasant effort to entertain or to be entertained'(15). Nick the narrator, however, interprets Tom's restless drifting as having a certain purpose: 'Tom would drift on forever seeking, a little wistfully, for the dramatic turbulence of some irrecoverable football game'(7); also, he interprets Daisy's hope to retrieve her white girlhood as something worth entertaining, although to attain a purpose, Nick the narrator might cynically tell us, is not easy for Tom and Daisy, for those who are enormously wealthy, for those who reached 'an acute limited excellence'(7) in their youth.

ARTHURIAN AND OTHER STUDIES

There is also Myrtle Wilson, who is never satisfied with the life in the valley of ashes as a wife to a man who isn't 'fit to lick [her] shoe'(42): at her first chance she becomes Tom's mistress to realise her dream, a dream of behaving herself like a lady in material affluence. Here, it is not Myrtle's immoral relation with Tom that Nick critically tells; it is rather the crowded small room of her New York apartment and the snobbish way she satisfactorily entertains her guests. Nick is quite tolerant of immoral behaviour when it has a lot to do with achieving one's ambition to live like a rich person; but, when it has to do with satisfying oneself too easily, he is prompted to express his criticism.

At Gatsby's party also, what Nick notices first is that young Englishmen, well-dressed but hungry-looking, talk earnestly to 'solid and prosperous Americans'(50). He immediately notices what is behind the young men's behaviour; their behaviour is based upon their conviction that 'the easy money in the vicinity'(50) is theirs for a few words in the right key.

The three parties he attends, where Nick sensitively perceives people's hope and dream, all end rather violently with the suggestion of the reality's oppression against human dreams: Nick had to feel 'confused and a little disgusted'(25) after leaving the Buchanans' because of the tension generated by the intrusion of the 'fifth guest's shrill metallic'(20) sound; Myrtle's party ended with Tom's breaking her nose; and, a new coupé, soon after leaving Gatsby's drive, was 'violently shorn of one wheel'(65) in the ditch beside the road.

Nick's attitude in depicting Gatsby's party, however, is a little different from that in depicting the two other parties. In the opening of Chapter 3, Nick, before entering into the minute description of the preparations for the party, briefly gives the reader the appearance of Gatsby's parties through the summer; moth-like gathering of men and women on weekends, the servants' toil of repairing the ravages of the night before, and the arrival of a large quantity of oranges and lemons on Fridays and piling up their pulpless halves like a pyramid on Mondays. In this way he already notices the outcome of dream-like events and even their emptiness, but he is nevertheless obliged to tell the sensuous enchantment of gaudy and meretricious beauty, an enchantment which is still alive in his memory after two years; he, by changing the tense to the present, makes the reader realise what a strong impact the fanciful reality of Gatsby's party had on him.

We have so far seen Nick the narrator reveal remarkably, if not honestly, qualities of Nick the character: from his self-introduction at the outset to the indirect presentation of his tendencies through his reaction to people and their circumstances. Nick tends to rationalize other people's behaviour on his own criteria, which are based upon his own desire for success, chiefly for material wealth. When he, as in the case of Tom and Daisy, finds his criteria difficult to be applicable, or when he

THE NARRATOR'S FUNCTION IN *THE GREAT GATSBY*

finds a certain person's behaviour beyond his understanding, then he tries other directions and causes to satisfy his curiosity.

Gatsby, an enormously successful man who holds a gaudy party every weekend, is not the kind of person who can conform to his standard of understanding: he says '[Y]oung men didn't – at least in my provincial inexperience I believed they didn't – drift coolly out of nowhere and buy a palace on Long Island Sound'(60). This is why Nick begins to seek for the identity of Gatsby; and, in retracing the vague hints of Gatsby's identity, he is also to reconstruct his own experiences in the East, where he happens to be deeply involved with Gatsby.

Nick the narrator tries punctiliously to give the reader the information on Gatsby as Nick the character obtains it;[3] and this is the only way he knows to convince the reader and himself how he was frustrated after the experiences in the East and why he justifies the existence of Jay Gatsby. Information on Gatsby, therefore, reliable or not, is gradually presented to the reader with his due comment. Nick, for instance, tells that, though he first denied the credibility of Gatsby's own tale of his life like 'a young rajah in all the capitals of Europe'(79), he had to accept it as true after he saw the proofs, a medal from Montenegro and a picture of Oxford, and yet betrays that even then he could not wholly convince himself of the existence of Gatsby; it is not until he heard Gatsby's relation with Daisy in the past and his hope for reunion with her from Jordan: Nick comments that '[Gatsby] came alive to [him], delivered suddenly from the womb of his purposeless splendor'(95). Nick thus recognises a purpose in Gatsby's behaviour, but the 'modesty'(95) of Gatsby's demand, which is shown in asking Nick's, or a mere stranger's help for a chance meeting with Daisy at his house after five years of his painstaking efforts to purchase a gorgeous mansion just across the bay from Daisy's, is still beyond his understanding.

The reunion of Daisy and Gatsby provides Nick with a good opportunity to observe Gatsby's reaction to the situation he must have long dreamed. Seeing changes in Gatsby's reaction from embarrassment to unreasoning joy, from unreasoning joy to the state of, as it were, an overwound clock running down, Nick is now in a position to realise that '[Gatsby] had been full of the idea so long, dreamed it right through to the end, waited . . . at an inconceivable pitch of intensity'(111). Perceiving the return of bewilderment, then, Nick further rationalises that the real Daisy must have been surpassed by the unreal Daisy Gatsby's illusion had produced with colossal vitality.

Following the reunion scene, Gatsby's real past, which he tells Nick much later when 'Jay Gatsby' has broken up and 'the long secret extrava-

---

3   The only exception is when the narrator thinks it better to give 'the strange story of [Gatsby's] youth with Dan Cody' (177) earlier to explode 'first wild rumors about his antecedents' (121–2).

ARTHURIAN AND OTHER STUDIES

ganza [is] played out'(177), is inserted by Nick the narrator[4] 'with the idea of exploding those first wild rumors about his antecedents'(121–2); the insertion is also intended to give the reader a more accurate image of Gatsby's identity, an image of an aspiring young man which conforms to Nick's standard of understanding and consequently enables Nick to interpret and rationalise Gatsby's behaviour by his own criteria.

Nick's freedom of interpretation about Gatsby thus obtained further enables him to use his imagination. His interpretation of Gatsby's desire to retrieve Daisy, to make her obliterate four years and to get married with her just as if the marriage had taken place five years ago, is this: '[Gatsby] wanted to recover something, some idea of himself perhaps, that had gone into loving Daisy. . . [If] he could once return to a certain starting place . . . he could find out what that thing was. . .'(133). Nick, in this way, finds a significant motive in Gatsby's pursuit of 'Daisy'. Whether the real Daisy is worth seeking for or not, the Daisy in Gatsby's aspiration, Nick thinks, becomes a symbol of wealth by which 'the youth and mystery'(179) is imprisoned and reserved, and the key for Gatsby to reorganise his life and to regain his forgotten dream.

Nick tells that what Gatsby said then reminded him of 'something – an elusive rhythm, a fragment of lost words, that [he] had heard somewhere a long time ago'(134). Gatsby here seems to be fully within the range of Nick's understanding. This is because the Gatsby the reader sees is Nick's Gatsby, the one Nick sees, or the one he wants him to be. In other words, as Daisy is a product of 'the colossal vitality of [Gatsby's] illusion'(116), so Jay Gatsby is a product not of the 17 year-old James Gats but that of Nick Carraway. Hence, it is natural that Nick should favourably evaluate and accept Gatsby's dream even if he has an unaffected scorn for everything Gatsby represents; Gatsby's dream reflects Nick's own hope for life.

On the last night before he leaves East, Nick, thinking of Gatsby, broods on 'the old, unknown world'(218), on the dream and wonder of Dutch sailors arriving for the first time in this New World. He meditates as follows:

> Gatsby believed in the green light, the orgastic future that year by year recedes before us. It eluded us then, but that's no matter – to-morrow we will run faster, stretch out our arms farther. . . And one fine morning –

---

[4] Kenneth Eble in 'The Craft of Revision: *The Great Gatsby*', *American Literature*, XXXVI (Autumn, 1964), points out that the Gatsby 'of his self-created present is contrasted with the Gatsby of his real past'(323) by this major structural change. Since this transposition among many is the only case where the evidence of transposing is retained in the work, we can suppose that there should be some more significant meanings for the narrator in the insertion of Gatsby's real past.

THE NARRATOR'S FUNCTION IN *THE GREAT GATSBY*

So we beat on, boats against the current, borne back ceaselessly into the
past.   (218)

Gatsby in this meditation is finally identified with Nick the narrator,
with every modern man, with the author himself: F. Scott Fitzgerald,
who, assigning Nick the narrator a function to tell Gatsby's abortive
dream, reveals, in effect, the situation of the modern man, a man who,
clutching with hope at his dream commensurate to his capacity, should
live in this hopeless world, in this seemingly hopeless and purposeless
world.

The Significance of Latin Teaching in British Education

ANTONY DICKINSON

'THE GREAT USE OF LATIN IS THAT IT IS NO USE AT ALL.' Thus spoke a Second Leader in *The Times Educational Supplement* some time in the 1950s. The column went on to explain this antithesis by pointing out that, of all subjects taught in British Secondary schools, Latin teaching alone was totally uninfluenced by any forces from outside the school. Neither teacher nor student saw any direct connection with future employment and little, if any, connection with future leisure or social activity; no one else was concerned with what was taught or how it was taught. Other teachers must worry about changes in technology and science, politics, social mores and so on, but the Latin teacher is unfettered; his only concern is his pupils and their mental development. He is at liberty to frame his course of study solely with the aim of producing the most beneficial intellectual experience for his pupils.

Total academic freedom!

May I rest my case for the defence of Latin there?

Unfortunately not. Events have shown the judgement unsound.

To proceed strikes, for me, a personal note which gives me little joy. But yet, it is not entirely personal, for my experience is inevitably associated with a changing British life-style over the span of my own career.

Briefly, I entered my profession in 1952, firmly convinced that Latin was the 'Queen of Subjects' and that all other subjects were of lesser status. I retired in the mid-1980s and, within a couple of years, Latin was dropped from the curriculum. The school could do perfectly well without it – and me.

That should be sufficient factual evidence to prove that Latin (and my professional life) was of no use at all. Past pupils have claimed that their knowledge of Latin was of use to them here and there in later studies of various sorts, but these are mere 'spin-off' benefits, not commensurate with the time and effort put into their Latin.

There is evidence on a more academic plane, too. Educationalists have tried many times at various points in my career to define the essential purpose of the teaching of the Latin language: 'transfer of training'; a key to a wonderful literature; a view of a certain dignified, lofty beauty; a

ARTHURIAN AND OTHER STUDIES

study of our roots; the aesthetic joy of expressing thought in such a meticulously precise language; and many others. None of these, in my chalk-laden, time-table confined, experience, holds a great deal of practical water.

This lack of convincingly-stated, 'water-tight', aims came home painfully to me when, just before my retirement, a new Headmaster asked all his teachers to state in writing the Aims and Objectives of their teaching and to assess their success. This I just could not do. Mountaineers climb mountains because they are there. I taught Latin for precisely the same reason (and it was the best and most beautiful mountain, any way!). If my pupils felt a sense of achievement and had experienced some pleasure on the climb – and passed their exams – I had succeeded. Full stop. No one wants to go beyond the summit.

But that assessment fails lamentably to come up to the standards demanded by modern educational criteria. By these standards, I could find no way to prove that the teaching of the Latin language was of any use at all.

How should one feel at the end of such a career? Have I depressed you sufficiently so far?

But the winter – even a winter of discontent – is followed by spring, in this case a very idiosyncratic spring.

This 'spring' is Professor Noguchi (quem honoris causa nomino). His idiosyncracies include an affectionate nature and a warm heart, the shrewdness to see that there is, here, a story half-told, together with a grossly inflated idea of my knowledge and intellectual capacities and the power to inspire me to 'look around myself' here and there in order to try to find out where I, a retired Latin teacher, fit so dismally into the overall picture of cultural and historical significance.

It was my good fortune to make contact with Mr Earl K. Robinson, lecturer in Education at Queen's University, Belfast, who led me on to a thesis submitted to his Department by Miss Maureen Brown.[1] That useful thesis carried me back to the mid-1800s (an important period, as I shall show later in some detail, in the history of primary and secondary education in Britain) and also brought to my notice R. R. Bolgar's perceptive article on classical education.[2] There is, here, a looking back to the Renaissance; then, a leap to Robert Graves's 'Claudius the God' which contains a Claudian observation on Romano-Greek philosophy, and that brought my mind back to Thales of Miletos in the 7th Century

---

[1] See her 'A Consideration of Recent Development in the Teaching of Ancient History in Schools – with Particular Reference to the Change of Emphasis from Derivative Works to Primary Sources' (B. A. Thesis, Queen's University, Belfast, 1983).

[2] See his 'The Classical Curriculum and its Links with the Renaissance', *Didaskalos*, IV, 1 (1972), 18.

THE SIGNIFICANCE OF LATIN TEACHING

B. C. Further back than that in West European civilisation one cannot go. That far back one must go to understand Latin and Britain.

Up to that time, men understood the Universe around them in terms of the whims and fancies of the immortal gods; fertility of crops, cattle and humans depended on divine favour; storm and fair weather was the work of Zeus; Poseidon ruled the sea and made earthquakes; and so through all the phenomena of nature and the infinite variety of human experience and emotion.

One can only surmise how it came about that, in that affluent city of Miletos on the Eastern shore of the Aegean Sea, Thales had the time and the inclination to sit and think. He thought that Man could calmly observe his environment and by thinking – or, more accurately, by a process of logical argument – could arrive at an understanding of the nature of the Universe and of the laws governing its functioning, explaining all that was and all that happened without reference to any supernatural powers.

Thus began the search for knowledge and truth. Thus began Western civilisation.

Thales was followed by a succession of thinking minds, each with a different and, perhaps, more sophisticated theory; atoms, rarefaction and condensation, the four elements of fire, air, water and earth and so on.

Then, in the 5th Century B. C., came Socrates. He regarded the study of the physical world as a waste of time; no amount of understanding could prevent a storm flattening the crops and causing a famine; 'the proper study of Man is Man'. He examined the attitudes, beliefs and values held by men and, by a process of question and answer, determined their truth and validity. The mainstream of philosophy was thus directed into the study of human behaviour.

From this grew the concept of the pursuit of 'virtue', the perfectly lived life, by means of philosophically-based guidelines. Nothing in this world is perfect. There is no man who is perfectly wise, no man who is perfectly courageous, no man who is perfectly just, no man who is perfectly 'virtuous'. But it is the duty of every man to seek and strive to be as perfect a man as the study of philosophy can make him. This is the pursuit of virtue.

Two other facets of Greek philosophy are relevant.

One is the issue of *The Republic* by Socrates's pupil, Plato, in which he outlines a perfect political system. He recommends that children should, at a young age, be separated into two classes by intellectual ability. The lower class should be sufficiently educated to become hewers of wood and drawers of water, the craftsmen, tailors, cobblers and so on. The most intelligent should be most carefully educated and nurtured to become the governors of the republic.

The other facet is the study of the physical universe which, however, continued most notably in the Greek colony of Alexandria. Here continued learned meditation on a wide range of 'scientific' subjects, but these studies were treated as purely cerebral exercise for the improvement of the intellectual powers of the student rather than for any benefit they might bestow on mankind at large.

I have made no mention of Archimedes and his Principle or of the schoolboy's friend, Pythagoras, with the square on his hypotenuse, but I must pass on, as historians do, to the Romans.

The Romans were a pragmatic people. If a certain thing worked and had been shown through time to work, that was the right way to do it. They had ample manpower through conquest and slavery to perform all necessary menial tasks. They knew that their divine mission was to rule and civilise the world:

> tu regere imperio populos, Romane, memento,
> hae tibi erunt artes, pacisque imponere morem.
> parcere subiectis et debellare superbos. (Vergil)

> (Remember, O Roman, to rule the nations with your authority and to impose a life-style of peace – these will be your special skills – and to deal mercifully with those you have brought low and to thrash in war those who stand up to you.)

If they won the favour of their gods and had the examples of their past heroes to follow, what need had they of the new-fangled notions of the 'Graeculi'? But time came when the mass of Romans began to feel that the ancient gods of the state were too distant and too inaccessible to be of any help in the conduct of private and personal life. While the common people turned to the mystic religions of the Near East – Isis and the other Egyptian gods, Mithras from Persia, even Christianity –, the upper, educated strata of society found themselves greatly helped by various Greek philosophies, notably Epicureanism and Stoicism (to the Emperor Claudius's reported distress).

The most effective Roman propagator of Greek philosophy was Marcus Tullius Cicero. Apart from his political and legal speeches, models for all time, and his private correspondence, it was his philosophical writings – for example, 'de Amicitia' (on Friendship) and 'de Officiis' (on Duty) – which exerted deep influence over many hundreds of years. At one time it was said that the only two books required for the education of a young English gentleman were the Bible and 'Tully's Offices'.

It is a sad chance that, for the modern British school pupil, 'History' is modern only in the sense that it leads up to himself; 'Latin' is something from a distinct and long-dead other world. In between came the Dark Ages when nothing existed and nothing happened. No connection is made. It is hard for our school pupil to realise that the Latin language persisted in use for many centuries. For the common people, Latin continued, diversified by local speech, and became the Romance languages. For the educated, it continued as the vehicle for cultured, learned international communication. As Bolgar shows in the above-mentioned *Didaskalos* article, far more works in Latin survive from the Renaissance (end 15th Century to mid 17th Century) than from the Classical period. Many are seminal to the development of modern society. Traces of this educated person's Latin persist today in the jargon of the medical and legal professions. It seems but yesterday that the Mass of the Roman Catholic Church abandoned Latin for the vernacular.

Here I must raise my ignorant hat in passing salute to those gifted persons (Chaucer I met at school; Malory I had to look up) who first wrote works of art in the English vernacular. Concerning these gifted persons, there are people in far distant lands (inter alios) who are more able to speak than I am. I blush and pass on.

I pass on to late Georgian and, particularly, Victorian Britain. Here, the threads of history seemed to come together; here, the threads of the present discourse seem to meet. From the past, Victorian Britain absorbed – and sincerely believed in – certain of these traditional ideas.

One of these ideas was that it was a beneficial condition of the human race that a few should be the rulers, the majority should be the ruled (Plato's *Republic*). From this it follows that wealth and education were right and necessary for those few; that it was acceptable that the majority should keep their station in near-poverty and ignorance.

A second idea, derived from Greek thought, (and for 'rulers' only) was that the purpose of education was the refinement of mental powers. (A colleague, reminiscing about his school days, remarked with a cold shudder that he found the translation of a passage of English into acceptable Latin the most terrifyingly pure intellectual experience of his life). Culture was the instilling of such qualities as grace, elegance, nobility, aesthetic sensibility, restraint and a compelling ability in the use of language (I am cynical enough to hesitate to use the Romano-Greek word 'virtue'). It was beneath contempt to consider the acquisition of education and culture merely as a means to secure remunerative employment.

A third idea stems from the Humanists of the Renaissance, the idea that all cultural excellence is to be found in the ancient world of Greece and Rome.

To this social and cultural inheritance must be added a totally new factor: the consideration that Britain was now the mistress of a worldwide empire.

The parallels were so close that there was now no doubt that the Roman Empire was reborn in the British Empire. Rome had brought together in harmony, peace and prosperity peoples of many diverse cultures and languages. It could be done again. Parliament at Westminster was the Roman Senate renewed: its members aspired to be Roman Senators with all their majesty, and also indeed, with all their sense of responsibility – responsibility for the welfare of all those they were appointed to govern.

What was more natural than that the schools of the gentry should provide an education consisting almost entirely of the study of the Classics?

Here was a curriculum combining rigorous mental training with the presentation of the use of language in its most highly esteemed and refined forms. This was the quintessential 'Arts' subject. Combined with that, the Classics also presented, for those of the next generation who were destined to undertake the responsibilities of government, Imperial administration and military enforcement of the Queen's Peace, clear pictures – not eulogies – of men of stature who had confronted these very problems in days gone by and of the qualities of the nation from whom these men had sprung.

Thus could Winston Churchill declare 'Boys should be allowed to study the Classics as an honour'. Thus did Classics become the 'Queen of Subjects', a fit study for those destined to rule.

At this point in time, vast social changes switch the educational focus to the needs of the mass of people. If I were to refresh my memory of these changes, I would open my school history book at the chapter headed 'Industrial Revolution' where I would read about the production of iron by the use of coke rather than charcoal, about James Watt and the steam engine, about huge factories and dark Satanic mills, about migration into suddenly growing towns, about improved sewers and water supplies, about Prince Albert's interest in good housing for the artisan, about the Crystal Palace and the Great Exhibition and about the establishment of the concept that science and engineering could raise the condition of the whole human race to unheard-of dignity.

This social upheaval made it clear that the labour market had a huge demand for manpower that offered not merely muscle but also some ability to read and to write and to make accurate calculations. Here was the driving force for the emergence of universal education; elementary education became compulsory in 1870.

The education of the socially elite still held the high ground in public and governmental esteem. In 1864, the Clarendon Commission, reporting on the Public Schools (the most expensive), insisted that 'The Classical Languages and Literature should continue to hold the principal place in the course of study.' Even in schools a little less eminent, the Classics occupied anything up to two thirds of the timetable.

The later 19th Century saw the emergence of an increasingly numerous middle class, seeking prestige and influence. They saw an education of a standard higher than the basic '3 Rs' as highly desirable.

By 1868, the Taunton Report drew these three levels of aspiration into one document, acknowledging that the new 'merchant class' required an education 'to equip their children for a world, dependent on industrial production and foreign trade'. The report outlined three strata of education:

1. Upper class; up to 19; a little less Classics plus Maths, Modern Language and Science;
2. Merchant Class; up to 16; less Classics; more Modern Subjects;
3. Working Class; up to 14; cheap elementary instruction; 'A clerk's education'.

The social evolution over the last hundred years plus has been sweeping. The Taunton Report identified three classes of society, each with a form of education suited to its needs. In the 1992 General Election, Mr John Major appeared in public announcing the dawn of the 'Class-less society', in which a man (and, increasingly, a woman) with the humblest of backgrounds can, in theory and frequently in practice, rise by his opportunities and by his talents to the highest eminence. Both Mr Major and Mrs Thatcher made much of that in their own cases.

It is illuminating to consider the history of my own family in the context of the development of society and education. My father's ancestors were tin-miners; his father was a police sergeant; he himself, after an elementary education, started as clerk to a coal-merchant and finished as an eminent stock-broker; his sons had a Public School and University education. I think he was sad that we both became teachers but we were most grateful that such was possible.

During these years, the story of the teaching of Latin has been the story of a steadily-fought rearguard action. Some would say that such an exclusive pursuit should have no place in modern society. Others wish to see it brought down from its lofty citadel and spread more widely through the populace (the Labour Party expressed such an intent in one of its early manifestoes; in the middle of this century, every school set up as a Grammar School, even a small rural one such as my own, was still finding that the inclusion of Latin in its curriculum was a bulwark of its status and a powerful means of attracting pupils).

On the 'defending' side of this rearguard action were those who blindly accepted Classics as the only true and traditional education; there were those, too, who had great personal enthusiasm for the benefits of the study, for the mental development afforded by this linguistic engagement and for the nobility of Classical literature and men. But I suspect a paucity, among them, of persons able to prove, on any sort of scientific basis, the precise benefits bestowed.

In 1903 the Classical Association was formed and, in 1969, there appeared the Joint Association of Classical Teachers (JACT). Both these bodies have laboured mightily in the defence of Classics. JACT, in particular, has led the way in formulating courses of study adapted to modern needs.

On the 'attacking' side, one does not so much find persons (though there is one Comprehensive School head who is alleged to have stated 'Latin is nothing more than a very long and very expensive intelligence test'). One finds, rather, pressures – pressures to include within the school curriculum ever more subjects, ever more 'high tech' on the one hand, and ever more closely relevant matters to modern living on the other (Road Safety, Aids prevention and lately even 'How to preserve your marriage'). The immediate and important effect of these pressures upon the teaching of Latin (Greek has almost disappeared) is the reduction of time allocation and the shortening for most pupils of the course to a bare three years. This has meant that the goalposts have had to be shifted. No longer can one aspire to such a grasp of the linguistics that one may indulge in the lofty art form of composing Ciceronian prose, let alone Vergilian hexameters. If a modern pupil can, with much assistance, stagger through a minute selection of original Latin and gain a smattering of Roman history and daily life, that is the ultimate, or was so when I retired.

I have come all the way from Thales of Miletos to the present day. I have viewed the heights of Classics teaching in the Victorian age. I have seen the teaching even of Latin cease in many schools such as my own (Down High School, near Belfast). An article headed 'Goodbye to All That?' in *The Sunday Times* of 3 May 1992 reports that the number of children in boarding schools has dropped dramatically for the first time in a decade ('boarding schools' implies predominately Public Schools, the bastions of Classical teaching). I quote: 'With the end of Empire, there are no longer legions of families who need to ship their children back to the homeland from the outposts of Asia and Africa to be given the kind of education which would fit them in their turn to govern Asia and Africa.'

How shall I value my own career? Did I spend my time converting intelligent country children into incipient members of the upper classes, into 'gentry'? Did I waste their time while I drummed into them a great deal of useless nonsense? Or did I, at least, teach them, by using words and language, to use their brains in every aspect of their thinking lives, in a way which no other subject can teach them? These three questions involve three possibilities.

Modern view and fashion will discard the first possibility as no longer relevant and will pick the second possibility. The third possibility remains, right out of educational, social and political fashion at the moment. I have a conviction, based solely on the observation of the workings of my own antiquated and rusty mind and, I emphasise, with

THE SIGNIFICANCE OF LATIN TEACHING

no possible shadow of proof, that the third possibility has some grain of validity in it. Could it be that, for that reason, Latin will return one day to educational favour? I am not quite ready yet to join the schoolboys chorusing:

'Latin's as dead as dead as can be.
First it killed the Romans and now it's killing me.'

Hauberk and Helm in Malory's
Le Morte Darthur

DEREK BREWER

Armour and weapons are intrinsic to medieval romance and romantic history. Malory's *Le Morte Darthur* is inconceivable without them, for knight-errantry is of the essence of the action. The present essay, from work in progress, presents just two examples of Malory's treatment of armour, as a tribute to the long and distinguished work of Professor Noguchi in relation to Malory.

Some paradoxes immediately emerge. Although Malory has many incidental references to armour he is no more interested in it than he is in the technique of single combat or the tactics and strategy of battle. Again, he relies heavily on sources, but he treats them with magisterial independence. He is a literary genius who is not interested in normal literary effects. He cuts out realistic detail, personal dialogue and literary devices. For example he is not interested in the ancient and immensely wide-spread 'arming topos'.[1] His interest is deep but narrow. He focuses on simple events of a very limited kind, based on armed combat, to construct a long chain of events which paradoxically become deeply complex, to illustrate that chivalric ethos which in his eyes was once the glory of Arthur and England.

I take just two examples to illustrate these aspects: Malory's references to the hauberk and the helm.

The hauberk was originally the main defensive armour for the body, made usually of mail, as copiously illustrated in the Bayeux Tapestry. Some form of garment, usually a quilted jacket known under various names, for example 'aketon', was worn under it. Though essential to the wearing of armour Malory never mentions this latter. From the mid-thirteenth century onwards plates of iron or steel might be attached to the hauberk, either on top or beneath it, along with other accoutrements of plate to protect elbows, arms, knees, legs and feet. In the fourteenth century the hauberk was often a cloth or leather garment lined with metal plates,[2] or the hauberk remained of mail with various arrange-

---

[1] Derek Brewer, 'The Arming of the Warrior in European Literature and Chaucer', *Tradition and Innovation in Chaucer* (London: Macmillan), pp. 142–60.

[2] For the historical development of armour I have mainly used C. Blair, *European Armour circa 1066 to circa 1700* (London: Batsford, rpt. 1972).

ments of plates set on top. The plates evolved into more elaborately clasped casings and the hauberk was shortened from reaching to the knees so that it covered only the trunk, and was known as the haubergeon. By Malory's own time the hauberk proper would have been virtually unknown.

The word, from Old French, is found in Middle English from c.1300 but uses are historical, poetical or metaphorical. 'Habergeoun' was the practical word. Malory refers to a hauberk(s) 17 times. The first occurrence of 'hauberk' in *Le Morte Darthur* is during Balin and Balan's fatal battle, in which they fought so fiercely that their 'hauberkes [were] unnailled, that naked they were on every syde' (2) 89/35.[3] This is the first occurrence of 'unnailled' so far recorded in English (*O.E.D.*) and the word seems to have been suggested by whatever French source Malory was using: for example Cambridge University MS. Add. 7071 referred to by Vinaver as a possible source, has at the relevant passage concerning the desperate fight between Balin and Balan 'li hauberc estaient desmaille e rompue e li escu si empire . . . Il sentre feroient e descouuert sor les chars nues' (f.277ʳ). Malory picks up both the dismantling of the hauberk and the reference to naked flesh. That this manuscript was in English hands in the fifteenth century is shown by the remark in English in a fifteenth-century hand at the foot of f.273ʳ, 'Turne the leef ouer', and the verso is blank. (It would be nice to think the manuscript was Malory's own. He must have read exactly such books.) The Huth manuscript (ed. G. Paris et J. Ulrich, SATF II, 1886, pp. 50–1) has similar though more wordy references to 'li hauberc desmaillie et dessevré . . . desmailliet et desrompu . . . sour les chars nues'. Here Malory brilliantly compresses a long account and selects the telling detail.

'Hauberc' seems to be the normal word used for body-armour in the thirteenth-century French romances, but Malory adds a reference to the thick mails of the hauberks (3) 111/36 – 112/3.

The three occurrences of the word 'hauberk' in the story of Arthur's war with Rome, at (5) 190/4, 209/32, 230/6, are quite independent of the source, the alliterative *Morte Arthure*. Malory is encouraged by the nature of his source but not dominated by it. The first occurrence is attributed to Lancelot, in a passage considerably changed from the poem. There Lancelot makes no reference to his lands bordering the enemies' land, but offers to lend 'sex score helmes' (380). Malory turns this into 'twenty

---

3 The text is from *The Works of Sir Thomas Malory*, ed. E. Vinaver, 3rd ed. revised P. J. C. Field (Oxford: 1990), but page and line references to this are preceded in brackets by the number of the books into which Caxton divided his edition. My debt to Vinaver and now to Mr Field is of course immense. This work could not have been done without constant reference not only to the text but to *A Concordance to the Works of Sir Thomas Malory*, ed. T. Kato (University of Tokyo Press, 1974) (in which Professor Shunichi Noguchi also receives honourable mention), and the *The Middle English Dictionary* (*M.E.D.*). I record my indebtedness and gratitude to both.

thousand helmys in haubirkes attyred', which out-Herods Herod in alliteration and numbers. Malory seems carried away by the gusto of his source to pile Pelion on Ossa. The word 'hauberk' appears in the *Morte Arthure* at lines 1156, 2078, 2700, but none of these references is picked up by Malory. His next use tells how Sir Idres 'brought fyve hondred good men in haubirkes attyred' (5) 209/32, which is based on *Morte Arthure's* 'Wyth fyue hundrethe men appon faire stedes' where Malory has again introduced 'hauberks' and 'attyred' thus creating an archaic flavour and rhythm. At (5) 230/6 Malory adds and archaicises even more radically. The *Morte Arthure* has Gawain cutting and smiting, with a passage full of details of armour current both in the fourteenth century and in Malory's day – ailette, rerebrace, couter, silvered vambrace, visor, aventail and rich velvet surcoat (2557–73). Hauberks are not mentioned. Malory abandons all these and gives us 'thorowoute the thycke haubirke made of sure mayles, and the rubyes that were ryche, he russled hem in sundir' (5) 230/5–7: 'in sundir' comes from the poem, like the later reference to the liver. As Malory abbreviates so he both extracts the essence and heightens the effect. The single concrete and archaic detail of the 'thick hauberk' summarises all the bits of armour which he knew but was not concerned with; the rich rubies sum up the richness of armour, perhaps in an archaising spirit, for precious stones were set on the helm up to the end of the twelfth century, and only occasionally later. (Though the Black Prince's bascinet had a circlet set with precious stones according to the representation on the effigy.) The last three references (9) 518/2, (10) 625/9, (10) 625/32 give us two collocations 'shield and hauberk', then in the third case 'helm and hauberk' (which harks back to (5) 190/4). All these references occur in the Tristram story and successfully sum up destructive fighting. It is as if for Malory in his historical romance the hauberk, made of 'thick mail', is the archetypal piece of body-armour, as it was for the earlier French romances. It is not envisaged in practical detail as worn under plate, or as being mainly of plate, though as early as the late fourteenth century Chaucer tells us that Sir Thopas's hauberk is of plate (*The Canterbury Tales* VII 863–5). We are free to imagine some sort of oldfashioned mixture of mail and plate, or not to visualise at all except in the vaguest way, and accompanied with appropriate feeling.

The helm or helmet was a crucial part of the knight's armour. Malory favours the word 'helm', of which in singular and plural there are over 200 instances, against only 16 of 'helmet(te)' all in the singular. 'Helm' from Old English is first recorded in Middle English in the early thirteenth century in Layamon's *Brut* and is used constantly throughout the medieval period. 'Helmet', which is an early example of an English word with a French suffix (cf. 'kitchenette') is first recorded in the middle of the fifteenth century. There are few fifteenth-century references and Malory is thus one of the earliest users of the word. It has superseded the word 'helm' in modern English presumably because it is less specifically associated with medieval armour, but there is no detectable difference of meaning or nuance between 'helm' and 'helmet' in Malory. The variation seems quite unconscious.

The history of the development of the helm in actual life is complex. Apart from the purely incidental references to bascinet and coif Malory gives no hint of the presence of a helm worn underneath the 'great helm', but it is clear that he always thinks of the helm (or helmet) as a 'great helm' because when wearing it the knight's face cannot be seen.

The great helm from the thirteenth century onwards was large, cylindrical, and with a flat top, though the shape changed considerably in time, eventually becoming very elaborate. Malory seems to think of the simpler shape. The helm was padded and worn over first a padded fabric arming cap, then mail coif, and then probably a bascinet. It was fixed with laces and chinstrap.[4] How easily it could be sliced through by a sword in real life as often as in Malory is uncertain. More probable, if less romantic, is the story of how the greatest of all jousters in the thirteenth century, William Marshal, ended up after a joust with his head inside the helm on an anvil while the blacksmith tried to beat the helm back into shape so that it could be removed, or, in Malory's term, 'raced off'.[5] (Barber and Barker p. 152). Padded though the helm was, and with underhelm, Henry of Lancaster in his *Livre de Seyntz Medecines* (1354) says that the practised jouster is known by his misshapen nose, battered so often against the front of his helm.[6] How far long speeches made from a closed helm could ever be heard is never considered in French romance (where they are endemic) or by Malory.

Good examples of these helms, which often had great crests never mentioned by Malory, may be seen in the Tower of London Armories. Perhaps best of all is the great helm of the Black Prince (ob. 1376) preserved at Canterbury Cathedral. The fullest readily available description of this is in *Age of Chivalry*, ed. Alexander and Binski, p. 480.[7] See also the summary account by Blair, pp. 169–71. This helm would be worn over the visorless bascinet which has its coronal set with gems and its attendant cape of mail, shown in the Black Prince's tomb effigy in Canterbury Cathedral. The use of the great helm, with its flamboyant crest, was probably already becoming less frequent in battle by the third quarter of the fourteenth century, though it continued for many years to be used in tournaments. In this respect Malory's imagination may well have been stimulated by any tournaments he may have seen, though

4 W. Reid, *The Lore of Arms* (London: Mitchell Beazley Ltd., 1976), p. 43.
5 R. Barber and J. Barker, *Tournaments: Jousts Chivalry and Pageants in the Middle Ages* (Woodbridge: Boydell, 1989).
6 Reid, *op.cit.* p. 41.
7 *Age of Chivalry: Art in Plantagenet England 1200–1400*, ed. J. Alexander and P. Binski, Royal Academy of Arts (London: Weidenfeld and Nicolson, 1987).

when a helm was knocked off in a fifteenth-century tournament the victim was not decapitated. In practical terms the great helm was heavy and hot, so that it was not put on until fighting was at hand. When it was put on the knight was unrecognisable. Hence the development of heraldic blazons on shield and surcoat, but also the invaluable anonymity which occurs again and again in Arthurian romance, the occasion of so much uncertainty and, as in the case of the fight between the brothers Balin and Balan, of tragedy. Hence too the subtleties of whether or not a knight should be prepared to give his name when asked, a piece of etiquette which to consider would take us too far afield.

The helm acquired the movable facial protection called the visor at the end of the thirteenth century. This was hinged, took on a variety of shapes, and from the fourteenth century might be attached to the bascinet, making the great helm unnecessary. The visor was the upper part of the facial protection which corresponded to the bevor as the lower part, and the visor therefore needed to be lifted up to give fuller vision. When it was lowered, vision was (just) possible through various arrangements of slits. There were also ventilation holes on the right side of the great helm (which was less exposed to attack), as in the case of the Black Prince's helm, or in the visor. From the end of the thirteenth century the helm was often provided with a guard-chain, so that it could be carried by a knight dangling from his shoulder and thus ready for instant use. The Black Prince's helm retains a fragment of its chain.

To what extent does the helm in *Le Morte Darthur* fit into these hard realities? Somewhat confusingly, it must be said. There are two essential points. First in *Le Morte Darthur*, a knight frequently, if not quite always, wears his helm and is consequently unrecognisable, in a way most improbable in ordinary life. For example, when Lancelot is on the magic ship in the story of the Grail, and becomes somewhat weary of it, so that he goes ashore 'to play hym by the waters syde', a strange knight rides up. Eventually they declare to each other their names. They are father and son. Lancelot kneels to Galahad, asks his blessing 'And aftir that toke of hys helme and kyssed hym' (17) 1012/19. We may assume Galahad was also at first wearing, and then took off, his helm. Such are the ways of romance. They wore their helms almost all the time. On a number of occasions knights remove their helms on learning each other's names and kiss in friendship.

On the other hand, Tristram is on one occasion after arming himself given by La Beall Isoude 'a good helme' (10) 694/22. Dinadan then travelling with him eventually 'carries' i.e. wears Tristram's helm. For this he is attacked and unhorsed and his victor sends a varlet 'to unbuckyll his helme' (10) 704/26. This implies a firm fastening, though no guard-chain is mentioned. It must be assumed that a knight could at need unbuckle his own helm.

A knight could quickly don his helmet on some occasions. Again in the Tristram story, Tristram and Palomydes come across a knight sleep-ing by a tree, lacking no piece of harness 'save hys helme lay undir his hede', obviously as a pillow, and as seen in so many contemporary tomb effigies. 'What shall we do?' says Tristram. 'Awake him' says Palomydes. So Tristram prods him with the butt of his spear, 'And so the knyght arose up hastely, and put his helme uppon his hede, and mowntyd uppon his horse, and gate a grete speare in his honde'. He forthwith knocks both Tristram and Palomydes off their horses (10) 563/6–31. The strange knight cuts a swathe through various knights of the Round Table, but turns out to be none other than Lancelot, a white knight with a covered shield i.e. with a blazon unseen, (10) 571/9018. He should have been recognised at first as he was not wearing his helm, since his face could have been seen, but Malory has been careless. In his source the strange knight is genuinely unknown but as Vinaver remarks Malory dislikes anonymity and so makes him Lancelot, at the cost of consider-able inconsistency, and blemishing of character.

The most common event in combat is for the victor to 'race' off his opponent's helm and often decapitate him. Helms are also often 'unlaced' by the victor. This must be taken as romance short-hand for a quite elaborate process, having regard to the mail attached to the bascinet under the great helm. Malory never mentions this. A strong man with a heavy sword could presumably cut through the mail of the camail. Illustrations of the great Maciejowski Bible, now in New York, of c. 1250 show many cases of swords and axes shearing through helms and mail (Reid p. 44). *The Gloucester Chronicle A*, 4577, of about 1300 notes 'Thoru hauberc and thoru is coler, that nere nothing souple, He smot of is heued' (quot *M.E.D* s.v. coler). This collar would have been of mail, probably attached to the hauberk, perhaps a camail. To slice through mail was readily assumed to be possible, once the helm was off.

In the phrase 'The buff syde of the helm' (7) 348/25, 'buff' as an adjective is a nonce-word, glossed by Field in the *Works* (3rd Edition), as the 'blow-receiving (side of the helm)', i.e. the left side, which is prob-ably based on *M.E.D.* The word 'buff' is only elsewhere recorded in *M.E.D.* as a noun again glossed by context to mean a 'buffet', of which 'buff' seems to be a shortened form. The only other quotation in *M.E.D.* is of the noun, in *The Avowing of Arthur*, a low-grade English hunting poem of the early fifteenth century. Malory may have picked up the adjectival use from his possible English source or it could be a soldier's colloquialism. Its use in the story of Gareth reinforces the sense of the popular, folktale, English flavour of the story. Of course Malory might have invented the adjectival use from the colloquial noun.

The elaborate crest of the helm, so noticeable in illustrations of armour, and, for example, on the great helm of the Black Prince, reached fanciful extremes in the latter part of the fifteenth century. Malory pays no attention. He mentions the crest of the helm once only merely to mean the top (5) 223/20. The glamour of armour is irrelevant to him.

Knights might wear ladies' tokens on their helms, though these are not strictly part of armour. Malory's only significant mention of this practice is when Lancelot carries the sleeve of the Fair Maid of Ascolot on his helm as a disguise, because he had never before been known to do such a thing (18) 1071/13–17.

Malory invokes the power of the imagination. He assumes that his reader has a general notion of armour. We focus on the essential elements of quest and encounter, contest and reconciliation, with all the representative and symbolic power of simple elements. The visual screen of the imagination is much more irregular than pictures in real life (which is why great stories lose so much in film or television where every detail has to be realised to the last corner). The screen of the imagination is naturally enough a more extreme version of ordinary vision, which is so highly selective of points of interest and disregards so much in the potentially observable field. Malory relies on this. He visualises very little and the reader visualises very little. A visual hint is enough for feeling and imagination. Hence many inconsistencies, large and small, do not trouble the experienced reader. We take the will for the deed.

Hunting, Hawking, and Textual Criticism in Malory's *Morte Darthur*

P. J. C. FIELD

Whatever medium they work in, all copyists tend to corrupt what they are reproducing. This will happen whether the copyist uses a quill pen or a word-processor, but naturally tends to happen more often when the copyist is unfamiliar with the subject of the work copied, and especially when that subject is one, such as the law, seamanship, or architecture, that generates an extensive private vocabulary.

To this rule of universal professional depravity, Malory's scribes were no exception. In particular, the scribes who copied the unique manuscript of the *Morte Darthur*, the Winchester manuscript, seem to have been more concerned with producing attractive-looking copy than with accuracy,[1] so it is not surprising that they made mistakes in matters in which Malory was knowledgeable and they, we may assume, were not. They made such mistakes, for instance, over words to do with warfare and weapons.[2] Chivalric romance alone might have made Malory familiar with some of the jargon of warfare, but we know that he experienced the reality as well, in the northern campaign of 1462–3, in local skirmishes in the Midlands about 1450, and perhaps before that in the dying phases of the war against the French in Gascony:[3] from their errors we may guess that his copyists had little familiarity with either.

Malory also seems to have known more about another pair of subjects, hunting and hawking, than his scribes, and it is aspects of those subjects that this paper will particularly address. His book shows his enthusiasm not merely for the pursuits themselves but for the jargon of their devotees, which he praises as one of the distinguishing marks of a gentleman:

---

[1] See *The Winchester Malory: A Facsimile*, ed. N. R. Ker, E.E.T.S., s.s. 4 (London, 1976), p. xvii; Sir Thomas Malory, *Works*, ed. Eugène Vinaver and P. J. C. Field, 3 vols. (Oxford, 1990), pp. 1755–63 (notes to pp. 266.23–4, 426.32, 918.33–4).

[2] *Works*, pp. 1753–62 (notes to pp. 27.4, 703.31, 8644.22).

[3] See P. J. C. Field, 'The Last Years of Sir Thomas Malory', *Bulletin of the John Rylands Library*, 64 (1981–2), 433–56. We may also notice that Malory's epitaph described him as *valens miles*, a phrase that claims distinction in arms: London, British Library, MS. Cotton Vitellius F.xii, fol. 284^r.

ARTHURIAN AND OTHER STUDIES

[Sir Trystram] began good mesures of blowynge of beestes of venery and beestes of chaace and all maner of vermaynes, and all the tearmys we have yet of hawkynge and huntynge. And therefore the booke of venery, of hawkynge and huntynge is called "The Booke of Sir Trystrams". Wherefore, as me semyth, all jantyllmen that beryth olde armys ought of ryght to honoure Sir Trystrams for the goodly tearmys that jantylmen have and use and shall do unto the Day of Dome, that thereby in a maner all men of worshyp may discover a jantylman frome a yoman, and a yoman frome a vylayne.[4]

What Malory said in that passage was plainly important to him: he repeated a substantial part of it some hundreds of pages further on in his story.[5]

Malory's enthusiasm for hunting and hawking appears also in a tendency, working against a more general tendency to reduce his sources by anything up to five-sixths, to add to his story material concerned with those pursuits. Sometimes he does no more than make his source's phrasing more specific. So, for instance, when the French prose *Tristan* has its hero hunt *un cerf moult grant et molt merveilleux*, Malory replaces that ungentlemanly vagueness with *an herte of grece*. The *hart of grece* was specifically a hart still fat with summer feeding, hunted, according to *The Book of St Albans*, in a season that ran from 24 June to 14 September.[6] At other times, Malory adds larger hunting elements to his story, as in the opening of the "Great Tournament" episode, where Sir Launcelot is wounded in a hunting accident. Whereas the French *Mort Artu* gives the hunt in half a dozen lines, Malory expands it to a page packed with technical terms.[7] In both cases the hunting detail helps to characterise the Arthurian world as Malory sees it, but in neither is it necessary to the action. It may be that, as has recently been argued, one kind of hunting was too much for Malory as author: the pursuit of that imaginary bundle of self-contradictions, the Questing Beast.[8] But with more realistic forms of hunting, it is not surprising that we can at various points in the *Morte Darthur* see a contrast between authorial authenticity and scribal error,

---

4 *Works*, p. 375.18. I have slightly modified the punctuation of the passage.
5 *Works*, pp. 682.28–683.4.
6 See *Works*, p. 780.4 and Commentary, and John Cummins, *The Hound and the Hawk: The Art of Medieval Hunting* (London, 1988), p. 33.
7 *Works*, p. 1104, *La Mort le Roi Artu*, ed. Jean Frappier (Genèva, 1964), § 64. One reason for thinking Malory wrote *The Wedding of Sir Gawain and Dame Ragnell* is that, unlike its analogues, it has at the beginning a hunting scene, described in some detail: cf. P. J. C. Field, 'Malory and *The Wedding of Sir Gawain and Dame Ragnell'*, *Archiv für Studium der neueren Sprachen*, 219 (1982), 374–81.
8 Catherine Batt, 'Malory's Questing Beast and the Implications of Author as Translator', *The Medieval Translator: The Theory and Practice of Translation in the Middle Ages*, ed. Roger Ellis and others (Cambridge, 1989), pp. 142–66, esp. 150–4.

and infer a contrast between knowledge on the one side and ignorance on the other.[9]

It may appear odd therefore that in a recent examination of one of the most striking hunting scenes in the *Morte Darthur*, Claude Luttrell finds it obscure and confused compared with its source.[10] The Malorian passage is Arthur's wedding-feast, and its source the corresponding passage in the French Post-Vulgate *Suite du Merlin*.[11] I should like to argue that, if the passage is read with the close attention that has distinguished Professor Noguchi's contributions to Malory studies, then, with one exception which may be the product of scribal error, nearly all the apparent confusions can be resolved.

As Dr Luttrell himself observes, some of what he feels to be obscurities come about because Malory chose to tell his story in a different way from his source.[12] In the *Suite*, for instance, the quest of each of the three knights sent out from Arthur's feast is neatly rounded off by his being described presenting to the court the object that he has been sent to fetch, whereas in Malory those objects are not explicitly mentioned on the knights' return. This, as Dr Luttrell remarks, reflects the fact that Malory is more concerned with the quests themselves than with their nominal objects. We might add that Malory is also much concerned with the honour or dishonour each knight gains from his adventures: each quest ends with a quasi-judicial inquisition into the quester's 'worship', with evidence given on oath, formal proofs offered, and the magician Merlin hovering ready to confound any misrepresentation. This provides Malory with a concluding focus alternative to that in his source, but Dr Luttrell is nevertheless right to observe that patterning is less important in the *Morte Darthur* than in the *Suite*.

That reduced element of patterning in the *Morte Darthur* is also seen when the hart is not killed, as it is in the *Suite* and other versions of the tale closer to mythology, by the hounds that have been pursuing it from the beginning. Dr Luttrell appears to feel that in both cases, and perhaps generally, less patterning means an inferior story. If he does feel this, he goes too far. In myth, continuity and patterning in the action contribute appreciably to our sense that the story has an inner significance; but there is no reason to suppose Malory was trying to write a myth-like story, here or elsewhere. Whatever effects he and the author of the *Suite*

---

[9] *Works*, pp. 1754–65 (notes to pp. 42.7, 821.12, 1104.21, and 1104.24). An excellent recent account of the two subjects will be found in Cummins, *op. cit.*

[10] 'The Arthurian Hunt with a White Bratchet', *Arthurian Literature IX* (1989), 57–80, esp. 76–80.

[11] *Works*, pp. 102.24–103.24; *Suite* (from the Huth manuscript) in *Merlin*, ed. Gaston Paris and Jacob Ulrich, 2 vols. (Paris, 1886), II, 77–81; and (edited by Jill Mann from Cambridge University Library MS. Add. 7071, fols. 284^b–285^c) in *Aspects of Malory*, ed. Toshiyuki Takamiya and Derek Brewer (Cambridge, 1981), pp. 197–9.

[12] Luttrell, p. 76.

had in mind, clear patterns of events are peculiarly appropriate to the story of the *Suite*, where divine providence is of great importance: they are less so in the *Morte Darthur*, whose narrative exhibits some of the brute incoherence of history. It is a distinctive part of the character of Malory's book that we feel that its events may be purposive, but that the purpose is hard to discern: the narrator rarely tells us what those purposes are, and may himself not know them.

Dr Luttrell has a second objection to the events of the episode: that the way they are related is not sufficiently continuous. Among other things, he feels it as a weakness in Malory's book that the white hart and its pursuing hounds are described entering Arthur's court but not leaving it, that just as Gawayne comes up with the hart the pursuing hounds (by whose cry he has been following it) disappear without explanation, and that Gawayne then brings the hart down by releasing greyhounds of his own, of which we have been told nothing before.

I would argue that these things too are appropriate to the *Morte Darthur*. Malory had developed a kind of story-telling that suited his kind of tale, a swift-moving narrative focussing on what participants and readers would have felt to be the high points of the action. It is a conspicuous feature of this kind of narrative that it leaves the 'low points' (if we may so call them) to be inferred, and we will misread it if we compel our imaginations to exclude everything that has not been made to some degree explicit. At the beginning of this episode, for instance, we are told nothing of King Arthur's wedding party leaving the church of St Stephen's in Camelot for the wedding feast.[13] In a more consecutive kind of narrative, we would have to assume from that the wedding feast, which makes use of the Round Table itself and other substantial items of furniture such as benches to sit on and 'sydebourdis' to sit at, was taking place in St Stephen's. Malory's kind of narrative must be read differently. We must be prepared to allow for the royal wedding party having travelled from cathedral to the palace in the kind of ceremonial procession that was used in real royal ceremonies in Malory's time; but, although it must be possible for us to imagine what happens at such low points, and we must therefore acknowledge that it is a fault if what the story implies at those points is inconsistent either with what is made explicit or with what we should imagine elsewhere, we will also misread the narrative if we often indulge our imaginations with such detail. The narrative method Malory is using here aims at conciseness and speed, relating a great deal in very few words. We need to feel that more is happening than we can fully comprehend, and that depends on our being aware as we read of the omitted 'low points', but not pausing to work it out in full.

[13] Cf. *Works*, pp. 102.24–103.1.

On particular occasions, this narrative method can have other special advantages as well. We may see one of them in the interruption to the wedding-feast, where keeping to the high points can help us to share the excitement, confusion, and suspense that would have been felt by participants. Arthur's court has been warned by Merlin to expect a marvellous adventure, and they see one. A white hart is a remarkable creature in itself, but becomes even more remarkable when pursued by a pack of hounds in full cry through a king's dining-hall. The court (we must assume) give this event the attention it deserves; but are then distracted by the dispute between the knight and the huntress over the white brachet. It is a measure of their distraction that they (and we with them) do not notice the final departure of that remarkable hunt from their hall.

A second special advantage of Malory's method can be in showing readers what is important. We may see this if we consider Gawayne's greyhounds, for instance, as a sign not of authorial confusion, as Dr Luttrell would have it, but of a kind of naturalism. Supernatural hounds may never lose their quarry, but hounds that are of this world can, and in this case do, and disappear from the story. We then find Gawayne properly provided against that eventuality. This is another 'low point': we should no doubt assume, if the question comes up in our minds, that the original pack has got lost, as hounds sometimes do, and that Gawayne had got himself some greyhounds before he set out. We may also assume that Malory was silent about these things because to have related them would have slowed down the pace of the narrative, and also because they were not sufficiently important compared with the things that he does tell us about. The acquisition of greyhounds at the beginning of the quest for instance, is less important than that the quest was advised by Merlin, commanded by King Arthur, and formally accepted by Gawayne, that Gawayne armed himself properly, and that his quest was the first he made after he was knighted. The implications of this may guide us, if guidance were needed, against attributing to the *Morte Darthur* a full-blown philosophical naturalism, or (since Malory is no philosopher) a common-sense equivalent of that philosophy. We should not, that is, despite Malory's enthusiasm for hunting, proceed from the fact that in his story the greyhounds kill the hart to the assumption that the quest would have failed without them: the way the story is told hints that knightliness would have found some other way. Or perhaps, calling to mind another passage in which Malory as narrator argues that *worshyp in armys may never be foyled*,[14] we should say that the story implies that Malory hoped and wished to believe that knightliness would have found another way.

---

[14] *Works*, p. 1119.27–8.

In this episode, Malory makes his story a good deal shorter than that in his source; but here as elsewhere he goes against that general trend towards abbreviation in bringing the Arthurian world to life as a one in which hunting and hawking are important. He does this at one of those points that Dr Luttrell has picked out as discrepant, not only by introducing Gawayne's hounds, but by specifying that they were grey-hounds. In Malory's day greyhounds were not racing dogs bred to pursue an electric hare they must not be allowed to catch, but one of the principal breeds of 'gazehounds', hunting dogs that pursued a real quarry by sight rather than by scent.[15] Another of Dr Luttrell's discrepancies may also show Malory bringing hunting realities into his story, when the first person Gawayne speaks to on his quest for the white hart says he has seen it pursued by hounds *and a whyght brachett was allwey nexte hym*.[16] When the hart first ran into the king's hall, the hounds that pursued it were led by a white brachet. This, to an enthusiastic hunter, would be very plausible: the main pack is said to consist of black run-ning-hounds, and ordinary running-hounds, if they were to keep up with a quarry, often needed guidance from a specialist scenting-hound, of which the most frequently used types were lymers and brachets.[17] However, the white brachet that led the pack into the king's hall was carried off by a knight who is now being pursued by one of Sir Gawayne's fellow-questers. Dr Luttrell sees the second white brachet as 'another self' of the first. That is surely over-literary. The *Morte Darthur* shows a great deal of interest in hunting and very little in 'other selves'. It seems more likely that he introduced the second brachet because his sense of the realities of hunting told him that in a long chase ordinary running hounds would probably lose a deer unless they had a lead from a brachet, and that brachets, or the best of them, were commonly white.[18] Even if this is true, however, Dr Luttrell seems right in seeing the out-come as contradictory. The apparent contradictions that I have called 'low points' can only be resolved if they can be reconciled (on consider-ation, if necessary) with the remainder of the story in a way that is internal to that story. Malory's enthusiasm for hunting has apparently supplied the brachet, and perhaps even specified its colour, without grasping that he had taken over a story in which the appearance of a second brachet in a masterless pack was very unlikely indeed, even when every allowance was made for the literary world of the *Morte Darthur* being one in which readers come to expect the possible as well as the probable. Malory needed to make it possible for his readers to see

[15] See Cummins, ch. 1.

[16] *Works*, p. 104.5–6.

[17] Cummins, pp. 12–31 and 47.

[18] The evidence suggests a brachet was a fairly small dog, perhaps only spaniel-sized, with pendulous ears, and often white with patches of red or black: Cummins, p. 47.

some plausible way in which a second brachet could have joined the pack. Since he did not, he left them with a real contradiction.

Dr Luttrell lists another passage of which he apparently feels that the same might be said: Merlin says the object of Gawayne's quest is to be the hart itself, but Gawayne actually brings back only its head.[19] I would argue that the text that Dr Luttrell is using characterises Gawayne consistently as an unchivalrous knight, but that that text is in fact suspect. Let us look first at the way it characterises Gawayne. In this episode, Gawayne, even when he cannot be said to fail, comes out of his adventures with very little credit, in contrast to his fellow-questers, one of whom emerges with honour from everything he undertakes, and the other of whom does so in most things. For Gawayne to bring back only part of what he was sent for would provide an objective correlative for his partial success, particularly as he owes even that partial success to the mercy of his enemies, who, when they allow him to leave, present him with *the hartes hede because hit was in the queste*. In that wording, Dr Luttrell presumably took *hit* as referring to *hede*, which is the most natural way to take it. The resulting reading contradicts what Merlin says and so creates a contradiction; but it is possible to take it as referring to *hart*, in which case Gawayne's captors would be giving him part of what he was sent for and refusing him the rest.

Gawayne's captors make him display one of his failures by carrying back to Camelot the headless body of a lady he had accidentally killed, and it might be thought Malory wanted to make him display his other shortcomings in his quest in a similar way. However, if we take the readings of Malory's source into account, another and to my mind a more attractive possibility appears. The *Suite* makes it clear, both when Gauvain is allocated his mission and when he is released by his enemies, that his quest is not for the hart but for its head alone.[20] There is no obvious reason why Malory should have altered that, particularly when his enthusiasm for hunting would have made him very aware of practical difficulties in transporting the whole carcass of a deer rather than its head. The author of the *Suite* consistently shows Gauvain as an unworthy knight, and the climax of his demonstration is his having Gauvain's quest end with the dramatic image, which Malory adopted, of the quester returning carrying the lady's headless corpse. There is no sign that Malory wanted to change the character of Gawayne as he found it, but even if he had been determined to deepen Gawayne's disgrace, he would not have done so to any appreciable extent by showing him failing to bring back the carcass of a deer. Even if Malory had not been shifting the emphasis of his story in the way Dr Luttrell noticed away from the formal object of the quest and towards the totality of

[19] *Works*, p. 103.19.
[20] *Merlin*, ed. Paris and Ulrich, II, 79, 95.

adventures, the much-commented-on presence of a human corpse must much outweigh in the story the unremarked absence of an animal carcass.

Under these circumstances, it seems much more likely that initial reading in the *Morte Darthur* was created not by an authorial decision but by an scribal error, committed by a scribe who lacked Malory's enthusiasm for hunting and who, when his copy dealt with it, became less rather than more alert. I would suggest that in the account of Gawayne being assigned his charge, the scribe omitted a phrase corresponding to one in Malory's source, and that the standard text should be emended to restore it, and to have Merlin say that Gawayne *must brynge agayne <the hede of> the whyght herte*. Since the error appears in both the extant texts, the scribe who did that must have been the scribe of the archetype or one of his predecessors, and his error would have been of a very common kind (often produced by boredom), the eye-skip or *saut du même au même*. If that is how it happened, it is not at all surprising that the scribe should not have been sufficiently alert a few pages later to notice the discrepancy his inattention had created.

For Malory, as what he says about Sir Tristram shows, hunting and hawking went together; but hawking is the less important of the two. However, just as hunting can extend to the mythical Questing Beast, so hawking can extend to dragons: the dragon Arthur dreams of during his cross-Channel voyage is described partly in hawking terms.[21] This provides us with another contrast between authorial knowledge and scribal ignorance leading to scribal error. When the dragon 'comes in the wind like a falcon' to attack a bear, and the bear sinks his teeth into the dragon's front, Malory speaks of the dragon's *breste and brayle* (his breast and stomach) being covered with blood. The word *brayle*, however, has to be recovered with the help of the reading of his source, the alliterative *Morte Arthure*, since the scribe of the Winchester manuscript, presumably because he was unfamiliar with terms of falconry, rendered the word as *brayre*.[22]

The most important episode concerned with hawking in the *Morte Darthur* is one of those in the fourth tale, the "Tale of Sir Launcelot du Lake". Sir Launcelot, riding out seeking adventures, becomes aware as he passes a castle of an escaped falcon flying with her lunes trailing. These catch round a branch of an elm tree and leave her dangling, whereupon a lady comes out of the castle and persuades Launcelot to take off his armour, climb the tree, and rescue the *fayre faucon perygot*.[23] When he is up the tree, her husband appears in full armour and tries to

---

[21] *Works*, pp. 196–7.
[22] The Caxton text has lost the word by abbreviation.
[23] *Works*, p. 282.19.

kill Launcelot, but Launcelot kills him instead, and rides off with the lady's reproaches in his ears. The episode contains several difficulties, which are the harder to resolve because, unlike most of the *Morte Darthur*, this episode has no known source. Malory may have invented it outright, or it may have been suggested to him by a romance not among his usual sources. One possibility is Girart d'Amiens's *Escanor*, where in one episode a sorceress uses a hawk to decoy and trap Gauvain, so that he is only able finally to escape by fighting twenty armed knights.[24] The changes that would have been involved – transferring an adventure from another hero to Launcelot, and stripping off magical elements – were congenial to Malory, but if *Escanor* lies behind his episode, it must be called an inspiration than a source: it is certainly too far from Malory's text to be useful for textual criticism in the way his major sources are.

In this passage, the meaning of *perygot* is remarkably obscure: the usual dictionaries and glossaries offer nothing helpful, and friends, acquaintances, and obliging strangers with various kinds of expertise in France, French, and falconry have been left at a loss.[25] The obvious meaning is *Périgord*: both the manuscript and Caxton texts of the *Morte Darthur* use exactly the same spelling here and at the much later point when Lancelot gives what is certainly the earldom of Périgord to one of his followers:[26] neither uses that word-form for anything else. Périgord is the more likely because there is some evidence that Malory may have known, indeed may have been to, the area round Périgord. He names a great many French territories in that area in the second *perygot* passage, and before the days of maps the obvious explanation for knowing them is personal experience; moreover, when he was a young man with a career to make, the English government of Gascony appointed his first cousin Sir Philip Chetwynd as mayor of one of the towns in the area, Bayonne, and commissioned Sir Philip to recruit a force to defend it.[27] The custom of the age would have made Sir Philip look for his officers first among his own family and social circle.

Most editors omit *perygot* from their glossaries, but, none of them having given reasons, we cannot tell whether they did so because they did not know what the word means or because they thought it a proper name, presumably Périgord. Until recently, the only editor to have glossed it was James Spisak,[28] who rendered it as 'peregrine'. That is not

---

[24] Girart d'Amiens, *Escanor*, ed. H. Michelant (Tübingen, 1886), ll. 1805–2986. Dr Peter Noble's description of *Escanor* in a conference paper made me aware of these similarities.

[25] I am particularly obliged to Dr R. W. Burchfield, Mrs Rachel Hands, and Dr John Cummins for trying to shed light on the problem.

[26] *Works*, p. 1205.6.

[27] *Proceedings and Ordinances of the Privy Council of England*, ed. Sir [Nicholas] Harris Nicholas, 7 vols. (London: Public Records Commission, 1834–7), V, 193–4.

[28] *Caxton's Malory*, ed. James W. Spisak, 2 vols. (Berkeley, California, 1983).

its meaning, but it raises the possibility that *perygot* might be a scribal error for *peregryne*. It is unlikely to be an ordinary scribal error, because the process of substitution is in the wrong direction. The classic scribal error of *difficilior lectio* substitutes a more familiar word for a less familiar one, and in Malory's England a peregrine falcon was a well-known part of a popular sport, whereas Périgord was a very little-known part of a foreign country. We have no reason to suppose that whatever special reasons made Malory aware of Périgord applied to his scribes as well. If therefore anybody substituted *perygot* for *peregryne*, the most likely candidate is Malory himself. It is a fact of textual criticism that both scribes and authors sometimes substitute a word that is not clearly better-known for another that sounds like it because of private associations that we may not be able to guess at, especially when the writer is dead.[29] It is also possible, however, that there was such a thing as a Périgord falcon, an unfamiliar object for which Malory was using a very unfamiliar word: since Malory was so proud of his knowledge of the technical terms of hawking and hunting, he could well have used a piece of jargon so specialised that no-one else has ever written it down. It is the function of textual criticism to weigh up the probabilities.

Weighing up probabilities is complicated because my correspondents disagreed about how promising an area Périgord would have been for falcons in the late Middle Ages, and because, even if it could be shown (which would be difficult) that there were no falcons at all in Périgord in the period, that fact need not have prevented a phrase like *Périgord falcon* from coming into being. Although its obvious meaning is a falcon *from* Périgord, other meanings are possible: a falcon trained, for instance, in a method devised in Périgord. When revising the Oxford English Texts edition of Malory for its third edition, the balance of the evidence persuaded me that it was most likely that the scribes had reproduced accurately what Malory wrote, and that the most straightforward sense was the one Malory was most likely to have intended: I therefore glossed *perygot* as 'from Périgord'.

However, even if the scribes did their duty at that point, a scribe certainly failed in it elsewhere in the episode (if we can for brevity's sake count Caxton's compositor as an honorary scribe). In the Winchester manuscript Sir Launcelot notices the falcon because he *herde bellys rynge*: in the Caxton text he *herde two bellys rynge*.[30] These readings cannot both be right, hence the scribal error. The natural suspect is the Winchester manuscript scribe rather than Caxton's compositor, since omission is (in general) easier than insertion, and short words are particularly easily omitted, whether by visual oversight or aural lapse or by an break in the

---

[29] Sebastiano Timpanaro, *The Freudian Slip*, trans. Kate Soper (London, 1976), pp. 63–76 and *passim*.

[30] *Works*, p. 282.13.

HUNTING, HAWKING, AND TEXTUAL CRITICISM IN MALORY

rhythm of copying.[31] Indeed the oddity of *two* in the Caxton text is itself evidence – though not very strong evidence – for its authenticity: there is no apparent reason why that particular number should have been intruded into a text that did not contain it. On their own, these considerations are hardly sufficient grounds for emending the text, but they can be strengthened by a recent study of medieval hunting and hawking, which shows that in the Middle Ages hawk bells were normally made in pairs, and that according to one authority, the pairs were made to ring a semi-tone apart.[32] If that was so, any knight who shared Malory's gentlemanly interest in field sports would no doubt soon have learned to distinguish the sound made by the two bells of a trained hawk in flight, and when he heard them to look towards the sound for a sporting spectacle that he could relish. There would be nothing surprising then about Sir Launcelot identifying the sound of *two* bells and taking a special interest in their source. Malory himself could also be expected to have known the significance of the number, but his scribes' mistakes in matters concerned with hunting and hawking elsewhere suggest that they would not, and therefore that they would have been likely to omit it. The *two* therefore appears to be authorial, and should be kept in Caxton-based editions and restored in those based on the Winchester manuscript.

The points considered in this essay have necessarily been miscellaneous, but if one general consideration emerges from them, apart from Malory's knowledge of and enthusiasm for hunting and hawking, it is that only the fullest knowledge of recondite matters and the most careful consideration of texts can enable us to understand great literature fully or to repair the ravages the time inflicts on it.

---

[31] This last phenomenon might be described by the useful term *arrhythmia*, which Eugène Vinaver coined in a rather more restricted sense: see his 'Principles of Textual Emendation', in *Studies in French Language and Mediæval Literature presented to Professor Mildred K. Pope* (Manchester, 1939), pp. 351–69.
[32] Cummins, pp. 200–1.

Malory's "Noble Tale of Sir Launcelot du Lake", the Vulgate *Lancelot*, and the Post-Vulgate *Roman du Graal*

EDWARD   DONALD   KENNEDY

Malory based his third tale "The Noble Tale of Sir Launcelot du Lake" primarily upon several episodes of the third and final division of the Vulgate *Lancelot* known as the *Agravain*; to these he added some material for which there appears to be no source and some from another French prose romance the *Perlesvaus*.[1] It is the shortest of the eight tales that make up *Le Morte Darthur* and also one of the tales in which Malory handled his sources with most originality. It has been cited on both sides of the once volatile controversy over unity, with some arguing that it contributed substantially to Malory's 'hoole book'[2] and others that it is independent of Malory's other tales.[3] Vinaver, who believed it to be an independent romance, found it a 'puzzling work' (1410), and, indeed, if Malory had considered it a romance with no relation to the others, he might have been expected to have made more use of the longest and most popular of his sources. Vinaver's explanation that Malory at this stage in the composition of his romances 'had as yet developed no ambition except that of telling a good story, preferably a short one' (1412) expresses his conviction that it had no relation to any of the other tales. However, Malory's lack of interest in writing a long romance seems an

---

[1]   See Eugène Vinaver, ed., *The Works of Sir Thomas Malory*, 3rd ed., rev. P. J. C. Field (Oxford: Clarendon Press, 1990), p. 1413, and Albert E. Hartung, 'Narrative Technique, Characterization, and the Sources in Malory's "Tale of Sir Lancelot" ', *Studies in Philology*, 70 (1973), 252–68. Subsequent references to Vinaver's edition will appear within parentheses in the text.

[2]   See R. M. Lumiansky, ' "The Tale of Lancelot": Prelude to Adultery', *Malory's Originality: A Critical Study of Le Morte Darthur*, ed. R. M. Lumiansky (Baltimore: Johns Hopkins University Press, 1964), pp. 91–8; Gilbert R. Davis, 'Malory's "Tale of Sir Lancelot" and the Question of Unity in the *Morte Darthur*', *Papers of the Michigan Academy of Science, Arts, and Letters*, 49 (1964), 523–30; Charles Moorman, 'The Relation of Books I and III of Malory's "Morte Darthur" ', *Mediaeval Studies*, 22 (1960), 361–6.

[3]   In addition to Vinaver's edition, see Robert H. Wilson, 'How Many Books Did Malory Write?', *University of Texas Studies in English*, 30 (1951), p. 21; David R. Miller, 'Sir Thomas Malory's *A Noble Tale of Sir Launcelot du Lake* Reconsidered', *Quondam et Futurus: A Journal of Arthurian Interpretations*, 1 (1991), 25–43. Although Wilson argued for the unity of Malory's book, he believed that Malory may have begun writing independent romances.

inadequate explanation for its brevity, since Malory in his first tale had already written a romance several times as long. Moreover, the selection of episodes from the Vulgate *Lancelot* that were separated by material Malory chose not to adapt and that were supplemented by one episode from the *Perlesvaus* and some apparently original material suggests that Malory had, when writing his "Launcelot", considerably more interest in the composition of this tale than Vinaver's comment about Malory's lack of ambition indicates.

The extent of Malory's familiarity with the Vulgate *Lancelot* and the question of why Malory did not make more use of it in his "Launcelot" are problems that merit examination; but also important is the possible influence that another Arthurian romance, the post-Vulgate *Roman du Graal*, had on the composition of this tale. This romance, the first part of which was the major source for Malory's first tale and which gave him a number of suggestions for other parts of his book, had a relatively brief section devoted to Lancelot that functioned as a transition between earlier and later parts of the book. Using the Post-Vulgate *Roman* as a model, Malory probably wrote his "Launcelot" as a brief tale whose episodes were chosen primarily for their relevance to earlier and later parts of *Morte Darthur*.

Malory and the Vulgate *Lancelot*

Although the episodes from the Vulgate *Lancelot* that Malory adapted for his third tale were limited to the final *Agravain* section (see Vinaver's and Field's notes, *Works*, 1408–13), he was also familiar with the other two parts. He includes a brief adaptation of the second *Chevalier de la Charrette* section as a part of his seventh tale "Sir Launcelot and Queen Guinevere", and although he did not include episodes from the first or *Galehaut* section, he had at some time read it. He adds allusions in his fifth tale, the "Tristram", to Lancelot's early days as a knight that do not appear to have been in his source, the *Tristan en prose* and that were apparently derived from the *Galehaut* (see *Works*, 459, ll. 32 ff.; 466, ll. 23 ff.); and in the "Launcelot" the giants Lancelot fights are armed 'with two horryble clubbys' (271), a detail that probably came from a fight that Lancelot has with giants in the *Galehaut*.[4] Furthermore, in the poisoned

---

[4] In the *Agravain* section of the Vulgate *Lancelot*, upon which the fight in the "Launcelot" is based, the giants are armed with swords. Vinaver assumed that Malory derived the clubs from the account of Arthur's fight with a giant in the alliterative *Morte Arthure*; but the clubs could have been suggested by an earlier fight in the *Galehaut* where two giants carry clubs. See my 'Malory and his English Sources', *Aspects of Malory*, ed. T. Takamiya and D. Brewer (Cambridge: Brewer, 1981), pp. 34–5.

apple episode of the seventh tale, Lancelot recalls the day Arthur had made him a knight: 'ye ar the man that gaff me the hygh Order of Knyghthode, and that day my lady, youre quene, ded me worshyp. And ellis had I bene shamed, for that same day that ye made me knyght, thorow my hastynes I loste my swerde, and my lady, youre quene, founde hit, . . . and gave me my swerde whan I had nede thereto' (1058). This scene that Lancelot recalls does not appear earlier in *Morte Darthur*; it is instead a somewhat inaccurate report of a scene in the *Galehaut* in which Lancelot rides away before Arthur can belt the sword on him because he hopes to be knighted by the queen. Arthur also forgets that he has not carried out this important part of the ceremony, and Guenevere later sends Lancelot the sword.[5] Malory may not have had access to the *Galehaut* when he wrote his seventh tale and perhaps did not remember the scene accurately, or since the scene in the *Galehaut* reflects poorly on King Arthur, Malory possibly modified the account by eliminating Arthur's memory lapse and having Lancelot accept blame for it himself.

Assuming that Malory had at some time read all three parts of the Vulgate *Lancelot* and had access to at least the last two parts of it (the *Charrette* and the *Agravain*) when writing *Morte Darthur*, why he did not use more of it for his "Launcelot" is puzzling. The possibility that Malory had a manuscript of his source containing only the episodes that appear in his tale is, as Vinaver admits, 'not very realistic', and Vinaver felt that the best explanation for Malory's choice of episodes was his desire to give 'a moderately continuous account of Lancelot's adventures and so avoid the typical "cyclic" method of interweaving a variety of different themes' (1408). This probably has some validity since the use of episodic as opposed to interwoven structure was favoured not only by Malory but by some other English and French writers of the later Middle Ages;[6] but that is probably not the whole explanation. While no one knew more or wrote more perceptively about Malory's work than Vinaver, his criticism was at times restricted by his belief that Malory's tales were independent romances; and although some of his critics went too far in trying to force Malory's book into the mold of a modern novel

---

[5] See *Lancelot do Lac: The Non-Cyclic Old French Prose Romance*, ed. Elspeth Kennedy (Oxford: Clarendon Press, 1980), 1. 163–74; trans. as *Lancelot of the Lake*, by C. Corley, World's Classics (Oxford: Oxford University Press, 1989), pp. 78–92.

[6] Malory was not the innovator in narrative technique that Vinaver thought he was. For earlier medieval English writers who avoid *entrelacement*, see Larry D. Benson, *Malory's Morte Darthur* (Cambridge, MA: Harvard University Press, 1976), pp. 39–64; R. M. Lumiansky, ' "The Tale of Lancelot and Guenevere": Suspense', *Malory's Originality*, pp. 216–7. Jane H. M. Taylor has discussed a similar technique in the fourteenth-century French *Perceforest*: 'each episode must be a finished whole . . . in which beginning and ending . . . take precedence over continuity, thematic or structural'. ('The Fourteenth Century: Context, Text and Intertext', *The Legacy of Chrétien de Troyes*, ed. N. J. Lacy, D. Kelly and K. Busby (Amsterdam: Rodopi, 1987), 1. 327).

with chronological consistency,[7] others have argued persuasively that the eight tales form 'a sequential whole, a work, not the *Works* of the title of Vinaver's edition'.[8]

If Malory planned a series of tales about Arthur's kingdom and if the "Launcelot" was to appear early in that series, Malory would have eliminated much of the material in the *Agravain* not simply because he wanted to tell a good story briefly or was trying to avoid interwoven narrative, but because it would not have been suitable at this early stage in his sequence of tales.[9] The *Galehaut*, which Malory might have been expected to use for the early career of Lancelot, offers a frequently negative portrait of Arthur as a weak king; and judging from the changes Malory made elsewhere in his source's portrayals of Arthur, he would have found much of the material in this section inappropriate to his book.[10] Furthermore, if Malory intended to write a book that emphasised Arthur and which had Lancelot as a character that was for his book 'both essential and secondary',[11] any attempt to adapt into his account much of a long romance[12] which has Lancelot as the protagonist would have obscured Malory's emphasis upon Arthur.

[7] See the essays in *Malory's Originality* and Charles Moorman, 'Internal Chronology in Malory's *Morte Darthur*', *J.E.G.P.*, 60 (1961), 240–9. Also see Ellyn Olefsky's response to Moorman's article 'Chronology, Factual Consistency, and the Problem of Unity in Malory', *J.E.G.P.*, 68 (1969), 57–73 and R. H. Wilson, 'Chronology in Malory', *Studies in Language, Literature and Culture of the Middle Ages and Later*, ed. E. B. Atwood and A. A. Hill (Austin: University of Texas, 1969), pp. 324–34.

[8] Derek Brewer, 'The Image of Lancelot: Chrétien and Malory', *Spätmittelalterliche Artusliteratur*, ed. K. H. Göller, Beiträge zur Englischen und Amerikanischen Literatur 3 (Paderhorn: Schöningh, 1984), pp. 109–10. Also see Brewer's 'the hoole book', *Essays on Malory*, ed. J. A. W. Bennett (Oxford: Clarendon Press, 1963), pp. 41–63, and R. H. Wilson, 'How Many Books Did Malory Write?', pp. 1–23.

[9] As Wilson pointed out, in the Vulgate *Lancelot* the first two episodes Malory uses are interwoven with the account of Lancelot's begetting Galahad on Pelles's daughter and an account of an imprisonment by Morgan le Fay during which he paints pictures showing the development of his love for Guenevere on the walls of his cell. Malory chose not to incorporate the latter account, which in the Vulgate Cycle provides an important link between the *Lancelot* and the *Mort Artu*, and the story of Pelles's daughter occurs much later in Malory's book. Wilson, 'Notes on Malory's Sources', *Modern Language Notes*, 66 (1950), 24.

[10] See Elspeth Kennedy, 'King Arthur in the First Part of the Prose *Lancelot*', *Medieval Miscellany Presented to Eugène Vinaver*, ed. F. Whitehead, A. H. Diverres and F. E. Sutcliffe (Manchester: Manchester University Press, 1965), pp. 186–95; 'Études sur le Lancelot en prose: 2: Le Roi Arthur dans le *Lancelot en prose*', *Romania*, 105 (1984), 46–62; also see my 'Malory's King Mark and King Arthur', *Mediaeval Studies*, 37 (1975), 190–234.

[11] Brewer, 'Image of Lancelot', p. 110.

[12] The Vulgate *Lancelot* consists of eight volumes of text in the edition of A. Micha, *Lancelot: Roman en prose du XIIIᵉ siècle* (Paris and Geneva: Droz, 1978–1983).

Malory and the Post-Vulgate *Roman du Graal*

The Post-Vulgate *Roman du Graal*, which Vinaver described as 'in many ways the most remarkable achievement in early French romantic fiction',[13] would have given Malory a good model for a series of Arthurian tales with an abbreviated account of Lancelot. This work, parts of which survive in French and parts in Spanish and Portuguese translations,[14] was written between 1230 and 1240 primarily as an adaptation of four parts of the Vulgate Cycle: the Vulgate *Estoire del Saint Graal*; the first part of the Vulgate *Merlin* known as the prose version of Robert de Boron's *Merlin*; the *Queste del Saint Graal*; and the *Mort Artu*. The author added his own continuation to the Robert de Boron *Merlin* that is generally given the title *Suite du Merlin*. His version of the *Queste* is considerably different from the Vulgate *Queste* in that the author associates Galaad's quest with the completion of the story of Balain's dolorous stroke that he had written for the *Suite du Merlin* and also introduces Tristan into the story, an innovation that made this version of the *Queste* suitable for adaptation into a later version of the *Tristan en prose*. He omits most of the Vulgate *Lancelot*, since, as he explains in the *Suite du Merlin*, the 'grant hystore de Lanscelot' would make the middle portion of his book three times as long as the other two parts.[15] Fanni Bogdanow, who has done most of the scholarly work on this romance, suggests, however, that the author omitted the greater part of the *Lancelot* not only to keep the three parts of his work of equal length, but also to keep the emphasis in his romance on Arthur rather than on Lancelot. Bogdanow describes this romance as 'the Epic of Arthur – the story of the rise and fall of the *roiaume aventureus*', and observes that Vinaver's words about Malory's giving Arthur the 'importance and dignity of a real hero' could apply equally well to the achievement of the author of the *Roman du Graal*.[16] This romance also presents Arthurian chivalry more positively

---

[13] Vinaver, 'Introduction', *Le Roman de Balain*, ed. M. D. Legge (Manchester: Manchester U P, 1942), p. xii.

[14] The Huth manuscript of the Post-Vulgate *Suite du Merlin* was published as *Merlin: Roman en prose du XIIIᵉ siècle*, ed. G. Paris and J. Ulrich, SATF, 2 vols (Paris, 1886). Also see Fanni Bogdanow, *The Romance of the Grail: A Study of the Structure and Genesis of a Thirteenth-Century Arthurian Prose Romance* (Manchester: Manchester University Press, 1966), pp. 12–3, pp. 228–70 for her editions of some of the fragments, and pp. 271–89 for a list of manuscripts and early prints, including the Spanish and Portuguese translations. Her *La Folie Lancelot* (Tübingen: Niemeyer, 1965) is an edition of the part of the Post-Vulgate *Lancelot* that survives in French.

[15] See *Merlin*, ed. Paris and Ulrich, II, 57. Also Bogdanow, *Grail*, pp. 61–2, 62 n. 1; and Bogdanow, ed., *Folie Lancelot*, p. xiv.

[16] Bogdanow, *Folie*, p. xxvii; Bogdanow, *Grail*, pp. 203, 200. Vinaver, *Malory* (1929; rpt. Oxford: Clarendon Press, 1970), p. 91; Vinaver wrote this before the discovery of the Winchester Manuscript when he considered *Morte Darthur* to be one book.

ARTHURIAN AND OTHER STUDIES

than does the Vulgate Cycle, and this may help account for its appeal to Spanish adaptors.[17]

In the Vulgate Cycle the *Merlin* led to the *Lancelot*, and the *Lancelot* to the *Queste del Saint Graal* and the *Mort Artu*; in the Post-Vulgate *Roman*, in order to link the *Suite du Merlin* with the Post-Vulgate *Queste* without lessening the emphasis upon Arthur, the author wrote a relatively short *Lancelot* that consisted of episodes from the Vulgate *Lancelot* combined with some from an early version of the *Tristan en prose* and with some, such as adventures of the knight Erec, of the author's own invention. His intent was to choose episodes that would complete stories or fulfil prophecies from the *Suite du Merlin* and provide a transition from the *Suite du Merlin* to the *Queste* and *Mort Artu* sections of his romance. Material adapted from the *Tristan en prose* included Gaheriet's slaying of his mother (which had been prophesied in the *Suite du Merlin*) and Gauvain's slaying of Pellinor's sons Lamorat and Drian (which completes the story begun in the *Suite du Merlin* by Pellinor's killing Gauvain's father Loth). In selecting episodes from the Vulgate *Lancelot*, the author of the Post-Vulgate *Roman*, like Malory, had no interest in the early career of Lancelot, in the first kiss of Lancelot and Guenevere or in the story of Lancelot's friendship with Galehaut; he, like Malory, selected episodes from the last part of the Vulgate *Lancelot*, the *Agravain*. He included adventures that anticipate the Grail Quest, such as Guenevere's banishing Lancelot from court after Lancelot mistakes Pelles's daughter for Guenevere, Lancelot's subsequent madness, his being healed by the Grail at Corbenic, and his staying for ten years with his son Galaad on the *Isle de Joie*. After this Lancelot returns to court, and this apparently marked the end of the *Lancelot* section of the Post-Vulgate *Roman*.[18] Besides writing a romance that emphasised Arthur and his kingdom instead of Lancelot, the author also created a romance highly critical of *fin' amour* in general and of the love of Lancelot and Guenevere in particular: 'the famous story of adulterous love, though not ignored, was given little place, . . . illicit amours were condemned as sin'.[19] Episodes from the *Agravain* emphasise the harmful effect the sinful love for

---

[17] J. B. Hall writes: 'The *Suite du Merlin* seeks to defend and justify chivalry and indeed reads in places like a manual on the origins, rights and duties of knighthood' and adds that the pro-chivalric ethos of the Post-Vulgate *Roman* probably accounts for its being translated into Spanish ('*La Matière Arthurienne espagnole*: The Ethos of the French Post-Vulgate *Roman du Graal* and the Castilian *Baladro del sabio Merlin* and *Demanda del Sancto Grial*', *Revue de Littérature Comparée* 56 (1982), pp. 425, 435–6).

[18] Bogdanow, *Folie*, p. xix.

[19] Bogdanow, *Folie*, p. xxvii; Bogdanow, 'The *Suite du Merlin* and the Post-Vulgate *Roman du Graal*', *Arthurian Literature in the Middle Ages*, ed. R. S. Loomis (Oxford: Clarendon Press, 1959), p. 332. The author's negative attitude toward Lancelot is also apparent in this romance's version of the *Mort Artu*. See Bogdanow, 'The Changing Vision of Arthur's Death', *Dies Illa: Death in the Middle Ages*, ed. J. H. M. Taylor (Liverpool: Francis Cairns, 1984), pp. 113–4.

Guenevere had on Lancelot, and the author alludes to Lancelot's future failure on the Grail Quest because of this love.

Malory based his first tale upon the Post-Vulgate *Suite du Merlin*; he also appears to have known the *Lancelot* part of the Post-Vulgate *Roman* that was intended to link the *Suite du Merlin* with the Post-Vulgate version of the *Queste*. The explicit to Malory's first tale includes the statement, 'And this booke endyth whereas sir Launcelot and sir Trystrams com to courte' (180). As both Vinaver and Bogdanow have pointed out, since Lancelot and Tristram do not come to court at the end of Malory's first tale, the allusion to 'this booke endyth' in all likelihood refers to Malory's source which must have continued beyond the point at which Malory stopped writing. Bogdanow believes that Malory's source for his first tale ended when Lancelot returned to court after staying on the *Isle de Joie*,[20] an event that occurs near the end of the *Lancelot* section of the Post-Vulgate *Roman*. Malory's reference to Tristram's coming to court, however, suggests that Malory's source for his first tale extended further and included the beginning of the Post-Vulgate *Queste*, which tells of Tristan leaving Iseult and going to court for Arthur's feast in honour of Galaad.[21] Thus Malory apparently had the *Lancelot* section of the Post-Vulgate *Roman* and the beginning of its Grail quest on hand when he wrote his first tale. He would also have known, at perhaps a later time, the rest of the Post-Vulgate *Queste* since it was the version of the *Queste del Saint Graal* that was incorporated into a later version of the *Tristan en prose* and that Malory rejected in favour of the Vulgate *Queste* ('Here endyth the secunde boke off syr Trystram de Lyones . . . But here ys no rehersall of the thirde booke [i.e. the *Queste* in the *Tristan*]. But here folowyth the noble tale off the Sankegreall' (845)).

Although the manuscript of the Post-Vulgate *Roman* that Malory used for his first tale would have been insufficient for a 'hoole book' of Arthur, some material in it would have appealed to him more than much of what he found in the Vulgate Cycle. While the Vulgate *Lancelot*, the *Queste del Saint Graal* and *Mort Artu*[22] emphasise Lancelot and give Arthur and his kingdom only secondary importance, Malory's book, like the Post-Vulgate *Roman*, emphasises Arthur and the fall of his kingdom.

---

[20] Bogdanow, *Grail*, p. 87 n. 1. See pp. 64–6 for a summary of these events in the Post-Vulgate *Roman*. Bogdanow derived her suggestion from Vinaver, *Works*, p. 1364.

[21] For the beginning of the Post-Vulgate *Queste*, see Bogdanow, *Grail*, p. 92; E. Löseth, *Le Roman en prose de Tristan* (Paris: Bouillon, 1891), ¶393, 393a, 394, 394a (pp. 281–2). Thomas C. Rumble argued that Malory's allusion to Tristram was in 'deliberate anticipation' of Tristram's role in Malory's fifth tale 'since Tristram plays no significant part in any of the extant cyclic versions of the Arthurian story' ('The First *Explicit* in Malory's *Morte Darthur*', *Modern Language Notes* 71 (1956), 566). Rumble, however, writing before the publication of Bogdanow's book, was not aware of Tristram's role in the Post-Vulgate *Roman du Graal*.

[22] The romances that make up what is now the first two parts of the Vulgate Cycle, the *Estoire del Saint Graal* and the *Merlin*, were written after the last three.

ARTHURIAN AND OTHER STUDIES

Malory's concept of Arthur, probably originally formed by the portraits in English chronicles and possibly Lydgate's *Fall of Princes*,[23] is generally positive; and he seems at times to have been struggling against the more negative portrait found in his other French sources.[24] Moreover, Malory's enthusiasm for the 'high order of knighthood' is incompatible with the negative portrait of knighthood often found in the Vulgate Cycle, particularly in the *Agravain* section of the *Lancelot* and the *Queste del Saint Graal*.[25] In its admiration for King Arthur and chivalry Malory's book is closer to the Post-Vulgate *Roman* than it is to the Vulgate Cycle.

The Post-Vulgate *Roman* could have given Malory several suggestions for his later tales. Although Lancelot's accidental slaying of Gareth appears in both the Vulgate and Post-Vulgate versions of the *Mort Artu*, Malory's presentation of the close bond of friendship between Lancelot and Gareth in his fourth tale, the "Gareth",[26] was probably suggested by a statement in the Post-Vulgate *Suite du Merlin* that Gaheriet would be slain by the man he loved most, Lancelot.[27] Similarly allusions to Tristan in the Post-Vulgate *Suite du Merlin* and *Queste*, as well as the inclusion of episodes from the *Tristan en prose* in the *Lancelot* section of the Post-Vulgate *Roman*, could have suggested the inclusion of Malory's "Tristram" before his "Sankegreall". Since references to the death of King Mark are relatively rare in Arthurian romance,[28] Malory's mention-

---

[23] For Malory's use of Hardyng's chronicle, see my 'Malory and his English Sources', pp. 42–8 and notes there on earlier scholarship; for Lydgate, see John Withrington, 'The Arthurian Epitaph in Malory's *Morte Darthur*', *Arthurian Literature VII* (1987), 123–44. It would be surprising if Malory had not also known some version of the prose *Brut* since it survives in about 50 French manuscripts and over 170 English ones.

[24] See my 'Malory's King Mark and King Arthur', pp. 190–234; 'Malory and his English Sources', pp. 49–55, and my comments on Malory at the conclusion of 'The Stanzaic *Morte Arthur*: The Adaptation of a French Romance for an English Audience', forthcoming in *Culture and the King: The Social Implications of the Arthurian Legend*, ed. James Carley and Martin B. Shichtman. For Arthur in the cyclic and non-cyclic versions of the *Lancelot en prose*, see Elspeth Kennedy, n. 10 above.

[25] On differences between Malory's version of the Grail story and the French Quest, see especially Sandra Ness Ihle, *Malory's Grail Quest: Invention and Adaptation in Medieval Prose Romance* (Madison: University of Wisconsin Press, 1983), pp. 110–60; Dhira B. Mahoney, 'The Truest and Holiest Tale: Malory's Transformation of *La Queste del Saint Graal*', *Studies in Malory*, ed. J. W. Spisak (Kalamazoo, Michigan: Medieval Institute Publications, 1985), pp. 109–28; Mary Hynes-Berry, 'A Tale "Breffly Drawyne oute of Freynshe" ', *Aspects of Malory*, pp. 93–106. On the negative conception of chivalry in the *Agravain* section of the *Lancelot* and in the *Queste*, see Elspeth Kennedy, *Lancelot and the Grail: A Study of the Prose Lancelot* (Oxford: Clarendon Press, 1986), pp. 302–3 and Bogdanow, *Grail*, pp. 197–8.

[26] 'Lorde, the grete chere that sir Launcelot made of sir Gareth and he of hym! For there was no knyght that sir Gareth loved so well as he dud sir Launcelot; and ever for the most party he wolde ever be in sir Launcelottis company' (360; also 295, 296, 297, 299–300).

[27] See *Die Abenteuer Gawains, Ywains und le Morholts mit den drei Jungfrauen*, ed. H. O. Sommer, Beihefte zur *Zeitschrift für romanische Philologie*, 47 (Halle: Niemever, 1913), p. 125; Bogdanow, *Grail*, p. 138.

[28] An account of Mark's death does not occur in the known manuscripts of the *Tristan en*

ing this near the end of his seventh tale in the account of the healing of Sir Urry was probably suggested by the Post-Vulgate author's announcement in the *Suite du Merlin* that his book will end with the death of Mark.[29] The Post-Vulgate *Roman* also influenced Malory's conception of the Grail quest. Bogdanow writes that the main point of the Post-Vulgate *Queste* is to show how Galaad completed the adventures begun in the *Suite du Merlin* by Balain's Dolorous Stroke.[30] Although Malory's source for his "Sankegreall", the Vulgate *Queste*, has no allusion to the Balain story, Malory's version does: after Galahad pulls the sword from the stone, he says, 'Now have I the swerde that somtyme was the good knyghtes Balyns le Saveaige, . . . and with thys swerde he slew hys brothir Balan, and . . . eythir slew othir thorow a dolerous stroke that Balyn gaff unto kynge Pelles, the whych ys nat yett hole, nor naught shall be tyll that I hele hym' (863). This was intended to remind readers of the reasons for the Grail Quest given in Malory's first tale, and the allusion is derived ultimately from the Post-Vulgate *Suite du Merlin*.

Although Malory may never have read the Post-Vulgate *Mort Artu*, what he knew of the earlier parts of the Post-Vulgate *Roman* influenced his conception of the Arthurian tragedy. Jill Mann's study of Malory's adaptation of the Post-Vulgate *Suite du Merlin* emphasises that much that happens in Malory's account is inexplicable and must be attributed to chance or 'adventure'. The story of Balin and Balan in the first tale is dominated by mischance; it 'offers a miniature version of the tragedy which is to engulf the whole Arthurian world, and shows that Malory had already conceived the terms in which he was to describe that tragedy'.[31] She cites instances in the final tale of characters' 'taking the adventure': Agravaine's ominous threat to reveal the adultery: 'Falle whatsumever falle may . . . I woll disclose hit to the kynge' (1162); Arthur's desire to avenge himself on Mordred: 'Now tyde me dethe, tyde me lyff . . . he shall never ascape myne hondes! For at a bettir avayle shall I never have hym' (1237). Chance happenings, as well as characters taking chances, also play an important role in Malory's tragedy:

---

prose; it occurs in the Spanish and Portuguese translations of the Post-Vulgate *Roman*, in a French manuscript fragment of the Post-Vulgate *Roman*, in some Italian versions of the *Tristan en prose*, and in Malory. See Bogdanow, *Grail*, p. 140 n. 3 and E. G. Gardner, *The Arthurian Legend in Italian Literature* (1930; rpt. New York: Farrar, Straus, & Giroux, 1971), pp. 186, 205, 263–4, 300–2. Malory's version of Mark's death is different from the others in that he has Mark killed by the son of Alexander the Orphan: 'Sir Bellynger revenged the deth of hys fadir . . . for he slewe kynge Marke' (1150). In the Post-Vulgate *Roman* he is killed by Paulart, a character that does not appear in Malory. Malory may not have read the Post-Vulgate *Mort Artu*, but even if he had, he would have been unlikely to bring in a new character Paulart for this purpose. The French fragment is edited in Bogdanow, *Grail*, pp. 264–70.

29 '. . . a chelui point meisme qu'il devise de la mort le roi March': *Merlin*, I, 280; Bogdanow, *Grail*, pp. 61, 139.

30 Bogdanow, *Grail*, p. 203.

31 Mann, ' "Taking the Adventure": Malory and the *Suite du Merlin'*, *Aspects of Malory*, p. 75.

Lancelot's chance slaying of Gareth (derived from the Vulgate *Mort Artu*), the chance appearance of an adder and a knight instinctively drawing a sword to kill it (derived from the English stanzaic *Morte Arthur*), and allusions to the 'unhappy' day, 'unhappy' acts, and 'unhappy' knights (see pp. 1161.7, 9, 32; 1183.25; 1236.28–9).

One of the most significant elements of chance is the role that Arthur's incest with his half-sister plays in both the Post-Vulgate *Roman* and in Malory. In the Post-Vulgate *Roman*, although Arthur is treated sympathetically as one who did not realise that the woman was his sister, his death caused by his son/nephew Mordred is a direct consequence of his sin. Such emphasis on incest is a significant departure from the Vulgate Cycle, and the story of incest in the Post-Vulgate *Roman* is, in Bogdanow's words, an 'example of the *mescheance* which overshadows Logres', and shows that 'pure accidents unleash catastrophes'.[32] Malory also treats Arthur sympathetically; and he too in his final tale emphasises Arthur's incest more than either of his two major sources, the Vulgate *Mort Artu* or the stanzaic *Morte Arthur*: 'bycause sir Mordred was kynge Arthurs son, he gaff hym the rule off hys londe and off hys wyff' (1211); Mordred wishes to marry Guenevere 'which was hys unclys wyff and hys fadirs wyff' (1227); the Bishop of Canterbury rebukes him for wanting to marry his 'fadirs wyff' (1228); when Arthur prepares to land at Dover, Mordred intends 'to beate hys owne fadir fro hys owne londys' and waits 'to lette hys owne fadir to londe upon the londe that he was kynge over' (1229); Mordred does not believe Arthur wants a truce because 'I know well my fadir woll be avenged uppon me' (1235); and the dying Mordred 'smote his fadir, kynge Arthure, with hys swerde' (1237).[33] Such allusions in the final tale remind Malory's readers of the role of mischance in the downfall of Arthur's kingdom, that

---

[32] Bogdanow, *Grail*, p. 150.

[33] The Vulgate *Mort Artu* simply mentions on three occasions that Mordred was Arthur's son (*La Mort le Roi Artu*, ed. J. Frappier, 3rd ed. (Geneva, 1964), pp. 172, 211, 245). The author was apparently relying upon the audience's recalling a brief allusion to the incest in the *Agravain* section of the Vulgate *Lancelot*. Anyone who did not recall this allusion would not have known that Arthur had committed incest. Boccaccio, for example, who drew upon the Vulgate *Mort Artu* for his account of Arthur in his *De Casibus Virorum Illustrium*, apparently was unfamiliar with the story; he describes Mordred as Arthur's son 'by a concubine' (see Gardner, *Italian Literature*, p. 235). (Allusions to the incest were included in the later additions to the Vulgate Cycle, the *Estoire del Saint Graal* and the *Merlin*.) The stanzaic *Morte* refers to the incest on two occasions: there Arthur's knights advise Arthur to appoint Mordred regent since he was the 'kynges soster sone . . . / And eke hys owne sonne', and when Mordred tries to take over the kingdom, the poet writes that 'Hys faders wyfe than wold he wedde' and the Archbishop of Canterbury rebukes Mordred for trying to wed his 'faders wyffe' (*Le Morte Arthur*, ed. Shunichi Noguchi (Tokyo: Centre for Mediaeval English Studies, University of Tokyo, 1990), ll. 2955–6, 2987, 3006). One of Malory's allusions to incest was based on the stanzaic *Morte*. I once believed that Malory placed less emphasis on incest than the Vulgate *Mort Artu* and that he was influenced in this by the stanzaic *Morte* (see my 'Malory and his English Sources', p. 49); I was wrong.

mistakes by good men can indeed unleash catastrophes, and thus represent another way the Post-Vulgate *Roman* could have influenced Malory.

Sandra Ihle has discussed yet another important difference between Malory's conception of the tragedy and that of the author of the Vulgate *Mort Artu*, and this difference too could reflect Malory's reading of the Post-Vulgate *Roman*. Ihle emphasises that ultimately the tragedy in Malory's account is caused by the treachery of the worst individuals in society: Arthur's world is destroyed 'not by God, fate, or providence, or even by unwitting actions of the best of men, but by the deliberate treachery of the worst'.[34] And, in fact, even where mischance plays a role, deliberate actions of individuals are the immediate causes: Arthur by mischance commits the sin of incest with his half-sister, but Mordred's treachery causes the tragedy; Lancelot by mischance slays Gareth, but Gawain's desire for revenge against Lancelot causes the war; a knight by mischance draws a sword to kill the adder, but the other knights' rash will to fight causes the final battle. Ihle points particularly to Malory's placing the blame for the tragedy upon Agravain and Mordred:[35] 'here I go unto the morte Arthur, and that caused sir Aggravayne' (1154); 'so thys season hit befelle in the moneth of May a grete angur and unhappe that stynted nat tylle the floure of chyvalry . . . was destroyed and slayne. And all was longe uppon two unhappy knyghtis whych were named sir Aggravayne and sir Mordred . . . For thys sir Aggravayne and sir Mordred had ever a prevy hate unto the quene . . . and to sir Launcelot' (1161); Arthur also blames not Lancelot and Guenevere but Agravain and Mordred: 'A, Aggravayne, Aggravayne! . . . Jesu forgyff hit thy soule, for thyne evyll wyll that thou haddist and sir Mordred, thy brothir, unto sir Launcelot hath caused all this sorow' (1184). Bogdanow, without allusion to Malory, makes similar observations about the destruction of Arthur's kingdom in the Post-Vulgate *Roman*: she points out that Arthur does not blame God or Fortune for the calamity and that practically all references to Fortune that were in the Vulgate *Mort Artu* have been omitted. Arthur becomes the 'helpless victim of an internal strife for which he was in no way responsible'. Arthur's nephews deliberately attempt to stir up hatred between Arthur and Lancelot. Bogdanow remarks too that this work 'stresses the pathos of the death of so many good knights caused by the machinations of one bad man [Mordred]'. In the Post-Vulgate *Roman*'s account of the final battle Arthur says, 'Ah! God, what mischance that a traitor should kill so many good and loyal knights.'[36]

---

[34] Ihle, 'The Art of Adaptation in Malory's Books Seven and Eight', *Interpretations* 15 (1984), 83; for a similar view, see C. M. Adderley, 'Malory's Portrayal of Sir Launcelot', *Language Quarterly*, 29 (1991), 47: Arthur's society is ruined 'not so much by its own flaws as by villains external to the society and its ruling code of chivalry'.

[35] Ihle, 'Adaptation', p. 81.

[36] Bogdanow, *Grail*, p. 151; 'Changing Vision', cited n. 19, p. 113. Another similarity in the

Admittedly some of the similarities, such as Malory's omission of so many references to God and Fortune in the Vulgate *Mort Artu* and increased sympathy for Arthur could be due to Malory's other major source for his final tale, the stanzaic *Morte Arthur* as well as to Malory's own conception of Arthur's character; but some of the ideas, such as the added emphasis on mischance, incest, and Mordred's responsibility, could have come from the early part of the Post-Vulgate *Roman* that Malory definitely knew.

Since the Post-Vulgate *Roman* appears to have suggested a number of ideas that Malory later incorporated into tales drawn from other sources, it in all likelihood also gave him a model for a series of Arthurian tales with an abbreviated *Lancelot* that helped link earlier and later parts of the book. It was not, however, a model that he could follow so far as content for his "Launcelot" was concerned; and although Malory and the author of the Post-Vulgate *Roman* both based their story of Lancelot upon the *Agravain* section of the Vulgate *Lancelot*, Malory chose different episodes. There are several good reasons for this. Malory probably knew at an early stage in the writing of his book what would be appropriate for earlier and later tales. P. J. C. Field's theory that *Morte Darthur* was probably written during Malory's final imprisonment 'to a coherent plan and with the help of a splendid library of Arthurian sources' that was unlikely to have been available at more than one prison[37] is certainly possible; for although how Malory acquired his sources is unknown,[38] there could not have been many prisons where Malory would have obtained the books he needed for his work. If the major sources were all available at one prison, Malory may well have known what he planned to include in his later tales before he wrote most of the early ones,[39] and

---

accounts is that while in the Vulgate *Mort Artu* Arthur awaits Mordred with fear and Mordred strikes first, in both the Post-Vulgate *Roman* and Malory's *Morte Darthur* Arthur seeks Mordred out and strikes the first blow. This similarity, however, is one that also appears in the stanzaic *Morte Arthur*, and this English work is the obvious source for this in Malory. See Bogdanow, *Grail*, p. 151; Malory, *Works*, 1236–7; stanzaic *Morte Arthur*, ll. 3389–99.

[37] Field, 'The Last Years of Sir Thomas Malory', *Bulletin of the John Rylands Library*, 64 (1981–82), 438–9.

[38] For a judicious and fairly recent discussion of this problem, see Carol Meale, 'Manuscripts, Readers and Patrons in Fifteenth-Century England: Sir Thomas Malory and Arthurian Romance', *Arthurian Literature IV* (1984), 93–126.

[39] The first tale may have been written some time before the earlier ones. Its explicit, besides indicating that Malory's source contained material not included in the tale, also suggests that Malory may have had to stop writing rather abruptly: 'Who that woll make ony more lette hym seke other bookis of kynge Arthure or of Sir Launcelot or Sir Trystrams; for this was drawyn by a knyght presoner . . . that God sende hym good recover' (180). Vinaver believed that Malory 'thought of the work as having been completed at this point' (1365), and he thought that this explicit offered evidence that the first tale was a romance independent of any of the others. Although this interpretation is questionable, his suggestion that 'there must have elapsed an interval of time long enough to enable

episodes in the "Launcelot" may have been chosen with later tales in mind. Malory's selection of episodes different from those found in the *Lancelot* of the Post-Vulgate *Roman* could have been due in part to the fact that much of the material that the author of the Post-Vulgate *Roman* adapted from both the *Tristan en prose* and the Vulgate *Lancelot* (Gaheriet's murder of his mother, the murder of Lamorat, the story of Lancelot and the mother of Galahad, Guenevere's rebuke of Lancelot and his consequent insanity) was available in the manuscript of the *Tristan en prose* that he used for his fifth tale;[40] and some of the material, such as the adventures of the knight Erec, who does not appear in Malory's other sources, would have been irrelevant to his book.

A still more important reason for Malory's not using the same material as that used by the author of the Post-Vulgate *Roman*, however, would be that Malory did not share the Post-Vulgate author's negative view of Lancelot and his love for Guenevere. The episodes that the author of the Post-Vulgate *Roman* adapted from the Vulgate *Lancelot* stress the folly, misfortune, and shame of Lancelot's love for Guenevere.[41] Malory, on the other hand, chose episodes that prepare for Lancelot's role as the best of Arthur's knights. Although at the end of the eighth tale, both Guenevere and Lancelot nobly accept responsibility for their part in the tragedy ('Thorow thys same man and me hath all thys warre be wrought . . . thorow oure love that we have loved togydir ys my moste noble lorde slayne' (1252); '. . . whan I remembre me how by my defaute and myn orgule and my pryde that they [Arthur and Guenevere] were bothe layed ful lowe . . .' (1256)), Malory, as Ihle points out,[42] never blames them, nor does Arthur. Malory's attitude toward their love was far more complex than that of the author of the Post-Vulgate *Roman*. Thus if he wished to give his readers at an early point in his book a positive attitude toward the love of Lancelot and Guenevere and to prepare for Lancelot's role as Arthur's greatest knight, he would have had to choose episodes different from those in the *Lancelot* section of the Post-Vulgate *Roman*.

[Malory] . . . to lay his hand on fresh material' (xxi) is possible. Occasional errors in the first tale, such as the prediction that four knights would achieve the Grail (180), as well as weaknesses in the writing (see Brewer, 'Malory: The Traditional Writer and the Archaic Mind', *Arthurian Literature I* (1981), 97), suggest that it is an early work. Although other tales have been suggested as having been written prior to the first tale, the evidence for this, in my opinion, is weak (see my 'Malory and his English Sources', pp. 28–39, p. 189 n. 5.) Also see my 'The Arthur-Guenevere Relationship in Malory's *Morte Darthur*', *Studies in the Literary Imagination*, 4 (1971), 29–40, for further evidence that the first tale was written before the others.

40 The version of the *Tristan en prose* that Malory used contained interpolated material (e.g. the story of the conception of Galaad) from the Vulgate *Lancelot*. See Vinaver, *Works*, p. 1524.

41 See Bogdanow, *Grail*, pp. 213–4; and for the negative portrait of Lancelot in the Post-Vulgate *Mort Artu*, see Bogdanow, 'Changing Vision', pp. 113–4.

42 Ihle, 'Adaptation', p. 81.

Malory's "Noble Tale of Sir Launcelot du Lake"

Malory's "Launcelot" consists primarily of adventures that show Lancelot's prowess. After an introduction for which there is no known source, Malory, drawing upon the *Agravain*, tells of the capture of Lancelot's cousin Lionel and his brother Ector by the knight Tarquyn and of Lancelot himself by Morgan le Fay and three queens. Bagdemagus's daughter frees Lancelot when he promises to help her father at a tournament. After doing this by defeating, among others, Mordred and Mador de la Porte, Lancelot fights and kills Tarquyn, as well as another knight, Perys de Foreste Savage. Lancelot then fights and kills two giants. He rescues Kay by overcoming three knights whom he sends to surrender to the Queen, defeats three others whom he also sends to the Queen, and then defeats four of Arthur's knights. In the next episode, derived from the *Perlesvaus*, Lancelot goes to the Chapel Perelous to find a sword and piece of cloth to heal a wounded knight, Melyot de Logyrs. At the chapel he meets Hallewes the Sorseres who wants Lancelot to kiss her; fortunately he refuses, for if he had done so, he would have died: Hallewes hoped to embalm his body so that everyday she could have 'clypped' and 'kyssed' him. After Lancelot leaves Hallewes, she dies of grief, and Lancelot goes on to heal the wounded Melyot with the sword and cloth he found at the chapel. In the next episode, which is possibly original with Malory, a lady persuades Lancelot to climb a tree to retrieve her hawk; when he does, her husband sir Phelot attempts to kill the unarmed Lancelot, but Lancelot tears off a branch of the tree, knocks Phelot unconscious, takes his sword from him, and kills him with it. Malory then turns back to the Vulgate *Lancelot* for an episode in which Lancelot is unable to keep a husband Sir Pedyvere from cutting off his wife's head. Lancelot, however, sends Pedyvere to Guenevere for sentencing, and she sends him on a pilgrimage to Rome after which Pedyvere becomes 'an holy man and an hermyte'. The conclusion to the tale is based to some extent upon an episode in the Vulgate *Lancelot* in which Lancelot tells Arthur's court of his adventures on a quest.[43]

Scholars frequently refer to two types of medieval readers of Arthurian romance. Many Arthurian works were written for those who had considerable knowledge of Arthurian literature, and these works allude to earlier works familiar to their readers. Many of the later romances, on the other hand, rely less upon outward allusions and include as many of the Arthurian adventures as possible within a single work, so that instead of relying upon allusions to other texts, the cycle becomes an

---

[43] Vinaver thought Malory had invented the conclusion, but Field, in his revision of Vinaver's edition, points out that it is based on the Vulgate *Lancelot*. See *Works*, p. 1426.

intertextual system in itself.[44] Malory's book appears to have been written for both types of reader. Karl Uitti's statement with regard to French romance that 'each romance text by definition responds to a previous romance text or even to the body of earlier romance texts in general'[45] applies also to romances written in England where French Arthurian romances were widely read. By the fifteenth century, there had been a long tradition of both French and English Arthurian literature that Malory's readers would have known. The reputation of Lancelot as the greatest of Arthur's knights and lover of Guenevere would have been, in Derek Brewer's words, a 'set of facts coming from the past'.[46] Yet at the same time Malory was writing a compilation, unique in English, but similar to the compilations by the thirteenth-century author of the Post-Vulgate *Roman* and Malory's fifteenth-century contemporaries Micheau Gonnot in France and Ulrich Füetrer in Germany which re-told the Arthurian stories 'within the framework of one great book'.[47] If the tales are understood to have references forward and backward to other tales in the series, Malory's choice of episodes for his "Launcelot" becomes more understandable than it does if he is seen as a writer of independent romances; and like the French cycles his tales serve to some extent as their own intertextual system. Earlier authors of Arthurian romance were by no means unanimous in their presentations of such matters as the character of King Arthur or their interpretations of the love of Lancelot and Guenevere. Arthur could be a great conqueror or a *roi fainéant*;[48] the love of Lancelot and Guenevere could be interpreted positively (as in the non-cyclic *Lancelot do Lac* and presumably Chrétien's *Charrette*) or negatively (as in the *Agravain* section of the Vulgate *Lancelot*, the Vulgate *Queste*, and the Post-Vulgate *Roman*). As Elspeth Kennedy has shown in her discussion of the non-cyclic and Vulgate versions of the *Lancelot en prose*,[49] context can indeed affect the way a reader interprets the events of a romance. Malory therefore had to provide some guidance for interpretation within his own text.

---

[44] See Matilda Tomaryn Bruckner, 'Intertextuality', *The Legacy of Chrétien de Troyes*, p. 239; E. Jane Burns, *Arthurian Fictions: Rereading the Vulgate Cycle* (Columbus: Ohio State U P, 1985), pp. 7–34; Elspeth Kennedy, 'The Re-Writing and Re-reading of a Text: The Evolution of the "Prose Lancelot" ', *The Changing Face of Arthurian Romance*, ed. A. Adams, A. H. Diverres, K. Stern, and K. Varty (Cambridge: Boydell & Brewer, 1986), p. 2; Douglas Kelly, *The Art of Medieval French Romance* (Madison: University of Wisconsin, 1992), pp. 311–3.

[45] Uitti, 'Renewal and Undermining of Old French Romance: *Jehan de Saintré*', *Romance: Generic Transformation from Chrétien de Troyes to Cervantes*, ed. Kevin Brownlee and Marina Scordilis Brownlee (Hanover, New Hampshire: University Press of New England, 1985), p. 141.

[46] Brewer, 'Traditional Writer', p. 95.

[47] The phrase is Elspeth Kennedy's; she is here referring to the fifteenth-century compilation of Micheau Gonnot, not Malory ('Re-Writing and Re-reading', p. 9).

[48] See, for example, Barbara Nelson Sargent-Baur, 'Dux bellorum/ rex militum/ roi fainéant: la transformation d'Arthur au XIIᵉ siècle', *Moyen Age*, 90 (1984), 357–73.

[49] See Elspeth Kennedy, *Lancelot and the Grail*, cited n. 25.

Lancelot's adventures in this tale – fighting Tarquyn, giants and other villains, rescuing ladies, showing mercy and justice to his enemies – establish, as many scholars have pointed out, Lancelot's reputation as a man of courage, strength, honour, goodness, and generosity, the model knight against whom others will be compared. The tale develops the portrait of Lancelot as a great knight that Malory had begun, without source authority, in his second tale that told of Arthur's Roman campaign (see *Works*, pp. 189–90, 212–24, 245). As Benson has observed, the adventures in the third tale present a Lancelot who is the best knight in the world and prepare for his adventures in virtually all of the later tales.[50] Lancelot achieves, as Malory writes at the end of the tale, 'the grettyste name of ony knyght of the worlde' (287).

Malory includes several references in this tale to the love of Lancelot and Guenevere, references that, so far as anyone knows, are not in Malory's sources. In the introduction to the tale, Malory writes: 'Wherefore quene Gwenyvere had hym in greate favoure aboven all other knyghtis, and so he loved the quene agayne aboven all other ladyes dayes of his lyff, and for hir he dud many dedys of armys and saved her frome the fyre thorow his noble chevalry' (253). Then characters that Lancelot meets refer to the love: Morgan le Fay and the other queens that imprison Lancelot tell him: 'we know well there can no lady have thy love but one, and that is quene Gwenyvere' (257); after Lancelot kills sir Perys de Foreste Savage, the lady riding with Lancelot says, 'hit is noysed that ye love quene Gwenyvere, and that she hath ordeyned by enchauntement that ye shall never love none othir but hir' (270); and Hallewes the Sorseres tells Lancelot 'there may no woman have thy love but quene Gwenyver'(281).

Lancelot denies being Guenevere's lover on the first occasion, dodges the question on the second but implies he is not her lover, and ignores it on the third. He tells Morgan and her friends that Guenevere 'is the treweste lady unto hir lorde lyvynge' (258); concerning the lady's reference to rumours about his love for Guenevere, he replies, 'I may nat warne peple to speke of me what hit pleasyth hem' and then goes on to give a lengthy explanation of why he is not married or does not have a paramour:

> But for to be a weddyd man, I thynke hit nat, for than I muste couche with hir and leve armys and turnamentis, batellys and adventures. And as for to sey to take my pleasaunce with paramours, that woll I refuse: in prencipall for drede of God, for knyghtes that bene adventures

---

[50] On Lancelot's character in Malory, see especially Benson, *Malory*, pp. 65–91; Brewer, 'The Presentation of the Character of Lancelot: Chrétien to Malory', *Arthurian Literature III* (1983), 35–42 and 'Malory's "Proving" of Sir Lancelot', *Changing Face of Arthurian Romance*, pp. 123–36; for some qualifications and recognition of his failure in this tale, however, see Felicity Riddy, *Sir Thomas Malory* (Leiden: Brill, 1987), p. 49.

MALORY'S "NOBLE TALE OF SIR LAUNCELOT DU LAKE"

sholde nat be advoutrers [adulterers] nothir lecherous, for than they be nat happy nother fortunate unto the werrys; for other they shall be overcom with a sympler knyght than they be hemself, other ellys they shall sle by unhappe and hir cursednesse bettir men than they be hemself. And so who that usyth paramours shall be unhappy, and all thynge unhappy that is aboute them (270–1).[51]

Such comments have convinced most scholars who have written on this tale that, at this point in the book at least, Lancelot should be taken at his word. Vinaver believed that Malory ignored the 'traditional courtly background of the Lancelot story' and dismissed Lancelot's 'literary past' (1408, 1414). Others have agreed. The relationship between Lancelot and Guenevere in this tale has been described as 'platonic'; the tale is a 'prelude to adultery', for although Lancelot loves Guenevere, she 'has as yet given him no indication that she will grant him her love; he therefore can maintain . . . that Guenevere is completely true to Arthur'; Lancelot is 'worshipping his lady from afar' as a 'young courtly lover, even though he has not as yet been accepted as such by Guinevere'; Lancelot's 'virginity, although never explicitly stated in the text, is unquestionable'; the love is the 'virtuous love of friendship' and Lancelot is a 'perfectly chaste' knight who 'would not carry on an adulterous affair with the queen'; although he is 'something of a sex symbol' and although he is 'lying about his relationship with the queen' and his love is 'shrouded in ambiguity', Lancelot 'remains chaste' and his attitude 'in affairs of the heart and the flesh . . . is abstemious and ascetic'. Davis expresses a minority opinion in firmly maintaining that Lancelot is lying. Brewer once described Lancelot as a liar, but in later articles qualified this by pointing out that Lancelot's replies leave 'the question of his adultery open'.[52]

This latter view is the only one that seems tenable: although Malory

---

[51] Brewer has in fact pointed to some serious implications in Lancelot's explanation of why he is not a wedded man and why he does not have a paramour: 'Guinevere is, after all, Lancelot's paramour, though the word is never applied to her; and Lancelot does slay men who are, like Gareth, in at least one respect, better than himself; and Lancelot does cause misfortune to all about him, because through him and Guinevere are the greatest king and the flower of knights destroyed' ('The Presentation of the Character of Lancelot', p. 46).

[52] Wilson, 'Malory's Early Knowledge of Arthurian Romance', *University of Texas Studies in English*, 29 (1950), 41; Lumiansky, ' "The Tale of Lancelot": Prelude to Adultery', pp. 95–6; Charles Moorman, *The Book of King Arthur* (Lexington: University of Kentucky Press, 1965), p. 18; Janet Jesmok, ' "A Knyght Wyveles": The Young Lancelot in Malory's *Morte Darthur*', *Modern Language Quarterly*, 42 (1981), 316; Beverly Kennedy, *Knighthood in the Morte Darthur* (Cambridge: Brewer, 1985), pp. 111–3 and 'Malory's Lancelot: "Trewest Lover of a Synful Man" ', *Viator*, 12 (1981), 417–9; McCarthy, *Reading the Morte Darthur* (Cambridge: Brewer, 1988), pp. 23–4; Davis, 'Question of Unity', pp. 528–9; Brewer, ed. "Introduction", *Malory: The Morte Darthur*, York Medieval Texts (London: Edward Arnold, 1968), p. 29; 'The Presentation of the Character of Lancelot', p. 43; 'Proving', pp. 131–2.

says at the outset that Lancelot loves Guenevere, the third tale gives no information about the extent to which the love between the two has progressed. Malory was not free to ignore the adultery of Lancelot and Guenevere; the story was too well known, and nothing short of a denial of the love by Malory himself (not by Lancelot) would have repressed it. Allusions to the love that characters in the third tale make would surely have reminded his readers of it. In fact, Malory's addition of such allusions would appear to be fulfilments of Merlin's warning to Arthur in the first tale that 'Launcelot scholde love hir, and sche hym agayne' (97). Lancelot's denials tell us nothing. If Lancelot were not the Queen's lover, he would deny it; if he were the Queen's lover, he would also deny it. It is, in fact, difficult to imagine Malory's having Lancelot announce to strangers that the Queen is his mistress; readers would be unlikely to have a favourable impression of a Lancelot who did. As Brewer points out, the necessity of protecting a lady's honour would always demand a denial.[53] (Agravain, not Lancelot, is the one that Malory describes as being 'ever opynne-mowthed' [1045].) Later, in the final tale even Bors does not know if Lancelot, when discovered with the Queen, 'ded ryght othir wronge' (1171); and in that tale Lancelot tells Arthur essentially what he told Morgan le Fay in the third tale: 'my lady, quene Gwenyver, ys as trew a lady unto youre person as ys ony lady lyvynge unto her lorde . . . take youre quene unto youre good grace, for she ys both tru and good' (1188). This statement comes after Lancelot in the 'Knight of the Cart' episode of the seventh tale 'wente to bedde with the quene and . . . toke hys plesaunce and hys lykynge untyll hit was the dawnyng of the day' (1131) and echoes fairly closely Lancelot's assertion to Morgan le Fay in the "Launcelot" that Guenevere 'is the treweste lady unto hir lorde lyvynge' (258).

While Lancelot's denials in the third tale tell us nothing about whether he and Guenevere have as yet consummated their relationship, they do tell us that Lancelot is loyal to the queen and that he is concerned with preserving her honour as the wife of Arthur. Lancelot's loyalty to Guenevere is also reflected in Lancelot's repeatedly sending knights that he defeats back to Guenevere (not to Arthur) and in Malory's changing a scene in which Lancelot in the French Vulgate, thinking that a strange knight who enters his tent is a lady, forgets Guenevere and embraces the knight.[54] Loyalty is one of Malory's basic concerns throughout *Morte*

---

[53] On the importance of chastity and honour, see Brewer, "Introduction", *Morte Darthur*, p. 29.

[54] In Malory's version of this scene Lancelot is sleeping in a pavilion; the knight Belleus enters and thinks Lancelot is his 'lemman'; Lancelot awakens because he feels a 'rough berde kyssyng hym' and the two knights begin to fight (259–60). In what was apparently in the Vulgate *Lancelot* at this point (see Vinaver's note, *Works*, p. 1417), when the knight begins to kiss Lancelot, Lancelot thinks the knight is a lady and embraces him. This suggestion of disloyalty to Guenevere is something Malory apparently wished to avoid.

Darthur; however, as Shunichi Noguchi has pointed out, it is a virtue that often presents a 'serious conflict with the ordinary, often self-assertive distinction of right and wrong'.[55] A loyal individual may have to lie; a treacherous one may be eager to tell the truth. (Characters committed to truth in *Morte Darthur*, we should remember, include Mark, Morgan le Fay, Agravaine and Mordred (see *Works*, pp. 555, 617, 1161–3).) Malory's emphasis upon loyalty in this tale, in fact, points to a clear distinction between the allusions to the love in Malory's "Launcelot" and the allusions in the Post-Vulgate *Roman*: references to the love there were intended to show the detrimental effect of love upon Lancelot's character and to foreshadow his failure on the Grail Quest; in Malory they demonstrate his loyalty to Guenevere. The love of Lancelot and Guenevere in *Morte Darthur* is complex. Derek Brewer once listed some of the qualities that made it, although criminal, virtuous: gentleness, service, unselfishness, kindness, and faithfulness.[56] To these could be added respect and loyalty:[57] Guenevere is Lancelot's 'moste nobelest Crysten quene' whom he never failed 'in ryght nor in wronge' (1166). Fighting for someone in right or in wrong can be seen as morally questionable; it can also be seen as loyal and good. The love of Lancelot and Guenevere has both virtue and sin in it, but the lovers are ultimately more sinned against than sinning. One of the primary functions of Malory's "Launcelot" is to establish the reader's positive attitude toward that love by associating it with the virtue of loyalty.[58]

Some episodes in the "Launcelot" recall events in the first tale and others parallel events in later tales, although it is admittedly difficult to know if Malory was deliberately drawing parallels or if he was simply following the practice of other romance writers in composing episodes that are similar to one another and that are familiar from other works.[59] Thus Morgan le Fay's role as an enemy of Lancelot in the third tale reminds readers of her role as an enemy of Arthur in the first tale, and her allusion to Lancelot's love for Guenevere anticipates her efforts to expose the adultery later in Malory's "Tristram". Pedyvere's cutting his lady's head off in the "Launcelot" and having to take it back to court as penance reminds us of the similar situation involving Gawain in the first

---

[55] Noguchi, 'Malory and the Consolation of Style', *Studies in English Literature, English Number* (1971), p. 42.

[56] Brewer, "Introduction", *Morte Darthur*, p. 25.

[57] Brewer remarks: 'Since honour concerns loyalty, and Launcelot in any version of his story must love Gwenyvere, Malory fully endorses the love between them' (Brewer, 'Proving', p. 131). On Malory's positive attitude toward the love also see Ihle, 'Adaptation', pp. 80–1.

[58] On Lancelot's loyalty to Guenevere in the later tales, see McCarthy, *Reading*, pp. 70–1.

[59] Benson has discussed Malory's creation of such parallels between his tales: 'A common pattern of action – a proof-of-knighthood theme – provides the shape of the narrative, which is composed of episodes familiar from other works. Only a few of the details in the scene are new' (*Malory*, p. 71).

ARTHURIAN AND OTHER STUDIES

tale.[60] When Malory tells us in his introduction to the "Launcelot" that Lancelot saved Guenevere 'from the fyre thorow his noble chevalry' (253), he is anticipating Lancelot's role in the seventh and eighth tales. Lancelot's being released from Morgan le Fay's prison by Bagdemagus's daughter anticipates his later deliverance in the "Knight of the Cart" episode of the seventh tale by an anonymous maiden.[61] In fighting Mordred and Mador de la Porte on behalf of Bagdemagus in this tale, Lancelot is fighting enemies he will oppose in the final tales. Malory may have turned from the Vulgate *Lancelot* to the *Perlesvaus* for the Chapel Perilous episode to provide parallels with later events: others have noticed that Lancelot's healing of the wounded knight Melyot antici-pates both Galahad's healing of the maimed king in the sixth tale and Lancelot's healing of Sir Urry in the seventh.[62] Moreover, when Hallewes the Sorseres, unable to win Lancelot from Guenevere, fails in her efforts to kill him and embrace his embalmed body, she 'toke suche sorow that she deyde within a fourtenyte' (281). This reminder of Lancelot's loyalty to Guenevere and the death of a lady because of her immoderate love for Lancelot offers a grotesque parallel to the story of Elaine of Ascolot [Astolot], who in the seventh tale also fails to win Lancelot from Guenevere and dies because of grief over love 'oute of mesure' (1094). Whether all of these parallels were intentional is difficult to say; but if, as is likely, Malory knew before he had written much of his book what sources were available to him, he may have planned some of them.

The final episodes of this tale offer evidence of such planning. If seen simply as concluding episodes, they are unusual, since, as Felicity Riddy has pointed out, they do not give the sense of an ending that readers expect from final episodes in a romance.[63] It is, however, easier to justify their occurrence at the end of the "Launcelot" if their primary function is to anticipate adventures in later tales. Both of Lancelot's final adventures in this tale show him facing unchivalric, treacherous characters and being unprepared to handle them. They to some extent parallel Lancelot's encounters with treacherous individuals later in the book. In the first of these episodes, after a lady asks Lancelot to retrieve her falcon from a tree, the unarmed Lancelot is attacked by her husband, Sir Phelot. Lamenting that 'ever a knyght sholde dey wepynles', Lancelot breaks a

---

[60] Beverly Kennedy believes that Malory was showing that both Pedyvere and Gawain were similarly vicious knights (*Knighthood*, pp. 123–5); the events are similar; but Ga-wain's cutting the lady's head off was, as Kennedy acknowledges, accidental, while Pedyvere's was deliberate (cf. *Works*, pp. 106 and 285).

[61] In the *Charrette* of the Vulgate *Lancelot* Malory's anonymous maiden is Bagdemagus's daughter (see Vinaver's note, *Works*, p. 1610), and readers familiar with that account in the source would probably have recognised the parallel.

[62] Benson, *Malory*, pp. 88–9; Moorman, 'The Relation of Books I and III of Malory's "Morte Darthur" ', cited n. 2 above.

[63] Riddy, *Malory*, p. 48.

bough off the tree he is in, and leaps to the ground: 'than sir Phelot laysshed at hym egerly to have slayne hym, but sir Launcelot put away the stroke with the rowgh spyke, and therewith toke hym on the hede, that downe he felle in a sowghe to the grounde.' Lancelot then takes Phelot's sword and 'strake his necke in two pecys' because he 'wolde have had me slayne with treson' (283–4). So far no source has been found for this story. Beverly Kennedy finds this account similar to the later treachery of Gawain when in the "Tristram" he plots to ambush Lamorak.[64] The ambush of Lamorak could indeed have suggested this episode to Malory, particularly since it is one of the episodes that the author of the Post-Vulgate *Roman* borrowed from the *Tristan en prose* and added to the *Lancelot* section of his romance.[65] However, another analogy occurs in Malory's final tale when the unarmed Lancelot is unexpectedly trapped in Guenevere's room by Mordred, Agravain, and twelve other knights of the Round Table. Lancelot fears that he will 'be thus shamefully slayne, for lake of myne armour', but he manages to open the bedroom door wide enough for only one knight to enter: '. . . sir Collgrevaunce of Goore . . . wyth a swerde strake at sir Launcelot myghtyly, and so he [Lancelot] put asyde the stroke, and gaff hym such a buffette uppon the helmet that he felle grovelyng dede wythin the chambir dore . . . than sir Launcelot . . . was lyghtly armed in Collgrevaunce armoure' (1166–7). In both cases Lancelot has no armour, is treacherously caught off guard, and must win in an unconventional way.

In the last episode, Lancelot attempts to rescue a lady from Sir Pedyvere, but Pedyvere tricks him into looking away and when he does so, strikes off the lady's head. Lancelot tells Pedyvere, 'take this lady and the hede, and bere it uppon the . . . and never . . . reste tyll thou com to my lady, quene Gwenyver.' Guenevere tells him to take the body to Rome and receive penance from the Pope: 'And . . . whan he com unto Rome the Pope there bade hym go agayne unto quene Gwenyver, . . . And after thys knyght sir Pedyvere fell to grete goodnesse and was an holy man and an hermyte' (285–6). This episode is based on an adventure in the Vulgate *Lancelot*, but there the knight does not become a holy man. This final adventure, as Riddy suggests, seems an odd choice for a conclusion, for it is not a triumph, but a defeat for Lancelot. Lancelot's failure to protect the lady is, in Guenevere's words, 'a grete rebuke unto sir Launcelot, but natwythstondyng his worshyp is knowyn in many dyverse contreis' (286). As Riddy points out, 'The ideas of "rebuke" and "worshyp" are held here in a contradiction that "natwythstondyng" fails to resolve: whatever excuses are made for Lancelot this adventure is at best ambivalent.' Moreover, it qualifies Malory's final words about Lancelot in this tale: 'so at that tyme sir Launcelot had the grettyste name

---

[64] Kennedy, *Knighthood*, p. 122.
[65] See *Folie Lancelot*, pp. 76–81.

of ony knyght of the worlde, and moste was he honoured of hyghe and lowe' (287).[66] If Malory, however, was thinking of the "Launcelot" as a tale that would prepare for adventures later on, it is appropriate that the final praise for Lancelot be somewhat qualified: he will suffer even greater humiliation on the Grail Quest where he will confess that 'now I take uppon me the adventures to seke of holy thyngs, . . . myne olde synne hyndryth me and shamyth me' (896). Malory's Lancelot is not a perfect knight and praise for him is qualified: he is the best of 'ony erthly synfull man' (934), and his son Galahad must remind him to 'remembir of this worlde unstable' (1035). The reader is reminded as the "Launcelot" ends that the man with 'the grettyste name of ony knyght of the worlde' will not always triumph. There is, furthermore, a parallel between Pedyvere, the treacherous enemy of ladies, and Launcelot, the honourable protector of ladies, that is almost as unexpected as that between the sorceress Hallewes and Elaine of Ascolot. While Guenevere causes Pedyvere to become a holy man at the end of this tale, she will at the end of the eighth tale cause Lancelot to do the same. While Lancelot's love for her results in his failure on the Grail Quest, his love for her will lead ultimately to his salvation. After Arthur's death, Lancelot hopes to marry her and take her to his kingdom. Her decision, however, to lead a life of penance as a nun leads to his decision to withdraw from the world as well: 'And therfore, lady, sythen ye have taken you to perfeccion, I must nedys take me to perfection, of ryght' (1253). Because of Guenevere Lancelot, like Pedyvere, becomes a holy man.

Since Lancelot was such a well-known and popular character, Malory's tale about him was, in all likelihood, written as a short romance in order to prepare the reader for Lancelot's role in later tales but yet not obscure Malory's emphasis in his book upon King Arthur. The *Lancelot* section of the Post-Vulgate *Roman du Graal* would have given Malory an example for such a romance. The explicit to Malory's first tale suggests that Malory knew this section of the Post-Vulgate *Roman du Graal* as well as its *Suite du Merlin*. Like Malory's "Launcelot," the Post-Vulgate *Lancelot* is based on episodes taken from two prose romances: both Malory and the Post-Vulgate *Roman* drew upon the *Agravain* section of the Vulgate *Lancelot*; Malory used for his second romance the *Perlesvaus*, and the Post-Vulgate *Roman* used the *Tristan en prose*. Both authors supplemented their sources with some apparently original material. The function of the story of Lancelot in both works – to provide links with earlier and later parts of the book – is similar. Malory chose episodes different from those in the Post-Vulgate *Roman* in part because some of the episodes would appear later in his "Tristram", some would have

---

[66] Riddy, *Malory*, p. 49.

been irrelevant to his book, and some presented an interpretation of the story different from and alien to his own. While Malory would have agreed with the Post-Vulgate *Roman*'s admiration for Arthur and for chivalry and its emphasis on mischance rather than Fortune, its condemnation of the love of Lancelot and Guenevere as sinful and degrading would have been incompatible with his own more positive and complex conception of a love that, although adulterous, had many admirable qualities, one of the chief of which was loyalty. For Malory the function of the "Launcelot" would have been to emphasise Lancelot's role as the greatest knight of the world, to show his love for and loyalty to Guenevere, to provide parallels to earlier and later events, and, in the final episodes, to suggest that Lancelot could fail as well as succeed.

Chaucer and Malory: Signs of the Times

GREGORY K. JEMBER

I have rather ambitiously chosen Chaucer and Malory as the subjects of this essay. Immediately, one might pointedly ask, what basis of comparison between them can there possibly be? Chaucer is, after all, noted principally for his poetry; Malory's medium was prose. Although Chaucer knew romance literature well enough to parody it, he apparently had little interest in Arthuriana, the only exception being the *Wife of Bath's Tale*, and even there Arthur's household is merely the setting of the story. Malory, alternatively, devoted himself entirely to the legends of Arthur and his knights. And finally, the two writers were not even of the same generation. But perhaps such obvious differences cloud our ability to see a deeper cultural relationship between them.

One obvious characteristic that Chaucer and Malory have in common is their method of composition. They were not, in the modern sense of the phrase, 'creative writers'. From a medieval point of view, both were literary craftsmen, shapers of pre-existing stories. The newness of their art derives principally from the ways in which they transform their inheritance as they translate, arrange, alter, and adorn their source materials. But even though their methods are at least late-medieval, the changes they work often provide insight into the psychology of Renaissance – 'modern' – society. Chaucer for better or worse commands the title 'father of English poetry', or as Spenser put it, 'well of English undefyled, / On Fames eternall beadroll worthie to be fyled'. But Chaucer is also the father of other things, such as English literary humanism. He is, therefore, one of the last medieval poets and arguably the first Renaissance poet in England. Malory, on the other hand, easily commands the title 'father of English prose', but his work, like Chaucer's, also evidences the gradual growth and transformation of the medieval mind. In the following pages I intend to analyse some features of their joint movement from medieval to Renaissance. I shall limit my discussion principally to Chaucer's *Canon's Yeoman's Tale*[1] and selected passages from Malory.[2]

---

[1] My text is *The Complete Poetry and Prose of Geoffrey Chaucer*, ed. John H. Fisher, 2nd ed. (New York: Holt, Rinehart and Winston, Inc., 1989). All references to Chaucer's text are to this edition.

[2] My text is *The Works of Sir Thomas Malory*, 3 vols., ed. Eugène Vinaver, 2nd ed. 3 vols. (Oxford: Clarendon Press, 1967). All references to Malory's text are to this edition.

ARTHURIAN AND OTHER STUDIES

The prologue of the *Canon's Yeoman's Tale* begins as follows:

> Whan ended was the lyf of Seinte Cecile,
> Er we hadde riden fully fyve mile,
> At Boghtoun-under-Blee us gan atake
> A man that clothed was in clothes blake,
> And undernethe he hadde a whyt surplys.
> His hakeney, that was al pomely grys,
> So swatte that it wonder was to see;
> It semed as he had priked miles three.
> The horse eek that his yeman rood upon
> So swatte that unnethe myghte it gon.
> Aboute the peytrel stood the foom ful hye;
> He was of foom al flekked as a pye.   (VIII, 554–65)

In these opening lines, Chaucer – quite typically – manages to accomplish several things. First, he gives us a very specific physical location: Boughton-under-Blean, a town in a forest about five miles from Canterbury. This location tells us that the pilgrims are on the final leg of their journey and thus very close to their spiritual goal, the shrine of St. Thomas à Becket. Within Blean Forest the pilgrims are overtaken by two riders, a Canon and his Yeoman. These two men, unknown to the pilgrims and uninvited by them, burst in upon the scene. Their horses – quite possibly stolen – are covered with sweat from being overridden and can barely continue. Clearly, these are men on the run. As Trevor Whittock notes, 'The opening description of the arrival of Canon and Yeoman on the scene begins at once to establish the symbolic implications of the incident. The frenzy of their pursuit of alchemy is already given an "objective correlative" in the sweating horses.'[3]

We may infer that the Canon and his Yeoman are running *from* something. Perhaps, having been exposed as frauds, they are running from the people of Ospringe, which, as Skeat suggested, would have been the customary place to take lodgings on the journey from London to Canterbury. In a broader sense, however, they are fleeing ordinary civilisation and all the people that they have been cheating. And their destination is uncertain.

Although the Yeoman mentions Canterbury (VIII, 624), he does not state explicitly that Canterbury is their goal. When it is clear to the Canon that the Yeoman intends to unmask him, all Chaucer tells us is that the Canon 'fledde awey for verray sorwe and shame' (VIII, 702). The final destination of the Yeoman is also unclear. He simply tells the

---

[3] *A Reading of the Canterbury Tales* (Cambridge: Cambridge University Press, 1970), pp. 262–3.

CHAUCER AND MALORY: SIGNS OF THE TIMES

pilgrims that he will complete his tale 'er that I fro yow wende' (VIII, 970). The pair do explain, however, why they have chosen to overtake the pilgrims:

> "God save," quod he, "this joly compaignye!
> Faste have I priked," quod he, "for youre sake,
> By cause that I wolde yow atake,
> To riden in some myrie compaignye."
> His yeman eek was ful of curteisye
> And seyde, "Sires, now in the morwe-tyde
> Out of youre hostelrie I saugh yow ryde,
> And warned heer my lord and my soverayn,
> Which that to ryden with yow is ful fayn
> For his desport; he loveth daliaunce."   (VIII, 583–92)

The reasons they give – pleasant company and conversation – are hardly plausible, as the Host's probing later shows. The tantalising bit of information we learn here is that it was the *Yeoman* who advised the Canon to take up the pursuit of the pilgrims. What motivated him to do so?

If indeed they are on the run, he may have thought that travelling with a band of pilgrims would provide them with good cover and the safety of numbers. Alternatively, the Yeoman may have considered it his duty to search out new sources of revenue and, upon seeing the gullible band of pilgrims, reasoned they might be easy 'game'. A third possibility, however, the one that seems to me to be most reasonable and most 'Chaucerian', is that the Yeoman had been planning to expose the Canon for some time, in order to sever the relationship between them, and to do this in the company of a group of pilgrims would be uniquely opportune. The members of such a group would have no reason to bear him ill will, and the Canon, exposed as a fraud, would be forced to leave. This reading, of course, changes our perception of the Yeoman. No longer can we see him as the penniless (and penitent) suffering servant, defrauded by a wicked, conniving confidence man. We must remember that for seven years (VIII, 721) he has been studying his *craft*, so that he, too, may well be capable of dissimulation and deceit – and even wish to be his own master.

The Canon and the Yeoman, like so many of Chaucer's personalities, are extremes. They are compulsive and obsessive in their pursuit of the secrets of alchemy. But let me pause here a moment to deal with the question of what alchemy is and what it means. Raymond P. Tripp's account is brief and to the point: 'Clearly, the craft of alchemy, as a blend of spiritual symbolism and primitive chemistry, epitomises men's striving to transform their condition. However misdirected their yearning may become, the original impulse is positive, even though it concludes in the self-deceptive hope against hope that *next time* the work will

ARTHURIAN AND OTHER STUDIES

succeed in turning their leaden existence into the gold of happiness.'[4] I
am reminded here of a similar assertion by Carl Jung:

> Although their labours over the retort were a serious effort to elicit the
> secrets of chemical transformation, it was at the same time – and often
> in overwhelming degree – the reflection of a parallel psychic process
> which could be projected all the more easily into the unknown chem-
> istry of matter since that process is an unconscious phenomenon of
> nature, just like the mysterious alteration of substances. What the sym-
> bolism of alchemy expresses is the whole problem of the evolution of
> personality, . . . the so-called 'individuation process'.[5]

What this means essentially is that we are obliged to regard alchemy
both as a physical process as well as a psychological one. It is something
that people *do* and also something that people *are*. If we remember this,
then the alchemical imagery in the tale can be made to reveal even more
about the characters themselves.

The image of the exploding pot is a case in point:

> Ful ofte it happeth so
> The pot tobreketh, and farewel, al is go.
> Thise metals been of so greet violence
> Oure walles mowe nat make hem resistence,
> But if they weren wroght of lym and stoon;
> They percen so, and thurgh the wal they goon.
> And somme of hem synke into the ground –
> Thus han we lost by tymes many a pound –
> And somme are scatered al the floor aboute;
> Somme lepe into the roof.   (VIII, 906–15)

Regarding this scene, Joerg O. Fichte notes that 'however dangerous the
craft of alchemy may be to the individual, leading to disordered perception, moral blindness, and his possible destruction, the very "science" is
an abuse of nature. In order to point this out, Chaucer employs the
image of the explosion, by which uncontrollable natural energies are set
free.'[6] And Masahiko Kanno perceptively notes that 'Chaucer portrays

---

[4] 'Craft, Canonical Alchemy, and Continuity between *Beowulf* and the *Canterbury Tales*',
Language and Style in English Literature: Essays in Honour of Michio Masui, ed. Michio
Kawai (Tokyo: Eihōsha Ltd., 1991), p. 148. In this regard, cf. John Gardener, 'The Canon's
Yeoman's Prologue and Tale: An Interpretation', *Philological Quarterly*, 46: 1 (January 1967),
1–17.

[5] *Psychology and Alchemy*, trans. R. C. F. Hull, Bollingen Series 20 (Princeton: Princeton
University Press), pp. 34–5.

[6] *Chaucer's 'Art Poetical': A Study in Chaucerian Poetics* (Tübingen: Gunter Narr Verlag,
1980), p. 106. Fichte adds: 'This passage is important in the light of the edict issued by
Pope John XXII, denouncing the practice of alchemy as being against the laws of nature'
(p. 106).

134

CHAUCER AND MALORY: SIGNS OF THE TIMES

the tremendous explosion of the pot in the laboratory as if he were describing a *living thing*.[7] The point I wish to make here is that the explosion has dual significance. Indeed, 'uncontrollable natural energies are set free', but these are also the uncontrollable forces of irrationality which erupt under the pressures of rational containment.

As I suggested above, both the Canon and the Yeoman are compulsively irrational; the frenzy of their pursuit is unnatural; their grail is unattainable. Yet however damning of the Canon and of alchemy the Yeoman's words often are, he cannot bring himself to abandon hope:

> Syn he is goon, the foule feend hym quelle!
> For nevere heerafter wol I with hym meete
> For peny ne for pound, I yow biheete.
> He that me broghte first unto that game,
> Er that he dye, sorwe have he and shame.
> For it is ernest to me, by my feith;
> That feele I wel, what so any man seith.
> And yet for al my smert and al my grief,
> For al my sorwe, labour, and meschief,
> I koude nevere leve it in no wise.   (VIII, 705–14)

As Tripp succinctly puts it, the Yeoman's 'lashing out at the Canon is, truly, a lover's quarrel'.[8] But what the Yeoman seems to object to most is that the Canon doesn't take alchemy *seriously* enough. The collocation of 'ernest' and 'feith' in l. 710 is most telling because it suggests a connection between alchemy and religion. That is to say, alchemy *is* the Yeoman's religion, a religion of the impossible and the irrational. At the same time, however, the Yeoman never ceases to believe that mastery of alchemy is rationally possible.

The Yeoman has, in fact, learned a great deal. After giving a brief introduction to the terms and tools of his trade (VIII, 750–83), he says:

> Ther is also ful many another thyng
> That is unto oure craft apertenyng.
> Though I by ordre hem nat reherce kan
> By cause that I am a lewed man,
> Yet wol I telle hem as they come to mynde,
> Thogh I ne kan nat sette hem in hir kynde,   (VIII, 784–9)

After all his study and observation, he remains a 'lewed man'. He understands the pieces, he believes, but not how they make up the whole. 'Ascauns that craft is so light to leere –' (VIII, 838), it appears to be so

---

[7] 'Lexis and Structure in *The Canon's Yeoman's Tale*', *In Geardagum X: Essays on Medieval English Language and Literature*, ed. Gregory K. Jember (Denver: Society for New Language Study, 1989), p. 51. (Emphasis mine).

[8] Tripp, *ibid.*, p. 149.

ARTHURIAN AND OTHER STUDIES

easy, he says, but adds that ultimately all is vain. Then immediately he says: 'To lerne a lewed man this subtiltee – / Fy, spek nat therof, for it wol nat bee' (VIII, 844–5). His protest is unconvincing simply because for him there is no alternative to alchemy.

Well what is the point of all this? Or rather what point is Chaucer making in this unusual tale? In an increasingly rational society, science and religion are bound to enter into competition, and 'fact' and 'faith' and 'truth' become increasingly indistinguishable. If the church condemned alchemy as 'unnatural', perhaps she also saw in it the more fundamental threat it posed as an alternate religion. In this tale the Canon and even more, I think, the Yeoman are shown to be among the first of its priests.[9]

But Chaucer also demonstrates how easily the irrational can erupt within a society apparently unaware of its existence. The pilgrims form, after all, a social unit – a microcosm of late medieval English society, and a pilgrimage itself, furthermore, is a steady movement of people toward a specific goal. What Chaucer seems to be saying, quite simply, is that society as a whole is in the process of transformation. And in that process of transformation, folly and, in the broadest sense, spiritual error may burst in upon the scene. Indeed, this tale of alchemy and delusion is a sign of the times.

By way of introduction to my discussion of Malory, I should like to refer the reader to one of the loveliest and most haunting of English lyrics, the early sixteenth century "Corpus Christi Carol"[10]:

> Lully, lulley, lully, lulley,
> The fawcon hath born my mak away.

[9] In our own time, perhaps the most widely known 'High Priest of Science' is Carl Sagan. To him and to many like him, science is the only means of understanding ourselves and our universe. In *Cosmos* (New York: Ballantine Books, 1980), p. xix, he writes: 'Science is an ongoing process. It never ends. There is no single ultimate truth to be achieved, after which all the scientists can retire. And because this is so, the world is far more interesting, both for the scientists and for the millions of people in every nation who, while not professional scientists, are deeply interested in the methods and findings of science.' The history of science is proudly acclaimed as a history of progress and advancement. Viewed from a slightly different perspective, of course, one could see it as a history of error. Yet modern society has become mesmerised by science and by the belief that ultimately science can accomplish anything. The Canon, the Yeoman, and their dupes are similarly disposed. Any scientist's assertion tends to be regarded as fact, even when what the scientist has to say is well beyond his scope of expertise. A case in point is Sagan's utterly wrong-headed comment about the pronunciation of the name of one of Jupiter's moons, Io: 'Frequently pronounced "*eye*-oh" by Americans, because this is the preferred enunciation in the *Oxford English Dictionary*. But the British have no special wisdom here. The word is of Eastern Mediterranean origin and is pronounced throughout the rest of Europe, correctly, as "*ee*-oh"' (p. 125). Sagan's expertise assuredly does not include historical linguistics.

[10] The text is taken from *Medieval English Lyrics: A Critical Anthology*, ed. R. T. Davies (London: Faber and Faber, 1963), p. 272.

He bare him up, he bare him down,
He bare him into an orchard brown.

In that orchard ther was an hall,
That was hanged with purpill and pall.

And in that hall ther was a bed:
It was hanged with gold so red.

And in that bed ther lythe a knight,
His woundes bleding day and night.

By that bedes side ther kneleth a may,
And she wepeth both night and day.

And by that bedes side ther stondeth a ston,
'Corpus Christi' wreten theron.

The concluding two lines of this lyric are of special interest because they contain a device which Malory uses often throughout the *Morte*, namely the written sign. Malory uses signs to commemorate, to explain, to prophesy, and thereby to contain experience in much the same way that a modern Polaroid camera can be used instantly to capture significant moments. The haunted spontaneity with which signs appear parallels the appearance of the Canon and Yeoman. These signs are not supernatural, nor are they natural, but rather irrational eruptions of psychologically potentiated experience. A review of some of these instances will show what I mean.

The appearance of names in the sieges of the Round Table is one good example:

So within shorte tyme Merlion had founde such knyghtes that sholde fulfylle twenty and eyght knyghtes, but no mo wolde he fynde. Than the Bysshop of Caunturbiry was [f]ette, and he blyssed the segis with grete royalté and devocion, and there sette the eyght and twenty knyghtes in her segis. And whan thys was done Merlion seyde,

'Fayre sirres, ye muste all aryse and com to kynge Arthure for to do hym omage; he woll the better be in wylle to maynteyne you.'

And so they arose and dud their omage. And whan they were gone Merlion founde in every sege lettirs of golde that tolde the knyghtes namys that had sitte[n] there, but two segis were voyde.

(98.32–7; 99.1–7)

The names of the knights simply appear in their respective sieges. Although their appearance must have involved a supernatural agent, Malory makes no comment about how they got there. Yet the suddenness and autonomy of these signs is not without significance. The as it were objective spontaneity of the signs indicates the explosive power of the irrational. Supernatural agency becomes a projection of the unconscious. This appearance of names also occurs in the seating of Trystram and Galahad, though there the names appear before they are seated:

> Than wente kynge Arthure unto the seges aboute the Rounde Table, and loked on every syege whyche were voyde that lacked knyghtes. And then the kynge sye in the syege of sir Marhalt lettyrs that seyde: THIS IS THE SYEGE OF THE NOBLE KNYGHT SIR TRYSTRAMYS.
>
> (572.10–4)

Similarly, in the seating of Galahad we find:

> And anone he lad hym to the Syege Perelous where besyde sate sir Launcelot, and the good man lyffte up the clothe and founde there the lettirs that seyde thus:
> 'THYS YS THE SYEGE OF SIR GALAHAD THE HAWTE PRYNCE.'
> 'Sir,' seyde the olde knyght, 'weyte you well that place ys youres.'
>
> (860.8–13)

In these passages one can discover no sense of surprise or wonder concerning the appearance of the names. Merlin and the old knight simply find letters there; and Arthur simply sees them. These are, of course, occasions of great import which the signs confirm. This matter-of-fact treatment is consistent with Malory's rational approach to his stories. Vinaver notes that 'in one respect [Malory's] attitude seems to have been consistent throughout: he deliberately avoided, as far as he could, any excess of the supernatural . . . This reluctance to bring in the atmosphere of the irrational for its own sake shows itself in a variety of ways . . .'[11] This matter of names, therefore, might well be viewed as a situation in which Malory becomes psychological in order to avoid being supernatural.

The most striking appearance of a sign, it seems to me, occurs near the beginning of the *Tale of the Sankgreal*:

> So whan the kynge and all the knyghtes were com frome servyse the barownes aspyed in the segys of the Rounde Table all aboute wretyn with golde lettirs:
> 'HERE OUGHT TO SITTE HE', and 'HE OUGHT TO SITTE HYRE'.
> And thus they wente so longe tylle that they come to the Sege Perelous, where they founde lettirs newly wrytten of golde, which seyde:
> 'FOUR HONDRED WYNTIR AND FOUR AND FYFFTY ACOMPLYVYSSHED AFTIR THE PASSION OF OURE LORDE JESU CRYST OUGHTE THYS SYEGE TO BE FULFYLLED.'
> Than all they seyde,
> 'Thys ys a mervylous thynge and an adventures!'   (855.5–16)

---

[11] Vinaver, *ibid.*, p. 1278.

CHAUCER AND MALORY: SIGNS OF THE TIMES

What is 'marvelous' here, however, is not the *appearance* of the message but rather its content; for immediately thereafter, Launcelot pragmatically calculates the date of fulfilment. One might also note the word 'newly', which here and elsewhere[12] serves to underscore the immediate significance of the sign.

Written signs also figure prominently on tombs of the dead. Sometimes they are little more than simple epitaphs:

> And than the kyng lette putte h[e]m bothe in the erthe, and leyde the tombe uppon them, and wrote the namys of hem bothe on the tombe, how 'here lyeth Launceor, the kyngis son of Irelonde, that at hys owne rekeyste was slayne by the hondis of Balyne', and how 'this lady Columbe and peramour to hym slew hirself with hys swerde for dole and sorow.'   (71.27–31; 72.1–2)

Following the death of Berbeus, 'kynge Arthure lette bury this knyght rychely, and made mencion [on] his tombe how here was slayne Berbeus and by whom the trechory was done of the knyght⌈Garlon⌉'(80.21–3). So it is with the fated brothers Balan and Balyn:

> Thenne anone Balan dyed, but Balyn dyed not tyl the mydnyghte after. And so were they buryed bothe, and the lady lete make a mensyon of Balan how he was ther slayne by his broders handes, but she knewe not Balyns name.
> In the morne cam Merlyn and lete wryte Balyns name on the tombe with letters of gold that 'here lyeth Balyn le Saveage that was the knyght with the two swerdes and he that smote the dolorous stroke.'
> (91.4–11)

The instinct to commemorate is universal, as is the desire to be remembered. The fate of Uwayne is a poignant example:

> 'No force,' seyde sir Uwayne, 'sytthyn I shall dye this deth, of a much more worshipfuller mannes hande myght I nat dye. But whan ye com to the courte recommaunde me unto my lorde Arthur, and to all them that be leffte on lyve. And for olde brothirhode thynke on me.'
> Than began sir Gawayne to wepe, and also sir Ector. And than sir Uwayne bade hym draw oute the truncheon of the speare, and than sir Gawayne drew hit oute, and anone departed the soule frome the body.

---

[12] Compare, for example, the description of the tomb of King Bagdemagus:
  And on the morne he arose and hard masse, and afore an awter he founde a ryche tombe which was newly made. And than he toke hede and saw the sydys wryten with golde which seyde,
    'Here lyeth kyng Bagdemagus of Gore, which kynge Arthurs nevew slew,' and named hym sir Gawayne. (1020.3–8)

139

ARTHURIAN AND OTHER STUDIES

> Than sir Gawayne and sir Ector buryed hym as them ought to bury a
> kynges sonne and made hit wryten uppon hys tombe what was hys
> name and by whom he was slayne.　(945.7–18)

As these examples suggest, the appearance of a written sign often
coincides with the occurrence of a significant event. Occasionally, however, signs are used prophetically, or as a contemporary critic might put
it, they are used to inscribe significance. Merlin, for example, adds the
following prophecy to the writing on the tomb of Launceor and Lady
Columbe:

> 'Here shall be,' seyde Merlion, 'in this same place the grettist bateyle
> betwyxte two [knyghtes] that ever was or ever shall be, and the trewyst
> lovers; and yette none of hem shall slee other.'
> And there Merlion wrote hir namys uppon the tombe with lettirs of
> golde, that shall feyght in that place: which namys was Launcelot du
> Lake and Trystrams.　(72.5–11)

Similarly, a prophecy appears on the tomb of Peryne, slain by Garlon:
'And there the ermyte and Balyne buryed the knyght undir a ryche stone
and a tombe royall. And on the morne they founde letters of golde
wretyn how that sir Gawayne shall revenge his fadirs dethe ⌈kynge Lot⌉
on kynge Pellynore' (81.15–8). Even the prophetic, i.e. the irrational,
must be contained in a concrete – or, as is often the case, marble – form.

The signs I have cited up to this point have been, in general, relatively
short, lapidary inscriptions, but Malory also uses longer forms, though
sometimes only implied, as a narrative device. Following the death of
Percivale's sister:

> Than sir Percivale made a lettir of all that she had holpe them as in
> stronge aventures, and put it in hir [r]yght honde. And so leyde hir in a
> barge, and coverde hit with blacke sylke. And so the wynde arose and
> droff the barge frome the londe, and all maner of knyghtes behylde hit
> tyll hit was oute of ther syght.　(1004.8–13)

The letter is at once a personal memorial and a social communication,
since through the letter, information concerning the adventures of
various knights can be made more widely known: 'And there sir Launcelot tolde the kynge of hys aventures that befelle hym syne he departed.
And also he tolde hym of the aventures of sir Galahad, sir Percivale, and
sir Bors whych that he knew by the lettir of the ded mayden, and also as
sir Galahad had tolde hym' (1020.26–30). In this instance, there is no
need for Malory to repeat the contents of the letter – which must have
been of considerable length! – but at the end of the episode of "The
Poisoned Apple", he uses a lengthy inscription to summarise the plot in
detail:

CHAUCER AND MALORY: SIGNS OF THE TIMES

Than was sir Patryse buryed in the chirche of Westemynster in a towmbe, and thereuppon was wrytten: HERE LYETH SIR PATRYSE OF IRELONDE, SLAYNE BY SIR PYNELL LE SAVEAIGE THAT ENPOYSYNDE APPELIS TO HAVE SLAYNE SIR GAWAYNE, AND BY MYSSEFORTUNE SIR PATRYSE ETE ONE OF THE APPLIS, AND THAN SUDDENLY HE BRASTE. Also there was wrytyn uppon the tombe that quene Gwenyvere was appeled of treson of the deth of sir Patryse by sir Madore de la Porte, and there was made mencion how sir Launcelot fought with hym for quene Gwenyvere and overcom hym in playne batayle. All thys was wretyn uppon the tombe of sir Patryse in excusyng of the quene.   (1059.26–35; 1060.1–2)[13]

There are, to be sure, many other instances in which signs play a significant role in Malory's story-telling: the writing on Balyn's sword (91.21–6), the cross on Galahad's shield (881.4–13), the cross in the road (883.20–30), the cross in the pommel of Percival's sword (918.26–34; 919.1–2), and the writing in the ship (984.27–36), to list a few. All of the signs to which I have referred, taken together as a single narrative device, tell us not only something about style and technique in the *Morte*, but also something about Malory and his times. Malory's signs, thus, provide us with an equivalent of Chaucer's would-be alchemists, whose rational efforts to achieve the irrational signify the new numinosity of the Renaissance idiom.

Edmund Reiss has recently written: 'The full meaning of a sign lies beyond its obvious significance; and, furthermore, the full meaning of a work lies not only beyond the fictions it offers but any explicit interpretation of these fictions as well.'[14] In this essay I have tried to show how both Chaucer and Malory reflect the increasingly rational thinking of pre-Renaissance England. Chaucer's Canon and Yeoman signify a 'new' sort of person. They are rational beings who become irrational, because in their rationality, they are unwilling and unable to see the limits it necessarily imposes. The ubiquitous signs in Malory, on the other hand, in addition to their 'obvious significance' as narrative details, are also a rational means of containment for the otherwise inexplicable, a means of dealing with, in a word, the 'other'. They register an attempt to contain and understand the irrational and the numinous. Tripp writes: 'In the world of Canterbury and its emerging and potentially neo-pagan humanism, there is a danger that the terminology of craft, in a new

---

[13] On this passage, Vinaver (p. 1600) comments: 'Here M seems to go back to an earlier passage in the *Mort Artu* (p. 63) describing the burial of Gaheriz li Blans Karaheu (M's 'sir Patryse'). The inscription on the tomb was, according to the *Mort Artu*, "Ici gist Gaheriz li Blans de Haraheu, li freres Mador de la Porte, que la reine fist morir par venim." '

[14] 'Ambiguous Signs and Authorial Deceptions in Fourteenth-Century Fictions', *Sign, Sentence, Discourse: Language in Medieval Thought and Literature*, ed. Julian N. Wasserman and Lois Roney (Syracuse: Syracuse University Press, 1989), p. 118.

psychological key, will become the litany of a master religion – and that religion will become the master craft.'[15] In Malory's world, signs in general and those of the automatic, self-inscribing sort in particular are evidence of yet another psychological step in the Renaissance direction.

[15] Tripp, *ibid.*, p. 155.

Editor/Compositor at Work: the Case of Caxton's Malory*

TOSHIYUKI TAKAMIYA

In terms of textual importance, Caxton's *Morte Darthur*, printed in 1485, is far superior to, for example, Caxton's *Canterbury Tales*, which was published in 1478 and again in 1484. This is mainly because the former is roughly contemporary with Malory's original composition, completed in 1470, and thus contributes a great deal, together with the Winchester MS., to the establishment of the text which Malory originally wrote. In contrast, the latter work was printed almost a century after the original composition and so was not a very faithful reproduction of what Chaucer actually wrote. It is known that Caxton's edition of 1485 was considered the sole authority on the *Morte Darthur* for several centuries until 1934, when the unique MS. of the *Morte*, now British Library Additional MS. 59678, was found by Dr Walter Oakeshott at Winchester College and subsequently edited by Professor Eugène Vinaver under the rather radical title of *The Works of Sir Thomas Malory*. This was first published in 1947, and revised by Vinaver himself in 1967; the third edition, further corrected by Mr Peter Field, was published in 1990. As far as Caxton's text is concerned, H. O. Sommer's edition, published in 1889–91, claimed that it faithfully reproduced the original text, page for page and word for word, although this was not actually the case. Malory students therefore waited with avidity for James W. Spisak's critical edition of 1983, based on the Pierpont Morgan copy of the *Morte*. However, this turned out to be a rather poorly edited text, if judged by modern critical standards: there are no less than a thousand inadequacies in the edited text and some weaknesses in editorial method.[1] As far as textual accuracy is concerned, therefore, one should turn to the Scolar facsimile of the Pierpont Morgan copy, which was published in

---

* This is a revised version of a paper originally read at the XVIth International Arthurian Congress which was held at the University of Durham on 12 August 1990. A later version was read at the British Council Japan English Literature Seminar, which was held at Hakone on 21 September 1991 with Professor John Burrow as guest lecturer. I am most grateful to Dr Ian Doyle, Dr Lotte Hellinga, and Mr Nicolas Barker for reading an early draft of this paper, and to Dr Felicity Riddy for a stimulating comment. I am also indebted to Professor Andrew Armour for improving my English.

[1] See Toshiyuki Takamiya, 'Caxton's Malory Re-edited', *Poetica*, 21 & 22 (1983), 48–70.

ARTHURIAN AND OTHER STUDIES

1976 in time for the quincentenary celebrations of the advent of printing in England.

Perhaps by far the most significant development in Malory studies in the past two decades or so resulted from the discipline of bibliography. Minutely detailed, often detective-like research, conducted with scientific tools by Dr. Lotte Hellinga of the British Library, has revealed the intriguing fact that on some leaves of the Winchester MS. there are smudges of printing ink, and also some very faint offsets of printing types – Type 2 and Type 4 – which only Caxton possessed; the latter was actually used in printing the *Morte Darthur*. Fully reported in *The British Library Journal* in 1977 and revised in *Aspects of Malory* in 1981,[2] this sensational discovery, however, did not suggest that the relationship between the MS. and Caxton's *Morte* was as immediate as that between printer's copy and printed text, because we cannot find in the former any sign of casting off made by an editor or compositor. Rather it suggests that the MS. was at Caxton's printing shop where it was probably used by Caxton or his editors in preparations with a compositor's MS., which must now be lost.

In Caxton's *Morte* there are no less than eight instances of textual errors, in which a line appears twice, or in which one to three lines have been lost at the turn from one page to the next. There are also eight inadvertent repetition of a word or phrase, and four omissions of a single word, occurring at the very beginning of a page. Furthermore, I have found two instances in which the Pierpont Morgan copy reads differently from the John Rylands copy at the turn from one page to the next.

Omitting or repeating a word or line can happen with any copyist (whether for manuscript or print) through 'eye-skip', and the turn of a page, or the change from one forme to another makes it more likely not to be spotted – either by him or a corrector – even when copying/setting in sense order.[3] Nevertheless, it is hard to imagine why this kind of careless printing mistake was repeated so often in Caxton's *Morte*, at least if one assumes the compositor set the text in regular sequence according to his exemplar. Certainly the medieval scribe would have transcribed his exemplar which he saw before him in sequence, copying the recto of a certain leaf, and then proceeding to the verso of the same leaf, and to the recto of the next leaf, and so on. As Dr Paul Needham

---

[2] Lotte Hellinga and Hilton Kelliher, 'The Malory Manuscript', *The British Library Journal*, 3 (1977), 91–113; Lotte Hellinga, 'The Malory Manuscript and Caxton', *Aspects of Malory*, ed. Toshiyuki Takamiya and Derek Brewer (Cambridge: D. S. Brewer, 1981), pp. 127–41.

[3] For example, there is an instance of the word 'terram' lost at a page turn in the leading MS. of Symeon of Durham's *History of the Church of Durham*, Durham University Library, Cosin MS. V.II.6, f. 45$^{r/v}$ (c. 1104–8); the word survives in the contemporary B.L. Cotton MS. Faustina A.V., which must have been copied from the same exemplar. I am very grateful to Dr Ian Doyle for this information.

144

EDITOR/COMPOSITOR AT WORK

suggests, there is some evidence to indicate that, at the beginning of Caxton's printing career, he followed not only scribal practice but also that of his fellow printers by typesetting in textual order, one page after another.[4] This practice, however, changed radically around 1480, and Caxton's method of setting page after page changed to setting forme by forme. In the case of Caxton's *Morte*, printed in folio with each quire comprising four sheets, only page 4 verso and page 5 recto of each quire must have been set in textual order. Indeed there is no evidence of textual corruption at the turn of the page from 4 verso to 5 recto. As Dr Lotte Hellinga explains, 'Not until the mid-seventeenth century was a book normally set in the order in which the text could be read in the *exemplar*, for setting a book in textual order meant that a large stretch of it had to wait standing in type before a quire could be printed.'[5] In addition to smudges of printing ink and fingerprints, a compositor's copy used in this period usually bears marks for casting off, or the calculations of pages required for typesetting each quire, since it was necessary to combine pages that were to be printed on one side of a sheet. A number of manuscripts used as compositor's copy for English incunabules have recently come to light – described, for example, in Carol Meale's article[6] – but the only surviving manuscript that was used in Caxton's workshop is the Vatican MS. of Laurentius Traversanus, *Nova Rhetorica*, which carries typical marks for casting off, including numeral figures, dashes, wiggles, and dividing lines.[7] It is these marks that were sometimes misunderstood by a compositor or his companions while typesetting, thus resulting in the printing mistakes found at the turn of a page.

Although the Winchester MS. was not used as compositor's copy for Caxton's *Morte*, a detailed comparison of these two Malory texts will reveal the nature of those mistakes which occurred during the printing process, and thus enable us to partially reconstruct the now lost compositor's copy. As Dr Hellinga points out in her splendid review article of the two Malory facsimiles in *The Library*(1980) 'there proved to be some variation at most page ends',[8] which can be explained by the constant copyfitting problem faced by the compositor of prose text. Space does not suffice for me to discuss here all of the textual variants probably caused by printing practice; I shall therefore concentrate on obvious printing errors which occur at the turn of a page, because they

---

4 Paul Needham, *The Printer & The Pardoner* (Washington, D.C.: The Library of Congress, 1986).

5 Lotte Hellinga, *Caxton in Focus* (London: The British Library, 1982), p. 47.

6 Carol Meale, 'Wynkyn de Worde's Setting-Copy for *Ipomydon*', *Studies in Bibliography*, 35 (1982), 156–71.

7 José Ruysschaert, 'Les manuscrits autographes de deux oeuvres de Lorenzo Guglielmo Traversagni imprimées chez Caxton', *Bulletin of The John Rylands Library*, 36 (1953–4), 191–7; cf. *Caxton in Focus*, p. 46.

8 Lotte Hellinga, 'Two Malory Facsimiles', *The Library*, 6th ser., 2 (1980), 92–9.

ARTHURIAN AND OTHER STUDIES

can bring us closer to an understanding of what happened in the production of Caxton's work.

1.1. One word repeated: $c1^v \rightarrow c2^r$; $d2^v \rightarrow d3^r$; $p2^r \rightarrow p2^v$; $A8^r \rightarrow A8^v$; $B4^r \rightarrow B4^v$; $G1^v \rightarrow G2^r$ (two words); $R2^v \rightarrow R3^r$; $bb2^v \rightarrow bb3^r$.

1.2. One word omitted: $g3^r \rightarrow g3^v$ (departed | [and] fonde); $g5^v \rightarrow g6^r$ (somme | [cause] and); $o3^v \rightarrow o4^r$ (wende | [ye] wold); $r4^r \rightarrow r4^v$ (knyghte | [kepe] thyself).

Twelve cases of a single word being repeated or omitted can be explained if we assume that the word in question was marked for casting off in such a way that a compositor could not clearly tell whether it should be the last word of the page or the first word of the next. What happened in the case of 1.1 was that one compositor took the marked word as the final word of the page, while a second compositor took it as the first word of the next page, and they consequently printed it twice. Alternatively, it may have been the same compositor, who failed to notice the mistake because the two pages were not set in textual order. Similarly, in the case of 1.2, one compositor failed to set the word because he thought it was meant to be the first word of the next page, while a second compositor also ignored it, thinking it was meant to be the last word of the preceding page. Again this could have been the mistake of a single compositor.

1.3. One word or phrase dropped out of the Pierpont Morgan copy at the turn of a page: $p5^v \rightarrow p6^r$ (other [kynges and quenys] |); $A2^r \rightarrow A2^v$ (Arthur [what] | knyghte).

There are two instances in which the Pierpont Morgan copy reads differently from the John Rylands copy. The first can simply be attributed to the accidental dropping of the phrase 'kynges and quenys', which occupied the last line of the page, while printing the Pierpont Morgan copy, because fillings in the last line were not tight enough. As for the omission of the word 'what' on page 2 recto of the Morgan copy, James Spisak suggests compositorial emendation as follows: 'As the sheets were being collated for this gathering, a compositor noticed that the word "what" had been left out as he (or his partner) went to a new page – an understandable and common mistake. Rather than excise any of the text, he changed the "and" of the previous line to an ampersand in order to move the first word (haue) of the last line up one and make room for the word that had been left out.'[9] Spisak even suggests that 'someone was careful enough to replace letters and words that had dropped out for one reason or another.' If so, he was not careful enough to notice that the phrase 'kynges and quenys' had been left out.

[9] James W. Spisak, ed., *Caxton's Malory*, 2 vols. (Los Angeles: University of California Press, 1983), p. 616.

EDITOR/COMPOSITOR AT WORK

Next we have to deal with eight instances in which one to three lines were either omitted or repeated inadvertently. In the cast-off copy the beginning of the first line of a new page would be indicated by a stroke, sometimes two strokes, or a cross, marked within the text or in the margin. Again a compositor would sometimes find it difficult to interpret what the mark meant, which would result in the omission or repetition of the whole line at the turn of the page. This would explain cases 2.1 and 2.2.

2.1. o3^r → o3^v: Caxton's Book VII, Chapter 22 (one line repeated)
[o3^r] And thenne | he loked afore hym and there be apperceyued and sawe co|me an armed knyght with many lyghtes aboute hym / and [o3^v] *sawe come an armed kny3t with many lyghtes aboute hym* / & | (emphasis mine)
[British Library, MS. Additional 59678, f. 133^v] And þerwithall he loked before | hym *and* sawe an armed knyght w*ith* many lyght*es* aboute hym. *and* | . . .

Let us suppose that a cross was marked in the margin of the line 'sawe come and armed kny3t with many lyghtes about hym'. Whoever was responsible for setting page o3^r took the mark as indicating that the page had to be completed with the line, while the compositor setting page o3^v understood that it meant the beginning of a new page; hence the line was repeated.

2.2. D2^v → D3^r: X. 36 (one line omitted)
[D2^v] Alle this sawe a damoysel / and [D3^r] sawe the best knyghte iuste that euer he sawe /
[MS. f. 264^r] And all this sawe a damesell and *went to Morgan le fay* and | *tolde hir how she* saw the beste knyght iuste þat eu*er* she sawe | (emphasis mine)

In this case, the opposite occurred: the person composing page D2^v assumed that the line 'went to Morgan le Fay and told her how she' was to be printed at the beginning of the next page, while the compositor of page D3^r assumed it completed the preceding page; thus both ignored the whole line of text.

There are two instances of the omission of text (2.3 and 2.4 below) due to homoeoteleuton, which occurs more often than not in prose text having the same words repeated within fairly close range. This phenomenon – not uncommon in Caxton's *Morte* and occurring even at the turn of a page – can certainly be attributed to eye-skip on the part of a compositor, who failed to recognise the mark for casting off.

2.3. g7^r → g7^v: IV. 18–9 (about two lines omitted, due to homoeoteleuton)
[g7^r] . . . for I wylle brynge you thorow the forest [g7^v] And rode daye by day wel a seuen dayes or they fond ony a|uenture . . .

[MS. f. 61^r] . . . for I woll brynge you thorow þe foreste. *So they* | rode forth all iij and sir Marhaus toke with *hym his gret|tyste spere* and *so they rode thorow þe foreste* and rode day be | day well nye a vij dayes or they founde ony aventure. (emphases mine)

2.4. V3^v → V4^r: XVIII. 3 (one line omitted, due to homoeoteleuton)
[V3^v] and soo it befelle by mysfortune a good | knyght named Patryse cosyn vnto sire Mador de la porte to [V4^r] take a poysend Appel / And whanne he had eten hit /
[MS. f. 411^v] and so hit befylle by myssefortune a good kny3t sir Patryse | which was cosyn vnto sir Mador de la porte to*ke an appyll for [he] was en|chaffed with hete of wyne and hit myssehapped hym to* take a poysonde | apple And whan he had etyn hit . . . [emphasis mine]

2.5. D3^v → D4^r: X. 36 (three lines omitted)
[D3^v] And the*n*ne he wenyng to be strong ynou3 wold haue mou*n*ted
[D4^r] And soo she leyd sire Alysander in an hors lyttar and ledde |
[MS. f. 265^r] And whan he had | done this batayle he toke his horse *and wolde haue mown|ted vppon his horse but he myght nat for faynte* // And | than he seyde a Jesu *succoure me So by that com Morgan* | le fay and bade hym be of good comforte And so she layde | hym this Alysaundir in an horse lettir and so led hym | (emphasis mine)

2.6. aa2^v → aa3^r: XIX. 11 (three lines repeated)
[aa2^v] Soo dyd the Erle Lambaile | Soo dyd the erle Arystause [blank] Thenne came in syr Gawayne with his thre sones sir Grynga|llyn /syr Florence / & sir Louel / these two were begoten vpon sir [aa3^r] *dyd the erle Lambayle* | *Soo dyd the Erle Arystause* | *¶Thenne came in syre Gawayne with his thre sones syr gan|galayne* /syr Florence and syr Louel these two were goten vp | *on syr* Brandyles syster / and al they fayled / (emphasis mine)
[MS. f. 446^r] So ded the erle Arystause | Than cam in sir Gawayne wyth hys iij su*n*nes sir Gryngalyn sir | *Florence and sir* Lovell thes ij were begotyn vppon sir Braunde|lles syster and all they fayled

2.5 is an example of three lines being omitted; there must have been something wrong with this passage in the compositor's copy. In the case of 2.6, three lines are repeated on page aa2^v.

Last of all, but not least, there are two very interesting instances of one line being repeated with textual variation. In each case, the altered text appears towards the end rather than of the beginning of the text page.

2.7. g1^v → g2^r: IV. 11 (one line repeated with slight variation)
[g1^v] . . . entente that I | shold slee kynge Arthur her broder / For ye shall vnderstand [g2^r] *entente to slee kyng Arthur her broder* | *for ye shal vnder-stand*| (emphasis mine)
[MS. f. 54^r] . . . entente to sle kynge | Arthure hir brothir for ye shall vndirstonde þ*at* kynge | Arthur ys the man . . .

148

EDITOR/COMPOSITOR AT WORK

This would be caused by homoeoteleuton on 'Arthur' but was taken up by Dr Hellinga in *Caxton in Focus* as an obvious error in the production of a book which can shed light on how a compositor or editor dealt with text that he found troublesome: 'When he began setting page g 2 recto the compositor thought it was the line beginning with *entente*. Page g 1 verso probably had to be completed after page g 2 recto had been set and printed. The compositor had to invent some extra words and longer forms to fill up the space . . . On g 1 verso he managed to expand the length of his line by adding ten letters and introducing the use of a capital. It was evidently necessary to end the pages *exactly* as cast off, and yet to make it look like a page filled to normal length, a "seamless" transition to the following page. When the compositor ended page g 1 verso he thought the stroke in his exemplar indicated the line *following* the one beginning with *entente* as the spot where g 2 recto had started – wishful thinking, no doubt, as he had obviously too much space on his hands.'[10] Thus she has reconstructed the relevant part of the compositor's copy as follows:

. . . kynge Vryence wyf sente it me yesterday by a dwarf to this
×   entente to slee kyng Arthur her broder / for ye shall vnderstand
that kyng Arthur is the man in the world that she most hateth . . .

All that is left for the present analysis is 2.8, which may look similar in nature to what Hellinga discussed above, but is arguably far more interesting.

2.8. T3^r → T3^v: XVII. 15 (one line repeated with variations)
[T3^r] ¶Thenne felte he many handes aboute hym whiche tooke hym | vp / and bare hym oute of the chamber dore / withoute ony a|mendynge of his swoune / and lefte hym there semyng dede to [T3^v] *of the chamber dore and lefte hym there semynge dede to* al pe|ple / Soo vpon the morowe . . . (emphasis mine)
[MS. f. 401^v] Than felte he many hondys whych toke hym vp | and bare hym oute of the chambir doore and leffte hym þer | semynge dede to all people So vppon the morow . . .

This occurs in Caxton's Book XVII, Chapter 15 – an episode which deals with Sir Launcelot in 'The Tale of the Sank Greal'. As soon as he entered the room in which the Holy Grail was placed, Sir Launcelot felt as if he were struck by fire, and swooned. T3^r thus follows: 'Thenne felte he many handes aboute hym', etc. T3^v begins with the italicised sentence above, which does not coincide exactly with that on page T3^r, but with that in the Winchester MS., f. 401^v. What is remarkable about the reading

---

[10] *Caxton in Focus*, pp. 93–4.

149

on T3^r is that it contains two phrases – 'aboute hym' and 'withoute ony amendynge of his swoune' – neither of which is found in the MS.

The compositor obviously followed the mark in the margin of the compositor's copy, and began setting page T3^v with 'of the chambir dore'. Whether or not he was the same compositor who typeset page T3^r, the latter found it necessary to complete the page with 'semynge dede to', as suggested by the cast-off mark in the margin of the compositor's copy. The two strokes drawn immediately before 'Than felte he' in the compositor's copy suggested to him that this was the spot where a new paragraph should begin, and he used the paraph mark (¶) to start with, but here he confronted a difficult problem. He found he needed three lines of text to fill the full page of T3^r, although there were only two lines in the compositor's copy. Whether he actually asked Caxton for advice at this stage we do not know, but at any rate he had to invent the two phrases mentioned above, which he inserted in appropriate places on the page so as 'to make it look like a page filled to normal length, a "seamless" transition to the following page.'

The expression 'withoute ony amendynge of his swoune' is not found in the Winchester MS. Professor Vinaver suggests that '[Caxton's] reading may well be authentic, though it is not confirmed by [a French source]'.[11] Judging from the above argument and also from the fact that the gerund 'amendynge' is not used anywhere else in the Winchester MS., it is reasonable to assume that the phrase was inserted by the compositor. According to Dr Hellinga, this kind of minor textual change was possibly permitted at the compositor's discretion.

In 1990 Kiyokazu Mizobata edited an extremely useful *Concordance to Caxton's Own Prose*, based mainly on Norman Blake's text, with emendations which resulted from Mizobata's own collations.[12] This concordance reveals the intriguing fact that Caxton used in his own prose text 'amende' as many as sixteen times, with 'amendement' and 'amendyng' appearing once each. Therefore, the phrase in question – 'withoute ony amendynge'– can reasonably be considered as 'Caxtonian' diction.

In the same way that Dr Hellinga reconstructed just a small portion of the compositor's copy through analysis of 2.7, we are now able to repeat the process for 2.8, as follows:

> //Than felte he many hondys whych toke hym up and bare hym
> ✕ oute of the chambir doore / and leffte hym there semynge dede to
> all people / So vppon the morow . . .

---

11 *The Works of Sir Thomas Malory*, 3 vols., ed. Eugène Vinaver, 3rd ed. rev. P. J. C. Field (Oxford: Clarendon Press, 1990), p. 1579: note to p. 1016.14–5.

12 Kiyokazu Mizobata, ed., *A Concordance to Caxton's Own Prose* (Tokyo: Shohakusha, 1990); cf. Tomomi Kato, ed., *A Concordance to The Works of Sir Thomas Malory* (Tokyo: University of Tokyo Press, 1974).

EDITOR/COMPOSITOR AT WORK

This kind of printing mistake occurred simply because the compositor of page T3^r assumed the cast-off mark in the margin of the compositor's copy indicated the last line of the page, while the compositor of page T3^v took it to indicate the first line of a new page. Furthermore, by tracing how these printing errors took place, we should be able to calculate the length of each line of the compositor's copy. My reconstructed compositor's copy has about the same line length as that of Dr Hellinga. Judging from this work, it would appear that each line of the compositor's copy had slightly more letters than the lines of the Winchester MS.

Modernity of the Middle English Stanzaic Romance *Le Morte Arthur**

JÁN ŠIMKO

Professor Shunichi Noguchi has given us and himself a very welcome birthday present in the form of a new edition of the stanzaic *Le Morte Arthur*.[1] His publication of the text only, not including any critical apparatus except a glossary for the letter A (as a specimen), is the ninth edition of the poem to appear so far. While there had been as many as five editions issued between 1819 and 1912, what came afterwards was a wide time gap of sixty-two years before the appearance, in 1974, of Larry D. Benson's text, followed immediately, in 1975, by another edition prepared by P. F. Hissiger.[2] It was in answer to 'the presence of not a few inaccuracies' in the latter publication that Professor Noguchi was prompted to bring out his text.[3]

It is a source of great satisfaction to me that, in honouring Professor Noguchi's memorable anniversary, I have been able to use his edition as basis of the subsequent discussion. All page and line numbers concerning this poem refer to his publication.

The title, *Le Morte Arthur*, derives from the 'Explycit' following the last

---

* I wish to express my appreciation for his help in the preparation of this article to Professor David George of Urbana University, Urbana, Ohio. In translating some of the Middle English words, I have availed myself of the extensive 'Glossary' in P. F. Hissiger's edition of *Le Morte Arthur* (The Hague: Mouton. 1975), pp. 144–79.

[1] S. Noguchi, ed. *Le Morte Arthur* (Tokyo: Centre for Mediaeval English Studies, 1990).

[2] All the editions, prior to Noguchi's, of this stanzaic poem are as follows:
Le Morte Arthur, ed. Thomas Ponton (William Bulmer, 1819).
Le Morte Arthur, ed. F. J. Furnivall (London: Macmillan, 1864).
Le Morte Arthur, ed. J. Douglas Bruce, E.E.T.S., e.s. 88 (London: Oxford University Press, 1903).
Le Morte Arthur, ed. Andrew Boyle, in *Morte Arthur: Two Early English Romances* (London: Dent, 1912)
Le Morte Arthur, ed. Samuel B. Hemingway (New York: Houghton Mifflin, 1912).
King Arthur's Death: The Middle English Stanzaic Morte Arthur and Alliterative Morte Arthure, ed. Larry D. Benson (Indianapolis: Bobbs-Merill, 1974).
Le Morte Arthur, ed. P. F. Hissiger (The Hague: Mouton, 1975).
Le Morte DArthur (extract), in *Medieval English Romances*, Part Two, ed. A. V. C. Schmidt and Nicolas Jacobs (London: Hodder and Stoughton, 1980).

[3] Noguchi, *ibid.*, 'Preface'.

line, 3969. The poem is composed of 498 stanzas consisting, as a rule, of eight lines each. Nearly all lines have four feet prevailingly carrying the iambic rhythm. The rhyme pattern of most stanzas is abababab. Since about 42% of the lines contain alliteration, the origin of the poem is thought to be connected with the alliterative revival which took place in the North and North West Midlands of England in the fourteenth century.[4] The British Library Harley Manuscript 2252 of the poem is thought to have been written down in the late fifteenth century by two scribes.[5]

The following discussion pursues, basically, a double purpose, in so far as it aims at pointing out that:

(1) the main elements of the story have a generally human relevance,

and that

(2) the structural build-up of the poem is close to that of a tragedy.

Two Kinds of Human Relations – Exposition and Complication

The drift and the resolution of the plot lead to the conclusion that the structure of the story is conceived as if it were a multi-layered tragedy. Over two centuries before Shakespeare, whose *King Lear* (*c.* 1606) is the prototype of a tragedy where the main plot and the subplot intertwine and complement each other, the anonymous English poet of the *Le Morte Arthur*, composing his *oeuvre* at the very dawn of English Arthurian literature proper, produced an epic poem of a surprisingly well-knit complexity. The first episode relates Lancelot's encounter with the Maid of Astolat, who falls hopelessly in love with him. It places into sharp contrast two kinds of man-woman relationship. While Lancelot's encounters with the Maid take place in the open, the Lancelot-Guenevere relationship, in an effort to prevent discovery, must play itself 'out' inside Guenevere's room. Unfortunately, not even this stratagem can save it from exposure leading to a major catastrophe.

At the very beginning of the poem, in some of the first stanzas, Nos. 7–10, the precarious nature of the illicit Lancelot-Guenevere relationship is laid out in a nutshell. While King Arthur had gone to Winchester to take part in a tournament, 'Launcelot lefte ['remained'] withe the quene' (53). Not only was he sick (54) at the time but, on top of that, 'For love þ<a>t was theym bytwene/ He made inchessoun ['excuse'] for to abyde .../ .../ Sir Agraveyne for suche a nede /At home bylefte, .../ For men

---

[4] P. F. Hissiger, *ibid.*, p. 5.
[5] L. D. Benson, *King Arthur's Death* (see note 2), p. xii. Hissiger, *ibid.*, pp. 3 and 5.

told . . ./ That Launcelot by the quene lay;/ For to take them w<i>t<h> the dede/ He awaytes both nyght and day' (55–64).

When Lancelot enters the Queen's chamber, she is not particularly pleased: 'Launcelott, what dostow here w<i>t<h> me?/ . . ./ I drede we shall discoverid be / Off the love is us bytwene;/ Sir Agravayne at home is he,/ Nyght <and> day he waytes us two' (69–74).

These lines are full of ominous forebodings, including two warning references to the King's nephew Agravain. Guenevere's apprehensive words are transformed into dangerous reality when Agravain, from having been a shadowy observer or spy, jumps on the stage towards the middle of the poem. Disregarding his brother Gawain's urgent admonition warning him of possible dire consequences, should he accuse Lancelot of treason against the King (1688–711), Agravain nevertheless takes matters into his own hands when proclaiming openly: 'Launcelote lyes by the quene –/ Ageyne the k[yng]e tra[y]tor is he' (1682–3). One of the many instances of tragic irony in this poem is that Agravain falls victim to his own attack (1858), 'hoist with his own petar',[6] while the targets of his attack, Lancelot and Guenevere, survive to the end of the poem.

As a counterweight to the more or less conventional instance of a reciprocal courtly love affair, that of Lancelot and Guenevere, the poet presents the case of the one-sided and hopeless, that is, unreciprocated love of the young Maid of Astolat for Lancelot. This 'minor' case of love is not secretive or hidden but is open for everybody to see. In this case, Lancelot plays the morally correct knight or 'gentleman' by not exploiting, or taking advantage of, the girl's inexperience and vulnerable emotions but excuses himself from reciprocating her feelings of which he is well aware (189–90). Lancelot's valid explanation states that 'In another stede myne hert is sette –/ It is not at myne owne wille' (203–4). In other words, he is bound to another woman, Queen Guenevere, by bonds of chivalric loyalty and honour and it is beyond his will to change it.

Gawain, at that juncture Lancelot's friend still, offers an unexpectedly 'class-conscious' explanation of Lancelot's behaviour as of one who did not want that 'hys love laye/ In so low a place in vayne ['uselessly'],/ But on a pryse ['excellent'] lady' (1109–11), that is, the Queen. Some time earlier he also warns the Maid that 'no lady . . ./ . . ./ might hyr love hald hym fro' (588–91).

Lancelot, true to the aristocratic 'code of ethics' and the rules of feudal courtly love, is bound by loyalty and allegiance to 'his' beloved lady. In case he steps, however, beyond the ethically permissible limits, he is in danger of trespassing against two other allegiances or loyalties inextricably linked in this case: the feudal loyalty to the ruler, King Arthur, who happens to be Guenevere's husband, 'The noble kynge that made me

---

[6] *Hamlet* (V. iv. 208), ed. E. Hubler (New York: Signet, 1963).

knyght!' (2145), on the one hand, and as many as two biblical command-
ments, on the other: the sixth: 'Thou shalt not commit adultery', and the
ninth: 'Thou shalt not covet thy neighbor's wife.'

As to the Church's handling of cases of illicit liaisons, there is no word
about it throughout the poem, except by inference at the end, when
Guenevere, openly admitting sin and guilt, becomes a nun (3569) of her
own choice and unequivocally renounces all worldly pleasures, rejecting
even Lancelot's seemingly innocuous suggestion for parting with a
'kysse' (3713). Following her lead, Lancelot becomes a hermit. In contrast
to this case, however, there does come a strong condemnation from the
Archbishop of Canterbury of Mordred's outrageous intention to marry
Guenevere, while her husband Arthur, who happens also to be his –
incestuous – father, is still alive – in France (3002– 9).

Form and Meaning – Complication

Two stories, that of the *Maid of Astolat* and that of the *Poisoned Apple*,
are intertwined in the first part of the poem. This interlocked presentation of the double material has a great significance from the standpoint
of both structure and meaning. This intertwined 'double bill' adds con-
vincing logic to the ongoing 'ups and downs' in the Lancelot-Guenevere
relationship, which, in its turn, being the 'major' theme of the poem,
functions as the underlying unifying element or 'glue' holding the two
stories together and transcending them.

(a1) At the end of the first instalment of the *Maid's Story*, Lancelot is
somewhat annoyed at being castigated by Guenevere for his, basically
harmless, championing of, and alleged flirtation with, the Maid. He
leaves the court abruptly, upsetting Guenevere with his less than
friendly farewell: '. . . thou seest me nevir-mare' (771)! Lancelot's friends
blame her for that 'gaffe' and none of them, except his brother Bors,
volunteers to fight for her soon afterwards.

(b1) At the end of the first instalment of the next story, that of the
Poisoned Apple, Guenevere, unjustly accused of poisoning a dinner guest,
finds herself in mortal danger of being burnt at the stake in case that no
one volunteers to fight for her against her accuser, the poisoned man's
brother Mador.

(a2) The second instalment of the *Maid's Story* is about her tragic death.
It comes about as a result of her pining away in reaction to unrequited
love on the part of Lancelot. From a letter found on the Maid's dead
body, it becomes evident that, contrary to Gawain's earlier unwitting
misrepresentation about Lancelot's supposedly having chosen the Maid
as his 'le<m>man' ['sweetheart'; 637] – in reality Gawain was told about
it earlier by the Maid herself (582) – Lancelot has actually refused to be

MODERNITY OF THE MIDDLE ENGLISH *LE MORTE ARTHUR*

her sweetheart. Thus, Guenevere, herself a victim of misinformation, has castigated Lancelot unjustly (740–59) and lays now the blame for this mix-up on Gawain (1146–67).

(b2) In the second instalment of the *Poisoned Apple* story, Lancelot seizes the opportunity fully to restore, reassert and 'rehabilitate' himself: by defeating Sir Mador, thereby rescuing Guenevere from the threat of death at the stake, he has proved his unshaken loyalty to 'his' lady by his utmost unselfish sacrifice, his courage and prowess.

After Lancelot's defeat of Mador, which has saved the Queen from the horrible death by fire, a deceptive lull, a calming-down, a temporary break or intermission in the hectic, excited previous action seems to have set in.[7] In reality it is a case of the proverbial 'quiet before a storm', when the action is going to be whipped up to a feverish pitch, this time by Agravain's physical assault on Lancelot and Guenevere. In terms of drama, this is the climax or crisis in the narrative.

Variations on the Theme of Love – Climax or Crisis

The element that links the Lancelot-Guenevere story with that of the Maid of Astolat is love, its power and its effects. What the poet actually offers us are 'variations on the theme of love'.

On the one hand, love is presented as a positive, ennobling force, generating in its bearer or 'victim' both positive attitudes, such as loyalty and devotion, etc., and positive actions, such as selfless help and service to another person or persons in case of need, rescuing one's beloved or friend or companion from danger, etc. All these elements, aspects or features can be found in Lancelot's behaviour and actions.

Moreover, love is correctly shown by the poet to have also a positive non-sexual, non-erotic aspect, binding, for instance, two or more people sharing similar aims or ideals with a common bond of friendship, loyalty or, in the highest degree, of love itself. This can be called a humanitarian kind of love of one person for another or 'the love of one's neighbour'. This, too, makes Lancelot a noble warrior. When his own life is not in acute danger, he is capable of sparing his adversary, the way he handled Mador: after knocking him 'to grounde, . . ./ . . ./ he smyte no-more' (1597–1602) and even extended 'love' (1661) to him. It is with extreme mercy that Lancelot treats even Gawain, his later arch-foe, by twice refusing to kill him (2825; 2927–9) – for 'love' (2837), and it is in the name

---

[7] See R. M. Lumiansky, ' "The Tale of Lancelot and Guenevere": Suspense', *Malory's Originality*, ed. R. M. Lumiansky (Baltimore: The Johns Hopkins University Press, 1964).

157

of 'love' (2937) that he appeals to Arthur, after the war has moved to France, to go 'home and leve your werrynge' (2932).

The Lancelot-Gawain relationship is a most telling case in point. When Agravain threatens to expose Lancelot's love affair with Guenevere as treason against the King, Gawain vehemently opposes his brother's dangerous intentions in the name of 'The love that has bene bytwene us twoo;/ Launcelot shalle I nevyr betrayne,/ Behynde hys bake to be hys foo . . ./ . . ./ Shedde ther sholde be mykelle blode / For thys tale, yiffe it were tolde' (1701–9). The latter sentence is prophetic indeed and foretells the dire tragedy and downfall of Arthur's fellowship of knights.

Let us take the basic question: Should Arthur be told or not? 'To tell or not to tell, that is the question.' That 'Launcelote lyes by the quene' (1682) is shocking and intolerable to Agravain because, as he asserts, 'that wote all the curte bydene,/ And iche day it here and see' (1684–5), except, evidently, the King himself. By the time of Arthur's being told the 'naked' truth about the 'goings-on' in his household or *ménage*, 'behind his back', things have gone too far. Agravain's suggestion for a redress, namely, to catch the 'culprits' *in flagrante delicto*, miserably backfires, so much so that it is 'fire', that is, war which erupts instead.

Thus, love is shown in this case to have degenerated into a most destructive force, capable of leading to the downfall and ruin of a whole society. This cruel fate befell Troy, too.

Furthermore, the poem demonstrates that love can work havoc on a small scale, too. This is the case of the pitiful fate of the Maid of Astolat. She dies pining away from grief for unrequited love of Lancelot. Bad luck of young people in a love relationship often results in their suicides, and her tragedy is not an isolated or unique instance. This has been the case since the 'very tragical'[8] but venerably old Babylonian story of Pyramus and Thisby, the Greek story of Hero and Leander, going *via* Tristan and Isolde all the way to Romeo and Juliet and including our Maid. She is thus in 'good company'.

What is 'new' or surprising – or is it really? – in the Maid's case is how unrequited love has utterly twisted her character. Although she has, ironically, fallen in love with Lancelot considered 'the noblest knight' (1075), after his repeated refusals to be her 'leman' ['sweetheart'; 1086] the poor girl makes a complete turnaround and in a letter addressed 'To kyng Arthur and all his knight<is>' (1048) she maligns Lancelot that 'so churlysshe of maners in feld ne hale['hall']/ Ne know I none of frende ne fo' (1078–79).[9]

What is worse, moreover, is that, after the bloody and fatal collapse of

---

[8] W. Shakespeare, *A Midsummer Night's Dream* (V. i. 57), ed. Kittredge – Ribner (Waltham, Massachusetts: Ginn, 1971).

[9] See William Congreve, *The Mourning Bride* (1697), III. 8: 'Heaven has no rage like love to hatred turned, Nor hell a fury like a woman scorned.'

Agravain's attempt to entrap Lancelot and Guenevere, it is Lancelot's (former) friend and apologue Gawain, who turns abruptly into his chief accuser, detractor, and mortal enemy.

After the unfortunate killing of his three brothers, Gawain's professed 'love' (1701) for Lancelot degenerates into mortal enmity and implacable hatred. Gawain even dares to go so far as to taunt King Arthur himself with a sarcastic barb, as if implicating him in Lancelot's killing of his brothers: 'All for your love, s<y>r' (2679).

Gawain does not tire of trying to draw Lancelot into a fight by repeatedly hurling at him avalanches of provocative 'juicy' verbal insults offensive to a knight's honour, such as 'Trayto<ur> and coward' (2829; also 2774–7; 2867). The top of Gawain's abuse comes after the war has shifted to France: 'To Yngland will I not torne agayne/ Tylle he be hangid on a boughe' (2680–1). Altogether, Gawain hurls as many as eleven more or less extensive and abusive verbal attacks and threats at Lancelot.[10]

In France, Lancelot's two peace offers are rejected (2698–9; 2942–3), in spite of his emotional appeal to the King to 'thynke uppon a thynge . . ./ The love that hathe be us bytwene' (2936–7). Lancelot's moderate approach of 'myldenesse' (2602) and compromise is more or less in tune with the King's feelings, basically, of sadness, sorrow and futility about the war, which is, in spite of all, kept alive and going mainly because of Gawain's stubborn persistence in fighting and trying to exact revenge upon Lancelot. Although Gawain possesses his enormous strength thanks to the prayers of 'An holy man' (2803), he himself is anything but holy and may not be aware at all of the biblical injunction against revenge.[11]

For a long time, and at the risk of being taken for a coward (2132; 2777) – an absolutely awful thing to befall a feudal knight – Lancelot resists Gawain's insulting provocations and refuses to be drawn into a fight. Lancelot's behaviour here is in agreement with another New Testament admonition: 'Resist not evil: but whosoever shall smite thee on thy right cheek, turn to him the other also' (Matthew, 5:39).

When Lancelot does take up the fight at last, in each of their two encounters Gawain, in spite of his enormous strength (2802 ff.), is sorely wounded and knocked down, but Lancelot refuses to kill him (2815–25; 2910–29): 'I forbare ['did not kill'] the . . ./ For love and for the kyng<is> blode' (2836–7). As to the King, he at least concedes the great loss and futility of the war but also Lancelot's nobility even in war, especially

---

[10] See lines: 2010; 2076–7; 2119; 2274–7; 2406 ff.; 2426–7; 2676–83; 2774; 2829 ff.; 2866 ff.; 2919 ff.

[11] 'Vengeance is mine; I will repay, saith the Lord' (Romans, 12:19). 'Revenge is a kind of wild justice, which, the more man's nature runs to, the more ought law weed it out' (F. Bacon, *Essays*, IV, 1597).

after Lancelot has placed him back on horseback at Joyous Gard, after Arthur's being knocked down by Bors (2200–5). Ironically, by saving the King's life, Lancelot has actually prolonged the 'life' of the war.

This kind of behaviour is in perfect harmony with Christian morality, which appeals to people to love even their enemies: 'do good to them that hate you' (Matthew, 5:44). Lancelot lives in a society still ruled, in spite of the New Testament's admonition just quoted, by the pagan or even Old Testament practices of the 'eye-for-eye, tooth-for-tooth' (Exodus, 21:24) blood feud. Its observance was imposed upon the nobility by the aristocratic 'code of ethics.' Refusal or failure to abide by it would result in being ostracised by the fellow nobles.

How values were changing in the past is well illustrated in the stark contrast between Hamlet and Laertes. Laertes, very much concerned about his aristocratic honour, is intent on exacting revenge on Hamlet, at all cost, for the slaying, albeit accidental, of his father Polonius. Hamlet, on the other hand, the 'modern' man, is troubled by this 'old' approach to revenge and waits diligently for the appropriate moment when exacting revenge on Claudius for his intentional poisoning of Hamlet's father would not be considered wanton killing or murder but lawful punishment, which occurs only at the end of the play.

On the other hand, Lancelot is disingenuous when, after Agravain's disastrous plot to entrap him, he takes Guenevere to his residence at Joyous Gard and sends a message to the King offering to fight (2053–69) in order 'To prove . . . fals' the 'lyes . . . sayde hym uppon' (2052; 2066). He evidently means the horrible accusations hurled against him and the Queen in front of the King by Agravain (1728–35). The King knows better and counters that Lancelot 'ne myght prove it nev<er>-more' (2072). Moreover, Lancelot betrays a touch of self-centredness and selfishness, of course under extreme duress, when, during the Agravain assault on the Queen's room, he asks her whether there is any weapon there for him 'to save my lyffe?' (1827). On its face value, this may imply that he has either given her up or thrown her 'to the wolves' and just intends 'to save his skin', instead of defending her in the first place.

In spite of all, the positive value of Lancelot's sparing or saving one, two, three or even a few more human lives pales in contrast with his being the cause, or just one of the causes, of a devastating, ruinous war which has, moreover, erupted for wrong reasons, that is, based on a wrong premise. Namely, Lancelot has placed his personal interest – defending his untenable personal relationship with the Queen – before the common good, the interests of society or even one organisation, such as the Round Table.

It is appropriate that the function of peace maker is assumed in the poem by the Pope of Rome (2250 ff.). Although Lancelot does comply and bring the Queen back (2372 ff.), the wrangling between Lancelot, on the one hand, and Arthur, but especially Gawain, on the other, immediately erupts anew with full fury. Gawain has slyly promised to 'keep his peace' only during the span of time in which Lancelot is supposed to bring the Queen back (2334–7).

Afterwards, Lancelot's prematurely optimistic question as to whether 'we myght frendys be aȝeyne' (2423) is categorically rejected. Thereupon he decides to leave England and return to France. His legitimate follow-up question: 'May I saffly wone ['live'] ther' (2446), is also sharply rebuffed by Gawain: 'we shall after come full sone!' (2451). Although, thanks to papal mediation, a peace accord has been concluded, yet no sooner has Guenevere been returned by Lancelot than the English side breaks the peace agreement and sends its war machine over to France in pursuit of Lancelot, in order, as Arthur has urged his nobles, 'To brenne and sle and make all bare' (2507), which amounts to the infamous 'scorched earth policy'.

Mordred's *Coup d'État* – Peripety

While the war in France is in 'high gear', a totally unexpected real 'shocker', a 'bolt from the blue' hits Arthur: Mordred, who has been chosen governor of England while Arthur is in France (2522), instead of protecting the English throne for Arthur, has usurped it (2954 ff.). This is a gruesome story and the poet makes his anti-Mordred sentiments unmistakably clear.

Mordred, offspring of Arthur's incestuous relations with his sister (2955–6), is evidently possessed of a warped psyche. How else can we explain his shocking decision to marry his stepmother, the wife of his father the King, who, as he must well know, is still alive in France? His conscious intention to go through with this adulterous marriage is very much more reprehensible than Oedipus's marrying, totally unwittingly, his mother Jocasta. Even so, when Oedipus finds out the horrible truth about it, he inflicts a most gruesome punishment on himself by gouging out his eyes and going into exile. Mordred, of course, cannot be unaware from the very beginning of the moral turpitude involved in his intended (mis)marriage, for, in order to cover it up, he lets false letters be drawn up, spreading the lie about Arthur's supposed demise. As to the outrageous nature of his marriage plans, Mordred is warned in no uncertain terms by the Archbishop of Canterbury: 'Thy faders wyffe, whether thou be wood ['mad'],/ To wedd her now mayste thou noght./ Come Arthur evyr over the flood,/ Thow mayste be bold ['sure'] it wyll be boght ['suffered for']' (3006–9). Mordred takes offence at these sharp words daring 'to warne ['refuse to allow'] me of my wille' (3011), and he, in turn, dares to threaten the head of the English church with his going to be 'hangyd hye upon an hylle' (3015). Evidently, Mordred has no respect

ARTHURIAN AND OTHER STUDIES

either for the church law or the moral law, for that matter, and acts like a true autocrat whose 'wille' (3011) is the supreme law and authority in the land. Arthur Schopenhauer (1788–1860) may have formed his 'philosophy of the will' in response to instances of the will's 'willful' misuse like this. No wonder that even an archbishop can get frightened for his life: he flees 'to a wyldernesse' (3025), still existing in the England of six centuries ago, and becomes 'an ermyte' (3031). He does not remain alone, however. Towards the end he is joined by Lancelot (3754) and his brothers Bors (3816) and Ector (3908). Later on, it is this episcopal 'hermit', who has a dream about Lancelot's being borne to 'hevyn' (3879) by angels.

As a counterweight to his autocratic, dictatorial, even ruthless, self-willed behaviour, Mordred, displaying his 'other face', buys himself public favour. He dispenses 'grete yiftys' (2963) especially 'To erlys and to barons' (3044). Moreover, gifts make him 'stronge' (3159) militarily, too. This would then be the 'military-baronial complex' of those days worthwhile courting for support. Evidently for the satisfaction of the masses, who crave *panem et circenses*, 'Festys made he, many and fele' (2962). And, following his coronation at Canterbury, before, of course, the Archbishop of Canterbury's flight into the 'wyldernesse' (3025), Mordred 'A fourte-nyght held the feste in towne' (2983), as if prefiguring the modern-day presidential inauguration festivities.

The buying of public favour by the ruler falls under the unflattering heading of 'corruption'. Yes, there was corruption even in the supposedly ideal Arthurland! No wonder that by calculated acts like these Mordred manages to sway public opinion in his favour, so much so that 'They sayd w<i>t<h> hym was joye and wele,/ And in Arthurs tyme but sorow and woo;/ . . . / . . . Arthur lovyd noght but warynge / And . . ./ Ryght so he toke hys endynge' (2964–5; 2975–7), which brings to mind the biblical proverb: 'They have sown the wind, and they shall reap the whirlwind' (Hosea, 8:7).

It will be interesting to learn that, at this point in the progress of the story, Malory adds to his text one of the highly significant and very well known patriotic passages, which has no parallel in the poem:

> Lo, ye all Englishmen, see ye not what a mischief here was? For he that was the most king and noblest knight of the world, and most loved the fellowship of noble knights, and by him they all were upholden, and yet might not these Englishmen hold them content with him. Lo thus was the old custom and usages of this land, and men say that we of this land have not yet lost that custom. Alas! this is a great default of us Englishmen, for there may no thing us please no term.[12]

[12] *Malory: The Morte Darthur*, ed. D. S. Brewer, York Medieval Texts (London: Edward Arnold, 1968), p. 139.10–6. See also *The Tale of The Death of King Arthur*, ed. Eugène Vinaver (Oxford: Clarendon Press, 1955), note (on p. 117) to p. 64.12–30 and p. 65.1–2: '. . .

MODERNITY OF THE MIDDLE ENGLISH *LE MORTE ARTHUR*

In order for us to 'set the record straight' or 'to restore the balance', our poet voiced strong patriotic sentiments a century before Malory, at a time when the expression of such sentiments may have been rather unusual. When the Pope threatens that 'Ynglande entyrdyted shulde bene/ And torne to sorow for ther sake' (2268–9) in case Arthur does not conclude a peace treaty with Lancelot, the King does not want to oppose the Pope, for 'Wolde he noght that Ynglonde were shente ['ruined; disgraced']' (2273). When the English Bishop of Rochester, the Pope's emissary and negotiator, comes to see Lancelot in his residence at Joyous Gard, he repeats the same terms as mentioned above (2284–5). Thereupon he makes a strong emotional, patriotic appeal to Lancelot: 'Syr, lettes not Ynglande go to noght!' (2301). After his exile into 'a wyldernesse' (3025), the Archbishop of Canterbury-turned hermit, too, 'Often gan . . . wepe and wake/ For Yngland that had suche sorowis sare' (3032–3).

While one side of the 'coin' is filled with patriotism, the other side is, surprisingly, taken by xenophobia. When the royal council is debating who the 'beste steward . . ./ . . ./ . . . for Bretaynes sake' (2511–3) should be during Arthur's absence in France, they are aware of the importance of the matter, for 'mykelle they dred hem . . ./ That alyens the land wold take' (2514–5)! Have we not heard similar sentiments repeated recently?

This massive onslaught on people's minds and attitudes by the 'Mordred administration' could not fail to lead to serious moral consequences, for 'thus gan *ryght* to *wronge* goo' (2969; emphases mine). Indeed, after an absence from England of only about nine months,[13] Arthur discovers, to his dismay, as soon as he lands back at Dover, in his own kingdom, the unpleasant truth about the complete change of attitude towards him: 'Hys fele fo-men that he ther found,/ He wende byfore had bene hys frend' (3060–1). May we dare paraphrase: 'Fickleness, thy name is populace'?

When the war against Mordred seems to have begun somewhat to tilt in Arthur's favour, the pendulum of the initial public disfavour also begins to swing back into his favour, so much so that 'Unto hym came many a doughty knyght,/ For wyde in worlde theyse wordys sprange,/ That syr Arthur hade all the *ryght*,/ And Mordred warred on hym w<i>t<h> *wronge*' (3152–5; emphases mine).

As far as the King's character is concerned, the poem presents him as no Mordred-type of a willful 'Machiavellian' autocrat or tyrant at all. Arthur makes his important decisions in a surprisingly 'democratic'

---

the reference to popular discontent in M[alory] is clearly a reminiscence of contemporary events . . .' Also in Vinaver's *The Works of Sir Thomas Malory*, 3 vols., 2nd ed. (Oxford: Clarendon Press, 1967), note to pp. 1228.35–1229.18, and in my article 'Thomas Malory's Creed', *Studies in Language and Literature in Honor of Margaret Schlauch*, ed. M. Brahmer and S. Helsztynski, and J. Krzyzanowski (New York: Russell & Russell, 1971), pp. 437–44, esp. 440 ff.

13 See lines: 2762: half a year; 2858: two weeks; 2938: two months.

163

ARTHURIAN AND OTHER STUDIES

way, that is, first asking for, and taking, advice from, and in consultation with, others. The poem offers nine instances of this kind.[14]

Two points bear scrutiny. When his wife Guenevere is unjustly accused of poisoning a dinner guest, nobody, let alone her husband the King, the 'chief justice', cares to find out the truth about it. Without Lancelot's defeating Mador, she could have been burnt – innocent – at the stake! Ironically, the investigation starts only after the duel and the culprits are punished (1648–55; 1664–6).

After Agravain's disastrous attempt at Lancelot's entrapment, 'Kynge and all hys knyghtis . . ./ Toke there counselle' and decided that the Queen 'fo[r]brent shuld . . . bene' (1921–5). Malory, on the other hand, writes that the proofs of the bloody event were such as 'caused king Arthur to command the queen to the fire and there to be burnt.'[15]

Withdrawal from the Flesh to the Spirit – Resolution or *Dénouement*

The history, the achievements, and the outcome of 'the woeful tale of the most pitiable love of Lancelot and Guenevere' are assessed and summed up towards the end of the poem with a penetrating and most insightful confession by Guenevere. It is the more noteworthy when considering both the period of origin of the poem and the fact that this 'epilogue' or postscript is placed in the mouth of a woman, after Lancelot has found her as a nun in a convent:

> . . . throw thys ylke man [Lancelot] and me –/ For we togedyr han loved us dere –/ All thys sorowfull werre hathe be!/ My lord [Arthur] is slayne,. . ./ And many a doughty knyght . . . (3639–43).

Guenevere has correctly verbalised her realisation, although a belated

---

[14] See lines 29–32; 416; 1113–8; 1746–53; 1921–5; 2332; 2509–22; 2668; 3225.

[15] Brewer, *ibid.*, p. 110. See Vinaver's note to p. 17.9;20–2 on p. 102 of his *The Tale of The Death of King Arthur*: '. . . in *Le Morte Arthur* (1920–5), the Queen is sentenced to death by the barons, not by Arthur.' This is not borne out by the text of *Le Morte Arthur*. The same argument, with additional comments, is repeated in his three-volume edition, *The Works of Sir Thomas Malory* (1967), note to p. 1174.18;28–9: '. . . in *Le Morte Arthur* (1920–5), the Queen is sentenced to death by the barons, not by Arthur . . . The reason for the change is not that M[alory]'s Arthur is less humane, . . . but that M[alory]'s conception of kingship tends to transform a feudal overlord into a fifteenth-century monarch.' In the 1977 revised edition of *Malory: Works* (Oxford Standard Authors), Vinaver has a clearer formulation in the note to p. 682.10: '. . . in *Le Morte Arthur* (1920–5), the queen is sentenced to death by the barons, in Malory by Arthur: not because Malory's Arthur is less humane, but because Malory's conception of kingship includes prerogatives which would have been denied a feudal overlord.'

164

MODERNITY OF THE MIDDLE ENGLISH *LE MORTE ARTHUR*

one, after all the horrible devastation has been wrought – only 326 lines or 41 stanzas before the end – of a direct or cause-and-effect correlation between her illicit love affair with Lancelot and the resulting destructive wars of over one year's duration,[16] somewhat reminiscent of the causes and results of the ten-year-long Trojan war. There is, however, one significant difference to be noted. As the ancients believed, and our poet is no exception, one of the supposed survivors of the Trojan wars, Aeneas's great-grandson 'Br[u]t[us] owte of Troy [h]a[d] sought/ And made in Bretayne hys owne wo<n>ne ['dwelling']' (3376–7). This belief in the Brutus story led to the rise of the Arthurian literature. Although Arthur is 'dead' but believed by some to 'rise from the dead', this can be taken figuratively, as is seen in the enormous spread of Arthurian studies around the globe and as far afield as – Japan!

While not assigning to Lancelot any comparable declaration of such deep general truth as is pronounced by Guenevere just quoted, the poet seems to be favourably disposed towards her.[17] He presents her as intuitively cautious, as seen in her initial unease about Lancelot's visit to her room (69 ff.) and mainly, at the end, showing her on her own initiative and choice being greatly concerned to assume her personal responsibility for the salvation of her soul: 'My sowle hele I wyll' (3655). Guenevere's absolute espousal, at the end, of an ascetic life and of purely spiritual values is not unknown in real life, either. In 1556, at the age of fifty-six, Emperor Charles V, two years before his death, resigned the throne and retired to a Spanish convent. As to Lancelot, he only later, but then, although initially somewhat hesitantly, loyally follows Guenevere: 'The same desteny that yow is dyghte/ I will resseyve' (3687–8; also 3700).

Arthur, on the other hand, is not seen to undergo such positive spiritual metamorphosis or regeneration at all. After his mortal wounding by Mordred, Arthur is taken by his two surviving companions to a chapel where they pray that 'hys sowle . . ./ . . . lese not the blysse of hevyn' (3414–5). Arthur's last wish is concerned only with his body, that is, he asks to be taken to 'the vale of Aveloune/ . . . to hele me of my wounde' (3516–7). The mysterious ladies, who brought his dead body to the chapel of the Archbishop-hermit and buried it there, ask him to pray for the salvation of Arthur's soul (3544–7).

The very moving ending or finale or *dénouement* of the poem where the two principal 'culprits', Guenevere and Lancelot, in this order now, renounce all worldly pursuits, cannot but suggest the following

---

[16] To note 13 above, add line 2111: 'Seven-tene wokys and well mare' for the siege of Joyous Gard.

[17] The 'bysschope' tells Lancelot: 'Women ar frele ['frail'] of hyr entayle ['character, nature']' (2300), which sounds like Hamlet's: 'frailty, thy name is woman' (I. ii. 146). Several striking parallels between the two texts have been noticed.

165

conclusion. The poet wrote most probably for the 'entertainment' of his employers, the feudal aristocratic lords and ladies – this was not popular poetry, unlike the Robin Hood ballads. Had the love of Lancelot and Guenevere been considered acceptable as mere harmless 'entertainment', the poet would hardly have dared to present in such dark terms the tragic effects of the couple's illicit love as are leading to the destruction and ruin of the supposedly most ideal or idealized feudal aristocratic society imaginable, that of the Arthurian Round Table. At the same time, the poem also includes an implied but evident indictment and rejection of the dangerous and destructive practices engaged in under the umbrella of 'courtly love'.

On the other hand, however, in the same way as are one-sidedly slanted the adulterous liberties taken by Lancelot and Guenevere during their earlier pleasure-loving life: 'we in lykynge lyffed in fere ['together']'(3702), as is admitted by Lancelot, so are possibly one-sidedly slanted, too, their strict conclusions and the resulting radical decisions. In order to atone for their grave sins against themselves, society, and their religion, this one not previously paid heed to by them, they choose to give up completely, each separately this time, the uses – or, rather, the abuses – of this world and turn absolutely to a life of spiritual service, subjecting themselves to a thorough penance (3700; 3706). They hope thereby to cleanse their sin-and-guilt-ridden souls and thus achieve forgiveness, absolution, and finally eternal bliss in heaven (3660–1). Before their heart-rending final parting, they pledge to pray for each other (3670; 3692).

As to Lancelot, his admission to heaven is foreshadowed in the Archbishop-hermit's dream: '. . . angellis . . ./ Hym . . . bare upon hye' (3877–8). As if to make absolutely sure of this to happen, Lancelot's brother Ector and the other hermits pray to God: 'Brynge thys sowle unto Thy trone' (3944). Who would not immediately be reminded of Horatio's memorable words pronounced in the moment of Hamlet's death: '. . . flights of angels sing thee to thy rest' (V. ii. 361)? It is in similar terms that Gawain's admission to heaven has been adumbrated, too, this time in an earlier dream of Arthur's before a battle with Mordred. In it Gawain appears surrounded with a lot of people: 'All semyd angellys cam from hevyn' (3199).

As has been observed several times, the poet has endowed Guenevere with the admirable quality and ability of deep insights not only into her own detrimental role in her society but also as to the dangerous direction of society's development at large. As a clear-sighted and privileged member of the inner ruling circle, but not at all protected by those privileges *ad infinitum*, having come twice under the threat of a terrible death by being burnt at the stake (943; 1925), she has reached an utterly pessimistic outlook on life, thus anticipating modern-day existentialism by six centuries. She tells Lancelot: 'Thynke on thys world, how there is noght/ But warre and stryffe and batayle sore' (3720–1). Again, who would not hear this deep pronouncement echoed in dying Hamlet's reminder to Horatio about 'this harsh world' (V. ii. 349)? Guenevere's counsel for Lancelot to 'kepe thy reme from werre and wrake' (3666) is, no doubt, an admirable piece of advice for a ruler who should be concerned about the well-being of his country. If a privileged but troubled queen has found worldly life not worth living, it should come as no surprise that all the surviving rank-and-file knights, Bedwere (3565), Bors (3830 ff.), and Ector (3950) have joined the 'chief' hermit (3031), the previous Archbishop of Canterbury exiled ('flemyd', 3560) by the autocratic Mordred. The highest churchman in the land has himself decided that 'The worldys wele ther he wyll forsake' (3026). In fact, the poem speaks of 'ermytes sevyn' (3963) remaining at the end.

Nevertheless, in order not only for an individual person but also mankind at large to be able to get on between these extremes, it is necessary to proceed along Aristotle's and John Henry Newman's *via media*. The poem does not, however, advance any such suggestion, except, perhaps, in Lancelot's highly commendable principle put into practice by him whenever the situation under difficult conditions of his life has permitted, that is, 'myldenesse' (2602), which amounts to as much as 'moderation' and 'avoiding extremes'.

Unlike the endings of Shakespeare's tragedies, the poem is brought to a conclusion with no prospect or hope for a better life here on earth suggested or intimated. This is a most appropriate place to give the last word to Sir Thomas Malory. This will make clear the justifiably high credit which he deserves for his unique achievement and contribution to the development and maturing of the Arthurian story. It is generally recognised that in Tale VIII, which is the concluding part of his memorable volume, *Le Morte Darthur*, he follows closely our poem, except the very end, where he has added a highly significant and weighty conclusion. After the burial of Lancelot,

sir Constantine . . . was chosen king of England, and . . . worshipfully he ruled this royame. And then this king Constantine sent for the Bishop of Canterbury . . . And so he was restored unto his bishopric and left that hermitage.[18]

There is no undue need to point out our relief from the pervasive pessimism of the poem. Malory's positive, forward-looking conclusion restores the shaken balance and holds out a promise that truth and justice can prevail.

---

[18] Brewer, *ibid.*, p. 157. See Vinaver's note (on p. 134) to p. 94.29–31, in *The Tale of The Death of King Arthur* (1955): 'Probably a reminiscence of the alliterative *Morte Arthure*, l. 4316: "Constantyn . . . sall the corown bere." '

ARTHURIAN AND OTHER STUDIES

In Larry D. Benson's apt words, 'Malory is . . . intent upon emphasizing for his readers that the history of the Round Table does not end in despair.'[19] Shakespeare, too, has firmly embedded this salutary humanistic message in the endings of his tragedies.

All in all, however, I cannot but wholeheartedly concur with L. D. Benson's assessment placing the stanzaic romance *Le Morte Arthur* 'among the finest of our English medieval narrative poems' and valuing it as 'a brilliant' and 'first rate' work of art deserving serious attention.[20]

[19] Benson, *Malory's Morte Darthur* (Cambridge: Harvard University Press, 1976), p. 247.

[20] *King Arthur's Death: The Middle English Stanzaic Morte Arthur and Alliterative Morte Arthure*, ed. L. D. Benson (Indianapolis: Bobbs-Merril, 1974), pp. xi and xv.

The Structure and Tone of the Stanzaic *Morte Arthur*

TADAHIRO IKEGAMI

It is generally acknowledged that a very close relationship exists between the Stanzaic *Morte Arthur (SMA)* and *La Mort le Roi Artu (MA)* and also that the *MA* is the most probable source of the *SMA*.[1] By comparing the structure and tone of the *SMA* and the *MA*, I try in this paper to indicate the leading characteristics of the *SMA*. These characteristics themselves are shared by other Middle English romances.

The Old French *MA* makes use of *entrelacement* in its development of the lengthy narrative which it relates. As Jean Frappier explains, entrelacement is a kind of parallelism of a double or triple action,[2] in which 'every episode is interrupted by another which is broken off in order to continue the earlier narrative.'[3] The events are thus interwoven or knit together. The stories of Lancelot and of King Arthur are alternately told, and then afterwards the stories of Mordred and of Queen Guenevere are added. The *SMA* poet is a conscious composer, who writes in the minstrel style, and uses as his poetic form rhyming stanzas of eight four-stressed lines. This gives the romance a steady, detached form which is well-balanced with the lyrical mode. He concerns himself with the structure of the plot, drastically cutting the interlacing plot of the huge French prose narrative and dividing it into two self-contained parts, which will be discussed later. At the same time, he summarises the

---

[1] *Le Morte Arthur*, ed. J. Douglas Bruce, E.E.T.S., e.s. 88 (London: Oxford University Press, 1903; rpt. 1930), pp. xiii–xx. Robert H. Wilson, 'Malory, the Stanzaic *Morte Arthur*, and the *Morte Artu*', *Modern Philology*, 37 (1939–40), 125–38. E. Talbot Donaldson, 'Malory and the Stanzaic *Le Morte Arthur*', *Studies in Philology*, 47 (1950), 460–72. *Malory's Originality*, ed. Robert M. Lumiansky (Baltimore: The Johns Hopkins Univ. Press, 1964), pp. 205–32 and 233–74. Eugène Vinaver, ed., and P. J. C. Field, rev., *The Works of Sir Thomas Malory*, 3 vols., 3rd edition (Oxford: Clarendon Press, 1990), Vol. III, pp. 1585–94 and 1615–26. References to the stanzaic *Morte Arthur* in this paper are taken from *Le Morte Arthur: A Critical Edition*, ed. Paul F. Hissiger (The Hague: Mouton, 1975).

[2] *La Mort le Roi Artu*, ed. Jean Frappier (Geneva: Librairie Droz, 1954), pp. xiii–xiv. About 50 manuscripts of the *Mort Artu*, complete and fragmentary, are extant.

[3] Jean Frappier, 'The Vulgate Cycle', *Arthurian Literature in the Middle Ages*, ed. Roger Sherman Loomis (Oxford: Clarendon Press, 1959), pp. 298–9. E. Vinaver, *The Rise of Romance* (Oxford: Clarendon Press, 1971), pp. 68–98.

French source and uses reciprocally extended scenes.[4] The French story is now changed into an English four-thousand-line poem, with a simple and straightforward narrative with a clear chain of causes and effects. The date of composition of this English version is generally considered to be late fourteenth century.

I

First of all, I will examine what is omitted from the French source and how the original work is transformed into a Middle English romance. The English poet omits the following nine main episodes or events in the *MA*.

1. Morgan's castle (48–54)[5]

King Arthur visits his sister Morgan's castle and sees the murals that Lancelot had painted when he was a prisoner there long before. The sight of the paintings, which depict the story of Lancelot's guilty passion for the queen, rekindles Arthur's suspicions. Morgan urges him to avenge his shame and dishonour. The English poet omitted this part altogether, with the result that he condensed and simplified the story, strengthened the depiction of the triangle of Arthur, Guenevere and Lancelot, and weakened the representation of King Arthur among his knights and of the sin of the lovers.

2. Detailed court proceedings (66–9)

King Arthur requests Mador de la Porte, brother to the victim in the Poisoned Fruit episode, to grant him justice concerning the queen, who has been falsely accused of murdering his brother, Gaheris de Karahen. The name of the criminal – a knight called Avarlan who mortally hated Sir Gawain – is given and the reason why he committed such a crime is explained but the punishment for murder is not mentioned. In the *SMA*, however, he is executed.

3. Gawain's genuine grief and the burial of Gaheriet (99–102)

Gaheriet, Gawain's brother, is Arthur's favourite nephew and also one of the knights whom Lancelot most loves. His dead body is placed in St. Stephen's Cathedral next to his two brothers, Guerrehet and Agravain.

---

[4] Dieter Mehl, *The Middle English Romances of the Thirteenth and Fourteenth Centuries* (London: Routledge and Kegan Paul, 1969), p. 186.

[5] References to *La Mort le Roi Artu* here are taken from Jean Frappier's edition (Geneva, 1954). The numbers in parentheses indicate the section numbers shown in the French text. *The Death of King Arthur*, trans. James Cable (Harmondsworth: Penguin Books, 1971). This translation is based on Frappier's edition, and very good and useful. For the structure of the *Mort Artu*, see Jean Frappier, *Étude sur la Mort le Roi Artu* (Geneva: Librairie Droz, 1972), pp. 347–71.

THE STRUCTURE AND TONE OF THE STANZAIC *MORTE ARTHUR*

The king commands Gaheriet to guard the field where the fire has been lit. Gaheriet is unwittingly killed by Lancelot. Gawain's attitude towards Lancelot suddenly changes at this time and we notice that his character lacks measure and that he is self-important, self-willed and obstinate, so that even King Arthur is obliged to yield to his opinions.

4. The council of war against Lancelot (107–10)

King Arthur summons his men to Camelot to take counsel with them before the appointment of new members of the Round Table, and the next morning they leave there to attack Lancelot in the Joyeuse Garde. Other battle scenes are also minutely depicted.

5. Lancelot's shield (120–1)

After Lancelot brings the queen back to King Arthur, he calls a squire called Kanahin and commands him to carry his shield to St. Stephen's Cathedral and to leave it in a place where it can remain and be seen. Then he gives four pack horses loaded with riches to the church, a detail which the English poet uses later in a different way (3542 ff.).

6. Mordred's treachery in the kingdom of Logres (134–43)

King Arthur entrusts the queen and the land to Mordred and also entrusts him with the keys of all his treasures. Mordred plans a great act of treason, and the queen, fearing it, secretly enters the Tower of London and remains there. Mordred attacks fiercely, and she sends a messenger to Lancelot. The English poet provided an abridged version of this story later in ll. 2944 ff.

7. Main characters' ages (158)

Arthurian characters' ages are rarely mentioned and they seem to be ageless. When the battle of Ganues is told the main characters' ages are described: King Arthur is ninety-two years old, Sir Gawain seventy-six, and Lancelot is younger than Gawain by about twenty-one years, that is, he is about fifty-five. Queen Guenevere is at least fifty years old and a very beautiful lady (4).

8. The Romans' intrusion into King Arthur's territory (160–1)

While King Arthur invades Lancelot's Ganues, the Romans enter his territory and meet him with his men between Champagne and Burgundy. He kills the emperor and the men of Logres defeat them when the messenger sent by Queen Guenevere, with the news about Mordred, arrives before King Arthur.

Here the English poet makes alterations to Gawain's final actions. Three times Sir Gawain seeks combat with Lancelot, and actually fights twice but finally dies at the battle of Dover. His body is buried at Dover Castle in the *SMA*, whereas in the *MA* (158, 160–1, 163–75) Gawain fights against Lancelot only once, receives a deep wound to his head, and dies at Dover Castle, requesting the king to have his body carried to Camelot and placed in Gaheriet's tomb there.

171

9. Mordred's two sons (195–8)

Mordred leaves his two sons at Winchester to guard the city. After Lancelot hears the news of the death of the queen, he rides on with his company and attacks the men of Winchester, destroying them including Mordred's two sons.

Besides the problem of these omissions mentioned above, I will examine some interesting additions or alterations made by the poet.

A. Negotiations take place in the battle of Salisbury Plain (178–80)

After supper King Arthur rides onto the plain with the archbishop, who advises him not to fight Mordred but to turn back to Dover. Arthur rejects his advice, and says that he will never leave until God has granted victory to him or to Mordred. When he comes back to his tent, a boy conveys a message from Mordred and the battle is decided.

In the *SMA* (3340 ff.), after King Arthur's two dreams he sends bishops and barons to Mordred and negotiations take place, but unfortunately an adder glides forth on the ground and stings a knight, who draws a sword to kill it. Arthur's army see the drawn sword and a mortal battle begins. This episode will remind us of King Arthur's outburst, which reveals Mordred's illegitimate birth in front of many barons (164):

<< Ha! Mordret, or me fez tu connoistre que tu ies li serpenz que ge vi jadis eissir de mon ventre, qui ma terre ardoit et se prenoit a moi. . . .>>

B. The death of Arthur (191–3)

After he kills his son Mordred, the mortally wounded King Arthur comes to the Black Chapel where he spends the whole night in prayer. He takes Lucan the Butler, who is unarmed, and embraces him, holding him so tightly that his heart bursts and he dies. The dying Arthur and his knight Girflet ride to the shore, and he orders Girflet to throw his sword Excalibur into the lake on the hill. The command is given three times and Girflet fondly performs it; then the king asks him to leave him. As soon as he has left him, a heavy rain falls. When he has reached the hill, he takes cover under a tree there, looks back to where he has left the king and sees a ship, occupied by women, across the sea. He rides back very fast and arrives at the shore, where he sees the king among a group of ladies and recognises Morgan la fee. In a short time the ship leaves. The French text mentions nothing of King Arthur's going to Avalon to be healed of his wound (3515–7). Sir Bedwere, King Arthur's knight, plays the same part as Girflet in the *MA*, and finds a hermit before a newly-built tomb of the king and lives there with him (3520 ff.). In the *SMA*, too, Arthur's tomb is in a chapel, which later we recognise as Glastonbury Abbey when the story comes to deal with the death of Queen Gaynor (Guenevere)(3598–661).

THE STRUCTURE AND TONE OF THE STANZAIC *MORTE ARTHUR*

C. Lancelot's last meeting with the queen[6]

This is one of the most moving episodes in the *SMA* (3614–737), which may have been preserved in a lost French text. The *MA* tells of the queen fleeing into an abbey of nuns to stay there with them (169–70), of her taking a nun's habit when she hears that Mordred's sons have seized the country (195), and of her death, which Lancelot hears of before marching towards Winchester (197). The *MA* author, however, does not tell us that Lancelot finally happens to meet the queen at a convent in Amesbury and takes farewell of her for ever. When she sees him the queen confesses:

> Abbess, to you I knowlache here
> That throw thys ylke man and me,
> For we togedyr han loved us dere,
> All thys sorowfull werre hathe be.   (3638–41)

II

The Stanzaic *Morte Arthur* consists of two separate episodes of Lancelot's career, which are closely woven into one long, linear narrative without any digression. This poet apparently prefers action to description and lets characters and events speak for themselves.[7] As R. W. Ackerman observes,[8] one episode is the hero's entanglement with the Maid of Ascalot at the Winchester tournament and his rescue of the queen when she is falsely accused of the poisoning of a Scottish knight; the other is the discovery of the adultery of Lancelot and Gaynor and its tragic sequel – the siege of Benwick and the death of Arthur and his knights; and then the lovers' interview and separation and their penitential life and death. Here I propose that the poem is divided into two parts, each of which is again subdivided into three sections. Part One has

---

6   Jean Frappier suggests in *Arthurian Literature in the Middle Ages*, ed. R. S. Loomis (Oxford: Clarendon Press, 1959), p. 312, note 1, that MS. Palatinus Latinus 1967 (Rome, Biblioteca Apostolica Vaticana) tells of a last interview between Lancelot and the queen after she has become a nun; but it is a fragment and probably a different version from ours. See *Works*, Vol. III, pp. 1657–8, note to 1252.8–1253.27. John Beston and Rose Marie Beston, 'The Parting of Lancelot and Guinevere in the Stanzaic "Le Morte Arthur" ', *Journal of the Australasian Universities Language and Literature Association*, 40 (1973), 249–59. Sharon L. Jansen Jaech, 'The Parting of Lancelot and Gaynor: The Effect of Repetition in the Stanzaic *Morte Arthur*', *Interpretations*, 15:2 (1984), 59–69.

7   *Five Middle English Arthurian Romances*, trans. Valerie Krishna (New York: Garland, 1991), p. 8. *King Arthur's Death*, ed. Larry D. Benson (Indianapolis and New York: The Bobbs-Merrill Company, 1974), pp. xvi–xviii.

8   See his 'English Rimed and Prose Romances', in *Arthurian Literature*, ed. R. S. Loomis , *op. cit.*, pp. 489–91.

173

three sections: (1) 1–831, (2) 832–1418,[9] and (3) 1419–1671, and Part Two also has three sections: (1) 1672–2499, (2) 2500–3565, and (3) 3566–3969.[10]

The story begins with the tournament at Winchester and Agrawayn's suspicion of the love between Lancelot and Gaynor and ends in the deaths of the lovers. In the first half of the story the two main episodes of 'the Maid of Ascalot' and 'the Poisoned Apple' are interwoven in three sections, which lead to a judicial combat between Lancelot and Mador, and fortunately end with a defence against outside pressures and a restoration of public order, although the familial fellowship of the knights is moving towards ruin. In the longer second half, Agrawayn's resolution to warn King Arthur about Lancelot and Gaynor, and the discovery of their affair, give rise to a fatal opposition between Lancelot and both Arthur and Gawain, to Arthur's forces attacking Benwick, to Mordred's treachery, the death of Gawain, the confrontation of Arthur with Mordred, and the death of Arthur, followed by the religious life and death of Lancelot and Gaynor, both of whom, uninvolved in the war, survive.

There is a chain of causes and effects, and the story remains steady. Events occur very quickly and we see the gradual destruction of the fellowship of King Arthur and his knights. This catastrophe originates in human relations in society. As Vinaver remarks,[11] this human drama is determined by the clash of personalities between Lancelot and Gawain, Lancelot and Gaynor, and Lancelot and Arthur. Obviously Lancelot is confronted with difficult, divided loyalties, one represented by Lancelot's faithfulness to Gaynor, and the other by his fidelity to Arthur and Gawain, and he cannot solve this conflict until the end of the story.

Arthur is the principal focus of his knights: they gather around him, come back and go away. Lancelot is the perfect hero and lover, and the most powerful knight of the Round Table. He is the central figure of this romance; his presence, however, presents a potential internal threat to Arthur's court, although he is the ideal terrestrial knight. His thought and behaviour are based upon a courtly and chivalrous code. He acts as a 'strange' knight or incognito in the first half. He never wants to fight against Arthur, who has made him a knight. He sends a maiden as a messenger twice to make peace with Arthur, although everyone on his side desires war. There follows a very moving and pathetic scene during the war (115–6; 2166–205). Arthur draws near Lancelot and hits him with

---

[9] In this section, a leaf of the manuscript is missing after folio 102: ll. 1182–317.

[10] The Stanzaic *Morte Arthur* is preserved in an early sixteenth-century commonplace-book: London, British Library, MS. Harley 2252, folios 86–133ᵛ. The structural divisions I suggest here are supported by my examination of the manuscript. I find 15 section marks or vacant spaces left for the large initial letters on it: ll. 1, 424, 832, 952, 1048, 1096, 1419, 1632, 1672,1864, 1966, 2046, 2246, 2396, and 2500; but I do not find any space at all from l. 2500 to the end.

[11] See his *Works*, Vol. III, p. 1621, and Dieter Mehl, *op. cit.*, pp. 186–93.

THE STRUCTURE AND TONE OF THE STANZAIC *MORTE ARTHUR*

all his might, but Lancelot will not strike a blow in return; Bors hits Arthur's helmet and knocks him down to the ground, then urges him fiercely to strike Arthur, but instead he gets off his horse, helps Arthur to mount and asks him to go away.[12] The stanza describing the scene reads:

> "Allas," quod Launcelot, "wo is me
> That evyr shulde I se with syghte
> Byfore me hym unhorsyd bee,
> The noble kynge that made me knyght."
> He was than so corteise and fre,
> That downe of hys stede he lyghte;
> The kynge theron than horsys he,
> And bade hym fle yiffe that he myght.   (2190–7)

The poet weakens Arthur's importance as a symbol of chivalry, nobility and justice and instead intensifies the contrast and opposition between Lancelot and Gawain, who are essentially close friends. Lancelot is kind, courteous, and faithful to his lover, although his loyalty to Arthur may be considered to be defective in this respect, while the implicit duality of Gawain's character, excellent yet destructive, and his negative aspects, are made full use of in the second half. Gawain becomes Lancelot's fiercest enemy after his brothers Gaheriet and Gaheries, who are unarmed, are killed when Lancelot rescues Queen Gaynor. The names of 'Gaheriet and Gaheries' are used like a set phrase (1722, 1931, 1940, 1962). Gaheriet is less emphasised than in the *MA*, but he is shown as clearly as in the *MA*, when Gawain learns the news of the death of his beloved brother (1979, 1987, 1992). The good Gawain is immoderate in all things and becomes so self-willed, obstinate and intransigent that he becomes driven by an unreasonable desire for revenge upon Lancelot. He asks for combat with him three times even though he is wounded each time. Finally, before giving full play to his abilities, he dies in the field at Dover. His implacable quest for revenge is an old blood-feud and a destructive pursuit of earthly justice, which causes a public feud and makes friend fight against friend. Arthur's knights form a kind of large family. The development of internal pressures constitutes a very serious problem and will invite the collapse of Arthurian society itself.

The romance is mainly the story of Lancelot and Gaynor, but there is much of warfare in the background. Relations between men and women in such tales are treated romantically:

> Whan he come to the lady shene,
> He kissid and clypped that swete wyght;
> For sothe they nevyr wolde wene

---

[12] D. Mehl, *op. cit.*, p. 192.

ARTHURIAN AND OTHER STUDIES

That any treson was ther dyght.
So mykylle love was hem bytwene
That they noght departe myght;
To bede he gothe with the quene
And there he thoughte to dwelle alle nyght.   (1800–7)

The description in the *MA* is more realistic:

Si se deschauça et despoilla et se coucha avec la reïne. (90)

The passionate Maid of Ascalot is treated with an air of detachment, which reflects the feelings of the poet and of Lancelot.[13] He answers her coldly in the complicated conditions of the suspicions of Arthur, the jealousy of Gaynor, the misunderstanding of Gawain and his own devotion to the queen:[14]

"Lady," he sayd, "thou moste lette,
For me ne giff the nothynge ille.
In another stede myne hert is sette;
It is not at myne owne wille."   (201–4)

In contrast to these private cases, the human relations among the group of knights are given a more active and realistic treatment and give rise to more serious social problems. The poet makes a moral comment on men and war at the siege of the Joyus Garde:

He that byganne thys wrecchyd playe,
What wondyr thoughe he had grete synne.   (2212–3)

Although Lancelot and Gaynor are responsible for the destruction of Arthurian society, their affair constitutes a smaller and rather unimportant factor, and the much stronger human factor overwhelms it. Ironically, Lancelot comes to England again after the fatal war has ended. King Arthur and Gawain have died. Lancelot finally gives up worldly knighthood altogether, becomes a hermit, and, falling ill, dies after seven years of penitential life. Queen Gaynor also follows the same pattern, which suggests the final end of her terrestrial life.[15]

---

[13] George Kane, *Middle English Literature* (London: Methuen, 1951), pp. 65–9.

[14] D. Mehl, *op. cit.*, p. 190. Pamela Gradon, *Form and Style in Early English Literature* (London: Methuen, 1971), pp. 146–9.

[15] Richard A. Wertime, 'The Theme and Structure of the Stanzaic *Morte Arthur*', *P.M.L.A.*, 87 (1972), 1075–82. Velma B. Richmond, *The Popularity of Middle English Romance* (Bowling Green University Popular Press, 1975), pp. 129–42. Sherron E. Knopp, 'Artistic Design in the *Stanzaic Morte Arthur*', *E.L.H.*, 45 (1978), 563–81. *Medieval English Romance*, Part II, ed. A. V. C. Schmidt and N. Jacobs (London: Hodder and Stoughton, 1980), pp. 20–8. Lee C. Ramsey, *Chivalric Romances* (Bloomington: Indiana University Press, 1983), pp. 127–31. Peter Korrel, *An Arthurian Triangle* (Leiden: E.J.Brill, 1984), pp. 225–45. W. R. J. Barron, *English Medieval Romance* (London: Longmans, 1987), pp. 142–7.

THE STRUCTURE AND TONE OF THE STANZAIC *MORTE ARTHUR*

The audience was much concerned with morality and sought works of historical and moral worth at that time.[16] Using the traditional materials, the poet deals with serious social themes,[17] which may have faithfully reflected the Hundred Years' War. He rearranges the story of the French text, greatly abridges its plot, but as a whole follows it. This is a simple, straightforward and well-designed romance, built on links between the various scenes and on monologues and dialogues in the stanza form. We respond to the rather lyrical elegy on the fall of the knights of the Round Table inherent in the narrative, which is caused by human weaknesses, and see that the natural course of mortal human events depends upon individual choices and decisions, which have a strong influence on the community. The poem adheres to the European tradition, but is distinct from it, and establishes itself as an English Arthurian popular romance.

---

[16] Felicity Riddy, *Sir Thomas Malory* (Leiden: E.J.Brill, 1987), p. 8.
[17] Pamela Gradon, *op. cit.*, pp. 260–5.

De Worde's Displacement of Malory's Secularization

TSUYOSHI MUKAI

William Caxton's series of books on chivalry, *Godefrey of Boloyne* (1481), *The Book of the Ordre of Chyualry* (1484), *Le Morte Darthur* (1485), and *Charles the Great* (1485) were published to evoke in knightly readers 'the need', as J. R. Goodman puts it, 'for a reformation of English knighthood and the attractions of a crusade against the Turks'.[1] Set against the companion books, however, Malory's *Morte* seems to give a unique presentation of knighthood, and, of all four works, Malory's alone needed reprinting and has kept its readership up to the present. Presumably Malory's chivalric view contributes not a little to the lasting popularity of his Arthurian stories, but the reception of his chivalric view varies from printer to printer of early editions. How far, then, was Malory's view of knighthood deviated from the traditional one? In this essay, I shall first discuss the Malorian conception of knighthood and then, limiting myself to Wynkyn de Worde, examine the editor-printer's attitude towards the conception through his editorial work.

The *Ordre* regards knighthood as a combination of religion, war and gallantry, and states that the knights are chosen to fulfil these divinely-established duties: to maintain and enhance the holy faith, to defend one's lord, to maintain justice and work for the common profit, and to protect the weak or the helpless.[2] The conception of knighthood specified here stands as a precept by which the companion works by Caxton can be measured. The *Godefrey* and the *Charles the Great*, all of which deal with the chivalry of a crusade, harmonise with the strongly religious view of knighthood. But the *Morte* is somewhat discordant.

Malory admittedly shares with the chivalric manual of his time not a few conceptions, conceptions which are derived from the same tradition: that noble birth is requisite to knighthood;[3] that worship and honour are most easily won among perils;[4] and that loyalty is to be directed to one's

---

[1] See her 'Malory and Caxton's Chivalric Series, 1481–1485', *Studies in Malory*, ed. J. W. Spisak (Michigan: Western Michigan University, 1985), p. 266.

[2] For each knightly duty, see *The Book of the Ordre of Chyualry*, ed. A. T. P. Byles, E.E.T.S., o.s. 168 (London: Oxford University Press, 1926), pp. 24–5, 29, 30, and 38.

[3] See *Ordre*, p. 57.10–6, and Malory's *Tale of Gareth*.

[4] See *Ordre*, pp. 37 and 62, and Malory's description of knights who win worship by siding with the losing party in tournaments. Cf. Dinadan's antichivalric realism.

ARTHURIAN AND OTHER STUDIES

natural lord rather than to the King or the Crown.[5] But the oath which the knights of the Round Table swear annually during Pentecost reveals a breach from these shared conceptions. After giving riches and lands, King Arthur commands the knights:

> never to do outerage nothir mourthir, and allwayes to fle treson, and to gyff mercy unto hym that askith mercy, uppon payne of forfiture [of their] worship and lordship of kynge Arthure for evirmore; and allwayes to do ladyes, damesels, and jantilwomen and wydowes [socour:] strengthe hem in hir ryghtes, and never to enforce them, uppon payne of dethe. Also, that no man take no batayles in a wrongefull quarell for no love ne for no worldis goodis.[6]

E. Vinaver suggests that there is a similarity between the *Ordre* and the *Morte* in their didactic way of enumerating knightly obligations.[7] But the duties prescribed here are exclusively in terms of war and gallantry, and religious virtues are excluded from consideration.

Hardyng's *Chronicle* is also suggested by E. D. Kennedy as directly inspiring Malory's formulation of the knightly ideals.[8] The knights of the Round Table in the *Chronicle* are expected to maintain justice by arms, to defend the church, to protect the weak, and to maintain the common profit:

> . . . theyr rule was wronges to oppresse
> With their bodyes, where lawe myght not redresse,
>   The fayth, ye church, maydens, & widowes clene,
> Chyldren also that were in tender age,
> The cōmon profyte euer more to sustene.[9]

As in the case of the *Ordre*, faith in God and service to the church are emphasised as part of knightly office, and yet Malory here again does not respond to this aspect of chivalry offered in his immediate source.[10]

---

[5] See *Ordre*, p. 29.9–13, and Malory's retelling of Gareth's and Gaheris's loyalty to Lancelot rather than to Arthur at Guenevere's execution.

[6] *The Works of Sir Thomas Malory*, 3 vols., ed. E. Vinaver, 3rd ed., rev. P. J. C. Field (Oxford: Clarendon Press, 1990), p. 120.17–24.

[7] *Works*, p. 1335 (note to p. 120.11–28). Vinaver suggests that Malory's conception of chivalry here corresponds to Caxton's in the preface to the *Ordre of Chyualry*. Caxton recapitulates Arthurian chivalry as 'manhode, curtosye and gentylnesse'. These are, as we saw at the outset of this essay, essentially the same as those virtues recommended in the Pentecost oath, virtues which are, as L. Benson says, 'the basic virtues of knighthood, not very different from those proclaimed at the council of Clermont as a guide for the first crusaders, though now there is less emphasis on service to the church and more on the social virtues necessary to the maintenance of the "common good" ' (*Malory's Morte Darthur* (Cambridge: Harvard University Press, 1976), p. 149).

[8] E. D. Kennedy, 'Malory's Use of Hardyng's *Chronicle*', *Notes & Queries*, 214 (1969), 167–70.

[9] *The Chronicle of Iohn Hardyng*, ed. H. Ellis (London: Longman, 1812; rpt. New York: AMS Press, 1974), p. 124.

[10] B. Kennedy also points out that the 'omission of the Round Table knights' obligation to

180

Hardyng's *Chronicle* even contains a romantic, courtly definition of knighthood: a knight could be regarded as honourable if he were 'beloued as paramoure' by ladies (which 'caused knightes armes to exercyse').[11] This element of 'courtly love' is quite foreign to the priestly tone of the *Ordre*, the author of which had turned from courtier to apostle, and, now regretful for his youthful follies, avoids any reference to this romantic element in writing the work in question.[12] It might be that, in the above-mentioned annual oath, Malory is also alluding to the negative aspect of courtly love by saying that 'no man' should take 'no batayles in a wrongefull quarell for no love'. Malory, however, relates to us a number of episodes positively emphasising, as does the *Chronicle* to a lesser degree, a lady's love as a powerful source for eliciting feats of valour.[13] And yet Malory definitely rejects this aspect of love, love for 'paramours' (in the words of Lancelot): 'in prencipall for drede of God, for knyghtes that bene adventures sholde nat be advoutrers nothir lecherous'.[14] Lancelot initially offers a religious reason for refusing the love of paramours, but we should hear the logic of his reasoning. Lancelot, then, goes on to say:

for than they be nat happy nother fortunate unto the werrys; for . . . they shall be overcom with a sympler knyght than they be hemself, . . .[15]

Lancelot's logic is: to be adulterous, to be lecherous, is to be not happy, not fortunate, because such a lecherous knight 'shall be' defeated by a less brave knight. Lancelot seems to be shifting emphasis onto the resultant proposition and reversing the logic: he fears God because he 'shall be' beaten by a simpler knight; pragmatic reasons are thus strongly combined with religious reasons. Unlike Hardyng's *Chronicle*, the *Morte* is apparently in the same line as the *Ordre* as far as courtly love for ladies is concerned. But actually the *Morte* is subtly and decisively different from the chivalric manual by Ramon Lull – who renounces this kind of love as sinful on principle, while Malory avoids it on pragmatic, militaristic grounds.

---

sustain the Christian faith and the church was deliberate' (*Knighthood in the Morte Darthur* (Cambridge: D. S. Brewer, 1985), p. 67).

[11] *Chronicle*, p. 130.

[12] See 'Introduction' to the *Ordre of Chyualry*, p. xxxvii, and A. T. P. Byles, 'Medieval Courtesy Books and the Prose Romances of Chivalry', *Chivalry*, ed. E. Prestage (London: Knopf, 1928; rpt. New York: AMS Press, 1974), p. 189.

[13] One such example is Tristram's pronouncement, 'a knyght may never be of proues but yf he be a lovear' (*Works*, p. 689.5–6), and his actual valorous action at the critical moment when he fears he will never be able to see La Belle Isoud again (*Works*, p. 625.27–9). Equally relevant are King Arthur's words to Guenevere: 'Madame, . . . Ye shall cause me to be the more hardy, what adventure so befalle me' (*Works*, p. 127.16–8).

[14] *Works*, p. 270.33–5.

[15] *Works*, p. 270.35–7.

ARTHURIAN AND OTHER STUDIES

Malory's secular inclination in his view of knighthood becomes more obvious when the knightly observances are compared with what is, in the actual dubbing ceremony, prescribed to the knights of the Bath.[16] The extant description of the accolade runs:

> Lo, this is the ordre. Be ye stronge in the feith of Holy Cherche, and wydows and maydones oppressed releve as right commaundith. Yeve ye to everych his owne with all thy mynde above all thynge. Love and drede God. And above all other erthly thinges love the Kynge thy soverayn lord, hym and his defende unto thy powere. And be fore all worldly thynges putte hym in worshipp and thynges that be not to be taken beware to begynne.[17]

While a modern, nationalistic idea of loyalty is presented, the religious view of knighthood is taken over and acted out here in a more enforced form. In view of the common idea that the English chivalric institutions like this were regarded 'as the almost lineal descendant of Arthur's order',[18] Malory's enacting of statutes for the late 15th century 'hyghe Ordre of Knyghthode' stands out for its worldliness.

Caxton, in 1489, published another manual on knighthood, *The Book of Fayttes of Armes and of Chyualrye*, which, unlike the ethical manual *Ordre* (1484), was more or less a practical and utilitarian handbook on military affairs issued for a wider audience.[19] What attracts attention here is that, although, or, rather, because the handbook mainly treats soldiery, the author rounds it off by extending the discussion as far as the problem of the salvation of the soul. Christine de Pisan, deviating from Vegetius and depending upon Bonet, shows warriors both a direct way and an indirect way to heaven: first, 'the knyght or the man of armes/ that deyeth in the werre ayenst them of euyl byleue/ for thenhaunsing of the feyth of Ihesu Criste . . . goeth strayghte as a martyr vnto heuen'; secondly, 'yf a man of werre deyeth in a bataylle grownded vpon a iuste and gode quarelle/ for to help the ryght/ or that hit be for the true deffense of the lande/ or for the comonwele/ or for to kepe the fraunches and good customes of the place or countrey . . . he goeth right forthe in to paradyse

---

[16] As for the Order of the Bath, W. Segar writes: 'At the coronation of a King or Queen there are made Knights of the Bath, with long and curious Ceremonies, whereof I am not perfectly enformed' (*The Booke of Honor and Armes (1590) and Honor Military and Civil (1602)*, Facsimile Reproductions, (New York: Scholars' Facsimiles & Reprints, 1975), p. 22).

[17] *Three Fifteenth-Century Chronicles with Historical Memoranda by John Stowe*, ed. J. Gairdner, Camden Society, n.s. 28 (Westminster: J. B. Nichols and Sons, 1880), p. 113.

[18] M. Keen, *Chivalry* (New Haven: Yale University Press, 1984), p. 191.

[19] The *Ordre of Chyualry* is aimed for the noble gentlemen, whereas the *Fayttes* is published, as is shown in the epilogue, for 'euery estate hye & lowe that entende to the fayttes of werre'. For a general review of the chivalric manuals, see D. Bornestein, 'Military Manuals in Fifteenth-Century England', *Mediæval Studies*, 37 (1975), 469–77.

182

by and by.'[20] The incorporation of the spiritual problem into such a military manual indicates that the next world was one of the strong abiding concerns of the knights or men of arms, whose vocation was to kill people, as well as of fifteenth century people in general.

In a similar way the *Ordre* codifies knightly rules, presupposing spiritual salvation. But what about Malory's *Morte*?

Malory, who restricts the annual oath to the earthly virtues, is equally obsessed with the problem of spiritual salvation. He ends the whole story by granting Lancelot and Guenevere 'a good ende' and by referring to 'many bataylles' that other knights of the Round Table fought against 'the myscreantes, or Turkes'.[21] Malory, certainly, by describing Grail knights, knights-hermits and crusading knights, treats the kind of chivalry which the *Fayttes* calls the 'strayghte' way to heaven, but he depicts with much more earnest concern the earthly chivalry which steps up 'by and by' to God's bliss. As an 'earthly' man of arms and letters, he repeatedly expresses in his 'explicits' an earnest desire for 'good delyveraunce', indicating his imprisonment and suggesting his strong attachment to the worldly free life. We see, therefore, Malory, in his work, take an approving view of *this* world, striving in his way to reconcile earthly, though knightly, values and celestial values.

Malory's tenacious attachment to *this*-worldliness is exemplified by his attempt to secularise the religious disposition of the French source in the *Tale of the Holy Grail*. As Vinaver aptly remarks, 'Corbenic', in Malory's version, becomes 'a province of Camelot',[22] and the quest for the Grail is presented as an opportunity for adventure to 'have much erthly worship'.[23] Lancelot, in the original, is judged, in spite of his partial fulfilment of the Grail quest, as an utter failure because of 'la voie de luxure [the path of lust]'.[24] In Malory's tale, however, he is appraised as one who is partially successful and who can give a satisfied cry: 'Now I thanke God, . . . for Hys grete mercy of that I have sene, for hit suffisith me. For, as I suppose, no man in thys worlde have lyved bettir than I have done to enchyeve that I have done.'[25] Lancelot's earthly chivalry is not judged, in an either-or way, as desperately inferior to Galahad's heavenly chivalry; rather his noble and fallible conduct is interpreted in an engaging way as worthy of God's eventual grace.

Interestingly, there can be found phrases and expressions which seem to imply an effort on Malory's part to contradict his usual secularization.

---

[20] *The Book of Fayttes of Armes and Chyualrye*, ed. A. T. P. Byles, E.E.T.S., o.s. 189 (London: Oxford University Press, 1932), p. 282.16–28.

[21] *Works*, p. 1260.14.

[22] E. Vinaver, *Malory* (Oxford: Clarendon Press, 1929), p. 84.

[23] *Works*, p. 955.9.

[24] *La Queste Del Saint Graal*, ed. A. Pauphilet (Paris: Librairie Honoré Champion, 1980), p. 125.34.

[25] *Works*, p. 1018.3–6.

Galahad's prayer to God, 'I wold nat lyve in this wrecched worlde no lenger'; Galahad's farewell to Lancelot, 'bydde hym remembir of this worlde unstable'; Galahad's message through Bors to Lancelot, that he earnestly wishes Lancelot 'to remembir of thys unsyker worlde'; and Lancelot's painful question at Arthur's death, 'Who may truste thys world?':[26] all these are Malory's own additions and each utterance is considered as carrying a strongly critical view of the world. The only case that can be traced back to the original source is Galahad's prayer to God, but its French version, 'je trespasse de ceste terriene vie en la celestiel [I should pass from the earthly life to the eternal life]',[27] is neither as forthright nor as deprecatory as the English renunciation of 'this wrecched worlde'.

In effect, however, the interposed theme of 'contemptus mundi' stresses all the more the intensity of Malory's attachment to *this* world for its incongruity with his secularization. It is especially so when Lancelot makes a request (refused) to Guenevere for a farewell kiss in the convent and when later, informed of Arthur's death, he cries out, 'Alas! Who may truste thys world?' On this last occasion Lancelot looks as if he were sharing the Boethian view of the world, denying his noble knighthood which has most admirably accomplished Arthur's code of chivalry. He puts on a religious 'habyte' and serves God 'day and nyght with prayers and fastynges'.[28] But his motive for religious conversion, I would say with F. Riddy, is purely secular, because his renunciation of the world is motivated by Guenevere's rejection of him, not by his penitence.[29] Lancelot has an occasion at this stage of his life to appreciate the Boethian world, but he still remains and lives out his earthly life in *this* world. In Malory's view, God's bliss is promised and actually given to such as Lancelot.

As far as the preface to his edition of the *Morte* is concerned, Caxton seems to be able to appreciate the Malorian continuity between earthly and celestial values. In exhorting the reader to good conduct, the publisher discloses his view of salvation: 'But al is wryton for our doctryne, and for to beware that we falle not to vyce ne synne, but t'exersyse and folowe vertu, by whyche we may come and atteyne to good fame and renommé in thys lyf, and after thys shorte and transytorye lyf to come

---

[26] *Works*, pp. 1034.25–6, 1035.11–2, 1036.28, and 1254.12.

[27] *Queste*, p. 278.11–2.

[28] *Works*, p. 1254.16 and 18.

[29] F. Riddy says: 'His [Lancelot's] conversion is not born out of penitence, as Guinevere's, but is initiated by her rejection of him in the convent and is concluded by a wider insecurity' (*Sir Thomas Malory* (Leiden: E.J.Brill, 1987), p. 157). P. E. Tucker presents a different view: 'It is not for her [Guenevere's] sake that he renounces the world; it is rather that her renunciation leaves him free at last to make his' ('Chivalry in the *Morte*', *Essays on Malory*, ed. J. A. W. Bennett (Oxford: Clarendon Press, 1963), p. 99).

unto everlastyng blysse in heven.'[30] Caxton coordinates earthly fame and renown with heavenly bliss, and he is unfolding the possibility of an explanation of spiritual salvation in terms of secular ethics.

Unlike his master, Caxton, who published the book for a limited circle of people, for courtiers and aristocrats, Wynkyn de Worde reprinted the *Morte Darthur* in 1498, on his own initiative, to aim for a wider readership including 'comynaltee'.[31] For a fresh presentation of the *Morte*, he arranges the text in double columns, uses woodcuts for visual diversion and even silently makes textual alterations. One such attempt at textual revision is the famous long interpolation at Book 21:

> . . . Behold beholde: se how this mygh[t]ly conquerour Arthur/ whom in his humayne lyf/ all the worlde doubted/ ye also this noble quene Gueneuer/ that somtyme sate in her chare aourned wyth golde. perle & precious stones: now lye ful lowe in obscure fosse or pytte coueryd wyth cloddes of erth & clay ❧ Beholde also this myghty champyon Laūcelot/ pyerles of knyghthode: se now how he lyeth grouelynge on the colde moulde. now beynge so feble & faynt that somtyme was so terrible: how & in what manere oughte ye to be so desyrous of the mondayn̄ honour so daungerous . . . Also me semyth by the oft redyng therof. ye shal gretly desyre tacustome yourself in folowynge those gracyous knyghtly dedes. That is to saye/ to drede god/ & to loue ryghtwisnes/ faythfully & courageously to serue your souerayne prynce. And the more that god hàth geuen you the tryumfall honour/ the meker ye oughte to be/ euer feryng the vnstablynesse of this dysceyuable worlde./ And so I passe ouer/ & turn agayne to my matere.[32]

When this passage is examined in its narrative context, the editor-printer's interpolation is too abrupt and divergent to be dismissed as a mere outlet of his personal emotion. What is shown here in a homiletic tone is obviously incompatible with Malory's secular bias. Caxton in the preface envisages earthly renown as a possible prerequisite to salvation and, along with Malory, takes an approving view of worldly honour. De Worde in this interpolation, however, presents a downright disparagement of 'mondayn̄ honour' and draws readers' attention to its transitoriness. De Worde also acknowledges here the ennobling force of knightly deeds in the *Morte*, but, unlike Malory who shifts emphasis onto the earthly knightly virtues, he rather abruptly epitomises Arthurian chivalry in the light of the 'dread of God' as well as 'justice-keeping' and 'loyalty to the sovereign'. And at the conclusion of his long apostrophe, he admonishes the reader to be humble before God and to recognise 'this dysceyuable worlde'.

---

30 *Works*, p. cxlvi.
31 The John Rylands Library copy of W. de Worde's 1498 edition, folio 2ᵛ, right column, ll. 36–7.
32 *Ibid.*, folios E 3ᵛ, right column, l. 34 – E 4ʳ, left column, l. 36.

ARTHURIAN AND OTHER STUDIES

De Worde sympathises with what Malory seldom does. De Worde's 'the more that god hath geuen you the tryumfall honour /the meker ye oughte to be' is exactly an echo of what hermits admonish Lancelot to do throughout the Grail tale, and this clerical view, followed by a kindred notion 'the vnstablynesse of this dysceyuable worlde', forcibly modifies Malory's *Morte* with a commonplace medieval outlook of 'contemptus mundi'. Taking into consideration all these things which are set against Malory's departure from the conventional idea of chivalry, we would like to suggest that de Worde's didactic interpolation does not make good, spontaneous reading at the tragic moment but, rather, strikes a reader as a contrived, though purposeful, intrusion aimed at adjusting the religious and the chivalric view expressed in the *Morte* towards his own view, as an editor-printer, of what the contemporary mind should hold fast to.

As in the case of Caxton's strong, though cautious, stance about Arthur's historicity, we can posit social and cultural circumstances which de Worde may have been prompted to try to forestall even at the expense of sacrificing the proper reading of the Malorian passage. Those circumstances are, it can be said, the rising 'Renaissance humanism with its classical and Protestant affinities'.[33] The *Morte* has to face, on the one hand, Ascham's outright denunciation of the romance as treating 'open mans slaughter, and bold bawdrye',[34] and, on the other, the proscription of the book in the 1539 Tract:

> Englishmen have now in hand in every Church and place, almost every man the Holy Bible and New Testament in their mother tongue instead of the old fabulous and fantastical books of the Table Round, Launcelot du Lac &c., and such other, whose unpure filth and vain fabulocity the light of God has abolished utterly.[35]

De Worde, in recapitulating Arthurian chivalry, ignores Malory's 'all-wayes to do ladyes, damesels, and jantilwomen and wydowes socour', and adds 'to dread God' instead. This ingenious replacement may reasonably have been instigated by his consciousness of an unfavourable publishing milieu.

The didactic interpolation may also be due to de Worde's own personal disposition. This passage, which is placed after the catastrophe of a tragic love, would soon be recognised by Chaucerian readers to be much like the palinode of *Troilus and Criseyde* in its structural and thematic aspects. De Worde, who is known to have had a marked preference for religious works,[36] may well have noticed the Boethian recantation, when

[33] *Malory: The Critical Heritage*, ed. M. J. Parins (London: Routledge, 1988), p. 4.
[34] Parins, *ibid.*, p. 57.
[35] E. J. Sweeting, *Studies in Early Tudor Criticism* (Oxford: Basil Blackwell, 1940), p. 40.
[36] N. F. Blake, 'Wynkyn de Worde: Early Years', *Gutenberg Jahrbuch* (1971), 62–9.

DE WORDE'S DISPLACEMENT OF MALORY'S SECULARIZATION

he helped his master to publish *Troilus and Criseyde* in 1483 in Caxton's press, and then, later, the religious-minded de Worde, may have, in reprinting the *Morte*, been reminded of this recantation and have found it worthwhile to interpolate a similar passage in the text at a place corresponding to that taken up by Chaucer's palinode.

There is actually circumstantial evidence to make such an inference. De Worde published *Troilus and Criseyde* in 1517. Although it cost more labour in the casting-off and the typesetting work, he began to make the text by using a manuscript, not an earlier printed edition (i.e. Caxton's), as an exemplar. But he suddenly abandoned it at l. 547 of Book 1 and thereafter adopted Caxton's edition instead. The manuscript used belongs to the 'Ph*etc*' group,[37] lacking the two stanzas (ll. 1807–27 of Book 5) where Troilus's soul ascends to the eighth sphere and despises the 'wrecched world' out of preference for the 'pleyn felicite' in heaven. Several accounts of the composite nature of the text can be postulated. A likely and tempting one will be this: while typesetting, the printer found the manuscript defective in the concluding stanzas, which Chaucer added later in his revision and with which de Worde personally felt much sympathy; and he therefore searched for a better text. De Worde must have produced Chaucer's works with meticulous care as he, at Caxton's press, had witnessed a special respect among readers for the poet's text. Possibly this literary consideration may be a primary reason for changing exemplars, but his personal sympathy with Chaucer's palinode seems to have just as much to do with the textual anomaly.

Like Chaucer, de Worde interpolates his version of palinode in the final part of the whole story. But his displacing of values does not fit in with the movement of readers' dramatic response, nor is his homiletic tone resonant to the last in their minds. De Worde's interference is immediately followed, and its inappropriate didacticism is disclosed, by the bishop's dream of Lancelot's saintly death. The bishop's vision, 'the angellys' heaving up 'syr Launcelot unto heven', and the narrative reference to the 'swettest savour' around his corpse, all communicate to the reader a conviction that the best sinful knight is ultimately sanctified by God.[38] And once again the reader is assured by Ector's lament that Lancelot was an epitome of the earthly chivalry codified by the oath of the knights of the Round Table.

De Worde, as an editor-printer sensitive to the demands of the market, tried to normalise (and medievalise) Malory's idea of chivalry; but Malory's obsessive attachment to *this* world and his approving view of terrestrial chivalry, which are too powerful to be affected by such a didactic interpolation, keep on attracting a modern audience.

---

[37] See 'The Text of the "Troilus" ' of *Troilus and Criseyde*, ed. B. A. Windeatt (London: Longman, 1984), pp. 36–54.

[38] *Works*, p. 1258.9 and 17.

Some Scribal Differences in Malory*

TOMOMI KATO

The present study is based on the assumption that the Winchester MS. (W) (now BL Additional MS. 59678) is the almost evenly divided work of two scribes, A and B.[1] The proportion of words used in the dialogue (D) and the narrative part (N) is roughly 4 to 6.[2]

Already in 1968, Sandved made an extremely detailed morphological study of the verbs in Malory, using Caxton's and Vinaver's editions. Though his study is restricted to the verbal morphology, he came to the conclusion that 'Caxton displays a more regular and consistent system than WA (=scribe A in the Winchester MS.) and WB (=scribe B)'.[3]

Let us here take some words other than verbs to find what they reveal. In E. Vinaver's 1973 edition of *The Works of Sir Thomas Malory* (hereafter abbreviated as O^2), there are three variants of *al*, *all*, and *alle* whose respective instances are tabulated below.

Table I[4]

				A	B	C	P
al	46	(D 9	N37) /	0	1	17	28
all	2327	(889	1438) /	1030	1269	28	0
alle	47	(6	41) /	4	7	35	1
	2420	(904	1516)	1034	1277	80	29

---

* This is a revised version of my paper read at the fifth congress (December, 1989) of the Japan Society for Medieval English Studies. My thanks are due to Professor Hugh Wilkinson for correcting my English.

[1] Cf. N. R. Ker, *The Winchester Malory* (Oxford: Oxford University Press, 1976), p. xiv. Dr. Ker writes, 'Probably we shall not be far wrong in thinking that he (=scribe A) wrote nearly as much as scribe B.' Cf. also A. O. Sandved, *Studies in the Language of Caxton's Malory* (Oslo: Norwegian University Press, 1968), p. 15, Note 2.

[2] To be more exact, 43%:57%. Cf. T. Kato, ed., *A Concordance to the Works of Sir Thomas Malory* (Tokyo: University of Tokyo Press, 1974), p. 1659. This concordance edited on the basis of E. Vinaver's *The Works of Sir Thomas Malory* (Oxford: Clarendon Press, 1973) shows that the number of words in D is 146653 and that in N 196466, totalling 343119. Incidentally, Vinaver's 1973 edition with corrections and additions is hereafter referred to as O^2 and the revised edition by P. J. C. Field (Oxford: Clarendon Press, 1990) as O^3.

[3] See Sandved, *ibid.*, p. 435.

[4] C and P stand for the supplementary parts in O^2 and O^3 taken from Caxton's edition and the Pierpont Morgan Copy of Caxton respectively.

ARTHURIAN AND OTHER STUDIES

From this table we learn:

a. *Al* appears only in C and P except for 1 instance in B (695/8 in *O*³ or f. 286ʳ l. 10 in W).

b. Despite the fact that *all* is the most usual form, there are no instances in P.

c. *Alle* appears in A, B, C, and P. However, one of the instances in B is an emended form and the four in A are all emendations. Therefore this is a form that A may not have used himself.

d. There is something strange about the unique instance of *al* in B. As shown in the table, B's customary form is *all* and, unlike his practice of writing *all* with a space on both sides and a bar across the *ll*, the *al* in question is written as if it were some affix with no space required between it and the following *to* (he writes '. . . brake his speare alto shyvyrs') or as if he mistook it for such when he began to write *al*.

e. Another solitary example that attracts our attention is that of *alle* in P. In this case the addition of *-le* to the usual *al* seems to be a 'space-filler' (cf. P. Needham, ed. *The Pierpont Morgan Copy of Caxton*, The xxi book, Capitulum xii, l. 4 from the bottom).

f. *All* and its variants appear far more frequently in N than in D, and for some reason 20% less in A than in B. C has 3 variants as against B's 2 (excluding the erratic *al*), while A seems to use only 1 form, if we take into account the fact mentioned in c above.

Table II (i) and (ii) show the distribution of *allwayes* with its variants and that of *allway* and its variants respectively.

Table II(i)

	A				B			C			P
allwayes	52	(D16	N36)	/	26	(D9 N17)	26	(D7 N19)	0		0
allways	1 (	0	1)	/	1 (	0	1)	0			0
allweyes	5 (	4	1)	/	5 (	4	1)	0			0
alwayes	1 (	0	1)	/	0				1	(D0 N1)	0	
alweyes	3 (	0	3)	/	0				3 (	0	3)	0
	62 (	20	42)		32 (13	19)	26 (7	19)	4 (0	4)	

190

SOME SCRIBAL DIFFERENCES IN MALORY

Table II(ii)

	A					B			C		P
allway	14 (D8	N6)	/	6 (D2	N4)	8 (D6	N2)	0			0
allwey	10 (3	7)	/	8 (3	5)	2 (0	2)	0			0
alwey	1 (0	1)	/	0		0			1 (D0	N1)	0
	25 (11	14)		14 (5	9)	10 (6	4)	1 (0	1)		

a. (i) and (ii) show that *all-* forms are restricted to A and B, and *al-* forms to C, and that twice as many *-s* forms are found in N as in D. But (ii) does not reveal such a clear contrast between D and N.
b. In the case of the *-s* forms, B uses only 1 form as against A's 3 variants.
c. C has no instance of any of these forms in D.
d. A uses 5 variants in all, while B and C both use 3.

Table III is a tabulation of the usage found in the case of *child* and *children* and their variants.

Table III(i)

	A					B		C		P
child	13 (D 8 N 5)		/	0		0		13 (D8	N5)	0
childe	3 (3	0)	/	2 (D2	N 0)	1 (D1	N0)	0		0
chyld	1 (0	1)	/	1 (0	1)	0		0		0
chylde	65 (23	42)	/	21 (8	13)	44 (15	29)	0		0
	82 (34	48)	/	24 (10	14)	45 (16	29)	13 (8	5)	0

Table III(ii)

	A					B		C	P
children	2 (D0	N 2)	/	2 (D0	N2)	0		0	0
chyldern	2 (2	0)	/	0		2 (D2	N0)	0	0
chyldir	5 (2	3)	/	0		5 (2	3)	0	0
chyldirne	4 (2	2)	/	0		4 (2	2)	0	0
chyldren	5 (4	1)	/	2 (2	0)	3 (2	1)	0	0
chyldryn	2 (1	1)	/	0		2 (1	1)	0	0
chyldyrn	2 (1	1)	/	0		2 (1	1)	0	0
	22 (12	10)	/	4 (2	2)	18 (10	8)	0	0

a. (i) shows that C keeps to *child*, while the predominant form in A and B is *chylde*. But in B we have twice as many instances of this as in A.

ARTHURIAN AND OTHER STUDIES

b. In contrast to C, both A and B in (i) show a somewhat higher frequency in N than in D, a tendency which is absent in (ii).
c. There are two minority forms – *childe* (3) and *chyld* (1), with the former occurring only in D. *Childe* is found in 44/18 (A) of O^3 or at the very beginning of f. 18^r of W and in 45/37 (A) or in the fourth position in l. 5 of f. 18^v. In these two cases, there seems to be no special reason for A to adopt this minority form. The more so, it would seem, as A has a number of instances of his usual *chylde* occurring in the vicinity of these two cases. For the instance in 636/7, B seems to have an understandable reason. The word happens to come at the very end of f. 262^r, with the last three letters -*lde* jutting out beyond the ink-ruled line. The restriction in space may also have influenced A when he adopted *chyld* in 1124/3. This word appears in l. 29 on f. 437^r in the penultimate position, pushing out the -*ed* of *aspyed* to the next line. Thus 'thys chyld aspy/ed.'
d. When we come to (ii), we notice that B is almost chaotic in his spelling, with 6 variants among his 18 instances, while A has only 2 variants.

Let us take *fyrste* as our last example. This word has 4 variants as shown below.

Table IV

	A		B	C	P
first	28 (D14 N14) /25 (D12 N13)		1 (D1 N0)	2 (D1 N1)	0
firste	50 (23 27) /50 (23 27)		0	0	0
fyrst	22 (13 9) / 2 (1 1)		17 (12 5)	2 (0 2)	1 (0 1)
fyrste	64 (28 36) / 3 (2 1)		59 (26 33)	2 (0 2)	0
	164 (78 86) /80 (38 42)		77 (39 38)	6 (1 5)	1 (0 1)

a. What this table shows is that A and B have almost the same number of instances (80 to 77) and that, unlike C, their instances are well balanced between D and N.
b. A displays a strong preference for forms with -*i*-, i.e. *first* and *firste*, and B for forms with -*y*-, i.e. *fyrst* and *fyrste*. However, this is not to say that they always have similar spelling preferences in other cases. Take *aftir* and its variants for example. For *affter* and *after*, A has 22 and B 16 instances. For *afftir* and *aftir*, they have 189 and 215, and for *afftyr* and *aftyr* A has 1 and B 9. Thus in this case the contrast is not so sharp as in the present case.

Judging from the four tables, we may say that there seem to be no idiosyncratic tendencies which are strong enough to wield overall influence over their spellings. Their idiosyncrasies may or may not reveal themselves. It is true that in some cases their presence is clearly observable. Compare *then* with *thenne* in O^2. *Then* occurs 4 times in A and 6 times in B. *Thenne* is found 5 times in A as against 67 in C and 4 in P. However, all these 5 instances appear in the emended passages, which fact may justify us in assuming that *thenne* is non-existent for A. Sometimes we may suspect some interaction between A and B. More exhaustive investigation will make the situation clearer. At present, their idiosyncrasies, if any, seem sporadic.

Before going on to syntactic problems, I would like to mention some lexical phenomena in O^2. They concern the ratios of the instances in D and N. Taking into consideration the proportion of D to N (4:6) and Malory's comparatively homogeneous plots, it is puzzling for us to find words which show a considerable disparity in usage between D and N. On the other hand, *stronge*[5] (41% in D and 59% in N), *dayes* (37:63), *bretherne* (44:56), for example, are roughly conformable to the norm. But such words as *ado* (86:14), *but* (55:45), *ellys* (82:18), *fayth* (90:10), *foo* (93:7), *foly* (92:8), *moste* (68:32), *yf* (83:17), *speare* (8:92), *aftir* (25:75), *into* (21:79), etc. show great deviation from the norm. Some words are markedly of the D-type and others of the N-type. *False* (87:13), *fayre* (66:34), *traytoure* (93:7), *truly* (96:4) are among those which can be expected to belong to the D-type. But why are words like *foo*, *evyll* (79:21), *therefore* (92:8), *for* (72:28) so much a part of the D-type?

Let me quote some words showing the opposite tendency: *fortune* (21:79), *thenne* (7:93), *therewithall* (0:100), *passinge* (24:76), *passingly* (24:76), *up* (12:88). Even numerals and prepositions (also adverbs) show curiously diverse ratios. *One* (44:56), *two* (33:67), *three* (28:72), *four* (23:77); *fyve* (24:76), *six* (15:85), *seven* (45:55), *eyght* (32:68), *nine* (27:73), *ten* (28:72); *aftir* (25:75), *among* (25:75), *at* (37:63), *before* (19:81), *by* (39:61), *in* (41:59), *into* (21:79), *of* (44:56), *on* (31:72), *out* (27:73), *over* (25:75), *to* (44:56), *tyll* (32:68), *undir* (25:75), *untyll* (35:65), *with* (39:61), *withoute* (49:51), etc.

When analysed according to the usage found in A and B, the figures reveal a different picture from the above. But a presentation of this analysis is a matter that must wait for another occasion.

Next I would like to take up *make* and *bydde* when used as causative verbs to find whether there is any difference in the use of them made by A and B. These two verbs have been chosen as they allow of two constructions: V + O + bare inf. and V + O + to-inf.

Make as a causative verb appears in the following forms in O^2: *make, makith, makyth; made, maad,* and *mad.*

---

5   The following words are representative forms, to be understood as standing also for their variants.

Table V

make 23

bare inf. 8   13/15 (N C), 410/1 (N B), 490/20 (N A), 882/11 (D A), 915/25[6] (2D A), 930/24 (D B), 1113/5 (D A).

to-inf. 15   11/38 (D C), 18/28 (N C), 141/14 (N B), 167/15 (D B), 301/15 (D B), 331/32 (D B), 509/16 (D A), 588/29 (N B), 618/11 (D B), 690/5 (D B), 794/13 (D B), 888/34 (D A), 934/17 [7] (D A), 963/32 (D A), 1257/4 (N C).

makith 1

to-inf. 1   867/14 (D A).

makyth 3

to-inf. 3   167/10 (D B), 451/3 (D B), 459/21 (D B).

When totalled:

make + O + bare inf.	8(D	5 N3)/	A5	(D4 N1)	B2	(D1 N1)	C1	(D0 N1)		
make + O + to-inf.	19(	15	4)/	A5	(5	0)	B11	(9	2)	C3 (1	2)
	27(	20	7)/	A10 (9	1)	B13 (10	3)	C4 (1	3)		

Table VI

made 138

bare inf. 25   27/8 (N A), 34/23 (N A), 40/12 (N A), 82/34 (D A), 105/3 (N A), 113/35 (N A), 143/28 (N B), 169/6 (N B), 176/11 (N B), 286/35 (D B), 371/28 (N B), 396/33 (N B), 426/28[8] (N B), 474/31 (N A), 496/35 (2N A), 547/20 (N A), 655/29 (N B), 762/26 (N B), 973/16 (N A), 998/1 (D A), 1072/27 (N A), 1125/17 (N A),1178/8 (N A),1196/7 (N A).

to-inf. 113   11/14 (N C), 14/5 (N C), 16/24 (2N C), 26/27 (N A), 30/33 (N A), 31/4 (N A), 82/9 (N A), 107/5 (N A), 107/32 (N A), 119/19 (N A), 125/27 (N B), 126/24 (N B), 143/4 (N B), 145/2 (D B), 146/20 (D B), 177/23 (N B), 179/19 (N B), 222/17 (N B), 242/17 (N B), 261/7 (N B), 299/35 (N B), 314/27 (N B), 324/28 (N B), 326/7 (N B), 361/8 (N B), 361/10 (N B), 385/1 (N B), 393/32 (N B), 394/29 (N B), 423/9 (N B), 423/19 (N B), 426/34 (N B), 430/2 (N B), 430/12 (N B), 470/3 (N A), 473/31 (2N A), 475/6 (N A), 476/6 (N A), 490/9 (N A), 499/22 (N A), 503/5 (N A), 510/15 (N A), 517/35 (N A), 536/1 (N A), 562/20 (D B), 568/16 (N B), 588/19 (N B), 598/31

---

[6] 915/25 (2D A). This instance occurs in 915/25 in both O^2 and O^3 and it is found in the dialogue in A. 2 means that the instance contains two consecutive causative uses: '. . . make the beleve on her and leve thy baptym.' Incidentally, C has '. . . make the to bileve and leve . . .'.

[7] The instance appears in the emended part: '. . . make the ⌈to falle into the⌉ depe pitte . . .'.

[8] C reads '. . . hym to falle . . .'.

(N B), 600/9 (N B), 600/11 (N B), 607/14 (N B), 622/17 (N B),
627/6 (D B), 633/12 (N B), 639/13 (N B), 647/3 (N B), 654/17 (N
B), 655/29[9] (N B), 659/25 (N B), 665/19 (N B), 669/19 (N B), 676/4
(N B), 676/8 (N B), 676/11 (N B), 686/16 (N B), 748/31 (N B),
762/26 (N B), 771/24 (N B), 773/31 (D B), 794/21 (N B), 800/18 (N
B), 802/20 (N B), 813/34 (N B), 825/26 (D B), 840/29 (N B), 843/33
(N B), 855/25 (N A), 860/2 (N A), 862/3 (D A), 864/34 (2N A),
886/17 (D A), 888/17 (N A), 890/5 (N A), 917/22 (D A), 926/17 (D
A), 932/9[10](N A), 934/15 (D A), 956/21 (N A), 993/7 (D A), 993/17
(D A), 993/19 (D A), 998/5[11] (D A), 998/27 (N A), 1036/14 (N A),
1072/9 (N A),1076/12 (N A), 1085/18 (N A), 1085/19 (N A),
1085/21 (N A),1096/12 (N A), 1096/26 (N A), 1097/4 (N A),
1146/1 (N A),1178/9 (N A), 1190/20 (N A), 1221/18 (N A),
1227/6 (N A),1232/12 (N A), 1242/22 (N A), 1254/22 (N P).

maade 1

   to-inf. 1   16/29 (N C)

mad 1

   bare inf. 1   537/23 (N A)

The total of Table VI is as follows:

made + O + bare inf.	25(D	3	N22)/	A16(D	2	N14)	B 9(D1	N 8)	C0
made + O + to-inf.	113(	15	98)/	A52(	9	43)	B56(6	50)	C5(D0 N5)
	138(	18	120)/	A68(	11	57)	B65(7	58)	C5(0	5)

The grand total of Tables V and VI is as follows:

Table VII

make + O + bare inf.	33(D8	N25)/	A21(D6	N15)	B11(D2	N9)	C1(D0	N1)	
make + O + to-inf.	132(	30	102)/	A57(	14	43)	B67(	15	52) C8(1 7)
	165(	38	127)/	A78(	20	58)	B78(	17	61) C9(1 8)

From these three tables, the following can be found:

a. It is immediately apparent that, unlike in Modern English, the general rule is to use the to-infinitive – it occurs just 4 times as often as the bare infinitive (see Table VII). The sole exception to this rule is seen in A in Table V, where both uses happen to be equal in number (5 to 5).

---

[9] This passage has both the to-infinitive and the bare infinitive constructions: '. . . he . . . made her go to the Haute Prynce and to aske leve for hir knyght to do batayle.'

[10] O^2 and O^3 read '. . . made hym to alyght to reeste hym'. But C has '. . . to alyghte and to reste hym'.

[11] For 'made me to suffir', C has 'badde me suffir.'

195

ARTHURIAN AND OTHER STUDIES

b. It may be purely a matter of chance that we find the same number of example (15) in D in Tables V and VI, and also that in VI the ratio of D to N in both uses (3 to 22 and 15 to 98) is roughly the same – 1:7.

c. Comparing Tables V and VI, we find that A and B in Table V tend to provide more instances in D than in N. This tendency is dramatically reversed in Table VI.

d. In the case of B's totals in Tables V and VI (2 to 11 and 9 to 56 respectively), we can discern almost the same ratio of 1 to 6 in both. But this cannot be said with regard to A (5 to 5 and 16 to 52).

e. A tends to use the bare infinitive more often than B – nearly twice as often both in V and VI, totalling 21 instances as against 11. In the case of the to-infinitive, however, there seems to be no significant difference in VI (A52 to B56).

f. When we come to Table VII, it is of interest to note that both scribes employ the causative *make* exactly the same number of times (78).

g. All in all, A and B in VII show the opposite tendency in their use of the bare infinitive and the to-infinitive (A21 to B11 and A57 to B67). The main factors contributing to this tendency are the disparities in their use of the bare infinitive, especially in N, and their use of the to-infinitive in N. Their use of the to-infinitive in D shows a similar frequency of 14 to 15.

The verb *bydde* as a causative appears in seven forms: *bid, byd, bydde, byddyth; bad, badde,* and *bade.*

The details of the use of *bid, byd, bydde,* and *byddyth* are as follows (* indicates an instance with the to-infinitive):

Table VIII

bid 2	624/18 (D B), 678/8 (D B).
byd 6	12/5 (D C), *222/12 (D B), 539/2 (D A), 814/17 (D B), 819/18 (D B), 1056/8 (D A).
bydde 15	151/1 (D B), 204/19 (D B),*206/11 (D B), 206/12 (D B),*268/16 (D B), 311/4 (D B), 376/10 (D B), 380/35 (D B), 424/15 (D B), 424/21 (D B), 428/16 (D B), 727/16 (3D B), 1035/11 (D A).
byddyth 1	140/24 (D B).

When tabulated, this gives:

```
bydde + O + bare inf.   21(D21 N0)/A3(D3 N0) B17(D17 N0)  C1(D1 N0)
bydde + O + to-inf.      3(  3   0)/A0           B 3(  3   0) C0
                        ────────────────────────────────────────────
                        24( 24   0)/A3(  3   0) B20( 20   0) C1(  1   0)
```

196

SOME SCRIBAL DIFFERENCES IN MALORY

Table VIII shows that the instances with the bare inf. are 7 times as many as those with the to-inf. (21 to 3) and that in B they are more than 5 times as many as those in A (17 to 3). All the instances in Table VIII appear in D.

The 3 examples with the to-inf. are shown below. They are all of them found in B:

(1) 206/11 (D B) . . . I bydde hym in haste to remeve oute of my londys.
(2) 222/12 (D B) . . . and byd hir for my love to worche for my soule.
(3) 268/16 (D B) . . . I bydde them to take suche stuff there as they fynde.

The insertion of *to* in (1) and (2) may be attributable to the interposition of the phrases 'in haste' and 'for my love'. In (3) the rhythm may explain the presence of *to*.

In the following list are shown the instances of *bad*, *badde*, and *bade*:

Table IX

bad 3	9/24 (N C), 18/30 (N C), 18/39 (N C).
badde 4	7/33 (N C), 18/18 (N C), 18/30 (N C), 760/25 (N B).
bade 150	22/2 (N A), 30/5 (N A), 43/19 (N A), 48/33 (N A), 73/35 (2N A), 85/17 (N A), *91/17 (N A), 102/26 (N A), 105/6 (N A), 112/7 (N A), 127/13 (N B), 132/24 (N B), 141/13 (N B), 169/1 (N B), 174/18 (N B), 174/32 (N B), 178/13 (2N B), 209/1 (N B), 218/17[12] (3N B), 230/14 (N B), *253/22 (N B), 254/9 (N B), 255/19 (2N B), 276/19 (N B), 282/6 (N B), 285/8 (2N B), 286/15 (N B), 295/10 (N B), 295/25 (2N B), 295/28 (N B), 298/25 (N B), 301/11 (N B), 302/11 (N B), 303/7 (N B), *310/12 (N B), 323/36 (N B), 341/7 (N B), 347/32 (N B), 352/18 (D B), 356/19 (2N B), 358/7 (N B), 376/7 (N B), 388/4 (N B), 388/9 (2N B), 401/1 (N B), 405/27 (2N B), 406/25 (D B), 414/3 (N B), 432/25 (N B), 435/26 (D B), 436/3 (N B), 450/14 (2N B), 462/31 (N B), 463/11 (D B), 472/21 (N A), 508/12 (N A), 533/4 (N A), 539/16 (N A), 548/18 (2N A), 549/4 (2N A), 550/26 (2N A), 558/28 (2N A), 561/1 (N B), 581/1 (N B), 593/30 (N B), 615/29 (N B), 617/7 (N B), 620/17 (N B), 623/6 (N B), 633/26 (N B), 634/21 (N B), 634/34 (2N B), 638/16 (N B), 640/17 (N B), 641/26 (N B), 642/30 (N B), 644/9 (N B), 658/17 (N B), 664/25 (N B), 665/12 (N B), 677/36 (N B), 680/20 (N B), 691/5[13] (2N B), 703/18 (2N B), *716/26 (N B), 759/1 (N B), 772/2 (N B), 772/13 (N

---

[12] O^2 and O^3 both read: He dressed his peple and hyghe hym he bade, and take hym of the beste men of armys many sad hundrethis, 'and go before, and we woll folow aftir'. I prefer to punctuate the passage as follows: . . . many sad hundrethis and go before, 'and we woll folow aftir'. As regards 450/14 which reads: and within a whyle he overtoke sir Lamerok and bade hym turne, 'and leve that lady, for thou and I muste play a new play: . . .', I am inclined to read: . . . and bade hym turne and leve that lady, 'For thou and I . . .'

[13] 691/5 in O^2 was 'and made them turne and amende . . .', but O^3 read 'and [b]ade them . . .'

B), 801/13 (N B), 804/4 (N B), 811/26 (N B), 811/28 (2N B), 813/36
(N B), 814/13 (N B), 815/19 (2N B), 827/17 (N B), 828/32 (N B),
853/20 (2N A), 855/26 (N A), 880/11 (D A), 917/33 (N A), 945/13
(N A), *956/25 (N A), 959/35 (N A), 965/24 (N A), 974/21 (N A),
982/30 (N A), *983/7 (N A), 990/33 (D A), 996/22 (2N A), 1003/8
(N A), 1029/31 (2N A), 1031/20 (D A), 1033/4 (D A), 1034/2 (N A),
1057/14 (2N A), 1085/28 (N A), 1093/1 (N A), 1122/5 (N A),
1125/22 (2D A), *1136/29 (N A), 1215/26 (N A), 1215/27 (N A).

A tabulation of the examples listed yields the following results:

bade+O+bare inf.	148(D10 N138)/A50(D6 N44)	B92(D4 N88)	C6(D0 N6)	
bade+O+to-inf.	7(0 7)/A 4(0 4)	B 3(0 3)	C0	
	155(10 145)/A54(6 48)	B95(4 91)	C6(0 6)	

The grand total of Tables VIII and IX is as follows:

Table X

bydde+O+bare inf.	169(D31 N138)/A53(D9 N44)	B109(D21 N88)	C7(D1N6)	
bydde+O+to-inf.	10(3 7)/A 4(0 4)	B 6(3 3)	C0(0 0)	
	179(34 145)/A57(9 48)	B115(24 91)	C7(1 6)	

The figures in Table X show that the tendencies mentioned in Tables
VIII and IX are also reflected here:

a. The overwhelming predominance of the bare inf. construction is still
   more evident in Table IX. It is also characteristic that we find in D no
   examples with the to-inf. as against 10 with the bare inf., which are
   almost evenly divided between A and B (6 to 4).
b. For the to-inf. construction in IX, we have 7 instances in all which are
   restricted to N and are again evenly divided between A and B (4 to 3).
   Incidentally, the 6 examples with the bare-inf. in C are all found in N.
c. The most striking point in Table IX is the imbalance between A and B
   in their use of the bare inf. in N (44 to 88). B has twice as many
   instances as A.
d. Let me quote here the 7 instances having the to-inf., which may call
   for a word of comment:
   (1) 91/17   (NA) So Merlyn bade a knyght that stood before hym to
                      handyll that swerde, . . .
   (2) 253/22   (NB) and than he . . . bade his nevew, sir Lyonell, for to
                      make hym redy, . . .
   (3) 310/12   (NB) Than Bewmaynes bade the Rede Knyght to stonde
                      up, . . .

SOME SCRIBAL DIFFERENCES IN MALORY

(4) 956/25 (NA) he . . . bade a squyre to brynge hym watir, . . .
(5) 983/7 (NA) And so he bade the jantillwoman to ryde, . . .
(6) 716/26 (NB) they . . . bade them to make them redy, . . .
(7) 1136/29 (NA) she . . . bade hym to chose of the beste, . . .

In instances (1) to (5), we find that the verb *bid* is followed by an object composed of a word-group. In (1) the object is modified by a clause, in (2) by an appositive 'sir Lyonell'. In (3), (4), and (5) we have 'the Rede Knyght', 'a squyre' and 'the jantillwoman' respectively. These examples reveal a tendency for both scribes to use the to-infinitive construction when the object is a word-group. Apparently, (6) and (7) seem to run contrary to this tendency. But if we compare the sentences in question with the same sentences expressed without *to*, we can easily find the former to be more euphonious.

e. In the long list of examples given above, there are some that have two bare infinitives in succession, as in 73/35: Than Merlion bade hem ryse and make hem redy. There exist 25 examples of this construction, the breakdown of which is as follows: DA1, NA9, DB1, NB14. Here again, we may see a difference, though slight, in the use of this construction. It is a phenomenon of interest that only the bare infinitive seems to be used in succession. In the case of *make*, however, there are only 3 instances except for 1 in NC. These 3 are all from A, including 1 instance used with the to-infinitive.

f. We find in Table VIII that A has no instance of the to-infinitive construction as against 3 in B (cf. b above). But in Table X, we notice that though the use of to-infinitive is restricted to N (4) in the case of A, B has 3 instances each in D and N.

In the data presented here, I have tried to demonstrate that, as seen in the verbal morphology, there are some idiosyncratic tendencies in the spelling though they can sometimes be quite obscure. In the case of the syntax, idiosyncratic differences are also discernible, though not always. The scribal differences are more widespread than one might suppose. These facts may indicate that the Winchester Malory undertaken by scribes A and B underwent, as often happened, some scribal modification due to their idiosyncrasies.

On the Relationship Between the Winchester Malory and Caxton's Malory*

YUJI NAKAO

To begin with, I should like to provide some linguistic evidence which shows that the Winchester Malory (hereafter referred to as W) and Caxton's Malory (hereafter as C)[1] are more closely related to each other than would presumably be the case with two texts of a collateral relation.

The first to be pointed out is the distribution of {betwixt}, {betwix} and {between} between W and C.[2] A noticeable fact with regard to the distribution is that the majority of instances of {betwixt} in W corresponds to {betwix} in C, and {between} in W also to {between} in C. Apart from the Roman War episode, i.e. Book V,[3] {betwixt} (<betwyxt(e)>, <betwexte>, <bytwyxte>, <betwixte>) occurs 91 times and {between} (<betwene>) 29 times in W, but {betwix} does not occur at all in W. Of the 91 instances of {betwixt}, 75 correspond to {betwix} (<betwix(e)>, <betwyx(e)>) and 12 to {betwixt} (<betwyxt(e)>, <betwixt>) in C. As for the remaining four, three correspond to {between}(<bitwene>) in C and one occurs where C has no parallel word. On the other hand, of the 29 instances of {between} in W, as many as 26 cases also correspond to {between}(<betwene>, <bitwene>, <bytwene>) in C. And only in two cases, {between} in W corresponds to {betwix}(<betwix(e)>) in C. The single remaining instance occurs where C has no corresponding part.

Looking at these phenomena from the side of C, we notice that all the instances of {betwixt}(<betwyxt(e)>, <betwixt>) found in C correspond

---

* This is a revised version of a paper read at the fourth congress of the Japan Society for Medieval English Studies held at Doshisha University, Kyoto, on 4 December, 1988. Thanks are due to Professor Shunichi Noguchi, who presided over the session and made valuable comments on an earlier draft of this paper.

1 References to W and C are from E. Vinaver, ed., P. J. C. Field, rev., *The Works of Sir Thomas Malory*, 3 vols. 3rd ed. (Oxford: Clarendon Press, 1990) and H. O. Sommer, ed., *Le Morte Darthur by Syr Thomas Malory, The Original Edition of William Caxton now Reprinted and Edited by H. O. Sommer*, 3 vols. (London: David Nutt, 1889–91). The E.E.T.S. facsimile of W and the Scolar facsimile of C will also be consulted when necessary.

2 For more details, see my paper, 'On the Variant Readings with Regard to the Preposition between MS., B. L., add. 59678 and Caxton's Edition of *Le Morte Darthur* (in Japanese)', *Studies in Language and Culture* (Nagoya University), Vol. 1 (1980), 53–81.

3 The portions where parallel contexts are lacking in one text are not counted in the statistics, either.

ARTHURIAN AND OTHER STUDIES

to {betwixt}(<betwyxte>, <betwixte>) in W as well and the majority of {between}(<betwene>, <bitwene>, <bytwene>) found in C also correspond to {between}(<betwene>) in W. We also notice that almost all the examples of {betwix}(<betwix(e)>, <betwyx(e)>) found in C are those formed by removing /-t/ from {betwixt}(<betwyxt(e)>, <betwexte>, <bytwyxte>, <betwixte>) found in W. In Malory's and Caxton's time, {betwixt}, {betwix} and {between} were the elements liable to be interchanged in the process of textual transmission, so that such close correspondences as we have observed above cannot be thought to have occurred haphazardly.

The same is true of the four words, {sithen}, {sith}, {sin} and {sins}, which are freely interchangeable with one another, regardless of their uses as conjunction, adverb or preposition. What interests us is the relation of these words between the two texts (cf. Table 1):

Table 1

W		C	
{sithen} (<sitthen>, <sythyn>, <sitthyn>, <sytthen>, 77 <sythen>*, <sytthyn>)	→	{sithen} (<sythyn>, <sitthen> 67(87.0%) <sythen>, <sytthen>) {sith} (<syth(e)>) 10(12.9%)	
{sith} (<sith>, <syth>, <sythe>) 29	→	{sith} (<syth(e)>) 21 (72.4%) {sithen} (<sythen>) 5 (17.2%) {sin} (<syn>) 1 (3.4%) Ø 2 (6.9%)	
{sin} (<syn>, <syne>) 25	→	{sin} (<syn>) 23(92%) {sith} (<sith>, <sythe>) 2(8%)	
{sins} (<synnes>, <syns>, 7 <synes>)	→	{sins} (<syns>) 4(57.1%) {sithen} (<sythen>) 1(14.3%) {sin} (<syn>) 1(14.3%) Ø 1(14.3%)	

* One example of <sythem> is included. Cf. Vinaver: sythe[n].

As can be seen from Table 1 (which excludes from the statistics Book V and those portions where the correspondence is unobtainable due to lucunae or the lack of contexts in one text), 87%, 72%, 92% and 57% of these words in W are found to correspond respectively to the same words in C. They must be regarded as high percentages. In addition, it must also be noticed that all the examples of {sins} that exist in C are found to be identical in W; and, except for two cases, all the examples of {sin} in C correspond to W's {sin}. These phenomena, too, cannot be regarded as being of haphazard occurrence.

Furthermore, there is a close correlation between W and C with regard

202

to {afore}, {before}, {tofore}, {aforne}, {beforne} and {toforne} as well, as shown in Table 2. The statistics in Table 2 include only those parts of the texts in which the two have parallel passages:

Table 2

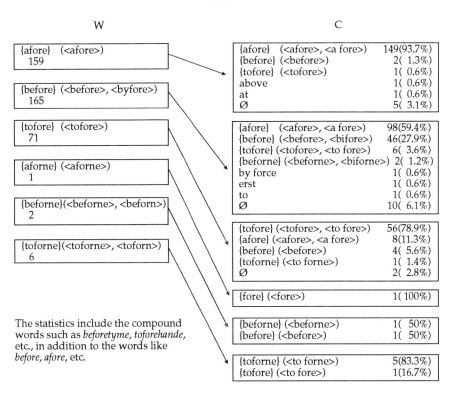

According to the table, {afore} occurs 159 times in those portions of W. Of these, 149 (that is 93.7%) correspond to the same word in C. It is of interest to find that many instances of W's {before} correspond to C's {afore}. But of the 165 instances of {before} in W, 46 correspond to {before} in C, and they constitute the majority of {before} that exist in C. There are only seven other instances (i.e. 2+4+1) of {before} in C that do not correspond to W's {before}. Moreover, there are six instances of {toforne} in W, five of which share {toforne} with C. We find only one instance of it in C that does not correspond to W's {toforne}.

Next we shall concern ourselves with the so-called 'do + the finite verb' construction. V. Engblom and A. Ellegård, for example, regard it as a genuine usage: to Engblom,[4] it is a prototype of the emphatic *do*, and to

---

[4] V. Engblom, *On the Origin and Early Development of the Auxiliary Do* (Lund: Gleerup, 1938), p. 45.

Ellegård,[5] it is a subsidiary factor in the establishment of the periphrastic *do*. On the other hand, A. Rynell[6] ascribes all the alleged instances to scribal errors or misprints because of their extremely scarce occurrence in any historical stage of English. I am with Rynell on this point.

Interestingly enough, one of the rare examples occurs in W. It reads: Than quene Gwenyver comended hym and so *did* all good knyghtes *made* muche of hym (W 660.30–1). E. Vinaver seems to regard this as being a scribal error, for he emends it to 'and so did all good knyghtes, <and> made muche of hym', choosing to preserve the past tense. In spite of Vinaver's note,[7] however, I prefer the other alternative, i.e. to emend *made* to *make*, because 'so + *do* + the anaphoric infinitive' construction[8] occurs several times in W. Be the matter as it may, the possibility of this rare expression being carried over to the Caxton text must be considered to be extremely low, if C is the text collateral to W. The reality is, however, that the Caxton text preserves the *'did* + made' construction as in the following: and soo *dyd* alle other good knyghtes *made* moche of hym (C 485.3).

Let us now turn our attention to the fact that marked elements in one text are found to be identical in the other text. The first is concerned with the two etymologically related words, {much} and {mickle}.[9] The former is in the great majority in both texts, so that the latter is clearly the marked form. Therefore we shall pay attention to the latter only. We find it seven times in W, four of which occur where C has no parallel passages, i.e. three in Book V and one in Book X.[10] So it is of great interest to know that all the remaining three correspond to the same word in C[11]: he enforced hym *myckyll* (W 1015.3) – he enforced hym *mykel* (C 710.32); praysynge hym *mykyll* (W 590.9) – praysynge hym *mykel* (C 434.2); *mykyll* she loved hym (W 905.11) – *mykel* she had loued hym (C 642.16).

Likewise, three instances of the prefix *i-/y-* with the past participle coincide with each other in the two versions, though there are fourteen and two additional ones in W and C: ye be well *ifounde* (W 995.7) – ye be *wely fonde* (C 699.35); I have the same *isought* (W 1084.1; MS. has a

---

5 A. Ellegård, *The Auxiliary Do: the Establishment and Regulation of its Use in English* (Stockholm: Almqvist & Wiksell, 1953), pp. 136–9.
6 A. Rynell 'On Alleged Constructions like *did wrote*', *Studier i Modern Språkvetenskap*, Ny Serie, Volym 2 (1964), 132–47.
7 Cf. Vinaver, *Works*, p. 1506.
8 For example: ye *know* me well inow by my shylde, and so *do* I *know* you by youre shylde (W 546.30). Though the passage in W 660.30–1 is somewhat different from this example (in that the same verb is not repeated), we have to pay attention to the fact that *make much of* is roughly synonymous with *commend*.
9 For details, see my paper, 'Many, *Much* and *Fele* in Malory', *Studies in English and Other Germanic Languages*, ed. M. Kanno and Y. Nakao (Tokyo: Kinseido, 1983), pp. 59–74.
10 W 204.10, W 204.27, W 234.15, and W 690.23 (cf. C 506.10).
11 There are, however, four additional instances of *mykel* in C which correspond to *much* in W: C 262.3, C 371.22, C 522.16 and C 661.4.

capital *I*.) – I haue the same *y sought* (C 754.1); *isette* with stonys (W 1196.17) – *y sette* with stones (C 822.32).

The frequency in use of the negative disjunctive is totally different in our two texts.[12] In W, the word that holds a large majority is *nother*, followed by *nor*, *ne* and *neyther*. On the contrary, it is *nor* that predominates in C, followed by *ne* and *neyther*. But curiously we find *no(u)ther* twice in C. It is not Caxton's own linguistic habit to use this word, as indicated in K. Mizobata's *Concordance to Caxton's Own Prose*,[13] where no instances of it are recorded. We are interested in knowing, therefore, where the two instances have come from. A comparison with the corresponding passages in W reveals that W has them directly or indirectly: And spare nat thy horse . . . *nother* for watir *nother* for londe (W 1124.2) – and spare not thy hors . . . *nouther* for water *neyther* for lond (C 775.21); I nevir forbade hit my frynde *nother* my foo (W 294.25) – I neuer deffended þᵗ none / *nother* my frende ne my foo (C 214.14). The two instances in question must have derived, in this way, from an exemplar that has *no(u)ther* in the corresponding contexts.

The last of our evidence is concerned with the significant correspondence of W's -*th* and -*s* to C's -*en* in the present indicative plural endings. This phenomenon is treated by A. O. Sandved and myself.[14] The predominant plural ending is -*ø* or -*e* in both W and C. Furthermore, W has 46 instances of -*th* and 12 of -*s* respectively,[15] with the exception of the Roman War episode. 34 out of the 46 instances of -*th* and one out of the 12 instances of -*s* correspond to -*en*[16] in C as in the following: e.g., man and woman *rejoysyth* and *gladith* of somer commynge (W 1161.3) – man and woman *reioycen* and *gladen* of somer comynge (C 797.3–4); all knyghtes *spekyth* of hym worship (W 580.7) – alle knyghtes *speken* of hym worsip (C 425.27); ye se what soddeyn adventures *befallys* (W 147.7) – ye see what auentures *befallen* (C 134.7). The sporadic occurrences of such dialectal forms as -*th* and -*s* in Caxton's exemplar, whatever it was, must have irritated Caxton the editor. He has replaced them by the full unlevelled Midland form in his edition. Thus the existence of -*en* in C must be due to Caxton's having put special emphasis on the fact that the finite forms with -*th* and -*s* found in his exemplar are, in fact, plural. We have

---

12 For detailed information, see my paper, 'The Coordinate Conjunctions – *nother, nouther, nor, neyther, ne, other, outher, or* and *eyther* – in Malory (in Japanese)', *Studies in Language and Culture* (Nagoya University), Vol. 1, No. 2 (1985), 15–36.

13 K. Mizobata, ed., *A Concordance to Caxton's Own Prose* (Tokyo: Shohakusha, 1990).

14 See A. O. Sandved, 'A Note on the Language of Caxton's Malory and that of the Winchester MS.', *English Studies* XL (1959), 113–4, idem, *Studies in the Language of Caxton's Malory and That of the Winchester Malory* (Oslo: Norwegian University Press, 1968), pp. 383–6, and Y. Nakao, 'Verbal Inflectional Endings in Malory (in Japanese)', *IVY, The Nagoya Review of English Studies*, 3 (1963), 15–30.

15 The verbs *be* and *have* are not included in the statistics.

16 One instance of <-yn> and two of <-n> are included among the predominant instances of <-en>.

only six instances of -*en* in C that do not correspond to W's -*th* or -*s*. These intricate correspondences would not have been preserved if C were collateral to W.

What have been shown so far are only samples. Much more similar evidence to prove that C is more intimately dependent on W will be brought forward. The above are sufficient, however, to excite attention to L. Hellinga's hypothesis.[17]

E. Vinaver's stemma[18] that assigns C a collateral relation to W has been seriously challenged by Hellinga's discovery that, on some pages of W, there are smudges which were caused by printing ink different from that used for writing, and on which offsets of certain letters of Caxton's type 2 and type 4 are discernible. This fact indicates that W was in Caxton's workshop for some years, though the lack of compositors' marks on it also indicates that it was not used as Caxton's direct exemplar. Presumably this lack can be ascribed to the fact that W was a precious manuscript which Caxton was under obligation to return to its owner in undamaged condition. On the basis of these facts, Hellinga postulates the relationship between the two versions as in the following:

> We must assume, then, that someone (either Caxton or another person) used the Malory manuscript that he had borrowed in order to prepare a revised version in manuscript; subsequently this was marked up for the compositors and used by them. This intermediate stage would now be lost.[19]

This assertion, founded on the undeniable material proof, cannot easily be ignored. Though it must be admitted that the evidence presented above in this paper is not of the kind to prove Hellinga's hypothesis directly, it shows at least that there are undoubtedly cases in which C cannot be regarded as independent of W, for the possibility of two collateral texts preserving such intricate affinities would not be high.

What comes to mind in this connection is A. McIntosh's reference to three types of ME scribes (i.e. Types A, B and C).[20] According to him,

---

[17] See L. Hellinga, 'The Malory Manuscript and Caxton', *Aspects of Malory*, ed. T. Takamiya and D. S. Brewer (Cambridge: D.S. Brewer, 1981), pp. 127–41.

[18] Vinaver presents the following stemma (*Works*, p. cvi):

Malory
|
X
Y   Z
| |
W   C

(Vinaver's stemma)

[19] L. Hellinga, *Caxton in Focus: the Beginning of Printing in England* (London: The British Library, 1982), p. 92.

[20] A. McIntosh, 'Word Geography in the Lexicography of Medieval English', *Middle English Dialectology: Essays on Some Principles and Problems*, ed. M. Laing (Aberdeen: The Univer-

ON THE WINCHESTER MALORY AND CAXTON'S MALORY

Type A is more or less faithful to the copy-text, Type B changes its language to their own dialects and Type C lies midway between the two. In order that the linguistic affinities referred to above might be kept unbroken between the two texts, it would be necessary that scribes Y, Z and W in Vinaver's stemma should all have been of McIntosh's Type A. That possibility, however, must be regarded as slight, for, as McIntosh says, Type A 'appears to happen only somewhat rarely.'[21]

In order to give final support to Hellinga's hypothesis, it remains for us to adduce further evidence. In this paper, we have to be content with emphasising the importance, on the basis of the data presented so far, of reexamining the textual evidence accumulated by scholars from an angle different from that shown by Vinaver's stemma. For example, we are interested in confirming, with reference to Vinaver's stemma, whether or not there will arise inconvenience if we replace X by W itself and, if we interpret Z as the manuscript prepared by Caxton or his staff, in cases where W's readings agree with X's against C's.[22] Likewise our interest is in getting to know whether, in cases where C's readings agree with X's against W's,[23] we can presume, without any serious contradiction, that Caxton consulted, and was influenced by, a manuscript other than W.

The speculation that Caxton used Malory's original manuscript as his exemplar (in addition to W) has recently been put forward by R. Griffith.[24] He emphasises that there existed a certain connection between Caxton the printer and Thomas Malory of Papworth St Agnes, whom he believes to have been the author of the Arthuriad. He thus argues that the author's own master manuscript 'made from drafts'[25] was delivered to Caxton for use as his exemplar. According to Griffith, the role that W played for Caxton was only 'for consultation in cases of hiatuses or questionable readings in his base text.'[26]

It is quite above my capability to judge who, of the three Malorys that lived at Papworth St Agnes, at Newbold Revel or in Yorkshire is the

---

sity Press, 1989), pp. 86–97; originally published in *Annals of New York Academy of Sciences* 211 (1973), 55–66.

[21] *Op. cit.*, p. 92.

[22] As the sample words, *nyght* and *whyche* that occur in W, for example, are presumed to be identical with those in X in his stemma, we can replace the string X–Z–C with W–Z–C, taking Z as Caxton's exemplar made on the basis of W.

[23] For example, it is worth while to consider if the scribal errors found in W such as the omission from *sire Tristram* to *sir Tristram* discussed by Vinaver (cf. *Works*, p. civ) were supplied by Caxton on the basis of a manuscript other than W.

[24] 'Caxton's Copy-Text for *Le Morte Darthur*: Tracing the Provenance', *Traditions and Innovations: Essays on British Literature of the Middle Ages and the Renaissance*, ed. D. G. Allen and R. A. White (Newark: University of Delaware Press, 1990), pp. 75–87.

[25] *Op. cit.*, p. 76.

[26] *Op. cit.*, p. 76.

most reasonable candidate for the author, or to say whether or not the copy Caxton is supposed to have used along with W is the author's master manuscript. But what interests me is his assumption that Caxton used W and the other manuscript, whatever it was. Our data, however, suggest that what Caxton depended upon chiefly was the text that did not undergo serious corruption from W. So it is highly probable that Caxton or his staff made the copy-text on the basis of W (making alterations in the text as editor).

Thus the extremely close linguistic affinities between W and C give support to Hellinga's view. On the other hand, it is necessary to postulate that Caxton used a manuscript other than W as well, in order to explain, for example, the passages from Geoffrey, Wace, etc., which exist in C's Book V but do not in the corresponding story in W. Another reason for making such postulation is in order to explain the better readings scattered throughout the other Books in the Caxton text. Accordingly my understanding is that C consists of at least three layers: the layer which is inherited from W itself, through the exemplar manuscript prepared, on the basis of W, by Caxton or some professional scribe(s) in Caxton's employ; the layer which reflects Caxton's own alterations as editor in orthography, morphology and syntax as well as the division into books and chapters; and the layer which comes from a manuscript other than W. Needless to say, the first layer of the three plays the most important role in bringing forth such linguistic correspondences as shown above.

Before closing this essay, a brief comment must be added, from a viewpoint of textual derivation, on the theory that Malory, rather than Caxton, revised the Roman War episode and, in addition, that Malory made alterations in the other portions as well, so that Caxton's Malory is Malory's second edition.[27] If such is really the case, we naturally have to conclude that the revision was made on the basis of Malory's original manuscript. Therefore, the putative manuscript X in Vinaver's stemma has to be split into two kinds: one that was revised by Malory and another that was copied from the original. Of course, W is the descendant from the latter and C from the former through some intermediate stages respectively. In such a stemma, the distance between W and C would be far more remote than what Vinaver shows in his stemma. That is untenable because of the data furnished so far.

---

[27] See, for example, J. Spisak, 'Malory Revises his Vocabulary', *Poetica* 17 (1984), 27–30, R. M. Lumiansky, 'Sir Thomas Malory's *Le Morte Darthur*, 1947–1987: Author, Title, Text', *Speculum* 62 (1987), 878–97 and C. Moorman, 'Caxton's *Morte Darthur*: Malory's Second Edition?', *Fifteenth Century Studies* 12 (1987), 99–113. For the present writer's view on this problem, see 'Does Malory Really Revise his Vocabulary? – Some Negative Evidence –', *Poetica*, 25 & 26 (1987), 93–109.

ON THE WINCHESTER MALORY AND CAXTON'S MALORY

I should like to conclude this essay by suggesting, as a problem for further enquiry, the importance of studying the textual pedigree between the two versions along a line other than indicated by Vinaver in his stemma.[28]

---

[28] The necessity for such studies is also suggested, for example, in G. A. Barthos, 'Caxton's Edition of Malory Based on a Source other than the Winchester Manuscript', *Notes & Queries*, 224 (1979), 9–10.

Texts of 'Be Cynestole' in Wulfstan's *Institutes of Polity**

TADAO KUBOUCHI

The fourth chapter entitled 'Be Cynestole' of Wulfstan's *Institutes of Polity*, edited by Karl Jost (Berne, 1959: pp. 55–8), is a revision by Wulfstan of lines 1204–20 of Ælfric's 'On the Old and New Testament' (written 1005–6)[1] in S. J. Crawford's edition of *The Old English Version of the Heptateuch, Ælfric's Treatise on the Old and New Testament and his Preface to Genesis*, (E.E.T.S., o.s. 160 (London, 1922, 1969), pp. 71–2). Jost prints texts in full from Corpus Christi College, Cambridge, 201 (MS. D) on pages 87 (l. 33)–88 (l. 8) and Oxford, Bodleian Library, Junius 121 (MS. X) on fols. 10b (l. 16)–11a (l. 19). However, he prints from British Library, Cotton Nero A.i (MS. G), f. 71ab (f. 71a, l. 13–f. 71b, l. 15), only the readings which are variant from those of Junius 121.

Although they in some way or other all represent what Dorothy Bethurum calls 'Archbishop Wulfstan's Commonplace Book',[2] these three manuscripts differ significantly in date of production. CCCC 201 (Ker 49 B) is dated in the mid-eleventh century, Junius 121 (Ker 338) in the third quarter of the eleventh century, and the B portion of Nero A.i (Ker 164), which contains the *Institutes*, at the beginning of the eleventh century.[3] Wulfstan died in 1023 and Nero A.i (part B) bears clear

---

* I am indebted to Professor Peter Clemoes for drawing my attention to the early English tradition beginning with King Alfred of the tripartite classification of society and for giving me a few copied pages from his forthcoming book, and to Dr Malcolm Parkes for invaluable advice and for a few copied pages from the pre-publication copy of his *Pause & Effect*. I am grateful to the authorities of the Bodleian Library, the British Library and the Corpus Christi College Cambridge Library for permission to reproduce the parts of their manuscripts which contain the texts treated here. I should like to take this opportunity to express my gratitude to Dr Bruce Mitchell, Professor Henry Loyn, Dr James Campbell, Professor Malcolm Godden, Dr Joyce Hill, Dr John Scahill, Professor Angus McIntosh, and Professor R. I. Page and the Research Group on Manuscript Evidence, the Parker Library, Corpus Christi College, Cambridge, for their generous and stimulating advice. I wish also to express my thanks to the British Academy and the British Council for their grants which enabled me to spend in England three months each in 1990 and 1991 to do research on the literary relationship between Wulfstan and Ælfric. This article is based on part of the product of those visits to England.

1 Clemoes (1959).

2 Bethurum (1942).

3 Cotton Nero A.i consists of two portions, part A (fols. 3–57; Ker 163) written about the

evidence that 'Wulfstan planned, ordered, supervised the construction of and corrected' it (H. R. Loyn (1971), p. 46). Its provenance also is notable.[4] In the introduction to her edition of *Sermo Lupi ad Anglos* (revised edition, University of Exeter, 1976; 3rd ed., London, 1963), Dorothy Whitelock observes, 'Though Liebermann thought a Canterbury origin possible, the manuscript [Nero A.i] must have been written at one of Wulfstan's sees, Worcester or York' (p. 1). She adds, furthermore, citing as evidence the erasure of a statement on f. 72b enjoining celibacy on priests to be replaced by a comment in favour of clerical marriage, 'This seems to fit York, where married priests were common in the eleventh century, better than monastic establishments such as Worcester and Canterbury' (p. 1, f.n. 5). Where the study of Wulfstan's original vocabulary, syntax or punctuation is concerned, priority should be given to manuscripts of York (and then Worcester) provenance and those written within his lifetime. We should always bear in mind the fact that the number of extant manuscripts of York provenance is deplorably small.[5] The eight other manuscripts in which Wulfstan's hand has been identified by N. R. Ker are also invaluable.[6] (H. R. Loyn adds pages from these manuscripts to his E.E.M.F. edition of Nero A.i, and lists them on p. 32.)

In what follows, therefore, are printed all the three manuscript texts in full and in semi-diplomatic form with the punctuation provided in the manuscripts. It is hoped that they will make clear how exemplary and informative Nero A.i is in terms of punctuation as well as how much closer the relationship is between Nero A.i and Junius 121 in terms of words and phrases than that between Nero A.i and CCCC 201:[7] while it is only a punctus that is used throughout the text in CCCC 201 and Junius 121, three principal punctuation marks are used in Nero A.i, a punctus placed at about mid-height (·), a punctus elevatus (⸵ or :) and a punctus versus (;). The occasional use of the punctus elevatus to give extra rhetorical force makes one certain that the homiletic element predominates even in the *Institutes*.[8] It is again hoped that the texts given below will show how rhythmically or heavily Wulfstan manuscripts on the whole are punctuated and finally how informative diplomatic or

---

middle of the eleventh century and part B (fols. 70–177; Ker 164) written at the beginning of the eleventh century.

[4] For Junius 121, a Worcester manuscript, see E. A. McIntyre (1978), and for the 'tremulous Worcester hand', see Franzen (1991). For the provenance of CCCC 201, see Whitelock (1976^r), p. 2.

[5] Ker (1971). See also Ker (1957), p. lvi and the introduction (especially pp. 24–5) to his E.E.M.F. edition of *The Pastoral Care* (Copenhagen: Rosenkilde and Bagger, 1956).

[6] Loyn (1971), p. 46, f.n. 3.

[7] Loyn (1971), pp. 25–6. For the general discussion of punctuation in Old and Middle English manuscripts, see Clemoes (1952), Parkes (1978), and Parkes (1992).

[8] Whitelock (1976^r), pp. 21 and 25–6.

TEXTS OF 'BE CYNESTOLE'

semi-diplomatic texts with manuscript punctuation are not only for palaeographical or prose rhythm studies, but also for syntactic ones.[9]

Ælfric, on whom Wulfstan is dependent, treats the subject of the three orders, i.e. 'bellatores, oratores and laboratores' two more times: *Ælfric's Lives of Saints* (ed. W. W. Skeat, E.E.T.S., o.s. 76, 82, 94 and 114 (London, 1881–1900), Life XXV, ll. 812–62); and *Die Hirtenbriefe Ælfrics in altenglischer und lateinischer Fassung* (ed. Bernhard Fehr, Bibliothek der angelsächsischen Prosa 9 (Hamburg, 1914), reprinted with a supplement to the introduction by Peter Clemoes (Darmstadt, 1966), Brief 2a (Ælfric's Latin letter to Wulfstan), XIV).[10] However, these two treatments have far less in common with Wulfstan texts: there are fewer words which are equivalent to those used by Wulfstan. Wulfstan's source, as Peter Clemoes points out, is clearly Ælfric's 'On the Old and New Testament'.[11] Ælfric's text from the sole MS. L (written in the second quarter of the eleventh century), i.e. Bodleian Library, Oxford, Laud Misc. 509 (Ker 344 art. 4), on f. 140ab, is given first below. Words in bold-faced type are those that Wulfstan made use of.[12]

L   (f. 140a, l. 15–f. 140b, l. 8; Crawford (1922, 1969), pp. 71–2, ll. 1204–20):

Witan sceoldon smeagan **mid wislicum** geþeahte . /
þonne on mancinne to micel yfel bið hwilc þæra /
stelenna þæs **cine stoles** wære to brocen . 7 betan /
ðone sona . Se **cine stol stynt on** þisum **þrim** stelum . /
Laboratores . bellatores . oratores . Laboratores sind /
þe `hig´[13] us **bigleofan tiliað** . yrðlingas . 7 æhte men to þam /
anum be-tæhte . **Oratores syndon þe** us **þingiað** to /
gode 7 cristen-dom fyrðriað **on cristenum** folcum . on /
godes þeow-dome to ðam gastlican ge-winne to þam /
anum be-tæhte us eallum **to þearfe** . **Bellatores sin/don**
þe ure burga healdað 7 éac urn(e) **eard** wið ⌈þ⌉on⌈e⌉ /
sigendne here feohtende **mid wæmnum** . swa swa paulus // <f. 140b>
sæde se þeoda lareow on his lareow-dome . Non sine cau/sa

---

[9] For the discussion of the relevance of investigations of manuscript punctuation for the syntactical study of Old English, see Mitchell (1980), Godden (1977), and Kubouchi (1983). For the discussion especially of the study of element order in Old and Middle English, see Kubouchi (1988).

[10] Clemoes (forthcoming), Ch. 11.

[11] *Ibid.*, Ch. 11.

[12] The signs used in the reproduced texts below are as follows: / indicates the end of a line in the manuscripts; // the end of a page or folio; `´ an interlinear insertion; ⌈ ⌉ an addition in a hand other than the original; and ( ) an erasure, deletion, or loss through fading. The period mark is used for the punctus irrespective of its height. Abbreviations are expanded in italics.

[13] A late hand adds `hig´ after 'þe' and transposes 'þe . . . tiliað' to follow 'betæhte' one line below.

213

portat miles gladium . & cetera . Ne byrð na se cniht /
butan intingan his swurd . he ys **godes** þen þe sylfum /
to þearfe on ðam yfelum wyrcendum to wræce ge-sett . /
On þisum þrim stelum **stynt** se **cyne-stol** . 7 gif an bið /
forud he fylð adun **sona** . þam oþrum stelum **to unðearfe** /
ge-wiss . **ac** hwæt gebyrað us embe þis to smeagenne /
þis sceolon smeagan þe þæs giman sceolon .

Wulfstan texts are given below. (K. Jost (1959), pp. 55–8)

G: BL, Cotton Nero A.1, f. 71a (l. 13)–f. 71b (l. 15). Ker 164 art. 1(iii).
D: CCCC 201, pp. 87 (l. 33)–88 (l. 8). Ker 49 B art. 42(iii).
X: Bodleian Library, Oxford, Junius 121, f. 10b (l. 16)–f. 11a (l. 19). Ker
338 art. 1(iv).

G **BE CY NESTOLE** :– /
D
X **BE CYNESTOLE** . / .iiii.

G	Ælc	riht	cyne stol ⁊	stent	on	þrim	stapelum . /
D	Ælc		cyne stol	stent	on	þrim	stapelum .
X	**ÆLC** . **RIHT** . **CYNE STOL** . **STENT** / on					þrym	stapelum .

G	þe fullice ariht	stænt ;	**An**	is .	Oratores ⁊ /		
D	þe fullice ariht	stent . /	**Án**	is .	Oratores .		
X	þe fullice a riht	steNT . /	án	is .	Oratores .		

G	7	oðer is . labo ratores ⁊	7	þridde is . bellatores ; /
D	And oðer is . Laboratores . And /			þridde is . Bellatores .
X	7	oðer is . Laboratores . /	7	ðridde is . Bellatores .

G	**Oratores** . syndon	gebed men .	þe gode scylan /
D	**Oratores** syndon	gebedmen .	/ þe gode sculon
X	**Oratores** sindon /	gebedmen	þe gode sculan

G	þeowian . 7 dæges	7 nihtes for ealne þeod/scype
D	þeowian . 7 dæges	7 nihtes for ealne þeodscipe . /
X	þeowian . 7 dæges /	7 nihtes for ealne þeod scipe

G	þingigan	georne ;	Laboratores . /
D	þingian	georne .	Laboratores .
X	þingian /	georne .	Laboratores

G	syndon weorc men ⁊		þe tilian	scylan	þæs /
D	sindon weorc men .		þe tilian /	sculon .	þæs
X	sindon weorcm⸢en⸣ //<f.11a>		þe tilian	sculon	þæs

214

TEXTS OF 'BE CYNESTOLE'

G þe eal þeod scype . big sceal libban ; /
D þe eal þeodscipe big sceal libban .
X ðe eall þeod scype big / sceall libban .

G **B**ellatores . syndon wigmen . þe eard /
D **B**ellatores / syndon wigmen . þe eard
X **B**ellatores . syndon wigm⌈en⌉ / þe eard

G scylon werian . wig lice mid wæpnum ; /
D sculon werian . wig lice mid wæpnum . /
X sculon werian . wiglice mid wæpnum . /

G **On** þyssum þrim stapelum . sceal ælc cynestol // . <71b>
D **On** þisum þrim stapelum sceal ælc cynestol
X **On** þyssum ðrym stapelum sceall ælc cyne/stol

G standan mid rihte . `on christenre þeode .' **7** awacie
D standan . mid rihte . / **7** awacige
X standan mid rihte on cristenre þeode . / **7** awácíe

G heora ænig ؛ / sona se stol scylfð ؛ 7 ful berste heora /
D heora ænig . sona se stol scilfð . 7 forberste heora /
X heora ænig . sona se stol scylfð . / 7 ful berste heora

G ænig . þonne hryst se stol nyþer . 7 *þæt* wyrð /
D ænig . // <p. 88> þonne rist se stol nyðer . 7 *þæt* wurð
X ænig . þonne hrysð se / stol nyðer . 7 *þæt* wyrð

G þære þeode eal `to' unþearfe ; **Ac** staþe lige man . /
D þare þeode eal to unþearfe . / **Ac** staðe lige man
X þære þeode eall to un/þearfe . **Ac** staþelige man

G 7 strangige ؛ and trym me hy georne . /
D 7 strangige . 7 trim me hi georne .
X 7 strangie . 7 trum/me hi georne .

G mid wislicre godes lage . 7 mid rihtlicre /
D mid wislicre / godes lage .
X mid wislicre godes lare . / 7 mid ríhtlicre

G worold lage . *þæt* wyrð þam þeod scype to lang/suman
D *þæt* wurð þam þeodscipe to lang suman
X woruld lage . *þæt* wyrð þam þeod/scype to lángsuman

215

G ræde ; 7   soð is *þæt* ic   secge *.* awacie /
D ræde . forða*m* / soð is *þæt* ic   secge . awacige
X ræde . 7   soð is *þæt* ic   / secge . awacige

G se chr*i*stendom *.* sona scylf*þ*   se cynedom ; /
D se cristendom . sona scylfð   se cynedo*m* . /
X se cristendóm   sona scylfð   / se cyne dom .

G 7   arære man unlaga   . ahwar on lande *.* /
D And arære man un laga   ahwar on lande .
X 7   arære man únlaga / ahwar on lande .

G oððon únsida lufige ahwar   to swyþe . /
D oððe   unsida   / ahwar   to swiðe .
X oððe   únsida lufige ahwar   / to swiðe .

G *þæt* cymð þære   þeode . eal to unþearfe ; /
D *þæt* cymð þare   þeode eal to un þearfe . /
X *þæt* cymð þære   þeode eall to un/þearfe .

G **Ac** do man swa hit þearf is *.* alecge man /
D **Ac** do man swa hit þeaf is . alecge man
X **Ac** dó man swa hit þearf is . alecge / man

G unriht . 7 rære   up godes riht *.* *þæt* mæg /
D unriht . 7 arære / up godes riht . *þæt* mæg
X únriht . 7 rære   up godes riht . *þæt* mæg /

G to þearfe   for gode 7 for worolde ; **AM***en* ; /
D to þearfe .   for gode 7 for worlde . am*en* . /
X to þearfe ⌈:⌉ for gode 7 for worulde . Am*en* . /

REFERENCES

Bethurum, Dorothy. 1942. 'Archbishop Wulfstan's Commonplace Book'. *P.M.L.A.* 57, pp. 916–29.

Cameron, Angus. 1973. 'A List of Old English Texts', *A Plan for the Dictionary of Old English*, ed. Roberta Frank and Angus Cameron (Toronto: University of Toronto Press), pp. 25–306.

Clemoes, Peter. 1952. 'Liturgical Influence on Punctuation in Late Old English and Early Middle English Manuscripts', *Department of Anglo-Saxon Occasional Papers* 1 (Cambridge), pp. 3–22; reprinted as *Old English Newsletter* Subsidia 4 (CEMERS, SUNY-Binghamton, 1980).

Clemoes, Peter. 1959. 'The Chronology of Ælfric's Works', *The Anglo-Saxons: Studies in Some Aspects of their History and Culture Presented to Bruce Dickins*, ed. Peter

TEXTS OF 'BE CYNESTOLE'

Clemoes (London: Bowes), pp. 212–47; reprinted as *Old English Newsletter* Subsidia 5 (CEMERS, SUNY-Binghamton, 1980).

Clemoes, Peter. Forthcoming. *Symbolic Action: Interactions of Thought and Language in Old English Poetry* (Cambridge: Cambridge University Press).

Crawford, S. J. ed. 1922. *The Old English Version of the Heptateuch, Ælfric's Treatise on the Old and New Testament and his Preface to Genesis*. E.E.T.S., o.s. 160 (London: Oxford University Press); reprinted with the text of two additional manuscripts transcribed by N. R. Ker (1969).

Franzen, Christine. 1991. *The Tremulous Hand of Worcester: A Study of Old English in the Thirteenth Century* (Oxford: Clarendon Press).

Godden, Malcolm. 1977. 'Old English', *Editing Medieval Texts English, French, and Latin Written in England: Papers Given at the Twelfth Annual Conference on Editorial Problems, University of Toronto, 5–6 November 1976*, ed. A. G. Rigg (New York & London: Garland), pp. 9–33.

Jost, Karl. 1959. *Die 'Institutes of Polity, Civil and Ecclesiastical': ein Werk Erzbischof Wulfstans von York*. Swiss Studies in English 47 (Berne: Francke).

Ker, N. R. 1957. *Catalogue of Manuscripts Containing Anglo-Saxon* (Oxford: Clarendon Press).

Ker, N. R. 1964. *Medieval Libraries of Great Britain: A List of Surviving Books*, second edition (Royal Historical Society Guides and Handbooks 3); First edition, 1941; *Supplement to the Second Edition*, ed. A. G. Watson (Royal Historical Society Guides and Handbooks 15) (London, 1987).

Ker, N. R. 1971. 'The Handwriting of Archbishop Wulfstan', *England before the Conquest: Studies in Primary Sources Presented to Dorothy Whitelock*, ed. Peter Clemoes and Kathleen Hughes (Cambridge: Cambridge University Press), pp. 315–31.

Kubouchi, Tadao. 1983. 'A Note on Prose Rhythm in Wulfstan's *De Falsis Dies* [sic]', *Poetica* 15 & 16, pp. 57–106.

Kubouchi, Tadao. 1988. 'Manuscript Punctuation, Prose Rhythm and S. . .V Element Order in Late Old English Orally-Delivered Prose', *Philologia Anglica: Essays Presented to Professor Yoshio Terasawa on the Occasion of His Sixtieth Birthday*, ed. K. Oshitari and others (Tokyo: Kenkyusha), pp. 71–87.

Loyn, H. R. ed. 1971. *A Wulfstan Manuscript Containing Institutes, Laws and Homilies: British Museum Cotton Nero A.I*. E.E.M.F. 17 (Copenhagen: Rosenkilde and Bagger).

McIntyre, E. A. 1978. *Early-Twelfth Century Worcester Cathedral Priory with Special Reference to the Manuscripts Written There* (D.Phil. thesis, Oxford).

Mitchell, Bruce. 1980. 'The Dangers of Disguise: Old English Texts in Modern Punctuation', *R.E.S.* 31, pp. 385–413; reprinted in Bruce Mitchell, *On Old English: Selected Papers* (Oxford: Blackwell, 1990).

Parkes, Malcolm. 1978. 'Punctuation, or Pause and Effect', *Medieval Eloquence: Studies in the Theory of Medieval Rhetoric*, ed. J. J. Murphy (Berkeley: University of California Press), pp. 127–42.

Parkes, Malcolm. 1992. *Pause & Effect: An Introduction to the History of Punctuation in the West* (London: Scolar Press).

Swanton, Michael. ed. and tr. 1975. *Anglo-Saxon Prose*. Everyman's University Library (London: Dent).

Thorpe, Benjamin. 1840. *Ancient Laws and Institutes of England; comprising Laws enacted under the Anglo-Saxon Kings from Aethelbriht to Cnut, with an English Translation of the Saxon . . . also, Monumenta Ecclesiastica Anglicana from the Seventh to the Tenth Century*, 2 vols. (London).

Whitelock, Dorothy. 1976. *Sermo Lupi ad Anglos*, revised edition (University of Exeter); third edition (London: Methuen, 1963; first edition, 1939).

Chaucer's Use of Words of Old Norse Origin

JUN SUDO

It is well-known that Chaucer was the first English poet that availed himself of dialectal words so as to create a stylistic effect. This was clearly illustrated in the *Reeve's Tale,* and as early as in 1934 this problem was admirably discussed by J. R. R. Tolkien. But how did Chaucer make use of Northern English words, especially loan-words from Old Norse in his other works? David Burnley said, 'the proportion of Norse words in Chaucer's vocabulary is quite small', in his *Guide to Chaucer's Language.*[1] In this paper I would like to reexamine this statement, and try to make a supplement to Burnley's claim.

1. Nouns

It is said that in Lincolnshire people in general still use many Scandinavian words such as 'lathe' for 'barn', and 'bairn' for 'child' in their daily life, to mention only a few. The word 'lathe' was already used by Chaucer in the *House of Fame*:

> For al mot out, other late or rathe,
> Alle the sheves in the *lathe.*   (*HF*, 2139–40)
>   (emphasis mine in this and the subsequent quotations)[2]

This northern colouring word is found in the *Reeve's Tale* again.

The noun 'bone' or 'boone' which means 'prayer, request, petition, or favour' may be said to stem from the Old Norse word 'bon'. This word was employed by Chaucer in his early poems:

> Throgh Juno, that had herd hir *bone,*
> That made hir to slepe sone.   (*BD*, 129–30)

> And seyde, "Graunte us, lady shene,
> Ech of us of thy grace a *bone!"*   (*HF*, 1536–7)

This word is found in the *Canterbury Tales*, too.

---

[1] See his *Guide to Chaucer's Language* (London: MacMillan, 1983), p. 146.

[2] All references to Chaucer's works are to *The Riverside Chaucer*, ed. Larry D. Benson (Boston: Houghton Mifflin, 1987).

ARTHURIAN AND OTHER STUDIES

> For thogh the signe shewed a delay,
> Yet wiste he wel that graunted was his *boone,* (: soone)
>
> > (*KnT*, A. 2268–9)

It is curious that the Old English counterpart 'ben' gave the form 'bene' in *King Horn*.

> 'King,' he sede, 'so kene
> Graunte me a *bene.'*   (*King Horn*, 507–8)[3]

The Modern English noun 'bull' was probably influenced by Dutch 'bulle', while the Middle English correspondence was 'bole', which was apparently adopted from Old Norse 'boli'.

> Right as the wylde *bole* bygynneth sprynge, (var. blood; lole)
> Now her, now ther, idarted to the herte,
>
> . . .
>
> Right so gan he aboute the chaumbre sterte,   (*Tr*, IV, 239–42)
> Cf. il *toro* (*Fil.*, 4, st, 27)
>
> Ful hye upon a chaar of gold stood he,
> With foure white *boles* in the trays.   (*KnT*, A, 2138–9)

Some words pertaining to the institutions of the Norsemen naturally entered the vocabulary of English, some of which were used by Chaucer. Such nouns as 'swayn', 'thral', and 'carl' are included here. The first noun 'swayn' was treated by Burnley in his book.[4] The second word 'thral' meaning 'slave' was adopted in the Old English period, and it seems that the word was prevalent in Chaucer's works:

> And throgh plesaunce become his *thral*
> With good wille, body, hert, and al.   (*BD*, 767–8)
>
> The faireste children of the blood roial
> Of Israel he leet do gelde anoon,
> And maked ech of hem to been his *thral.*   (*MkT*, B, 2151–3)

Only once did Chaucer make use of the newer loan-word from French: 'sclave':

> I kan namore, but that I wol the serve
> Right as thi *sclave,* whider so thow wende,   (*Tr*, III, 390–1)

But in Chaucer the noun was still rare. Then we find double forms of 'cherl' and 'carl', the latter of which came from Old Norse. The former

---

3   *King Horn* from *Specimens of Early English,* ed. Richard Morris, Pt I (Oxford: Clarendon Press, 1898), pp. 237–86.
4   See Burnley, *ibid.*, p. 151.

CHAUCER'S USE OF WORDS OF OLD NORSE ORIGIN

form 'cherl' is employed as often as forty times in the *Canterbury Tales*, while the latter Northern variant of 'carl' is seen four times. The northern form 'carl' seems to carry somewhat derogatory meanings.

The *O.E.D.* failed to record any example of 'won' from Chaucer, who used the word of Norse origin eight times in the rhyming positions. W. W. Skeat notes that this is one of the rather numerous words in Chaucer that have not been rightly understood.[5] The word 'woon' or 'won' probably came from ON *van*, which meant 'hope, expectation, or prospect'. Then in the phrases of 'ful good won' or 'ful great won' it came to signify 'resources, abundance' and the sense resulted from individual applications of 'what is hoped for'. What is more, the word 'won' appears only in the rhyming position:

> Of roses ther were gret *wone*,   (*RR*, 1673)

> "I have of sorwe so gret *won*
> That joye gete I never non,   (*BD*, 475–6)

> And whan he say ther was non other *woon*,
> He gan hire lymes dresse in swich manere
> As men don hem that shal ben layd on beere.   (*Tr*, IV, 1181–3)

The next example seems to have a meaning of 'dwelling place', or 'place':

> Thoo gan I up the hil to goon,
> And fond upon the cop a *woon*,   (*HF*, 1165–6)

The word 'sky' appears twice in the works of Chaucer. The word originally meant 'cloud' as is seen in the example from the *House of Fame*:

> And let a certeyn wynd to goo,
> That blew so hydously and hye
> That hyt ne lefte not a *skye*
> In alle the welken long and brod.   (*HF*, 1598–1601)

The word 'skye' was adopted from ON 'sky'. The word gradually came to mean 'the firmament', as in:

> Til I koude flee ful hye under the sky. (: by)   (*SqT*, F, 503)

In Chaucer the synonymous nouns such as 'welken', 'firmament', and 'heaven' were used. Among these, the word 'heaven' is most prevalent.

If Old English 'sceaða' came down to Middle English, the form would be '*shathe'. Besides, the original sense of the word 'sceaða' was 'one

---

5 Cf. *The Complete Works of Geoffrey Chaucer*, ed. W. W. Skeat, Vol. II (Oxford: Clarendon Press, repr., 1950), p. 492.

who works harm, injurer', which contained the semantic feature of the agent, as is seen in *Beowulf*:

> Þæt mid Scyldingum   *sceaðona* ic nat hwylc,   (*Beowulf*, 274)[6]

The Old Norse cognate noun 'skaði' did not have the distinctive feature of the agent, and it had the meaning of 'hurt, damage, harm or misfortune', which came to be blended with the native word in the Middle English period, although the Scandinavian characteristics were stronger in the Middle English noun 'scathe' both in form and in sense. A Chaucer example is:

> Criseyde, which that nevere dide hem *scathe*,
> Shal now no lenger in hire blisse bathe;   (*Tr*, IV, 207–8)

Chaucer's idiomatic use of the next 'and that was scathe' which seems to mean 'and that was a pity!' strikingly resembles the example found in *Sir Gawain and the Green Knight*:

> . . . bi Kryst, hit is *scape*
> Þat þou, leude, schal be lost, þat art of lyf noble!
> > (*Sir Gaw*, 674–5)[7]
> But she was somdel deef, *and that was scathe*.
> > (*Gen Prol*, A, 446)

In Chaucer we find the doublet forms of 'bush' and 'busk'. The latter is supposed to reflect Scandinavian influence and this northern form seems to be limited in the *Romaunt of the Rose* and the *Knight's Tale*:

> Or *bush*, or grass, or eryd lond;   (*HF*, 485)
> For ther is neither *busk* nor hay   (*RR*, 54)
> He stirte hym up out of the *buskes* thikke   (*KnT*, A, 1579)
> > (Ellesmere and Hengwrt MSS.)

In Chaucer's vocabulary we find a group of words which have meanings of 'fortune'. They may be said to include 'fortune, wyrd, destinee, fate, chaunce, aventure, cas, hap, lot, and sort'.[8] Among them the word 'hap' and its variants have their origin in Old Norse, and it seems that Chaucer employed it when he tried to translate Latin 'casus' and Old French 'cas' in his *Boece*. Chaucer did not use the word 'wyrd' in his *Canterbury Tales*. Instead he employed the word 'hap' both as a noun and a verb twenty-seven times:

---

[6] *Beowulf*, ed. Michael Swanton (Manchester: Manchester University Press, 1978).

[7] *Sir Gawain and the Green Knight*, ed. I. Gollancz, E.E.T.S., o.s. 210 (London: Oxford University Press, 1957).

[8] See Hiroyuki Matsumoto, 'Chaucer's Use of *Fortune* and its Related Terms', in *Key-Words Studies in Chaucer* 2, ed. Yoshio Terasawa (Tokyo: Centre for Mediaeval English Studies, 1987), pp. 17–73.

CHAUCER'S USE OF WORDS OF OLD NORSE ORIGIN

The oghte not to clepe it *hap,* but grace.   (*Tr,* I. 896)

And the next collocation seems to have some idiomatic usage:

Thoughte in his herte, "*Happe how happe may,*
Al sholde I dye, I wol hire herte seche!
. . ."   (*Tr,* V, 796–7)

The phrase has a meaning of 'whatever may happen':

Shal I clepe hyt *hap* other grace
That broght me there? Nay, but Fortune,   (*BD,* 810–1)

2. **Adjectives and Adverbs**

The native adjective of OE *wac* (> ME *woke*) was gradually replaced by the Scandinavian loan word 'waik', which was adopted from ON *veikr.* The earliest examples in English are found in the *Cursor Mundi.* In Chaucer the adjective 'wayk' is often juxtaposed with its synonymous adjectives, such as 'wayk and fieble', (*ParsT,* I, 310), 'thynne and wayk', (*Bo,* I, p. 6, 102) or 'wayk, and ek wery', (*LGW,* 2428) or 'weik and small' (*RR,* 225). It is as often used singly:

And *wayke* been the oxen in my plough.   (*KnT,* A, 887)

A curious form of the comparative degree of the adjective 'bad' is found in Chaucer's *Book of Duchess:*

Allas, how myghte I fare *werre*?   (*BD,* 616)

This form is directly descended from ON 'verra' (= worse), while Chaucer's usual form appears as 'worse':

I ferde the *worse* al the morwe
Aftir to thenken on hir sorwe.   (*BD,* 99–100)

The next rare form of 'stoore' is worth mention. The adjective 'stoore' meaning 'bold, great or proud' was borrowed from Old Norse 'storr'. Chaucer seems to have made use of this form only once in his works:

"O strange lady *stoore,* what dostow?"   (*MerchT,* E, 2367)

Another Scandinavian adjective 'wight' is found in Chaucer:[9]

---

[9] This adjective 'wight' is included into the same entry as the noun 'wight' meaning 'man', in Akio Oizumi's *Complete Concordance,* Vol. III (Hildesheim: Olms-Weidmann, 1991), p. 2310.

With any yong man, were he never so *wight*. (: myght)

(MkT, B, 3457)

Cf. He was fayr man, and swithe *wiht*. (: kniht)

(Havelok, 344)[10]

Other instances of adjective of Old Norse origin are:

Ne Dedalus with his playes *slye*; (: melodye)　　(*BD*, 570)

O, welaway! So *sleighe* arn clerkes olde　　(*Tr*, IV, 972)

The adjective forms of 'sleighe' and 'slye' are used together with the noun 'sleight', both of which came from Old Norse *slægr* and *slægð*. A Chaucer example is:

Ther nas baillif, ne hierde, nor oother hyne,
That he ne knew his *sleighte* and his covyne;

(Gen Prol, A, 603–4)

The set phrase of 'high and low' (the latter form 'low' came from Old Norse) is made use of by Chaucer:

In many a place, *lowe* and hie.　　(*RR*, A, 841)

What so he were, of heigh or *lough* estat,　　(*Gen Prol*, A, 522)

The Modern English adjective 'ill' has its origin in ON 'illr'. In Chaucer, the word is restricted in the *Reeve's Tale* and in the *Romaunt of the Rose*, B. Instead such adjectives as 'yvel, bad or sik' were employed by Chaucer.

The impressive alliterative phrase 'meek as a maid' (consisting of Old Norse adjective 'mjukr') is found in:

And of his port as *meeke* as is a mayde.　　(*Gen Prol*, A, 69)

In Chaucer the concept of 'beauty' and its antonym was expressed with the words of 'fair' and 'foul'. But the next example is of the rarest occurrence:

This *ugly* sergeant, in the same wyse (Hengwrt: *vggly*)
That he hire doghter caughte, right so he –　　(*ClT*, E, 673–4)

The adjective 'ugly' was adopted from ON *uggligr*.

The noun 'anger' and its adjectival derivative 'angry', which are descendent from Old Norse, were used by Chaucer very frequently. At the same time, the synonymous and more elegant word 'ire' taken from Old French occurs as often.

---

[10] *The Lay of Havelok the Dane*, ed. W.W. Skeat, 2nd ed. revised K. Sisam (Oxford: Clarendon Press, 1915).

Diane, which that wroth was and in *ire*
For Grekis nolde don hire sacrifice,   (*Tr*, V, 1464–5)

Thise wordes seyde he for the nones alle,
That with swich thing he myght hym *angry* maken,
And with *angre* don his wo to falle,   (*Tr*, I, 561–3)

We should note that the phrase 'in ire' is juxtaposed with its synonym 'wroth'.

One of the basic lexical items of our daily English concerning the size of a thing or man may be the adjective 'big'. This word is found in Chaucer, too. Perhaps Chaucer, as a Londoner, might not have any recognition of the word 'big' as a Norse word:

The MILLERE was a stout carl for the nones;
Ful *byg* he was of brawn, and eek of bones.
                                    (*Gen Prol*, A, 545–6)

Similarly:

And therto he was long and *big* of bones   (*KnT*, A, 1424)

Here we may include some adverbial words. One of the well-known battle scenes in Chaucer is found in the *Legend of the Good Women:*

And *heterly* they hurtelen al atones   (*LGW*, 638)

The adverb 'heterly' is the blending of OE 'hetelice' and ON 'hatrliga'. This word belongs to the vocabulary of alliterative poems as J. R. R. Tolkien noted. It seems that Chaucer intentionally tried to imitate the expression of alliterative school in this case.

Another Norse-derived adverb is found in the next examples:

Thise wordes seyd, she on hire armes two
Fil *gruf*, and gan to wepen pitously.   (*Tr*, IV, 911–2)

And with that word, withouten moore respit,
They fillen *gruf* and criden pitously,   (*KnT*, A, 948–9)

The phrase of 'fall gruf' means 'fall in a prone position, face down'.

3. Verbs

The verb 'baiten', which is the causative of 'bite', was borrowed from Old Norse 'beita'. Chaucer's use is found in:

On many a sory meel now may she *bayte*;   (*MLT*, B, 466)

The following use of the verb 'baiten' is of interest, because the verb is used figuratively:

ARTHURIAN AND OTHER STUDIES

> And in his walk ful faste he gan to wayten
> If knyght or squyer of his compaignie
> Gan for to syke, or lete his eighen *baiten*
> On any womman that he koude espye.   (*Tr*, I, 190–3)

Another example of Old Norse loan words is given by the verb 'greithen':

> She hadde no thought, by nyght ne day,
> Of nothing, but if it were oonly
> To *graythe* hir wel and uncouthly.   (*RR*, A, 582–4)

> Unto the Jewes swich an hate hadde he
> That he bad *greithen* his chaar ful hastily,   (*MkT*, B, 3783–4)

The verb 'greithen' which came from ON *greiða* means 'to make or get ready or arrange', and it was used in the *Reeve's Tale*, too.

In the famous description of the Wife of Bath in the *General Prologue*, a curious verb 'carpe' is found. This verb was not recorded in the *O.E.D.* as a Chaucerian example. The word had meanings of 'brag, boast, talk in a loud voice'. This verb was clearly borrowed from ON 'karpa' and belonged to the alliterative school. The famous description has:

> And on hir feet a paire of spores sharpe.
> In felaweshipe wel koude she laughe and *carpe*.
> (*Gen Prol*, A, 473–4)

The originally impersonal verb 'want' meaning 'lack' was adopted from ON 'vanta'. Chaucer seems to make a sporadic use of the verb:

> For hastif man ne *wanteth* nevere care.   (*Tr*, IV, 1568)

> Ful many a story, of which I touche shal
> A fewe, as of Calyxte and Athalante,
> And many a mayde of which the name I *wante*.   (*PF*, 285–7)

In the Commentary to the *Havelok the Dane*, Bennett and Smithers noted that the verb 'rowte' occurs in Middle English solely in Rolle and the *Catholicon Anglicum*, besides the *Havelok*.[11] But the word in question does appear in Chaucer, too:

> Whan tempest doth the shippes swalowe,
> And lat a man stonde, out of doute,
> A myle thens, and here hyt *route*;   (*HF*, 1036–8)

> The sterne wynd so loude gan to *route*
> That no wight oother noise myghte heere;   (*Tr*, III, 743–4)

[11] *Early Middle English Verse and Prose*, ed. J. A. W. Bennett and G. V. Smithers (Oxford: Clarendon Press, 1966), p. 290.

The verb 'route', which has the meaning of 'roar', reflects the ON verb 'rauta'.

In Chaucer's vocabulary we find the noun 'candle' descendent from OE 'candel' or 'condel' taken from Latin 'candela'. At the same time Chaucer availed himself of the Old Norse form of 'kindle' as a verb:

> Whan *kyndled* was the fyr, with pitous cheere
> Unto Dyane she spak as ye may heere: (*KnT*, A, 2295–6)

> Whiche been the verray develes officeres
> To *kyndle* and blowe the fyr of lecherye.   (*PardT*, C, 480–1)

Then, let us take the next examples into consideration:

> Lo, he that *leet* hymselven so konnynge,
> And scorned hem that Loves peynes dryen,   (*Tr*, I, 302–3)

> And I with that gan stille awey to goon,
> And *leet* therof *as* nothing wist had I.   (*Tr.*, II, 542–3)

The senses of the verb 'let' are quite complicated, but the meaning of 'consider, behave as, pretend' is influenced by the meaning of ON 'lata', because the preterite form 'let' of OE WS 'lætan' (Anglian 'lētan') happened to be the same as the preterite 'lēt' of ON 'lāta'.

One of the linguistic characteristics of the *Romaunt of the Rose* is the frequent use of Northern forms. Thus the next example is a good one:

> For syngyng moost she *gaf* hir to;   (*RR*, A, 757)

In other works the preterite form of the verb 'yeven' occurs as 'yaf' and its similar forms with the initial /j/ sound. But rarely do we find the Northern English form:

> That Theseus hath taken hym so neer
> That of his chambre he made hym a squier,
> And *gaf* hym gold to mayntene his degree.   (*KnT*, A, 1439–41)
> (Ellesmere, Hengwrt, and Cp MSS.)

As the present plural form of the verb 'be', the type 'ben' is of most frequent occurrence. But the less usual form 'arn', which reflects Scandinavian influence (cf. ON *erum*, Swedish *är*) is found here and there. In the *Troilus and Criseyde* the form 'ben' is used 284 times, while the northern form of 'arn' is employed merely three times:

> Thanne *arn* thise folk that han moost God in awe,   (*Tr*, I, 1006)

In the *Canterbury Tales* more than 800 times the forms 'been' and 'ben' are used but the form 'arn' occurs only four times. An example is:

ARTHURIAN AND OTHER STUDIES

Thise *arn* the wordes that the markys sayde
To this benigne, verray, feithful mayde:
>(*ClT*, E, 342–3) (Ellesmere and Hengwrt MSS.)

4. Function Words

In Chaucer's works the conjunction meaning 'before' has two variant forms: *er* and *or*. The former came from OE *ær*, and the latter from ON *ār*. See the Chaucerian variants:

>For I ne myghte, for bote ne bale,
>Slepe *or* I had red thys tale   (Fairfax 16; other MSS. *er*)
>>(*BD*, 227–8)
>And have my trouthe, but thow it fynde so
>I be thi boote, *or* that it be ful longe (var. *er*)   (*Tr*, I, 831–2)

These two variants are interchangeable, but we can say that in the *Troilus and Criseyde* the Northern form 'or' is often employed, while in the *Canterbury Tales* the other forms 'er' and 'ere' become far more dominant.

In his early poetry Chaucer did not employ the Scandinavian preposition 'til'. It is interesting that he made use of the Old Norse particle in the *Canterbury Tales*. For example, the next lines offer a good example:

>Ne that a monk, whan he is recchelees,
>Is likned *til* a fissh that is waterlees –   (*Gen Prol*, A, 179–80)
>>(Ellesmere and Hengwrt MSS.)

When we examine the verb 'turn' together with its prepositions, we find the following collocations:

1. turn *to* somebody, something.
2. turn *til* something, somebody.

Let me quote some typical instances:

>Now wol I *turne to* Arcite ageyn,   (*KnT*, A, 1488)

>And al his ernest *turneth til* a jape.   (*MillT*, A, 3390)

We may recall here that Chaucer, in the *Reeve's Tale* (A, 4039), used the phrase 'til and fra', instead of his own dialect form 'to and fro' (e.g. *Tr*, IV, 460) in order to create a dialectal atmosphere.

Other grammatical words from Old Norse such as 'same, both, though' had already taken root in London English, and Chaucer availed himself of these basic words very often.

5. **Other Northern Phrases**

A remarkable evidence of Old Norse traces is to be cited from Chaucer's *General Prologue*. In the description of the young Squire, we find:

> So hoote he lovede that *by nyghtertale*
> He sleep namoore than doth a nyghtyngale.
>
> (*Gen Prol*, A, 97–8)

The same expression may be quoted from the *Havelok the Dane*:

> Hwo mihte so mani stonde ageyn
> *Bi nihter-tale*, kniht or swein? (Laud MS.: *nither tale*)
>
> (*Havelok*, 2024–5)

This phrase seems to be a blending of ON 'a nattar-þeli' meaning 'at the dead of a night, at the darkest part of night', and another ON 'nattar-tale' with the sense of 'night-counting, night-number'. Be that as it may, the above phrase in Chaucer occurs only once.

Now let us turn to the next phrase:

> And al this thyng he tolde hym, *word and ende*,   (*Tr*, II, 1495)

This formula has its origin in an OE phrase 'ord and end', which has the meaning of '(from) beginning to end'. We may remember the Gothic 'and' had the meaning of 'to'. In the course of time the first element of this phrase was confused with ON *orð*, which means 'word', and it was substituted by the more familiar but semantically strange noun 'word'. Chaucer makes use of this phrase as a rhyme-tag.

Another alliterative set phrase 'thryve and thee' may be worth quoting here:

> Wel yvel mote they *thryve and thee*, (: be)   (*RR*, 1067)

The first part of this alliterative phrase came from ON 'thrifa', which is often used in Chaucer's optative sentences like 'So mote I thryve', etc.

Noteworthy is the following alliterative phrase:

> But wasten al that ye may *rape and renne*.   (*CYT*, G, 1422)

The *O.E.D.* records this phrase under the word 'rape (2)', which came from Old French 'raper' with the meaning of 'to take a thing by force'. But at the same time, we must pay attention to the fact that this is an alliterative phrase, and that the second element 'renne' has its origin in ON 'renna'. The first element of this phrase, therefore, may probably be connected with the Old Norse word 'hrapa', which meant 'to hurry'. As it stands, the phrase in question means 'to hurry and run'. On the other hand, there was an Old English phrase 'hrepian and hrinan' (which means 'to handle and touch'). It follows from this fact that the verb 'rape' with the significance of 'to hurry' descended from ON 'hrapa' is a false substitution for OE 'hrepian', while the other 'renne' proves to be a false replacement for OE 'hrinan' meaning 'to touch, lay hold of'. Then there occurred a contamination of 'rape (1)' meaning 'to hurry' and 'rape (2)' meaning 'to take a thing by force', and finally the above cited phrase came to signify 'seize and run away with, seize and carry away'. In this case, therefore, three kinds of phrases or words such as OE 'hrepian and hrinan' (= to handle and touch) and ON 'hrapa ok renna' (= to haste and run) and OF 'raper' (= to take a thing by force) were blended in form as well as in meaning.

Our final example offers a suggestive conclusion:

> And she shal out; thus seyden *here and howne*.   (*Tr*, IV, 210)

This purely alliterative formula has attracted scholars' attention, and both F. N. Robinson and B. A. Windeatt mentioned it as 'an unexplained phrase'.[12] Of several interpretations suggested by Chaucerian scholars, the best one will be that considering the phrase to be an alliterative set idiom which came from such a unit as ON 'herra ok hunn' meaning 'lord and boy, that is, high and low, everyone', and which fits the context in question perfectly. Zoëga's *Concise Dictionary of Old Icelandic* provides us with the word 'hunn (1)' which meant 'bear's cub, urchin, boy (poetical)'.

Chaucer might not perceive words borrowed from Old Norse as such. He probably thought that these were perfectly English vernacular. It did not matter whether the word in question came from Old Norse or Old English. What is more important is Chaucer's perception of the status of these basic and everyday words. Some of these Norse-derived words had definitely dialectal shades of meanings, but others belonged to the basic stratum of London English. It seems that Chaucer attempted to employ as many French words as possible in order to polish his poetic language, but he had to resort to words of Old Norse origin from time to time, because these Norse words had already permeated Chaucer's London English.

---

[12] *The Works of Geoffrey Chaucer*, 2nd edition, ed. F. N. Robinson (Boston: Houghton Mifflin, 1957), p. 828. *Troilus and Criseyde*, ed. B. A. Windeatt (London: Longman, 1984), p. 361.

'Myn deere herte' in Chaucer's
Troilus and Criseyde

FUMIKO OKA

The word for 'heart' may be found in any human language: for instance, according to J. Pokorny,[1] Indo-European ancestor language had $\hat{k}ered$- as a root of 'heart'; therefore, Armenian *sirt*, Instrumental *srti-v* 'heart' (*$\hat{k}erdi$-); Greek καοδία (Attic); Latin *cor* (*cord*), *cordis* 'heart', Gothic *haírto*, Old High German *herza*, Hittite *ka-ra-as* (*karts*) 'heart'. The Egyptian word *ab*, in its narrower sense of 'heart' denoted longing, desire, will, wisdom, courage, etc., and also there was soul connected with the heart, the *hāti* ('heart soul'). The Japanese word *kokoro* means seat of affections, and *shinzo*, physical organ.

I am greatly indebted to John Leyerle's penetrating study, 'The Heart and the Chain',[2] in which he takes up the words 'heart' and 'chain' as Chaucer's poetic nucleus, especially in *The Book of the Duchess, Troilus and Criseyde*, and *The Knight's Tale*. In this paper I will confine myself to words of 'heart' used as endearment in *Troilus and Criseyde*, where out of 335 instances of the word 'herte', 65 are used as endearment ('heart' as endearment dates back, according to the *O.E.D.*, to the first decade of the 14th century). I will examine their forms and distribution from Book I to Book V, with attention to the development of the story.

As the basic text, I used the Facsimile of Corpus Christi College Cambridge MS. 61, abbreviated as Cp (which is dated the first quarter of the 15th century, and on which Windeatt's edition mentioned below is based), with reference, when necessary, to St. John's College Cambridge MS. L.1, abbreviated as J (which is dated about 1425–50).[3] In comparing the *Troilus's* MSS. and in interpreting the text, I have been greatly helped by the invaluable notes in Windeatt's monumental edition (1984).[4]

---

1 Julius Pokorny, *Indogermanisches Etymologisches Wörterbuch* (München: Bern University Press, 1969), pp. 579–80.
2 See his article in *Chaucer's Troilus*, ed. S. A. Barney (London: Scolar Press, 1980), pp. 181–209.
3 *Troilus and Criseyde: A Facsimile of Corpus Christi College Cambridge MS 61*, with Introduction by M. B. Parkes and E. Salter (Cambridge: D.S.Brewer, 1978) and *St. John's College, Cambridge, Manuscript L. 1, A Facsimile*, Introduction by R. Beadle and J. Griffiths, (Oklahoma: Pilgrim Books and Boydell & Brewer, 1983).
4 *Geoffrey Chaucer: Troilus and Criseyde*, ed. B. A. Windeatt (London: Longman, 1984).

I

I begin with a list of forms of endearment-phrase with 'herte'. The 'herte' endearment occurs often with 'My'/ 'Myn':

My dere herte allas myn hele and hewe (Book I, l. 461: Cp 13a); My deere herte (II. 982; III. 803, 843, 888, 1110; IV. 853; V. 569); herte myn (III. 988, 1004, 1039, 1285, 1349, 1510; IV. 1214; V. 228, 939); My deer herte and al myn owen knyghte (II. 871); my deer herte and al my knyght (III. 996); my dere herte ſwete (III. 1525); Myn herte swete (III. 1278); myn herte deere (IV. 1574); dere herte myn (III. 1181); swete herte myn (III. 1173); my deere herte trewe (IV. 1528); myn owen ſwete herte (III. 147, 1183; IV. 1449; V. 1344, 1421); myne owene deere herte trewe (V. 1401); my swete herte deere (III. 1210); myn owene herte fre (IV. 1552); My gode hert myn (III. 1009 (BL MS Harley 1239, abbreviated as H3)).

Compare the use in the genitive:

myn owen hertes list . . . and al myn herte deere (III. 1303–4); Myn hertes lif (III. 1422); Myn owene hertes ſothfaſt ſuffiſaunce (IV. 1640); myn hertes lady[5] free (V. 1390 (J)); myn hertes day (V. 1405).

'Herte' as endearment occurs without personal pronoun:

dere herte (I. 535 (Boccaccio 'donna')); deere herte and al my knyght (III. 176); ſwete herte deere (III. 127; IV. 1209); herte ſwete (IV. 779, 1590); deere herte ſwete (V. 1189); herte deere (III. 1493 (Boccaccio 'Anima mia')); deere herte (III. 1347 (Boccaccio 'Amor mio'), IV. 759).

Compare the following designations (with genitive personal pronouns) used by the narrator:

his owen herte ſwete (III. 1820); hire herte deere (III. 1553); hire lief[6] and deere herte (III, 774); hire owen ſwete herte(V. 63); (with genitive nouns) his deer hertes queene (I. 817); His hertes lif (II. 1066).

Mention must also be made of Pandarus's encouraging and humorous address to Troilus (drawing him to Criseyde's bed), the equivalent of which is not found in Boccaccio:

thow wrecched mouſes herte (III. 736).

---

[5] In *Troilus and Criseyde*, out of 110 instances of 'lady', about 41 instances with 'my/ myn' are found. And they are sometimes in parallel with 'herte', or used as variants of 'herte' among MSS.

[6] As for 'lief', out of 14 instances in *Troilus and Criseyde*, 8 endearment uses are found.

II

Let us examine the functions of endearment-phrase with 'herte'. In Book I, out of 18 instances of 'herte', only 2 are used as endearment. One is:

461–2:   Cp 13a   My dere herte allas myn hele and hewe
                        And lif is loſt but ȝe wol on me rewe

This occurs in Troilus's soliloquy (in which 'myn hele and hewe' means 'my health and countenance') addressed to the absent Criseyde. He repeats his plea for pity: he will die if Criseyde does not take pity on him. It is the first instance of 'herte' endearment in his soliloquy.

535–6:   Cp 15a   O mercy dere herte and help me from
                        The deth

This, too, occurs in Troilus's soliloquy addressed to Criseyde. He is begging her mercy to rescue him from the 'death'.

In Book II, the first of 2 instances occurs in 'Cantus Antigone' (827–75).

869–75:   Cp 44b   But I with al myn herte and al my myghte
                        As I haue ſeyde wol loue vn to my laſte
                        My deer herte and al myn owen knyghte
                        In which myn herte growen is ſo faſte
                        And his in me that it ſhal euere laſte
                        Al dredde I firſt to loue hym to bigynne
                        Now woot I wel ther is no þil Inne
        J 29r   But I wᵗ alle myn herte Ⓒ al my myght
                        As I haue ſeide/ wol loue vn to my laſte
                        My ᵒʷⁿ[7] deere herte/ Ⓒ al myn owene knyght
                        In wecche myn herte groue is ſo faſte
                        And his in me/ þᵗ it ſhal eũe laſte
                        Al drede I firſt to loue hym/ to begynne
                        Now wot I wele ther is no þel Inne

It is in the last stanza of a most beautiful love-song from a lady to her knight. With this song sung by her niece Antigone, Criseyde's terror for love faded fast, and her conversion began. It is important that 'the theme of lovers' heart-exchange'[8] is sung here.

The other instance runs:

982:    Cp 47a   Whan ſhal I next my deere herte ſee

---

[7] Written over-line.
[8] For the theme of 'Exchange of Hearts', see Leyerle *op. cit.*, pp. 201–5.

which is Troilus's question addressed to Pandarus while they are talking about Criseyde: Troilus is impatiently asking Pandarus when and how he will once again be able to see Criseyde, who is now his 'deere herte'.

In Book III, the distribution of the 31 instances of 'herte' endearment is: Troilus to Criseyde (10), Pandarus to Troilus (1), Narrator (2); Criseyde to Pandarus (3), Pandarus to Criseyde(1), and Criseyde to Troilus (14). The first instance is:

69:      Cp 64a   ȝe ſwete herte allas I may nought riſe

which occurs in Troilus's answer to Criseyde, who, on this occasion of her first visit (with Pandarus) has formally addressed Prince Troilus, saying 'Sire,. . . it is Pandare and I.' The rather incongruous intimacy on the part of Troilus is pointed out by Windeatt, who notes as follows: '68–9 *Sire*: C addresses T formally (again, 75), but T blurts out an endearment'.[9] Troilus's 'blurting' way of speaking is yet to be found in:

97–8:   Cp 64b   Lo the alderfirſt word that hym aſterte
                   Was twyes mercy mercy ſwete herte

It is clear that he has not learnt the lesson on how to say a good phrase (or how to set his face). We shall see if there is any change in his way of speaking to Criseyde:

147:     Cp 65b   Lo this mene I myn owen ſwete herte

Troilus is now making a vow: he will be without a touch of vice, he will always offer his whole-hearted true service and devotion to her. And his offer to become her servant is accepted by her. All this is in full accordance with the due ceremony of homage in the medieval love service. (See also 127, 1173, 1181, 1278, 1285, 1347, and 1525, in which similar phrases are used by Troilus in speaking to Criseyde).

How does Criseyde, we ask now, use endearment in speaking to Troilus? The following is the first case:

176:     Cp 66a   . . . deer herte and al my knyght

For similar uses by Criseyde, see: 988, 996, 1003, 1009, 1039, 1110, 1183, 1210, 1303, 1304, 1349, 1493, and 1510.

774:     Cp 77a   And hym hire lief and deere herte calle

This is only one instance from Pandarus to Criseyde, referring to Troilus as 'hire lief and deere herte' in his persuasion.

---

[9]   Windeatt, *op. cit.*, p. 253.

Criseyde, on three occasions, uses the 'herte' endearment, not in speaking directly to Troilus, but in talking with Pandarus, calling Troilus her 'deere herte'. On one of these occasions she says:

803–4: Cp 77a My deere herte wolde me nought holde
So lightly fals allas conceytes wronge

This is spoken by Criseyde, when told by Pandarus that Troilus will come tonight, as he has been seriously suffering with her amorous rumour. An interesting variant is found here: MS. Phillipps 8252, now Huntington Library HM 114, has 'Now certes Eme' for Cp's 'My deere herte'.[10] The 2 other occasions are found in 843 and 888. Pandarus's use of 'mouſes herte' in his speech to Troilus (III. 736) has already been quoted.

The narrator also uses the 'herte' endearment, once in reference to Troilus who is Criseyde's 'herte deere':

1553: Cp 88b Deſiryng ofte to han hire herte deere

and once in reference to Criseyde, Troilus's 'owen herte ſwete':

1819–20: Cp 92b And Troilus in luſte and in quiete
Is with Criſeyde his owen herte ſwete

Here H3 has a variant:

And Troilus in luste and quiete
Is wyth Creseide hys one lady swete   (leaf 35)[11]

where the first line seems to scan better than in Cp, although 'one' in the second line is most probably a scribal mistake. One more case of variant occurs in:

1009: Cp 80a My good myn noot I for why ne how
J 56r   My goode myn/ noot I for why ne how

in both of which 'myn' is used as substantive. H3 (leaf 29)[12] is noteworthy here, because it uses 'hert' lacking in Cp and J:

My goode hert myn not I for why ne how

Book IV presents 19 instances, of which 15 are found in Criseyde's

---

[10] *Ibid.*, p. 291.
[11] *Parallel Texts of Chaucer's Troilus and Criseyde*, Pt. 2 (Chaucer Society, 1st series), p. 167.
[12] *Ibid.*, p. 139. Cf. Windeatt, *op.cit.*, p. 301.

speech (including soliloquy) to Troilus; 1 to Pandarus, 3 in Troilus's speech to Criseyde. In one of the 15 instances Criseyde says:

759–60:   Cp 194a   O deere herte eke, that I loue ſo
                        Who ſhal that ſorwe ſlen that ȝe ben Inne

Windeatt directs our attention to the fact that there is not Criseyde's concern for Troilus in *Filostrato*, 89/1–3:[13]

> Che farò io, dogliosa la mia vita,
> allor che più non ti potrò vedere?
> Che farò io da te, Troiol, partita?
>
> (What shall I do, my sorrowful life, when I cannot see you any more? What shall I do when I am parted from you, Troilo?)

Four similar uses are found in Criseyde's soliloquy: 779, 792, 795, and 796. Criseyde's use of the 'herte' endearment in her speech (directly addressed to Troilus) is found (cf. IV. 1214 below):

1216:   Cp 112a   ȝe herte myn that thonked be Cupide
            J 86r   Ye herte myn Ithonked be Cipride

Criseyde's use of the endearment recurs in her long proposal for solution of their difficulties:

1254:   Cp 112b   Lo herte myn wel woot ȝe this quod ſhe

For additional four instances, see 1274, 1311, 1334, 1352. A slight variant occurs in:

1527–8:   Cp 116a   Criſeyde with a ſike right in this wiſe
                        Anſwerde ywys my deere herte trewe
            J 90v   Criſeide hym wᵗ a ſik right in this wiſe
                        Anſwerd/ Iwis my deere herte trewe

both of which correspond to Boccaccio, *Fil*. 146/2: 'Caro mio bene e del mio cor diletto' ('my dear joy and delight of my heart').[14] There are also 3 instances: 1552, 1574, and 1590. Criseyde's very eloquent use of the 'herte' endearment in Book IV is indeed remarkable. Troilus's use here seems to be more restrained. He speaks to Criseyde:

1214–5:   Cp 112a   And he anſwerde lady myn Criſeyde
                        Lyue ȝe ȝeet and leet his ſwerde down glide

[13] *Giovanni Boccaccio, Il Filostrato*, ed. V. Pernicone, with Translation and Introduction by R. P. apRoberts and A. B. Seldis, Vol. 53, Series A, Garland Library of Medieval Literature (New York: Garland, 1986), pp. 232–3.

[14] Windeatt, *op. cit.*, p. 432.

'MYN DEERE HERTE' IN CHAUCER'S *TROILUS AND CRISEYDE*

J 86r   And he anſwerde herte myn Criſeide
          Lyue ye yit ℭ let his ſwerd down glide

(Cf. *Fil*, IV. 124/3 Dolce mio disiro 'my sweet desire'). The J variant
'herte' is supported by (Cambridge UL) MS. Gg, (BL) H3, and (Huntington) HM 114.[15] Criseyde's reply to Troilus (1216) was given above. For 2
other instances in Troilus's speech, see 1209 and 1449. Criseyde is found
using this endearment, in her speech to Pandarus, in reference to Troilus
as her 'deere herte':

858:      Cp 106a Than wol my deere herte ſeyn to me
          J 80r   What wil my deere herte ſeyn to me

Book V offers us 11 instances: 1 in Narration, 7 in Troilus's speech to
Criseyde, 1 in Troilus's speech to Pandarus, 1 in Diomede's speech to
Criseyde, 1 in Criseyde's speech to Troilus. Let us first see the narrator's,
referring to Troilus, who is still her own 'ſwete herte':

62–3:   Cp 120b What wonder is though hire ſore ſmerte
                   Whan ſhe forgoth hire owen ſwete herte
          J 93v   What wonder is though þᵗ hir ſoore ſmerte
                   Whan ſhe forgoth hir owene deere herte

in which Cp's 'ſwete' is supported by (BL) Add MS. 12044, (Pierpont
Morgan) M 814, (Durham UL) Cosin MS. V. 11, 13, (BL) Harley 2280,
(Bodley) Arch. Selden, Supra 56, and Thynne's edition (1532).[16] Troilus's
pathetic, regretful soliloquy (addressed to the absent Criseyde) runs:

228–9:   Cp 123a O herte myn Criſeyde O ſwete fo
                   O lady myn that I loue and namo

in which 'herte' endearment occurs in parallel with 'lady myn'.
   The following letter, addressed to Criseyde as Troilus's 'Right fresshe
flour', makes use of formulaic phrase:

1324:   Cp 141b Liketh зow to witen ſwete herte

which is in accordance with the standard phrasing (the opening formula)
of English letter writing.[17] Troilus's letter continues and ends thus:

---

[15] *Ibid.*, pp. 418–9.

[16] *Ibid.*, p. 449.

[17] As for the Formula of the 15th century English letter, there is an important study by
Norman Davis, 'The "Litera Troili" and English letters' in *Chaucer's Troilus, Essays in
Criticism*, ed. S. A. Barney (London: Scolar Press, 1980), pp. 145–58. Cf. Windeatt, *op. cit.*,
p. 523. For the reference, the following quotation is useful:
   Fifteenth-century letters in English of a formal, respectful kind very often
   open with a long sequence of conventional phrases and sentences

ARTHURIAN AND OTHER STUDIES

1415–21: Cp 142b With hele ſwich that but ȝe ȝeuen me
The ſame hele I ſhal none hele haue
In ȝow lith whan ȝow liste that it ſo be
The day in which me clothen ſhal my graue
And in ȝow my lif in ȝow myght forto ſaue
Me fro diſeſe of alle peynes ſmerte
And far now wel myn owen ſwete herte
le vre T[18]

J 113r With heele ſwich þᵗ but ye yiuen me
The ſame heele/ I ſhal non heele haue
In yow lieth when yow liste þᵗ it ſo be
The day/ on which me clothen ſhal my gue
In yow my lif/ in yow myght forto ſaue
Me from diſeſe/ of alle peynes ſmerte
And fare now wel myn owene ſwete herte
le vre T

This final portion of *Litera Troili*, containing five uses of 'herte' endearment by Troilus (the other four are: 1344, 1390, 1401, and 1405), is appropriately concluded, as we saw just now, with 'myn owne ſwete herte' (and Troilus's signature). The nostalgic tone of the letter was adumbrated by Troilus's reminiscence of Criseyde (in his dialogue with Pandarus):

> constructed with minor variations upon a regular pattern. Even when some of the possible components are not present the same order of the main items is observed. The full scale, seen best in letters from children to parents, includes seven divisions, some with subdivisions, thus: [1] a form of address most commonly beginning with the word 'Right' and an adjective of respect ('worshipful', 'worthy', 'well-beloved', &c.) and the appropriate noun ('sir', 'husband', 'father', &c.); [2] a formula commending the writer to the recipient, often accompanied by [2a] an expression of humility and, if the letter is to a parent, [2b] a request for a blessing – this usually introduced by a present participle and strengthened by an adverb or a phrase; [3] an expression of desire to hear of the recipient's welfare – this again introduced by a participle; [4] a prayer, introduced by a relative, for the continuation and increase of this welfare 'to your heart's desire', or the like; [5] a conditional clause deferentially offering news of the writer's welfare; [6] a report of the writer's good health 'at the making of this letter'; [7] thanks to God for it. (pp. 148–9)

[18] Davis's comment is quoted by Windeatt in his note on 'le vostre T[roilus]' in p. 529 as follows:

> It seems that it was in French, and no doubt in France, that the various expressions of respect and politeness were regularized into the system so generally observed in English letters of the fifteenth century. Some Chaucerian scribes, if not Chaucer himself, certainly associated the art of polite letter-writing with French...

But I should like to add further quotation (from Davis) his last 3 lines referring to Criseyde's letter:

> ... three manuscripts and Thynne's edition subscribe Troilus's letter 'Le vostre T(roilus)', and four manuscripts (only one of them among the previous three) and Thynne similarly subscribe Criseyde's. (p. 155)

'MYN DEERE HERTE' IN CHAUCER'S *TROILUS AND CRISEYDE*

569:     Cp 129b My dere herte laugh and 3onder pleye

Compare the following speech by Troilus (he is talking with Pandarus) about Criseyde's promise to return to Troy:

1188–90: Cp 140a She ſeyde I ſhal ben here if that I may
                  Er that the moone o deere herte ſwete
                  The Leoun paſſe out of this ariete

Quite a different man enters now, addressing Criseyde with the 'herte' endearment. This is Diomede, who says:

939:     Cp 135b But herte myn ſyn that I am 3oure man

Diomede, escorting her to her father in the camp of Greeks from Troy, is here boldly asking her to give him her heart.

This brief study of mine is best concluded with reference to *Litera Criseydis*:

1590–6: Cp 145b Cupides ſone enſample of goodly heede
                 O ſwerde of knyghthode, ſours of gentileſſe
                 How myght a wight in torment and in drede
                 And heleles, 3ow ſende as 3et gladneſſe
                 I herteles, I ſik I in diſtreſſe
                 Syn 3e with me nor I with 3ow may dele
                 3ow neyther ſende ich herte may nor hele

This letter, the last one from Criseyde to Troilus, has a beginning with long and exaggerated greetings, instead of the succinct 'heart' endearment. Its wordiness presents a very symbolic and fatal contrast with the expressiveness of Book I, 461 (already quoted): 'My dere herte allas myn hele and hewe'. Instead of 'herte' endearment she says here, 'Syn 3e with me nor I with 3ow may dele/ 3ow neyther ſende ich herte may nor hele' (V. 1596: Cp 145b).[19] The real meaning of the crucial word 'herteles' is, we

---

[19] In interpreting the closing part of Criseyde's letter, the following remark by Davis is helpful:

> So familiar was it that Margery Brews, in one of her 'Valentine' letters to John Paston III in 1477, was able to play upon the convention by denying the customary good health: '[1] Ryght reverent and wurschypfull and my ryght welebeloved Voluntyne, [2] I recommande me unto yowe full hertely, [3] desyring to here of yowr welefare, [4] whech I beseche Almyghty God long for to preserve unto hys plesure and yowr hertys desyre. [5] And yf it please yowe to here of my welefare, [6] I am not in good heele of body ner of herte, nor schall be tyll I here from yowe'. Indeed, in view especially of the poem by the Duke of Suffolk . . . , this turn can hardly be credited to Margery Brews's own ingenuity (or that of someone who helped her to write the letter, which is in the hand of her father's clerk); it must have become a new convention in its own right. (pp. 149–50)

may suppose, that the 'herte' of Troilus was driven away from the breast of Criseyde, as already suggested by Cassandra when interpreting Troilus's ill-omened dream.[20]

We can say, therefore, that the main story of *Troilus and Criseyde* begins with the exchange of the two 'hertes', Troilus's and Criseyde's, and ends with transportation of Troilus's stray 'herte'.[21]

---

[20] Cf. V. 1516–7: Cp 144a 'And thy lady wher ſo ſhe be ywis/ This Diomede hire herte hathe and ſhe his'.

[21] The following list shows the distribution of the occurrence of 'herte' endearment. (T=Troilus; C=Criseyde; A=Antigone's song; P=Pandarus; D=Diomede)

	T→C	C→T	A	T→P	P→T	P→C	C→P	D→C	Narrator	Total
Bk I	2									2
Bk II			1	1						2
Bk III	10	14			1	1	3		2	31
Bk IV	3	15					1			19
Bk V	7	1		1				1	1	11
Total	22	30	1	2	1	1	4	1	3	65

Negation in the Wycliffite Sermons

SHUICHI AITA

Negative expressions in Middle English have a variety of formal devices, which contain not merely a few well-known words beginning with *n*, but also other words and constructions which denote a negative meaning. These expressions may be influenced by the writer's individual locution and preference for different forms, and by characteristics of the work and also by contexts or situations. Negation is one of the most important factors of literary style, and greatly contributes to the intensive note of much medieval narrative.[1] This probably holds true of non-literary works as well, because, whatever genre the work may belong to, the writer's exaltation will be reflected in his idiosyncratic use of negative forms. In the Wycliffite Sermons,[2] the importance of the literal sense of the Bible is constantly emphasised to make a scathing attack on Wyclif's opponents and on ecclesiastical abuses.[3] An investigation of his negative expressions will reveal the quality of his language, though in a very limited way, as a reflection of his attitude towards what he believed to be in the wrong.

Not naturally exceeds other negative forms in number, but some interesting examples of *neuere* can be found as in the following:

16:60   vpon þes þre synnys haþ God mercy here, but vpon þe furþe
        synne God cesuþ *neuere* to punysche[4]

a rather free paraphrase of which is: God, by virtue of His forgiveness shown in the miracles of Christ resuscitating the dead, forgives the first three sins but never this fourth, the sin of bringing the coffin of a dead person who was at odds with God's law in order to bury him in the ground, because He condemns this act as consent to wickedness. *Neuere* in this case strengthens the negative import of the message: God definitely does *not* purpose to 'cease to punish' those deserving punishment. This emphatic negative adverb is employed in twenty-four of thirty

---

[1] G. Roscow, *Syntax and Style in Chaucer's Poetry* (Cambridge: D. S. Brewer, 1981), p. 141.

[2] The text used here is: 54 Sermons on the Sunday Gospels in *English Wycliffite Sermons I*, ed. A. Hudson (Oxford: Clarendon Press, 1983), pp. 223–474.

[3] E. W. Talbert, 'Works Generally Ascribed to Wyclif', *A Manual of the Writings in Middle English 1050–1500 Vol. 2*, ed., J. B. Severs (Connecticut: Archon Books, 1970), p. 360.

[4] The number 16:60 means that the citation is from Sermon 16, line 60.

examples which contain explicitly religious words such as 'God', 'heaven', and 'sin', and the Biblical modal *schal* with the sense of 'the prophetic-oracular future'.[5] The word *neuere* is thus so closely associated with religious contexts that it should not simply be called an 'adverb of negation',[6] and its frequent occurrence is due to the writer's determined expression against unholy and evil things.

While either *not* or *neuere* is used in a single negative sentence, the conjunction *ne*, which introduces a double negative construction, is ordinarily used in connecting two negative sentences. The following is a typical example:

> 46:85   he iugeþ *not* þe worþinesse of Godys body, *ne* worschipeþ *not* his ordenaunce.

This example suggests the possibility that the double negation does not necessarily imply any special intensity of negation,[7] because the double negation in the Wycliffite Sermons occurs almost always in a copulative *ne*-clause. This possibility will be proved by the fact that our corpus contains sixteen cases of this construction out of a total of nineteen copulative *ne*-clauses. Some degree of regularity in the uses of other non-emphatic double negatives is shown below:

> 32:29   *Ne* wiste 3e *not* þat I muste be in þe nedys of my Fadyr?
> 8:10   hit is *no* dowte *þat ne* syche men ben prophets.

The first is an example of a negative interrogative. G. Jack comments that 'in the Wycliffite Sermons *ne . . . not* usually occurs in interrogative clauses (nine of the thirteen instances in the sermons are found in this construction).'[8] The second is that of a sentence containing a *þat ne*-clause, on which A. Warner makes a detailed discussion.[9] An interesting case parallel to the latter type is:

> 8:15   *who* schulde dreden of hem *þat ne* þey ben false prophetys?

This construction is essentially the same as 8:10, because here, too, can be found an implied negation: 'we in effect do not admit that such men exist'.[10] The appearance of *ne* within a *þat*-clause is due to the force of

---

[5]   F. Th. Visser, *An Historical Syntax of the English Language III* (Leiden: Brill, 1969), p. 1590.

[6]   G. Jack, 'Negation in Later Middle English Prose', *Archivum Linguisticum*, Vol. 9 (1978), 58.

[7]   D. Burnley, *The Language of Chaucer* (London: Macmillan, 1989), p. 61.

[8]   See Jack , *ibid.*, p. 65. Other examples are 3:34, 14:13, and 22:17. There is an irregular one:
         37:100   *Wher* hit is *not* lewful to me to do myn owne þing as I wole?

[9]   See his *Complementation in Middle English and the Methodology of Historical Syntax* (University Park and London: The Pennsylvania State University Press, 1982), pp. 198–225. Other examples are 46:31 and 53:78.

[10]   G. Jack (1978, p. 60) cites the same kind of instance from *Boece* II, pr. 4, 72–5:

that scope of a negative element in the main clause which extends its influence over the complement clause. The same rule can be applied in analysing *no þing* in the following instances, where *no(o)*, instead of *any*, occurs probably by virtue of negative concord in negative clauses:[11]

> 40:66   Crist schulde *not* hurte hym at þe eyr, *ne* in his fallyng at þe eurþe, *ne* at *no þing* þat Crist mette.
>
> 43:99   And þus, ȝif men schulde not sewe Crist her, fore he muste neede suffre, *noo* cristene man schulde sewe Crist in *no þing* þat he dyde, . . .

As is apparent from the previously stated findings, the double negation in the Sermons occurs in some limited circumstances: in a copulative *ne*-clause, a negative sentence including a *þat ne*- clause, a negative interrogative and a negative declarative sentence having the latent *any*. Unlike these systematic double negative patterns (the example of 46:85 is, for instance, a most typical one), however, the following is a case in which the sentence is headed by *ne* in spite of the fact that there is no negative element in the preceding sentence:

> 24:60   And þus eche story of myracles of Crist may be moralisyd to a good witt. *Ne* hit is *no* perele to varien in suche wittis, so þat men vary not fro trewþ ne fro good lore, . . .

Here, it can be said that in addition to the use of the emphatic *neuere*, the construction *ne . . . not* is used to heighten a negative effect.[12]

To examine the characteristics of the negation in the Wycliffite Sermons from a different viewpoint, the comparison between the paraphrased passage of the Bible used in the Sermon and its original passage will be helpful. As previously shown, we have found twenty-four examples of *neuere*, among which there are four cases cited from the Bible, and in all these four cases, *not* in the original is replaced by *neuere* in the Sermons. An example is:[13]

> 6:12   But ȝif ȝour riȝtwisnesse passe a poynt þe feynud riȝtwis-nesse of scribes and of pharisees, ȝe schal *neuer* come to heuene.

> For *what man* is so sad or of so parfit welefulnesse, *that* he *ne* stryveth or pleyneth on som halve ayen the qualite of his estat? (emphases mine)

[11] See Jack, *ibid.*, p. 70.

[12] Another equivalent example is:
> 53:57   furst he schal meue mennys erys in sensible voyses and siþ he schal be slydon in and teche mennys þowtis in al þat Crist haþ spoke byfore in general wordys; *ne* þei schal *not* cese anoon to lerne more sutylly, but euere in þis lyȝf þei wexen more rype til þat þei comen to heuene, and þere knowe al fully.

[13] Other examples are 44:56, 47:90, and 49:15. Although the Biblical verses are drastically changed in these four examples, I shall not discuss such changes in this paper.

243

WB LV   but ȝour riȝtfullnesse be more plenteuouse than of scribis and of Farisees, ȝe schulen *not* entre into the kyngdom of heuenes (Matthew, 5:20)[14]

Such a replacement is due, it seems, partly to a systematic locution in the Sermons and partly to the writer's judgement on the contextual appropriateness of using the stronger negative. The following is an example of a negative interrogative sentence in which the double negation is used in the Biblical quotation in spite of the employment of a single negation in the Bible:

14:13   Iesus spak and seyde . . ., '*Ne* ben *not* ten made clene? [and] wher ben oþur neyne?. . .'
WB LV   Jesus answerde, and seide, Whether ten be *not* clensid, and where ben the nyne?. . . (Luke, 17:17)

Here, the wording of the Sermon is derived not from the writer's judgement of the context but from his syntactic preference: the *ne . . . not* construction, as we saw earlier, usually occurs in interrogative sentences.[15]

Although the Wycliffite Sermons were written in the period when the use of the double negation began to decline, they nevertheless make use of these systematic double negatives. There are, however, a few exceptional cases which cannot be explained by simply saying that they belong to the syntactic patterns of double negation that we regard as non-emphatic uses. The contrast between 25:10 and the equivalent Biblical verse of John 6:7 will give us a clue in understanding its irregular occurrence:

25:10   Philip seyde to Crist þat loues of two hundred pens *ne* suffysid *not* to hem, so þat echone myȝte taken a lytulwhat of breed.
WB LV   Filip answerde to hym, The looues of tweyn hundrid pans sufficen *not* to hem, that ech man take a litil what. (John, 6:7)

This utterance is Philip's reply to Christ's question to test him: 'wherof þei schulde bughge breed for to fede þis folc?' Philip, however, thinks that the crowd is so large that 'loues of two hundred pens' cannot possibly suffice for them. It is, therefore, more than probable that he expresses his doubt explicitly by making use of the non-systematic, that is, emphatic double negation. Though rare, the use of such double

---

[14] All quotations are from *The Holy Bible*, ed. R. J. Forshall and Sir F. Madden (London: Oxford University Press, 1850; rpt. New York: AMS Press , 1982). WB and LV mean the Wycliffite Bible and its Later Version respectively.

[15] See Note 8. The Biblical passage corresponding to 37:100 is:
    Whether it is *not* leueful to me to do that that Y wole? (Matthew, 20:15)

negation (emphatic) is noteworthy in that it indicates the writer's strongly rhetorical response to the original holy words in the Bible.[16] The preference for *neuere* over *not* in some circumstances, too, can be taken as a clear manifestation of the writer's pious stance. If I were one of Wyclif's followers, I, too, would convey the doctrines of Christ to our disbelieving opponents in strong and 'philologically truthful'[17] words, unless His true meaning is distorted by such a replacement of the ordinary words and constructions with those of a more passionate meaning in the Sermons.

[16] In his 'A Rhetorical Spoken Style of Middle English', *Studies in English Literature, English Number* (1968), 61–81, Y. Terasawa shows some syntactic evidence that the Sermon Translation was written in a 'rhetorical-spoken' style.
[17] S. Noguchi, 'Beowulf and "Sothfæstra Dom" ', *Philologia Anglica: Essays Presented to Professor Yoshio Terasawa on the Occasion of His Sixtieth Birthday* (Tokyo: Kenkyu-sha, 1988), p. 258.

Spelling Variations in
Cambridge, St John's College, MS. B 12 (34)*

YUZURU OKUMURA

In his luminous comment on the extant *Confessio Amantis* MSS., G. C. Macaulay remarks that the text of the MS. in the above title agrees very closely with that of the Fairfax MS.,[1] which has been recognised by Gower scholars as representing most faithfully the author's final version of the poem. Significantly, however, he also noted that this textual agreement 'is not equally observable in the earlier part of the poem, and indeed does not become at all marked until the fifth book.'[2] A linguistic fact which is of particular interest in this connection has been found out by J. J. Smith, who, analysing representative portions of Books III and VI of this MS., points out that there are noticeable differences between these passages in the spelling of certain items.[3] Since this MS., as Macaulay says, is written in one hand throughout,[4] these differences cannot be explained by the change of scribe. Smith suggests that they are due to a shift on the part of the exemplar, giving two grounds for his reasoning: firstly, a scribe, in the course of copying a long text, often becomes increasingly or decreasingly influenced by one and the same exemplar, but his spelling practice would in any case have settled down by Book III; and secondly, Macaulay's textual evidence implies that this MS. is based on more than one exemplars. In this paper, I shall first seek to confirm Smith's argument by clarifying where and how the scribe changed his spelling habit while producing this MS.; I shall then present some linguistic facts to corroborate Macaulay's textual evidence pointing to the close relationship between the latter half of this MS. and the Fairfax MS.; and finally, I shall suggest some possible explanations as to how the textual situation of this MS. originated.

---

* This is a revised version of a paper read at the 8th meeting of the East Branch of the Japan Society for Medieval English Studies, held at Tokyo Metropolitan University on the 27th of June, 1992. I am deeply grateful to Dr. Jeremy John Smith, who so kindly allowed me access to a microfilm copy of the manuscript and gave me many insightful comments and suggestions. Any errors made here, however, are entirely mine.

[1] *The English Works of John Gower*, ed. G. C. Macaulay, E.E.T.S., e.s. 81 and 82 (London: Oxford University Press, 1900), p. cxxxiii.

[2] *Ibid.*

[3] J. J. Smith, *Studies in the Language of some Manuscripts of Gower's Confessio Amantis* (Diss. PhD., Glasgow, 1985), Vol. I, pp. 91–3.

[4] Macaulay, *English Works*, p. cxxxix.

ARTHURIAN AND OTHER STUDIES

As noted by Smith, the shift in the spelling practice of this MS. is typically seen in the item 'WHICH',[5] and the variation of its forms is worth examining more closely. My examination has shown that *which* and its variants (*whiche, whych* and *wych*) appear as very minor variants in Prologue, Books I and II. The form *whech* and its variants (*wheche* and *weche*) are predominant in Prologue, Books I and II, and are exclusively used in Book III. This fact, viewed alone, might be explained by saying that the *i*-forms were the regular forms of the exemplar, and that the *e*-forms were the habitual forms of the scribe: in the earlier portions of the MS., the scribe used the *i*-forms under the influence of the exemplar; but, as he got used to copying, he increasingly replaced them with his own preferred forms, until in Book III he came to use the latter alone.[6] But this explanation is unsatisfactory, since in the middle of Book IV, the *i*-forms appear again, and quite suddenly become predominant in Book V, and are exclusively used in Book VI onwards except the sole example of *whech* in Book VII. If the scribe accepted only the *e*-forms and his exemplar used the *i*-forms consistently, it is difficult to explain why he again came to use the *i*-forms alone, the ones he once abandoned, in the latter half of the MS. An assumption that the scribe accepted only the *i*-forms is equally untenable, because it is difficult to explain why he entirely gave up his own forms in Book III. In any case, it seems unlikely that he reproduces the unfamiliar forms of the exemplar, considering the fact that he persistently uses *heo* for 'SHE' instead of *sche* used in all the other extant MSS. of the *Confessio Amantis*,[7] and replaces also regularly 'whilom' with 'som tyme' – a fact indicating that he is a scribe of B-type defined by A. McIntosh, i.e. a scribe who tends to translate the language of his exemplar into his own dialect.[8]

The most likely explanation of this scribal behaviour, then, seems to be found in the concept of 'constrained usage'.[9] Our MS. has been localised in Herefordshire in *A Linguistic Atlas of Late Mediaeval English* (hereafter

[5] Smith, *Studies*, Vol. I, p. 93.

[6] For a detailed discussion on various types of mediaeval scribal translations, see M. Benskin and M. Laing, 'Translations and *Mischsprachen* in Middle English Manuscripts', *So meny people longages and tonges: Philological Essays in Scots and Mediaeval English Presented to Angus McIntosh*, ed. M. Benskin and M. L. Samuels (Edinburgh: Middle English Dialect Project, 1981), pp. 55–106; now largely reproduced, with rearrangement, in the General Introduction to A. McIntosh, M. L. Samuels and M. Benskin, with the assistance of M. Laing and K. Williamson, *A Linguistic Atlas of Late Mediaeval English* (Aberdeen: Aberdeen University Press, 1986) (hereafter *L.A.L.M.E.*).

[7] Smith, *Studies*, Vol. II.

[8] A. McIntosh, 'Word Geography in the Lexicography of Mediaeval English', *Middle English Dialectology: Essays on some Principles and Problems*, ed. M. Laing (Aberdeen: Aberdeen University Press, 1989), p. 92 ; originally published in *Annals of the New York Academy of Sciences* 211 (1973), 55–66.

[9] Benskin and Laing, 'Translations and *Mischsprachen*', § 5.1. and *L.A.L.M.E.*, Vol. I, pp. 18–9.

248

SPELLING VARIATIONS

L.A.L.M.E.),[10] and the relevant map in the *Atlas* suggests that the *e*- and *i*-forms were both well-known to the scribe.[11] These two types of forms might have been equally acceptable to him, but more probably, the *i*-forms belonged to his 'active repertoire'[12] – the forms he used sponta-neously regardless of what he was copying, and the *e*-forms belonged to his 'passive repertoire'[13] – the forms he did not use spontaneously, but which he was well acquainted with in everyday usage and willing to reproduce when he found them used in his exemplar. In the beginning of the MS., the scribe allowed the *i*-forms, his own habitual ones, to appear in the copy-text he was now making, though he in the main reproduced the *e*-forms used in his exemplar, not finding them foreign to him; but, as the text proceeded, he was increasingly influenced by the usage of the exemplar, and began to suppress his own habitual forms in favour of the exemplar's. Later, he found the *i*-forms to be predominantly, or probably exclusively, used in his exemplar, and, since the new forms were exactly the same as his favourite, naturally began to reproduce them. Our scribe is thus very likely to have reproduced both types of spellings as he found them in his exemplar, though it should be emphasised that he was by no means a *literatim* copyist in the usual sense of the term. He was willing to follow his exemplar simply because the spellings of the exem-plar were acceptable to him as far as the item 'WHICH' was concerned. In fact, he might be taken here as something between a 'dialectal trans-lator' and a *literatim* copyist.

There can also be found a number of other items which show a similar pattern of shift from one type of form to the other. Until the middle of Book IV, the main form for the item 'IT' is *hit*, whereas the form is replaced by *it* in the rest of the MS. Likewise, the items 'BUT', 'GIVEN', 'IF' and 'YET' change their main form with roughly the same part of the MS. as a turning point: from *bote* to *bot*; from *ȝeue* to *ȝiue*; from *ȝef* to *ȝif*; and from *ȝet* to *ȝit*, respectively. We may also add the item 'SHALL (pl.)': the shift is not so clear-cut in this case, but we may note that the main form until the end of Book IV is *schal*, while *schul*, *schull* and *schulle* are predominant in Book V onwards. As in the case of the forms for 'WHICH', these shifts of form can probably be best explained by assum-ing that all of these forms belonged to our scribe's repertoire of spellings, and that the choice between them was largely influenced by the usage of the exemplar. This assumption is supported by the relevant maps in *L.A.L.M.E.*, which show that all these forms are readily expected of the Herefordshire dialect.[14]

---

[10] *L.A.L.M.E.*, LP 7450.
[11] *L.A.L.M.E.*, Vol. II, map 11.
[12] Benskin and Laing, 'Translations and *Mischsprachen*', § 2.2.1. and *L.A.L.M.E.*, Vol. I, p. 14.
[13] *Ibid.*
[14] *L.A.L.M.E.*, Vol. I, maps 24, 25, 430 and 431; and Vol. II, maps 22, 33, 40 and 91.

TABLE

Book	Book IV								
folio item	–80^{v}	81	82	83	84	85	86	87	88
IT	hit (((it)))[15]	it 3 hit 6	it 4 hit 2	it 3 hit 5	it 4 hit 1	it 14 hit 4	it 6 hit 8	it 11 hit 7	it 3 hit 6
IF	3ef (((if, iff, 3if)))	3ef 3 if 3 3if 0	3ef 1 if 2 3if 1	3ef 1 if 3 3if 0	3ef 0 if 2 3if 0	3ef 4 if 1 3if 0	3ef 3 if 0 3if 0	3ef 5 if 4 3if 0	3ef 7 if 4 3if 0
WHICH	whech[16] (((which)))	whech 3 which 0	whech 17 which 0	whech 15 which 1	whech 10 which 5	whech 8 which 13	whech 7 which 12	whech 5 which 11	whech 1 which 8
YET	3et (((3it)))	3et 2 3it 1	3et 0 3it 2	3et 3 3it 0	3et 0 3it 0	3et 3 3it 1	3et 0 3it 3	3et 3 3it 0	3et 1 3it 1
BUT	bote (((bot)))	bote 7 bot 4	bote 10 bot 0	bote 6 bot 0	bote 5 bot 0	bote 8 bot 1	bote 4 bot 1	bote 9 bot 0	bote 9 bot 1
GIVEN	3eue	—	—	—	—	3iue 1	—	—	—

In order to 'zero-in' on the place where the usage changes, the frequency of these forms is shown in Table I above. A glance at the table would show that the shift is not an abrupt but gradual one, and also that the place of the shift is different from item to item. Again, it seems appropriate to begin by examining closely the forms for the item 'WHICH', since the shift in this item is, unlike the others, thoroughgoing: the exclusive, not just predominant, use of one type of form is switched to the exclusive use of the other. The *i*-forms almost disappear on folio 50^{r} onwards (*whiche* appears once on folio 78^{r}), until *which* appears again, as we see in the table, on folio 83^{v}. The single instance of *whiche* on folio 78^{r} may be taken as an exceptional slip, but the appearance of *which* on folio 83^{v} should not be written off as such, since the *i*-forms begin to increase in number from then on. It will be noted as well that *it* for 'IT' and *3it* for 'YET' become predominant on folio 84 and folio 86, respectively. The forms for 'IF' and 'BUT' are much slower to change: *3if* replaces *3ef* at the end of Book IV; and *bot* replaces *bote* at the beginning of Book V. This, however, is readily accounted for by saying that our scribe was particularly fond of the forms *3ef* and *bote* and so took longer time to replace them with their alternatives. In view of the

---

[15] The brackets here have the following significances: three bracket (((. . .)))=rare form; one bracket (. . .)=up to about 1/3 of the forms for a given item; no brackets=main (i.e. usual) form.

[16] *Whech* here includes all the *e*-forms, and *which* the *i*-forms.

SPELLING VARIATIONS

		Book IV					Book V		
89	90	91	92	93	94^{r-v}	94^{v}	95	96	97^{r-}
it 1	it 6	it 3	it 7	it 7	it 9	it 5	it 9	it 12	it
hit 3	hit 10	hit 7	hit 3	hit 2	hit 0	hit 3	hit 3	hit 1	(((hit)))
3ef 0	3ef 1	3ef 3	3ef 3	3ef 0	3ef 0	3ef 0	3ef 0	3ef 0	3if
if 1	if 1	if 0	if 1	if 0	if 0	if 0	if 0	if 4	(if)
3if 0	3if 0	3if 0	3if 1	3if 3	3if 0	3if 0	3if 2	3if 8	
whech 3	whech 5	whech 5	whech 3	whech 0	whech 0	whech 0	whech 1	whech 0	which
which 11	which 11	which 13	which 10	which 8	which 7	which 2	which 11	which 7	(((whech)))
3et 1	3et 0	3et 1	3et 0	3et 0	3et 0	3et 0	3et 0	3et 0	3it
3it 2	3it 2	3it 2	3it 4	3it 5	3it 1	3it 0	3it 1	3it 3	(((3et)))
bote 9	bote 7	bote 13	bote 6	bote 5	bote 1	bote 4	bote 4	bote 1	bot
bot 0	bot 0	bot 0	bot 2	bot 1	bot 0	bot 2	bot 2	bot 9	(((bote)))
—	—	—	—	—	—	—	—	—	3iue (((3oue, etc.)))

extended length of the whole poem, therefore, all of these shifts can be said to have taken place within a fairly restricted stretch of text, and this strongly suggests that the spelling practice of the exemplar changed in the middle of Book IV or, if I may say more precisely, on or immediately before folio 83^{v}.

This is further reinforced by the distribution of minor variant forms. The following is a list of the forms which appear as very minor variants throughout the first half of our MS., but which disappear altogether in the second half, except that -ur and -us each appear in Book V:

uche 'EACH':   found in Prologue, Books I and III (4 times in all)
(-)huld '(-)HELD (sg.)':   found in Prologue, Books I, II and IV
  (9 times in all)
whan(ne) 'WHEN':   found in Prologue, Books I and IV (4 times in all)
-ur '-ER':   found in Books I, II, IV and V (5 times in all)
-us '-(E)S (sb. pl.)':   found in Prologue, Books I, II, III, IV and V
  (21 times in all)

It is plain that their appearance is encouraged by the usage of the first half of the exemplar.

There are also a group of forms which are attested only in the very early sections of the latter half of the MS., all as very minor variants:

hild 'HELD (sg.)':   found only once in Book V

251

hille 'HILL':   found only once in Book V

-redde 'DREAD, SPREAD (pt. sg.)':   found only in Books V and VI
(3 times in all)

togidre 'TOGETHER':   found only in Books IV (folios 90^v and 94^r) and
V (4 times in all)

The peculiar pattern of their distribution suggests that they are among the orthographic features of the second half of the exemplar, which were filtered out by our scribe after he got used to the new usage.

Also ascribable to the spelling habit of the second half of the exemplar is the sporadic form *(-)hield* '(-)HELD (sg.)', which is found in Books V, VII and VIII (ten times in all).

Linguistic evidence is thus sufficient, I think, to validate Smith's assumption. The spelling habit of the exemplar evidently changed in the middle of Book IV, and, since the orthography in each of the halves of our MS. is regular and consistent, it is highly probable that our MS. as a whole is in fact an example of a 'composite text',[17] its two halves copied either from two separate exemplars or from a single exemplar which is itself a 'composite text'. If our MS. derives from a single 'composite' type of MS., there are two further possibilities: either the exemplar-copy is based on two distinctive exemplars, or it is based on one exemplar but copied by two scribes, each of them using his own dialect. With linguistic evidence alone, we cannot say for sure which of these is more probable, but the textual content of our MS. will be illuminating here.

In his account of the textual transmission of the extant *Confessio Amantis* MSS., Macaulay has divided the relevant MSS. into three 'recensions',[18] but this does not mean that these forms of text are definitely independent of each other. Though belonging to different recensions, our MS. and the Fairfax MS. are very closely related textually, as is indicated by the following facts: firstly, the Fairfax MS. is 'an example of a manuscript which has passed from one group to another [i.e. from the first recension to the third] partly by erasure and partly by substitution of leaves, apparently made under the direction of the author'[19]; and secondly, our MS. 'stands alone among first recension copies in agreement with the Fairfax text.'[20] As mentioned at the outset of this discussion, however, Macaulay also points out that it is only in Book V onwards that this textual affinity between the two MSS. becomes prominent.[21] The text and the language of our MS. can thus be said to have changed almost simultaneously, and this would point to the conclusion

---

[17] Benskin and Laing, 'Translations and *Mischsprachen*', § 4.1. and *L.A.L.M.E.*, Vol. I, pp. 14–5.

[18] Macaulay, *English Works*, p. cxxviii.

[19] *Ibid.*, p. cxxx.

[20] *Ibid.*, p. cxxxiii.

[21] *Ibid.*, p. cxxxiii.

that the linguistic shift discussed above was brought about not because any one copy underlying our MS. was written by two scribes, but rather because two distinctive MSS. were put together at a certain stage of textual transmission. Admittedly, we can postulate any number of intermediate copies between our MS. and the exemplars which first introduced those contrastive spellings,[22] and the original exemplars might well have had many more instances of orthographic difference, which were eventually to be wiped out in our MS. through the processes of dialectal translation by the intervening scribes.

The close relationship between the two MSS. in Book V onwards, inferred from their textual resemblance, is confirmed by their linguistic resemblance. This can be seen in Table II below, which compares regular forms in our MS. with those in the Fairfax MS., the latter collected by Smith:[23]

TABLE II

MSS / item	St John's		Fairfax
	1st half	2nd half	
IT	hit	it	it
WHICH	whech wheche	which	which whiche
SHALL (pl.)	schal	schul schull schulle	schul schull schulle schullen
EITHER . . . OR	or . . . or (ouþer . . . or)	or . . . or	or . . . or
YET	ȝet	ȝit	ȝit
(-)HELD (sg.)	no example of (-)hield	10 examples of (-)hield	hield
BUT	bote	bot	bot

The Fairfax forms, which have been identified with those of Gower himself,[24] persistently appear, as Smith was able to show, in so many *Confessio Amantis* MSS. that they have become ' "traditional" in the

---

[22] Cf. note 26 below.

[23] Smith, *Studies*, Vol. I, pp. 42–4.

[24] M. L. Samuels and J. J. Smith, 'The Language of Gower', *The English of Chaucer and his Contemporaries*, ed. J. J. Smith (Aberdeen: Aberdeen University Press, 1988), pp. 13–22; originally published in *Neuphilologische Mitteilungen*, 82 (1981), 295–304.

spelling-systems of these MSS.'[25] In fact, not a few of them are attested throughout our MS., and there might have been more which were purged out in our MS. by the scribe. But the above table plainly shows that the influence of the Fairfax usage is more conspicuous in the second half of our MS., and this linguistic fact, together with Macaulay's textual evidence, makes it fairly certain that the second half of our MS. can be traced back to an exemplar which was very closely related to that of the Fairfax MS.[26]

Why, at a certain stage of textual history behind our MS., two distinctive exemplars were combined together is difficult to say precisely, but at least three possible reasons can be suggested here. One is that the first exemplar was lacking in the text corresponding to the latter half of the poem, and so the scribe had no other choice than switching to another exemplar to supplement the missing part. Another possibility will be that the two exemplars were put together utterly by accident. It is now known that exemplar-copies of such widely read works as the *Confessio Amantis* were often stored in the workshop as collections of loosely bound 'booklets'. After those exemplars were divided into booklets so that they might be copied out by several scribes simultaneously, those booklets were very likely to be mixed up with those which had originally belonged to other exemplars. There is further a third sort of explanation, which would seem to be attractive in view of the fact that 'there was', as mentioned above, 'a strong orthographic tradition within which the Gower MSS were produced.'[27] This tradition seems to have been established because, as Smith argues, the contemporary respect for Gower's works, indicated by the existence of Latin commentaries and also of elegant illuminations in MSS. of his works, 'attached itself even to the archetypal spellings of the Gower tradition.'[28] It appears highly probable, therefore, that copyists of Gower MSS. took extra care to use an exemplar which was as close as possible to the author's original, both textually and linguistically. The scribe who was responsible for the shift from one exemplar to the other was undoubtedly well aware of such circumstances, and when he obtained, by chance or after a persistent hunt, an exemplar which he knew was closer to the original, he had every reason to adopt it for portions yet to be copied, though he had

[25] J. J. Smith, 'Spelling and Tradition in Fifteenth-century Copies of Gower's *Confessio Amantis'*, *The English of Chaucer and his Contemporaries*, ed. J. J. Smith, p. 96.

[26] Indirect evidence to support this conclusion has already been found out by Smith; see Smith, 'Spelling and Tradition', pp. 104–7. As we have seen, Gower's idiosyncratic spellings, as attested in the Fairfax MS., tended to be handed down from one scribe to another, and so the survival of the contrast between the Fairfax and the non-Fairfax forms in our MS. does not in itself rule out the possibility that there were many intervening copies between our MS. and the two original exemplars.

[27] Smith, 'Spelling and Tradition', p. 98.

[28] *Ibid.*, p. 99.

SPELLING VARIATIONS

already come too far into the text to set afresh about copying it from the very beginning. If this last hypothesis is an acceptable one, then the spelling variations discussed here can be taken as a further confirmation of the prestigious status of Gower's authorial language and text, as represented in the Fairfax MS.

Caxton's Revisions: the *Game of Chess*, the *Mirror of the World*, and *Reynard the Fox*

KIYOKAZU MIZOBATA

In the prologues and epilogues to his English translations of French, Latin and Dutch texts (of which there are more than twenty) which Caxton the translator published in his lifetime, he often begged readers' pardon for his 'rude and simple' English, and entreated them to correct mistakes which they would find in his translations. These requests, which are in accordance with the conventional 'humility formula' of the day, can even be considered as an expression of his positive intent to improve his translations on the suggestions of his readers, and thus, such a positive intent on Caxton's side is, we expect, reflected in the second editions, which are reprints (with revisions) of the first editions.

Of all the Caxton translations only three were reprinted by himself: the *Game of Chess* (first issued in 1474[1] and reprinted with woodcuts in 1485), the *Mirror of the World* and *Reynard the Fox* (both of them first printed in 1481 and reprinted about 1489). How have the second editions of these works been estimated by Caxton scholars? N. F. Blake says: '[in the case of the second edition of the *Game of Chess*] the body of the text was simply touched up', because Caxton 'did not think it necessary to update the body of the text or otherwise correct it';[2] likewise, in publishing the second edition of *Reynard the Fox*, Caxton 'made very few changes' with 'no attempt to improve the style or language' of the first edition.[3] As for the *Mirror of the World*, O. H. Prior says: 'the differences between the first and second editions are very slight . . . On the whole it seems as if Caxton had taken greater pains over the first issue than over the second, in which misprints are numerous and abbreviations far more frequently used.'[4] In this paper we shall examine the morphological and syntactical

---

1 For this dating we referred to P. Needham, *The Printer & the Pardoner* (Washington: Library of Congress, 1986), Appendix D.

2 *Jacobus de Cesslis, The Game of Chess, translated and printed by William Caxton c.1483* (London: Scolar Press, 1976), Introduction.

3 N. F. Blake, 'English Versions of *Reynard the Fox* in the Fifteenth and Sixteenth Centuries', *William Caxton and English Literary Culture* (London: Hambledon Press, 1991), pp. 271–2.

4 O. H. Prior ed., *Caxton's Mirror of the World* (London: Oxford University Press, 1913), pp. vi–vii.

differences between the two editions of the above three works[5] in order that we may gain some idea of different printing-attitudes towards the revision of each text in Caxton's press.

First, typographical alterations. In the second edition of the *Game of Chess* very few typographical mistakes are found, and many of the morphological and syntactical mistakes of the first edition are corrected, whereas in the second editions of the *Mirror of the World* and *Reynard the Fox* we can notice many typographical mistakes, most of which were probably made through inserting wrong pieces of type, misreading certain types used in the first edition, and even misinterpreting its text.

With regard to morphological differences between the first and the second editions of the *Game of Chess* and the *Mirror of the World* (*Reynard the Fox* does not present noteworthy cases), we find some changes, in the second editions, which do not seem to be haphazard, but which can be taken as reflections of the compositor's intent. In the case of the *Mirror of the World*, the two editions reveal the compositors' own peculiarities in the use of *i* and *y*. As a whole, *i* is more frequently used in the first edition, while in the second *y* is very much favoured. In the first edition, word-forms such as 'thing', 'wise', 'without', 'will', 'said', 'with', 'wit' and 'like' are much more preferred than *y*-forms, which are much favoured forms in the second edition. In both editions, however, 'their', 'which', 'right' and 'science' favour *i*, and 'him', 'might', 'if' and 'nothing' favour *y*. In the ending of the preterite of weak verbs and in the gerund and the present and past participles, *y*-forms are much more common in the second edition. In the first edition 'people'/'peple' and 'philosopher'/'philosophre' interchange freely, but in the second edition 'people' (except for one instance of 'peple' as a verb) and 'philosopher' are consistently used throughout the text. In the *Game of Chess* some words are differently spaced through each edition: 'to fore' and 'an other' in the first edition, for example, are almost always typeset in the second edition as 'tofore' and 'another'. Each edition also has its own favourite orthography in certain words: in the second edition 'than' is altered to 'thenne' in 43 instances, 'allway'/'alleway' to 'alwey' in 39 instances, 'made' to 'maad' in 27 instances, 'peple' to 'people' in 15 instances and 'only' to 'onely' in 12 instances. Though 'hit' (personal pronoun) is often altered to 'it' in the first half of the second edition, such alterations become much fewer in the latter half. In the case of 'ben' (present indicative pl.) it is frequently replaced by 'be' only in the latter half of the second edition.

As to alterations in vocabulary, we find a few in the second editions of the *Game of Chess* and the *Mirror of the World*: in the *Game of Chess* 'fornier'

---

[5] In comparing the first editions of three texts with their second editions we used microfilms made by University Microfilms International: the *Game of Chess* (STC 4920, 4921), the *Mirror of the World* (STC 24762, 24763) and *Reynard the Fox* (STC 20919, 20920).

258

and 'compaignon' (derived from Old French), and 'oughwer' (der. from Old English) are changed to 'baker', 'companyoun' and 'ony where'; in the *Mirror of the World* 'maynee' and 'maynyes' (der. from Old French) become 'seruaūte' and 'seruaūtes'. In *Reynard the Fox* the following Dutch words are replaced by English words: 'dasse' by 'brocke' in six instances and by 'gray' in one instance; 'hāmes' and 'rore' by 'buttockes' and 'styre' respectively. Even English words are sometimes replaced by other English words: 'cryde' (originally French), 'lerynge' and 'yl' (originally Old Norse) by 'sayde', 'lernynge' and 'euyl'.[6]

What examples can we give for the syntactical differences between the first and the second editions of the three works? In each of the second editions are found syntactical alterations, probably intended to make readers grasp the meaning more easily: change of a subjectless construction into that of the *Subject plus Verb*, supplementation of the conjunction 'that', or restoration of the inverted construction of *Auxiliary plus Subject* to that of the *Subject plus Auxiliary*. Examples are:

(1) why chacest and smytest away thyse flyes
(1st ed., *Game of Chess*)
why chasest & smytest thou away thyse flyes
(2nd ed.)

(2) in suche wyse the oke was wyde open
(1st ed., *Reynard the Fox*)
in suche wyse that the oke was wyde open
(2nd ed.)

(3) thus shold they be more easyd
(1st ed., *Mirror of the World*)
thus they sholde be more eased
(2nd ed.)

In addition to these syntactical changes, the *Game of Chess* presents us with an alteration which was probably made by a meticulous compositor with a thorough knowledge of the text. In the following sentence, the misplacement of words 'foure thinges The first is wher' in the first edition results in disordered sentences, which would be overlooked by a compositor who is just glancing through the text of the first edition mechanically in order to typeset the second edition:

And foure thinges The first is wher ye shal vnderstande that ye ought to consydere here in fore that lxiiii poyntes ben sette in the eschequer
(1st ed., *Game of Chess*)
and ye shal vnderstonde that ye ought to considere here in foure

---

6   Cf. Blake, *op. cit.*, p. 268. Here he refers to the replacement of Dutch words and English words in the second edition of *Reynard the Fox*.

thynges The first is wher fore that lxiiii poyntes been sette in the
eschequer

(2nd ed.)

More important emendations, the kinds which can never be found in the
other two works, are the following:

(1) Ther is none that is so *synfull* as he that hath alle the world in
despyte For he is in pees that dredeth no man And he is ryche that
coueyteth no thynge

(1st ed., *Game of Chess*; emphasis mine)
there is none that is so *blisful* as he that hath al the world in despite
For he is in pees that dredith no man & he is riche that coueiteth no
thyng

(2nd ed.; emphasis mine)
(2) And the Juges ought to entende for to studie for y^e[*sic*]yf smythes
the carpētiers ye vignours and other craftymen saye that it is *most*
necessarye to studye for the comyn prouffit And gloryfye them in
their connyng and saye that they ben prouffitable Than shold the
Juges studie and contemplaire moche more than they in that that
shold be for the comyn wele

(1st ed., *Game of Chess*; emphasis mine)
And the Juges ought to entende for to studye For yf the smythes the
carpentiers the vignours and other craftymen say that it is *not* necessarye to studye for the comyn proffit And glorefye them in their
cōnyng and say that they ben proffitable than shold the Juges studye
and contemplaire moche more than they in that that shold be for the
comyn wele

(2nd ed.; emphasis mine)

We find that 'synfull', the first instance (1) in the first edition, and 'most',
the second instance (2) in the first edition, are causes of textual corruption, which prevents us from making a logical reading. But by replacing
each word with 'blisful' and 'not' respectively, a coherent text has been
produced in each instance of the second editions. Such emendations
would not have been made if the compositor had not been careful to
improve the text. The second edition of the *Game of Chess* is also different
from the second editions of the other two works in the treatment of the
doublet, a stylistic device frequently found in Caxton's translations and
which lends distinction to his English. In the first half of the second
edition there are six instances in which a single word-form is remade
into a doublet, but in the latter half eight doublets found in the first
edition are changed to single word-forms (no newly-made doublet can
be found there). This phenomenon seems to reflect the work of two
compositors with a different sense of style working simultaneously or, in
the case of a single compositor, the change of attitude of the compositor
towards textual revising. In the latter case, the compositor presumably

tried to make the text ornate by doublets, characteristic of Caxton's diction, but in the middle of his work he came, it seems, to have a different sense of style, and finding doublets wordy, he presumably began to replace them by single word-forms.

On the whole there are many changes between the first and the second editions of the *Game of Chess*, the *Mirror of the World* and *Reynard the Fox*. If we follow N. F. Blake's classification of textual changes,[7] most of them are 'typographical' mistakes or 'compositorial' changes, and we find very few 'editorial' changes in these editions. It seems as if Caxton or a master-printer had not taken a hand in textual revising. But when we closely examine their changes (other than typographical mistakes), we find that these changes are more than changes in spelling or in word-order which are rather haphazard: the second editions of the *Game of Chess* and the *Mirror of the World* have their own peculiarities in orthography, different from those of their first editions. In vocabulary it often happens that Old French words or Dutch words are replaced by their English equivalents in the second editions, a fact undoubtedly reflecting the compositor's attempt to make readers understand the text more easily; we can also find the same attempt in syntactical changes, though most of them are very simple ones which are mostly caused by the restoration of inverted word-order, or the supplementation of a subject or a conjunction.

Apart from the morphological and syntactical features of each work, there is a difference, in the attitude towards textual revising, between the *Game of Chess* and the other two works: the second edition of the *Game of Chess* has far fewer typographical mistakes than do the others; it is also characterised by those emendations and changes (the kinds scarcely found in the other works which impress us with the compositor's earnest concern for printing an accurate text). This different attitude may be attributed to the nature of the works: the *Mirror of the World* and *Reynard the Fox* belong to the category of moral or didactic works, whereas the *Game of Chess* comes under the category of courtly works. We can imagine that, in the later stages of Caxton's printing-life, moral and didactic works such as the *Mirror of the World* and *Reynard the Fox*

---

[7] *Ibid.*, pp. 270–1. Blake classified all the changes made between a text and its copy into three groups: (1) editorial, (2) compositorial and (3) typographical. A typographical change (group 3), which is a typographical mistake, can arise through the compositor actually picking up and inserting the wrong piece of type or through the compositor misreading a certain letter because its shape resembles that of another; a compositorial change (group 2), which is not a mistake, is a change made in the spelling or word order of the text, a change by which one variant spelling or syntactical usage is haphazardly replaced by another; editorial changes (group 1), which are made consistently through a text, reveal an attempt to eliminate a certain spelling, word or syntactical usage from a text.

were popular and in constant demand among the middle-class people[8]; that the reprinting of these editions, aimed for the reliable market of the bourgeoisie, therefore, may not have required such careful revision. Actually, as far as the typographical mistakes are concerned, the second editions of these works are inferior to the first ones.

In reprinting however, the *Game of Chess*, a piece of fashionable literature, it seems that it was necessary to do scrupulous revising and typesetting in order to respond to the quality standard of the courtly reading-public. The linguistic improvements and textual emendations found in the *Game of Chess* can be explained in terms of the difference of intended customers.

It is not likely that Caxton himself had a hand in the editing and the typesetting work of these second editions, but it is not utterly deniable that Caxton, the master, communicated his views of those works to the supervising editors and left them to execute the reprintings. In either case, the editors and compositors must have appreciated their master's attitude towards these texts and practised it in their work.

---

[8] Cf. H. S. Bennett, *English Books and Readers 1475–1557*, 2nd ed. (Cambridge: Cambridge University Press, 1969), pp. 109–10; Blake, 'Caxton's Reprints', *ibid.*, pp. 107–17.

Discourse Properties of Initial and Final
When-Clauses in English Written Narratives*

KAZUO FUKUDA

I

By *when*-clauses I mean those which perform the function of temporal adverbials, and not those which perform that of relative and interrogative adverbs. The motive for my choice is that the conjunction 'when', unlike 'as' and 'while', which are much more restricted in their use by the aspect of verbs contained in the clauses they introduce, is highly versatile in expressing temporal hypotaxis of simultaneity.[1] But why in narratives? Because in narratives time-sequence plays a crucial part, perhaps, a more crucial part than does space-to-space correspondence; time is constantly flowing, and so more changeable than space.[2] A story is developed forward, or sometimes backward, along a particular time-sequence. And it is considered that written narratives, as a carefully planned discourse, will show the temporal sequence most clearly.

R. Quirk and others say that the information in a subordinate clause is often placed in the background with respect to the main clause.[3] R. Tomlin proposes more radically that almost all subordinate clauses carry background information, while main clauses carry foreground information.[4] The problem is whether these remarks are actually tenable when

---

* I am especially grateful to Professor Shunichi Noguchi, Osaka University of Education, for his consistent encouragement that has been given to me since I was a graduate student, and for his insightful comments and suggestions on an earlier version of this paper. I would also like to express my thanks to all the members of *Studia Anglistica* for their honest, helpful comments, and to my colleagues at Niigata University, Professor William Plain and Associate Professor Keiichi Narita, for their willing help in the preparation of this paper. Responsibility for infelicities remains entirely my own.

1 For a detailed discussion about the relationships between conjunctions and the aspect of a verb, see J. R. Martin, 'Conjunction: The Logic of English Text', *Micro and Macro Connexity of Texts*, ed. Petöfi, J. S. and E. Sözer (Hamburg: Buske, 1983), pp. 1–72.

2 It should be noted that the spatial conjunction 'where' is not so frequently used as the temporal conjunction 'when'. This partly demonstrates the relative dominance of Time over Space in English subordinate clauses to describe actions and events.

3 R. Quirk and others, *A Comprehensive Grammar of the English Language* (London: Longman, 1985), 13.3.

4 R. Tomlin, 'Foreground-Background Information and the Syntax of Subordination', *Quantified Studies in Discourse*, special volume of *Text*, ed. T. Givón (1985), pp. 85–122. In

the subordinate clauses are initial and final *when*-clauses in English written narratives, not just on the level of a clause, but on the level of discourse as well.

Before going into a discoursal examination, let us first consider the Theme/Rheme structure both of a temporal prepositional phrase and of a temporal finite clause on the level of a clause. I will follow M. A. K. Halliday with respect to the definition of the notions of Theme (the Theme is a clause-initial element which serves as the point of departure of the message) and the Rheme (the Rheme is the remainder of the message, in which the Theme is developed).[5]

(1) <u>I work best at night</u>.
    Th   Rh

(2) <u>He turned pale</u> <u>when</u> <u>he saw me</u>.
    Th   Rh   Th Th Rh   (micro-structure)
    Th   Rh   (macro-structure)

(3) <u>At night I work best</u>.
    Th   Rh

(4) <u>When</u> <u>he saw me</u> <u>he turned pale</u>.
    Th Th Rh Th   Rh   (micro-structure)
    Th   Rh   (macro-structure)

The macro-structure as seen in (4) is suggested by M. A. K. Halliday,[6] which serves efficiently to analyse the message structure of hypotaxis, and allows us to concentrate upon the informational status of a clause as a whole, and not the micro-Theme/Rheme structure of individual constituents of a clause. The semantic function of the prepositional phrase 'at night' and that of the finite clause 'when he saw me' are, it should be noted, basically the same, in that both of them act as temporal adjuncts to add an explicit temporal frame to the rest of the message. All the cases of (1)–(4) seem to coincide very well with the general principle of the Functional Sentence Perspective (FSP) at least here on the clause level.[7] The important point is, however, that the degrees of Communicative

---

his experiment, the subjects were requested to produce oral and written narratives after seeing a voiceless video film. However, he does not mention the functional distinction between initial and final subordinate clauses.

5 M. A. K. Halliday, *An Introduction to Functional Grammar* (London: Edward Arnold, 1985), p. 38.

6 *Ibid.*, pp. 57–8.

7 The FSP theory has been developed by J. Firbas, 'On Defining the Theme in Functional Sentence Analysis', *Travaux Linguistique de Prague*, 1 (1964), 267–80, and 'Non-Thematic Subjects in Contemporary English', *Travaux Linguistique de Prague* 2 (1966), 239–56; and S. Kuno, 'Functional Sentence Perspective: A Case Study from Japanese and English', *Linguistic Inquiry*, Vol. 3, No. 3 (1972), 269–320. According to them, the linear order of informational structure is from Given to New, unless there is some special reason to violate it.

Dynamism (CD) of temporal elements are different between (1) and (2) on one hand, and (3) and (4) on the other.[8] The degree of CD is lower in (3) and (4) than in (1) and (2). In this paper, I will illustrate how initial and final *when*-clauses, in fact, differentiate in terms of the degree of CD, and will classify them into five types. At the same time, I will show that some of the types convey background information, while the others foreground information.[9]

II

In the case of Noun Phrase (NP) Themes, Given Themes are overwhelmingly pervasive as is shown by K. Fukuda.[10] This is because NP Themes can easily be referential items such as pronouns or definite NP's. Nevertheless, in the case of clausal Themes such as initial *when*-clauses, completely Given Themes like 'when he did it' are rare. By a clausal Theme I mean the whole of a preposed subordinate clause which consists of a Structural Theme (=Conjunction) plus the internal microstructure of the Theme/Rheme as shown in (4) above. The fact that a clausal Theme contains an internal Rheme is the main reason why a clausal Theme tends to carry newer information much more frequently than do NP Themes. In this paper, the term Given indicates not only Referential Givenness but also Givenness in a wider sense as is seen between propositions or between a proposition and its nominalization. I will propose the notion of the Immediate Relevancy-Chain (IR-Chain): a logico- semantic chain between one propositional content and another, which comprises in it the notion of inferability[11] or predictability in view of both linguistic and situational contexts distinguishable from the contexts of our general outlook upon the world. When there is an IR-Chain between two propositional contents, the second usually has a low degree of CD or informationally Given, except for a contrastive case.

---

[8] I will use the term Communicative Dynamism (CD), which is proposed and developed by J. Firbas, *ibid*. This term covers both the notion of information value and that of the Force of Forward-Chaining.

[9] Cf. S. A. Thompson, 'Grammar and Written Discourse: Initial and Final Purpose Clauses in English', in T. Givón (ed.), *ibid*., pp. 55–84. She proposes that initial and final purpose clauses are quite independent of each other; she does so by demonstrating that the use of the former requires the reader's expectation about the existence of some problem and about the corresponding solution to come in the main clause that follows, while the use of the latter does not presuppose such expectation.

[10] K. Fukuda, 'Some Observations on Thematic Progression', *Studia Anglistica*, 7 (1991), 10–34, where I discussed the feasibility of the models proposed by F. Daneš, 'Functional Sentence Perspective and the Organization of Text', *Functional Sentence Perspective*, ed. F. Daneš (The Hague, Paris: Mouton 1974), pp. 106–28.

[11] For a detailed discussion of the notion of Inferential Givenness, see E. F. Prince, 'Toward a Taxonomy of Given-New Information', *Radical Pragmatics*, ed. P. Cole (New York: Academic Press 1981), pp. 223–55.

ARTHURIAN AND OTHER STUDIES

I will classify initial *when*-clauses into two types: one functioning as a Given Theme and the other functioning as an informative Theme with Medium CD. Let us consider the first type: (in examples given hereafter, italics are added to *when*-clauses, and underlines to the elements which are related to Chaining, both by the present writer)

(5) . . . At ten o'clock <u>he left her alone</u>. And *when he had gone* Mary got up and locked the door . . .   (J. Steinbeck: "The White Quail")

The initial *when*-clause repeats a message very similar to that of the preceding underlined part.[12] This is one of the typical examples of a clausal Given Theme. The following example falls into the same category:

(6) . . . She didn't know how to combat it; but <u>her head ached terribly</u>. *When it ached its worst* he tried to make it up to her for refusing the poison. He kept a little pad soaked with Florida Water, and he patted it on her forehead . . .   (J. Steinbeck: "The White Quail")

Despite the focal point falling upon 'its worst' in the second half, the first half of the *when*-clause is no more than the repetition of the preceding underlined part. The IR-Chain, found between 'aching terribly' and 'aching its worst', makes the degree of CD of the main clause clearly higher than that of the *when*-clause. The next example also illustrates the IR-Chain:

(7) . . . She came in with such a proprietary haste, and looked around so possessively at the furniture that <u>I wondered if she lived here</u>. But *when I asked her* she laughed immoderately, repeated my question aloud, and told me she lived with a girl friend at a hotel . . .
(F. S. Fitzgerald: *The Great Gatsby*)

in which the underlined part makes it possible to interpret the initial *when*-clause as a Given Theme because of the IR-Chain between 'I wondered' and 'I asked'. Cases of (5)–(7), where it is possible to predict the content of the *when*-clause, can be classified into Type 1. Schematically,

---

[12] J. R. Martin (*ibid.*, p. 42) remarks that the potentially comparative *as if*-clauses cannot be preposed in the hypotaxis. This is generally correct, but it is, in fact, not impossible to prepose them when the IR-Chain between their content and that of the preceding discourse is very strong, as is seen in (5)–(7). This kind of linkage is one of the greatest factors in deciding which clause in various hypotactic clause complexes should be put in the initial position. The following is an example of an initial *as if*-clause. The phrase 'his absence' forms an IR-Chain between the preceding underlined proposition and its nominalisation.

ex.) The butler came back and murmured something close to Tom's ear, whereupon Tom frowned, pushed back his chair, <u>and without a word went inside</u>. *As if his absence quickened something within her* Daisy leaned forward again, her voice glowing and singing . . . (F. S. Fitzgerald: *The Great Gatsby*)

266

together with the distribution of CD, the Theme/Rheme structure of Type 1 is shown as follows:

Figure 1 (for Type 1)

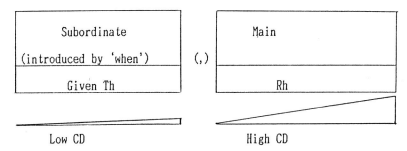

In the following examples, which belong to another type of initial *when*-clause, we cannot predict the content of the *when*-clause:

(8) . . . Mrs. Miller felt oddly excited, and *when the little girl glanced toward her*, she smiled warmly.   (T. Capote: "Miriam")

Here, despite the existence of referential items 'the little girl' and 'her', the information of the *when*-clause as a whole is newer than in Type 1, due to the existence of the new item 'glanced' which has no IR-Chain formed with the preceding discourse (now omitted). In other words, there is nothing in the preceding discourse that makes the use of the word 'glanced' predictable. The following is a typical example of a New Theme, brand-new because it appears as a story-opener:

(9) *When dear old Mrs. Hay went back to town after staying with the Burnells* she sent the children a doll's house. It was so big that the carter and Pat carried it into the courtyard, and there it stayed, propped up on two wooden boxes beside the feed-room door.
(K. Mansfield: "A Doll's House")

Such New Themes often appear in the story-initial position as well as at the beginning of chapters and paragraphs. There exists no IR-Chain at the beginning of a story, because of the absence of a preceding discourse. The reason why the reader can accept a story-initial New Theme is probably explained by referring to our extra-linguistic outlook. We can very naturally expect the existence of a temporal frame in narratives as well as a spatial frame when we start to read them. And, although the Theme is new and higher in the degree of CD, it still functions as a background temporal frame, and not as the focal point in the stream of the story. This is illustrated by the Referential Chain between 'a doll's house' and the Unmarked Given Theme of the following clause, 'It'. The following example shows how long and how informative a New Theme in the initial *when*-clause can be:

(10) ... *Even when the East excited me most, even when I was most keenly aware of its superiority to the bored, sprawling swollen towns beyond the Ohio with their interminable inquisitions which spared only the children and the very old* – <u>even then</u> it had always for me a quality of distortion. West Egg, especially, still figures in my more fantastic dreams . . .
(F. S. Fitzgerald: *The Great Gatsby*)

Several interesting features of (10) can be pointed out: first, the initial temporal frame is composed of two *when*-clauses; second, the juxtaposed *when*-clauses form a very long, informative New Theme; third, the expression 'even' highlights the informativeness of the two *when*-clauses; fourth, the long New Theme is rephrased by the following short Given Theme 'even then'; and finally, despite the informativeness of the *when*-clauses, there is no IR-Chain between the *when*-clauses and the discourse which follows (now omitted). Instead, the omitted passage concentrates upon the elaboration of the content of the main clause. Such a long, informative initial *when*-clause is probably characteristic of a carefully planned written discourse like narratives. The degree of CD of the New Theme in (8)–(10) is considered to be Medium, because of the conflict between the inherent positional status of Themes (=Given) and the actual informativeness of the clause in question. Examples (8)–(10) can be classified into Type 2 with the following schema:

Figure 2 (for Type 2)

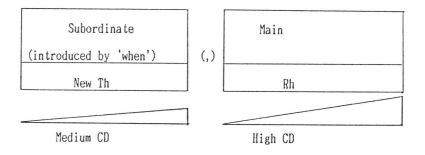

III

Let us turn our attention to final *when*-clauses, which can, according to the degree of CD, be classified into three types: Supplementary Given Rheme, New Rheme, and Co-Ordinative Informative *when*-clauses.

In the Supplementary type, which does not occur frequently, it is possible to predict the content of the final *when*-clauses. Consider the following example:

> (11) ... 'Promise me you'll <u>put out poison</u>.' She looked closely at him and saw a rebellious light come into his eyes. 'Promise.'
> 'Dear,' he apologized, 'Some dog might <u>get it</u>. Animals suffer terribly *when they get poison.*' (J. Steinbeck: "The White Quail")

in which the message of the *when*-clause, 'they get poison', can be easily predicted through the IR-Chain from the preceding underlined parts. Since the *when*-clause functions supplementarily, its degree of CD is not very high. The following example illustrates this supplementary function more explicitly:

> (12) ... 'Oh, Chips, I am so glad you are what you are. I <u>was</u> afraid you <u>were</u> a solicitor or a stock broker or a dentist or a man with a big cotton business in Manchester. *When I first met you*, <u>I mean</u>. Schoolmastering's so different, so important, don't you think? ...'
> (J. Hilton: *Good-bye, Mr. Chips*)

Although the punctuation makes the *when*-clause appear independent of the rest of the passage, the function of the *when*-clause is, in fact, supplementarily adding a temporal frame to the main clause existent in the preceding sentence. The use of the elaborative connective 'I mean' explicitly indicates the supplementary character of the *when*-clause. We can classify (11) and (12) into Type 3 (the term 'Topical Element' used in the figure indicates NP's or Circumstantial Adjuncts following M. A. K. Halliday[13]):

Figure 3 (for Type 3)

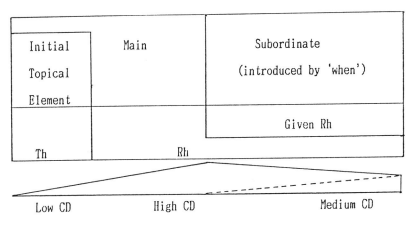

[13] Cf. M. A. K. Halliday, *ibid.*, p. 54.

In this diagram, the degree of Medium CD is due to the conflict between the inherent positional status of Rheme (=New) and the lack of actual informativeness of the supplementary clause. (The dotted line indicates the increasing degree of CD of the internal micro-Theme/Rheme structure of the *when*-clause, only to reach the point of Medium CD.)

Let us proceed to examine the *when*-clauses in the final position which function as a New Rheme. The informational status of the final *when*-clause in the following three examples is noticeably compatible with the inherent property of the Rhematic position in a clause. Note that *when*-clauses of this type tend to be longer, though their length is not a single factor contributing to the high degree of CD. Consider the following example:

> (13) . . . They rose *when she entered* – a small, fat woman in black, with a thin gold chain descending to her waist and vanishing into her belt, leaning on an ebony cane with a tarnished gold head . . .
>
> (W. Faulkner: "A Rose for Emily")

in which, despite the short *when*-clause, the degree of CD is high. The high degree here can be illustrated in this way: the succeeding lengthy description concentrates upon 'she', the woman who entered, not upon 'they', those who rose. This chaining pattern, including in it a backward Referential-Chain between 'she' in the *when*-clause and the following underlined part 'a small, fat woman', demonstrates the difference in the degree of CD of the *when*-clause of this type and the main clause. In this case, 'her entering' has a higher focal value than 'their rising'. The degree of CD of the former, therefore, is higher than that of the latter.

The following example is interesting with respect to the relation between the Referential Chain and the IR-Chain:

> (14) . . . Everyone was incredulous *when it was reported that he had a vocation for the priesthood.* Nevertheless it was true . . .
>
> (J. Joyce: "An Encounter")

in which the *when*-clause clearly has a higher degree of CD than the initial main clause. The message of the *when*-clause becomes the Referential, Unmarked Given Theme 'it' of the following clause, while the part 'everyone was incredulous' in the main clause links to the following Rheme 'was true' by means of the IR-Chain, though the Chain in this case is a contrastive one, with the result of the high CD of the phrase 'was true'. There is another example in which the degree of CD of the two *when*-clauses is heightened by the use of comparison:[14]

---

[14] A *than*-clause to indicate the standard for comparison is hard to prepose, unless it is accompanied by the adjective in the form of comparative degree. Therefore, it is generally a Rheme-Proper in the same way as *as if*-clauses mentioned in the note 12 above. Inciden-

(15) . . . Well, it would do him no harm to see what business really was like. Things seemed righter *when you did them* than *when you thought about them*. A little mental house-cleaning mightn't be a bad thing for Harry. . . .   (J. Steinbeck: "The White Quail")

The cases of (13)–(15) can be grouped into Type 4. Its schematic illustration is as follows: (the explanation of the dotted line is the same as in the schema of Type 3, but in this case the internal CD-Crescendo reaches the point of High CD)

Figure 4 (for Type 4)

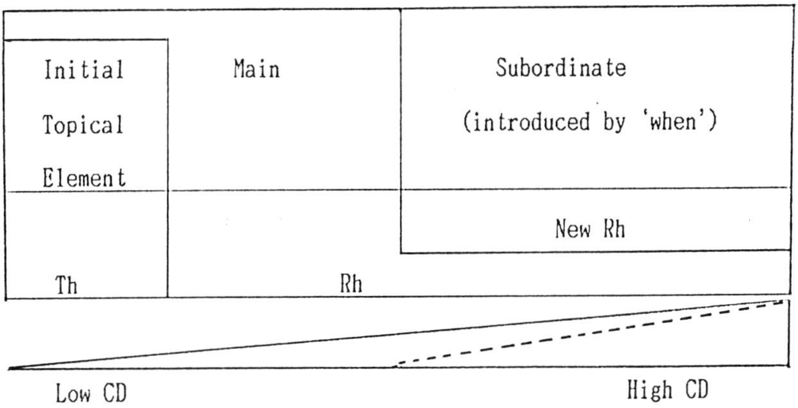

Finally let us examine the structure of those final *when*-clauses which are subtly different from Types 3 and 4, in which the clauses are used restrictively. Consider the following example, in which the final *when*-clause is used non-restrictively:

(16) . . . She excused his gloominess on the grounds that he was still growing up and his radical ideas on his lack of practical experience. She said he didn't yet know a thing about 'life,' that he hadn't even entered the real world – *when already he was as disenchanted with it as a man of fifty* . . .   (F. O'Connor: "Everything That Rises Must Converge")

In (16) the dash before the final *when*-clause appears to make the clause fall into the category of Type 3. There is, however, a crucial difference between the type represented by (16) and Type 3: the content of the *when*-clause in (16) cannot be predicted, while that of Type 3 can. Clearly

---

tally, temporal *until*-clauses are usually postposed if they express the resultative meaning 'and finally'. Such *until*-clauses should be interpreted as a non-restrictive use of a subordinate clause, thus a sort of co-ordination like the *when*-clauses of Type 5 discussed below.

the degree of CD of the *when*-clause in (16) is far higher than that of Type 3. The so-called relationship of Antithesis exists between the main clause and the *when*-clause.[15] The *when*-clause in (16) can, therefore, be paraphrased into 'but the fact was that . . .' Non-restrictive *when*-clauses semantically overlap with co-ordination just as in the case of the other non-restrictive use of conjunctions and relatives. The following example illustrates most clearly how similar non-restrictive use of the *when*-clause is to the use of co-ordinating conjunctions and how informative the final *when*-clause of this kind could be, especially in a carefully planned discourse such as written narratives:

(17) . . . One day she was picking her path among the puddles and crushed refuse of a market street in a strange city of a strange country, *when without warning, plain and clear in its true colors as if she looked through a frame upon a scene that had not stirred nor changed since the moment it happened, the episode of that far-off day leapt from its burial place before her mind's eye.* She was so unreasonably horrified she halted suddenly staring, the scene before her eyes dimmed by the vision back of them . . . (K. A. Porter: "The Grave")

The case of (17) shows that a non-restrictive *when*-clause functions as if it is a main clause. Can we still call such a *when*-clause (paraphrasable with 'and then') a subordinate or dependent clause? Given that the co-ordinative reading is correct, it is easier to understand the informativeness of the *when*-clause in (17), since the second of the co-ordinated clauses becomes a focal point.[16] We can classify (16) and (17) into Type 5. To this type, we should apply a Theme/Rheme schema different from the macro-structure so far applied to Types 1–4 above. The alternative is a micro-Theme/Rheme structure:

Figure 5 (for Type 5)

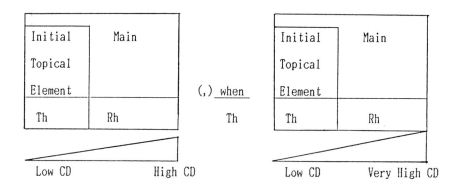

---
[15] Cf. R. Quirk and others, *ibid.*, 15.29.
[16] Cf. *ibid.*, 13.4 (note).

IV

Through the discussion above, I have identified five types of *when*-clauses, and demonstrated that initial and final *when*-clauses, conveying different weights of information, show different behaviour in chaining elements of co-occurring messages. In the light of formal syntax, subordinate clauses are simply subordinate to the main clauses. When we consider discourse properties such as Theme/Rheme, Referential Chain, IR-Chain, or the degree of CD, it becomes clear that subordinate clauses can be more informative than the main clauses as shown in the case of Types 4 and 5. Type 5 shows that formally subordinate clauses are highly informative, to such an extent that the nomenclature 'subordinate' seems inappropriate. It has also been found that Types 4 and 5 will work counter to R. Tomlin's conclusion that subordinate clauses almost always carry background information.

Another significant finding is the relationship between the general principle of FSP and the informational status of initial and final *when*-clauses. Type 1 agrees with this principle, though the frequency of occurrence is low. Type 2 also agrees with it, for the initial *when*-clause of Type 2 is interpreted as having a medium degree of CD and the main clause that follows usually has a higher degree of CD than the *when*-clause. Type 3 is the only case that is counter to the general FSP principle, since the *when*-clause does not convey culminated information despite its occupation of the final position. Type 4 agrees with the FSP principle as naturally as do Types 1 and 2. Finally, Type 5 has a strong independent status, and, like Type 4, its degree of CD is higher than that of the preceding main clause. Type 5 also agrees with the FSP principle, though, in this case, the Theme/Rheme structure is a conjoined micro-Theme/Rheme structure.

Type 2 and Type 4 occur with the highest frequency. They form a New Theme and a New Rheme, respectively. A clausal Temporal Theme is frequently New. M. A. K. Halliday groups together NP Themes and Temporal Themes into one category of Topical Themes,[17] and he is clearly right as far as his concept of Topichood or Topicity is concerned. The two kinds of Themes are, however, different from each other in respect of their informational status as a Theme.

[17] Cf. note 13 above.